# Evangelicals engaging in p

This book aims to introduce a distinctively evangelical voice to the discipline of practical theology. Evangelicals have sometimes seen practical theology as primarily a 'liberal' project. This collection, however, actively engages with practical theology from an evangelical perspective, both through discussion of the substantive issues and by providing examples of practical theology done by evangelicals in the classroom, the church, and beyond. This volume brings together established and emerging voices to debate the growing role which practical theology is playing in evangelical and Pentecostal circles. Chapters begin by addressing methodological concerns, before moving into areas of practice. Additionally, there are four short papers from students who make use of practical theology to reflect upon their own practice. Issues of authority and normativity are tackled head on in a way that will inform the debate both within and beyond evangelicalism. This book will, therefore, be of keen interest to scholars of practical, evangelical, and Pentecostal theology.

**Helen Morris** is Head of Postgraduate Studies at Moorlands College, UK.

**Helen Cameron** is a Research Fellow at the Centre for Baptist Studies, Regent's Park College, Oxford and a Research Fellow at Wesley House, Cambridge.

# Explorations in Practical, Pastoral and Empirical Theology

Series Editors: Leslie J. Francis, Jeff Astley, Martyn Percy and Nicola Slee

Theological reflection on the church's practice is now recognised as a significant element in theological studies in the academy and seminary. Routledge's series in practical, pastoral and empirical theology seeks to foster this resurgence of interest and encourage new developments in practical and applied aspects of theology worldwide. This timely series draws together a wide range of disciplinary approaches and empirical studies to embrace contemporary developments including: the expansion of research in empirical theology, psychological theology, ministry studies, public theology, Christian education and faith development; key issues of contemporary society such as health, ethics and the environment; and more traditional areas of concern such as pastoral care and counselling.

**Tragedies and Christian Congregations**
The Practical Theology of Trauma
*Edited by Megan Warner, Christopher Southgate, Carla A. Grosch-Miller and Hilary Ison*

**Disclosing Church**
An Ecclesiology Learned from Conversations in Practice
*Clare Watkins*

**The Sunday Assembly and Theologies of Suffering**
*Katie Cross*

**A Practical Christology for Pastoral Supervision**
*Geoff Broughton*

**Evangelicals Engaging in Practical Theology**
Theology that Impacts Church and World
*Edited by Helen Morris and Helen Cameron*

For more information and a full list of titles in the series, please visit: https://www.routledge.com/religion/series/APPETHEO

# Evangelicals engaging in practical theology
Theology that impacts church and world

Edited by
Helen Morris and Helen Cameron

Routledge
Taylor & Francis Group
LONDON AND NEW YORK

First published 2022
by Routledge
4 Park Square, Milton Park, Abingdon, Oxon OX14 4RN

and by Routledge
605 Third Avenue, New York, NY 10158

*Routledge is an imprint of the Taylor & Francis Group, an informa business*

© 2022 selection and editorial matter, Helen Morris and Helen Cameron; individual chapters, the contributors

The right of Helen Morris and Helen Cameron to be identified as the authors of the editorial material, and of the authors for their individual chapters, has been asserted in accordance with sections 77 and 78 of the Copyright, Designs and Patents Act 1988.

All rights reserved. No part of this book may be reprinted or reproduced or utilised in any form or by any electronic, mechanical, or other means, now known or hereafter invented, including photocopying and recording, or in any information storage or retrieval system, without permission in writing from the publishers.

*Trademark notice*: Product or corporate names may be trademarks or registered trademarks, and are used only for identification and explanation without intent to infringe.

*British Library Cataloguing-in-Publication Data*
A catalogue record for this book is available from the British Library

*Library of Congress Cataloging-in-Publication Data*
A catalog record has been requested for this book

ISBN: 978-0-367-54510-9 (hbk)
ISBN: 978-0-367-55748-5 (pbk)
ISBN: 978-1-003-09497-5 (ebk)

DOI: 10.4324/9781003094975

Typeset in Sabon
by Taylor & Francis Books

To Helen Cameron's mother Beth Cooper (1934–2021)

# Contents

*Acknowledgements* x
*List of contributors* xi

Introduction 1
HELEN MORRIS AND HELEN CAMERON

## PART I
## Engaging with the discipline 23

1 Practical theology and evangelicalism: Methodological considerations 25
ANDREW THOMAS

2 Prophetic imagination as a mode of practical theology 40
CHLOE LYNCH

3 The role of teleology in practical theology 56
ALISTAIR J. MCKITTERICK

4 A wonderful plan for my life? Pete Ward's "the Gospel and Change" in dialogue with Charles Taylor 70
HELEN MORRIS

## PART II
## Engaging with education 85

5 From the boy in the temple to the man on the road: The maturing role of practical theology in the life of the church 87
HELEN CAMERON

6 Evangelicals learning practical theology: Autobiographical reflections 100
ANDREW ROGERS

viii  Contents

7 Developing reflective practitioners: Engaging evangelical ordinands in theological reflection  116
LIZ HOARE

## PART III
## Engaging with practice  131

8 Educating for the common good: Engaging relational truth in a world of ideas  133
OLWYN MARK

9 Salvation's song  150
MATT SPENCER

## PART IV
## Engagement by students  167

10 Developing critical thinking within the context of a small group Bible study  169
ISAAC MCNISH

11 Theodrama: A contemporary application  177
SAMUEL NORMAN

12 Creating space: A reflection on chaplaincy work in a local day-hospice  185
FIONA MOORE

13 An Elim community pneumatologically engaged in corporate theological reflection  192
SHERYL ARTHUR

## PART V
## Theology that impacts church and world  201

14 Evangelical practical theology: Reviewing the past, analysing the present and anticipating the future  203
MARK J. CARTLEDGE

Conclusion  218
HELEN MORRIS AND HELEN CAMERON

| | |
|---|---|
| *Biography* | 225 |
| *Subject Index* | 245 |
| *Author Index* | 248 |
| *Biblical Index* | 254 |

# Acknowledgements

We would like to acknowledge the work of Helen Morris' colleagues at Moorlands College who worked with her on the conference which was the stimulus for this book and the Bible Society who worked in partnership with Moorlands in running this event.

We thank our contributors for working with us in a collaborative way, meeting the deadlines we set, and engaging with the purposes of this volume.

We are grateful to Kezia Johnson for providing editorial assistance.

We have valued the opportunity to collaborate on this volume and the stimulus to our own teaching, research, and writing that has flowed from that.

# Contributors

**Sheryl Arthur** is part-way through her doctorate in Practical Theology at the University of Roehampton, UK.

**Helen Cameron** is a Research Fellow at the Centre for Baptist Studies, Regent's Park College, Oxford and a Research Fellow at Wesley House, Cambridge.

**Mark J. Cartledge**, FRSA, is Principal of the London School of Theology and Professor of Practical Theology, UK.

**Liz Hoare** is Tutor for spiritual formation at Wycliffe Hall, Oxford where she has taught for thirteen years.

**Chloe Lynch** is Lecturer in Practical Theology at the London School of Theology, where she writes and teaches in the areas of leadership, ecclesiology, and spirituality.

**Olwyn Mark** is Lecturer in Practical Theology at Union Theological Colleg, Belfast.

**Alistair J. McKitterick** is a tutor and lecturer at Moorlands College, teaching practical theology, Christian spirituality, biblical theology, and hermeneutics.

**Isaac McNish** is a graduate of Moorlands College. He now works as a Mission Enabler for a rural Methodist Circuit in Cornwall.

**Fiona Moore** is a volunteer chaplain at a local day-hospice.

**Helen Morris** is Head of Postgraduate Studies at Moorlands College.

**Samuel Norman** is a recent graduate of Moorlands College and specialised in the area of missional leadership.

**Andrew Rogers** is Principal Lecturer in Practical Theology at the University of Roehampton, London, where he runs an open access ministerial formation programme and teaches on a professional doctorate in practical theology.

**Matt Spencer** is an ordained Salvation Army Officer, and has held appointments in The Salvation Army's Public Affairs and Social Policy Unit and on the teaching staff at William Booth College. Matt and wife Emma have led New

Addington Salvation Army Community Church since 2008, when Matt also founded SingCR0nise Community Choir.

**Andrew Thomas** divides his time between being the Senior Tutor at Moorlands College's South West centre and the Training Manager for South West Youth Ministries (SWYM).

# Introduction

*Helen Morris and Helen Cameron*

### Purpose and audience

This book has two main purposes. First, to give examples of practical theology written by people from across the evangelical and Pentecostal traditions in the UK. Second, to discuss the issues evangelicals raise when they engage in practical theology whether as practitioners, educators, or researchers.

The book has been edited with two main audiences in mind. The first audience is those already involved in studying, teaching, and researching in practical theology who wish to attend to the way in which evangelicals are engaging with the discipline. Practical theology is taught both in universities and in colleges that offer theological education to those preparing for ministry. University teachers often wish to illustrate the ways in which practical theologians engage with the Christian tradition in different ways. Those in theological education institutions desire to prepare ministers for the range of theological positions they will encounter. Students of practical theology are encouraged to engage with a range of ways of doing practical theology and so this book offers a variety of examples. For those engaging in research in practical theology there are examples of research undertaken by practical theologians.

The second audience is those who identify with the evangelical tradition but have not so far engaged with practical theology. This book hopes to introduce practical theology to this audience and discuss some of the issues it raises for evangelical scholars. By providing examples of practical theology, it aims to illustrate the contribution practical theology can make to the wider theological task whether undertaken in the university or the church.

### What is practical theology?

There are three definitions that are deployed by authors in this book. These definitions can therefore be seen as ones that resonate with evangelical writers.

The first is provided by John Swinton and Harriet Mowat in their highly valued textbook, *Practical Theology and Qualitative Research.* They are writing from the context of the University of Aberdeen but with the expectation

DOI: 10.4324/9781003094975-1

that many of their students will be studying practical theology because they are practitioners in the church.

They define practical theology as:

> critical, theological reflection on the practices of the Church as they interact with the practices of the world, with a view to ensuring and enabling faithful participation in God's redemptive practices in, to and for the world.[1]

This definition places God's redemptive practices as the focus for theology, something which evangelicals with their focus on the cross can identify with. The role of the church is also clear as one of the locations of the practices that are being reflected upon. The world is both a possible location for practice and the *telos* (goal) of God's redemptive practices.

A second definition is offered by the American scholar Bonnie Miller-McLemore in her introduction to the *Wiley-Blackwell Companion to Practical Theology* which she edited. Her definition reads:

> [P]ractical theology refers to an *activity* of believers seeking to sustain a life of reflective faith in the everyday, a *method* or way of analysing theology in practice used by religious leaders and by teachers and students across the theological curriculum, a *curricular area* in theological education focused on ministerial practice and subspecialties, and, finally, an *academic discipline* pursued by a smaller subset of scholars to support and sustain these first three enterprises.[2]

This definition has become popular because it shows the range of functions practical theology performs. This variety can be confusing for new students as different books tend to take one of these four functions as their starting point. This definition is also helpful because it highlights that other theological sub-disciplines, such as biblical studies, can perform the same four functions.

A final definition is that supplied by Pete Ward in his popular textbook, *Introducing Practical Theology*:

> I define practical theology as any way of thinking that takes both practice and theology seriously.[3]

Whilst Ward does not identify himself as evangelical by his academic affiliations, the introduction to his book raises a number of the concerns evangelicals bring to their study of practical theology. Ward argues that practical theology must do theology in the context of the church. Practical theology builds on ordinary ways of doing theology that are developed by taking part in the life of the church. Academic study builds on this but does not replace it. He goes on to argue that attempts to distinguish between practical theology that starts with practice and applied theology that starts with Scripture and doctrine are false.

Practice is seen through the beliefs and ideas that practitioners have gained by taking part in the church. The issues that believers bring to their study of Scripture and doctrine are shaped by their practice. Ward therefore rejects as a liberal assumption the idea that practice and theology can be separated.

In arguing for a broad definition of practical theology, Ward observes that material in other theological sub-disciplines and other academic fields can contribute to the task of practical theology thus making it wider than the key figures who self-identify as practical theologians. In line with his earlier work[4] Ward defines theology as 'sharing in the life of God.'[5] If relational engagement with God is the basis for theology, then prayer and worship have a central place in its practice and enable the theologian to develop both humility and confidence.

Ward's assessment signals that there is disagreement about how practical theology should be defined and that those disagreements are theological and not just matters of preference. In this brief discussion of three definitions of practical theology it is evident that evangelical writers favour definitions that take seriously the role of the church, the Christian tradition, and the relationship between the theologian and God.

## What is evangelical theology?

At the time of writing the word 'evangelical' is as contested a term as ever.[6] Michael F. Bird laments that 'the Evangelical label has become so broad as to be practically meaningless'[7]—although it is the term's association with particular political groups and expressions of Christianity that he sees as corrupt that troubles him more than the breadth *per se*. Mark Smith wryly notes that the definition of evangelicalism is so contested that the search for self-definition is one of the movement's defining features.[8] Nevertheless, neither Smith nor Bird seek to abandon the label. Rather they, like many others, recognise that although some of the apples have fallen far from the tree, the tree itself has deep and nourishing roots.[9] In his own definition, Bird, for example, uses the language of 'renewal' to describe the movement:

> When I refer to *evangelicalism*, I am referring to a historic and global phenomenon that seeks to achieve renewal in Christian churches by bringing the church into conformity to the gospel and by making the promotion of the gospel the chief mission of the church.[10]

Others affirm this focus on the gospel. Timothy Larsen contends that evangelicals are 'people of the gospel.'[11] Stanley Grenz concludes that the gospel is at the core of evangelicalism: 'to be "evangelical" means to be centred on the gospel.'[12] This gospel, in turn, is centred on the person and work of Christ. John Stackhouse maintains,

> [E]vangelical theology views Christ as the center of God's story—the most important thing God has ever done or said. The person and work of Christ

do not merely crown God's work of revelation and redemption as a sort of splendid ornament ... [but] ... constitute the defining chapter of the whole narrative, the hinge of history, the basis upon which everything else in creation makes sense.[13]

This emphasis on the saving work of Christ on the cross is reflected in Bebbington's 'quadrilateral of priorities,' consisting of conversionism, activism, biblicism, and crucicentrism.[14] Bebbington traces this quadrilateral, indeed evangelicalism's origins, to the eighteenth-century revivals. He acknowledges, however, continuity between the revivalists and the Reformers who preceded them.[15] Both the Reformers and revivalists maintained the divine inspiration and authority of Scripture as conveyed by Bebbington's 'biblicism'. Both emphasised justification by faith and the accompanying transformational new birth that is available through the sacrificial victory of Christ, as depicted through Bebbington's 'conversionism' and 'crucicentrism'. Moreover, although Bebbington sees a renewed assurance of salvation, enabled by Enlightenment confidence, as foundational to the missionary dynamism of the eighteenth-century revivals, Williams counters that their 'activism' was in continuity with the Reformers before them.[16] Therefore, regardless of where one locates the movement's roots, Bebbington's four priorities remains the most widely accepted definition of evangelicalism to date.[17] Indeed, even where Stackhouse endeavours to add a fifth distinctive, it is on the basis that the prioritising of the quadrilateral relativises other convictions—such as particular church structures and denominational affiliations. His addition of 'transdenominationalism' serves to reinforce, rather than undermine, Bebbington's assessment.[18]

Despite the wide acceptance of Bebbington's definition, much dispute remains. Rob Warner, for example, observes a bifurcation of English evangelicalism into 'conservatives' and 'entrepreneurs' in the mid- to late twentieth century. He contends that, whilst both affirm the quadrilateral, the conservatives have focused on biblicism and crucicentrism and the entrepreneurs on conversionism and activism. Prioritising the priorities differently has resulted in tension, conflict, and fragmentation.[19] Andrew Atherstone and David Ceri Jones observe that, when assessing evangelicalism more widely, scholars often identify a multiplicity of strands and offer a plethora of metaphors to depict this unity-in-diversity. They provide the examples of tribes, extended family, a mosaic, a kaleidoscope, streams and rivers within a single water course, and a '"rainbow" with a variety of hues.'[20] In addition, Alistair McGrath notes how evangelicalism's commitment to the authority of Scripture can sit in tension with its own traditions of interpretation. For instance, regarding the controversy generated by N. T. Wright's arguments about Paul's theology of justification McGrath asks,

Are evangelical New Testament scholars under some kind of family obligation to repeat what their forebears affirmed? Or are they under an absolute obligation to determine what Scripture says, even if this may prove to be in tension with what the evangelical tradition held, and held dearly?[21]

Accordingly, readers will observe differences in the flavour of evangelicalism reflected in this book. Some of the authors, for instance, write from a Pentecostal perspective.[22] The influence of Pentecostal and charismatic Christianity on global evangelicalism is significant. In particular, Larsen notes, these strands have brought pneumatology to the fore which, he observes, accords with the emphasis on the Spirit's work in the eighteenth-century revivals.[23] Readers will also detect the influence of charismatic Christianity on other authors in this volume. What the authors all share is a commitment to Scripture, hope in the transformative power of the good news of Jesus, and a conviction that theology empowered and enlivened by God's Spirit impacts both church and world.

## Evangelical engagement with practical theology: reservations and opportunities

In emphasising the role of Scripture within evangelicalism, Larsen maintains,

> Evangelicals believe that human beings are judged by the Bible and called to change in the light of it, rather than standing in judgement over the Bible and rejecting those parts that are not in line with their own sensibilities.[24]

As exemplified in Graham McFarlane's diagrammatic model of the 'evangelical quintilateral,'[25] whilst tradition, experience, reason, and the community all play an important role within evangelical theology, Scripture sits above these four components—albeit not independently, since no interpretation of Scripture occurs apart from the interpreter's particular location within this quintilateral.[26] Therefore, as Mark Noll contends, although there is much plurality within evangelical interpretations of the Bible, this disagreement in itself testifies to evangelicals' high regard for Scripture.[27] Liz Hoare and Benno van den Toren note that this high view of Scripture is the main reason for a reluctance within evangelical theological education to engage with practical theology, despite the emphasis within evangelicalism on practical Christian ministry and the local church. There is concern that the emphasis on experience within practical theology challenges evangelicalism's reliance on the Bible as God's redemptive truth.[28] For example, in assessing two prominent methodologies used within theological reflection, Helen Collins argues that these models' focus on 'experience, the present, critical incidents, other disciplines, and Enlightenment thinking' is accompanied by a corresponding neglect of 'the Bible, Christian experience, and God's agency.'[29] She maintains that such models 'are in tension with an evangelical, charismatic theology and with an intention to educate and form Christians for Christian ministry.'[30] Addressing practical theology more widely, Mark Cartledge concludes that, '[t]he majority of

6  *Helen Morris and Helen Cameron*

authors in academic practical theology either use Scripture in a limited manner or not at all.'[31] He clarifies that the work produced is theological, but sources other than direct engagement with the Bible are prioritised.[32]

This dearth of biblical engagement within published practical theology has prompted a reluctance amongst at least some evangelicals to engage with the discipline. Others, however, endeavour to challenge this deficiency, as Cartledge does in proposing a 'practical-theological' reading of Scripture.[33] Such challenges are to the benefit of both practical theology and evangelicalism. Writing in 2000, Alistair McGrath observed a 'widespread agreement within the evangelical theological community that evangelicals have not paid adequate attention to the issue of theological method'.[34] He clarifies that evangelicals do have a method, but this is often intuitive and unarticulated, much like an artist might produce their art without being able to specify exactly how they go about doing so. However, as McFarlane contends, every field of study and practice has its own methodology, 'grammar', and therefore it is important that evangelical theologians can identify and evaluate their particular method.[35] Grappling with which methodologies best enable biblical engagement within practical theology has the potential to elevate the use of the Bible within this discipline and encourage evangelical theologians to consider how their theologising can best inspire 'the mind of Christ' in thinking, words, and action.[36]

Therefore, despite the reservations identified above, there is much to be gained from evangelical engagement with practical theology. As the contents of this book testify, propelled by their activism to an ever-widening range of practice, evangelical churches and educators have then thought about how best to train those practitioners. Whereas formerly it had been possible to see the equipping with biblical theology and the development of practical skills as two parallel activities, there is now a desire for an integrated approach which has generated the turn to practical theology. In practical theology and the practice of theological reflection there is the potential to develop practitioners who can make active connections between their beliefs and actions and so further their impact on both church and world.

### Evangelicalism post-Trump

Sending this book to press in the aftermath of Donald Trump's departure from office as President of the USA we feel we must address the layers of meaning attached to the word evangelical. Practical theology aims to be a discipline that responds to the call for ever greater levels of reflexivity as times and contexts change. It is appropriate to pause and think about the layers of meaning in the word evangelical.

In the title of this book the word evangelical is used descriptively to refer to a wide and varied strand of theology that traces its roots to the Reformation and encompasses a range of church traditions both denominational and non-denominational. Earlier in this introduction we have highlighted the popular definition of Bebbington that indicates evangelicalism's emphases on the cross, the Bible, conversion, and activism. This book has chapters that critically examine all four of those markers. Evangelical theology is manifest in particular institutions, such as Moorlands College, whose 70th Anniversary occasioned the conference that catalysed this book. It is also manifest in theologians who would explicitly describe themselves as working within this strand, some embracing the description and others having a more critical relationship with it.

Beyond the descriptive, the word evangelical has always been, and is particularly at this time, a label for groups of people. Like all labels it carries baggage, some of which is relevant to some evangelicals in some places but not all of which is relevant to all evangelicals in all places. The evangelical movement tends to throw up prominent individuals who gather a following. The words and actions of those individuals are then seen as representing the views of their followers. In the USA, the label evangelical is applied to and claimed by some of those supporting political populism of the right. The speed and reach of social media mean that prominent evangelicals in other parts of the world feel a need to respond to the content of this labelling. There are then calls for them to withdraw support and condemn prominent individuals who espouse populism of the right. These pressures reflect the cultural dominance of the USA. They also reflect the growing recognition of Christianity as a world religion unable to deploy labels in fixed ways but subject to the same rapid, global, and fluctuating cultural identities as other faiths and ideologies.

Amongst Christians who identify as liberal there are those who have formerly identified as evangelical. Of these some have negative experiences of their time as evangelicals to share and have reached different evaluations of what they were taught in the past. Some of these evaluations are shared in the spirit of inquiry but others are deployed in debates that have both cultural as well as theological overtones. It is inevitable that whilst this book seeks to use the word evangelical in a theologically descriptive way, it will be read by some as contributing to these vital debates.

This book engages with the UK context and the preoccupations and concerns of evangelical practical theologians in that locale. Indeed, it has proved impossible to embrace the full diversity of evangelicalism even within that single context. In sticking with that limitation, the hope is that the book will provoke further publications by evangelical practical theologians who represent different elements of the UK context, and then evangelicals in other locations, so that a wider range of voices will be heard.

## Editors' opening reflexivity

As editors we want to briefly attempt to put something of our own evangelical engagement on the page. We hope this will provide some of the context for the editorial decisions we have made and supplement what we have said in our own chapters. We appreciate the way in which practical theology encourages the student, practitioner, teacher, and scholar to value their own voice and reflect upon the influences that have shaped it.

## Helen Cameron

I could have been a practical theologian much sooner if I hadn't been advised that, despite my undergraduate degree in theology, my interest in the life of the local church 'wasn't really theology' and that I should retrain as a social scientist. Fortunately, I found my first work in practical theology on a Master's programme at a Methodist institution that understood the value of inter-disciplinary partnership within practical theology. I am not complaining about this detour because formal qualifications in social policy came in very useful later in my career when I was lobbying politicians for changes in public policy to address injustice. As a member of The Salvation Army, which is an offshoot of Methodism, I am rooted in the Holiness tradition which places authority in Scripture but encourages a lively engagement with the Holy Spirit, activism in the world, and an international fellowship of believers. Being a woman who preaches goes back four generations in my family to the 1880s, so I don't suffer from doubts about the religious agency of women. However, the treatment of women in my tradition means I experience intellectual dissonance and engage in practices of solidarity and resistance.

None of this academic and church experience had led me to engage culturally with evangelicalism and so it was only in working at an Anglican theological college that I was pushed to say not only whether I was an evangelical but what sort of evangelical. Looking back over my writing in practical theology, it is my engagement with the Bible and my interest in the work of the Holy Spirit I would most readily identify as rooted in the Holiness Tradition. The fact that my working life has moved from the secular world to the university to the church and sometimes spanned those boundaries, I take as an outworking of the diaconal activism that is very much part of The Salvation Army. Coming from a non-learned tradition, I have done my academic theology as a guest in Methodist, Anglican, and Baptist institutions and so I have put more energy into helping my hosts articulate their theological tradition than giving voice to my own. I was therefore surprised when my co-editor invited me to speak at the Moorlands 70th Anniversary conference both as a practical theologian and a Salvationist. It was a helpful prompt to think more fully about my relationship to evangelical theology.

## Helen Morris

Having someone introduce you before speaking or preaching is always a risk and perhaps never more so than when the person knows you really well. So it was that my favourite introduction was given by my late grandma. I was preaching at her local church and her introduction started well: 'I am delighted that my granddaughter Helen is preaching this morning.' It then took an unexpected turn: 'I always remember how, when Helen was a small child, if she didn't get her own way, she would storm off to her room and slam the door behind her.' Great, thanks Gran, I remember thinking. Everyone will now be looking forward with great anticipation to hearing what the impetuous preacher has to say! She then went on to describe my conversion to faith in Jesus at the age of 11 and how, from her vantage point as my gran, she observed a marked change in my life from that point onwards. She didn't, and couldn't, have gone on to say that all stubbornness was relinquished from that point on. However, the change that she observed matched my own experience of God's gracious work in my life up to and following a classical evangelical presentation of the good news of Jesus Christ, in response to which I realised that I wasn't a Christian simply because other members of my family were but was being invited into a personal relationship with Jesus as Saviour and Lord.

Alongside this personal experience of Christian discipleship came a keen interest in the intellectual aspects of faith. The intellectual coherence of the Christian faith has long been important to me and so plaguing my Baptist minister father with theological questions as a child developed into more formal and academic study and teaching of theology as an adult. It is relatively recently in this formal setting that I have engaged with the academic discipline of practical theology. However, in relation to the first strand of Miller-McLemore's definition—'an activity of believers seeking to sustain a life of reflective faith in the everyday'[37]—I have engaged in practical theology throughout my Christian life. My ongoing encounter with Jesus as Lord and Saviour has propelled me to reflect on how Christian discipleship impacts a person's character and actions.

My more recent explorations of practical theology as a method, curricular area, and academic discipline has helped me to understand and articulate the reflexivity I undertook more intuitively in the past and has enabled greater criticality in my practical theologising. I have also experienced the tensions expressed by others within the evangelical tradition regarding the role of Scripture in practical theology.[38] It is for this reason that I was keen to provide a forum for evangelical practical theology within the 70th Anniversary of Moorlands College conference that prompted the publication of this book. I was delighted when Helen Cameron agreed to present the keynote address at this conference and offer her expertise in the editing of this book. My hope is that this book will enable evangelicals to explore how the discipline of practical theology can sharpen their lived expression of Christian discipleship as well as demonstrating the fruitfulness of evangelical engagement with practical theology within the wider field.

## Chapter summaries

The book is divided into five parts which give further insights into its purposes. The different parts contain theoretical arguments, reflections on practice from teachers of practical theology and practitioners in the church and world, and provocations to think differently about taken for granted ways of working. This range of different genres reflects the diversity of approaches encouraged by practical theology.

Part I contains four chapters engaging with the nature of practical theology as a discipline. Part II contains two reflections on practice from experienced teachers of practical theology and one provocation to question the way in which practical theology is taught. Part III offers two extended reflections on practice that span the boundary between church and world. Part IV contains four examples of work undertaken by students, three undergraduates and one doctoral student. These are there to encourage students that they too have a contribution to make to the discipline and that they are not just recipients of the wisdom of their teachers. Part V is an attempt to take an overview of the book's purposes. Mark Cartledge who has taught practical theology in both the USA and UK gives his perspective on the past, present, and future of practical theology. The book concludes with our reflection as editors on what we have learned from the book and how that might shape future engagements by evangelicals with practical theology.

*Part 1—Engaging with the discipline*

In chapter one, Andrew Thomas explores the tensions that exist between evangelicalism and practical theology, arguing that such tensions are largely related to methodology. He explores these tensions in reference to Bebbington's quadrilateral, arguing that such an analysis sheds light on evangelicals' objections to non-evangelical practical theology and, *vice versa*, why evangelicalism has come under critique from practical theologians. Thomas maintains that engagement with this mutual critique results in an enrichment of the four distinctives of evangelicalism expressed in Bebbington's quadrilateral. The evangelical focus on 'biblicism' is enriched by attention to the role of the Spirit in illuminating Scripture to the community of God's people. A pneumatological focus enables both evangelical and non-evangelical practical theologians to move beyond the impasse of where one should start, Scripture or experience, to a recognition of both the complex interplay between the two and, for evangelicals, the centrality of Scripture regardless of starting point. The evangelical distinctive of 'crucicentrism' provides an important qualification to an evangelical focus on biblical authority. Evangelicals should approach theology with the compassion and humility that is exemplified through Jesus' cruciform love. Such an attitude is encouraged when evangelicals see themselves as both under the authority of the text and ongoing participants in the grand narrative of the text. The evangelical focus on 'conversionism' is qualified by an appreciation of the richness and fullness of the gospel of Jesus Christ, in contrast to reductionist conceptions. Finally, the global impact of evangelicalism through its focus on 'activism' is qualified by a biblical critique of Western conceptions of time. Such analysis encourages a timefull approach to ministry, wherein Christ's followers walk at his speed—the 'three-mile-an-hour' speed of love.

In chapter two, Chloe Lynch proposes a mode of doing practical theology based on Walter Brueggemann's notion of 'prophetic imagination', which is derived from his assessment of the biblical prophet's engagement with the world. In this mode of practical theologising, the practical theologian, like the Old Testament prophet, presents an alternative reality to the 'dominant consciousness' (ideology of the age) that they confront. Their aim is to challenge the ideology and practices around them in light of their God-given perspective on the world and inspire the community of God's people towards God's promises of hope. The way things are often benefits the practical theologian—consumerism, for instance, profits those with the means to enjoy its fruits even whilst others are oppressed by it. Therefore, central to practical theology in the mode of prophetic imagination are the practices of repentance and lament. An experience of pain is therefore the first of the four 'pillars' on which prophetic imagination rests. The other three pillars are: memory of God's work and revelation in the past; appropriate language with which to express both lament and hope, drawn from the images and metaphors that have come before; and action based on the hope of God's promises, and his own fulfilment of these promises, such that the alternative reality seen through divine revelation becomes embedded in current reality—or, as God's kingdom comes on earth as it is in heaven. The role of imagination is key to this mode of doing practical theology. This is not imagination detached from reason or revelation but imagination that is Spirit-led and Christ-shaped and therefore able to reimagine how things could and should be in conformity with God's character and plans. The accountability and support of the community of God's people is vital in this enterprise. Lynch explores the interrelationship, and challenges, of the academy and church in this regard. Last, she offers her own doctoral studies—*Ecclesial Leadership as Friendship*, published by Routledge—as an example of what practical theology in the mode of prophetic imagination can look like in practice. Her own experience of 'sitting with pain' in this process bears testimony to the power of pathos in the practical theologian's task.

In chapter three, Alistair McKitterick addresses the role of teleology[39] in practical theology. He affirms the benefits of interdisciplinary dialogue with the natural and social sciences within practical theology but argues that, within this dialogue, theology has a distinctive ability to give an account of the *telos* (purpose or goal) of human life. Therefore, although the social sciences are important dialogue partners for practical theology in the indicative (descriptive) mood—when formulating a critical account of what is currently the case—it is only theology that can speak in the imperative to urge change or reinforce the status quo. Whilst theology alone can provide the required teleological foundations for practical theology, confusion and inaccuracy result from the prevalent misconception that God has just one *telos*. Drawing on David Kelsey, McKitterick argues that God has, in fact, at least three *teloi*—he argues for four. God's purpose in creation is distinct from his goal in redemption which, in turn, cannot be conflated with the end goal of eschatological consummation. The fourth *telos*, absent from Kelsey's assessment, is God's purpose in incarnation. McKitterick maintains that there would be greater clarity and criticality within practical theologising if practical theologians were more aware and explicit about which of the three (or four) irreducible *teloi* they adopt in any one scenario. To illustrate the difference this can make, he addresses the issue of transgenderism, arguing that if practical theology is to be of value to theologians and Christian ministers, it must be able to address the complex and difficult topics. McKitterick concludes by proposing that holding God's irreducible *teloi* in narrative tension in the story of Scripture, alongside the illumination and guidance of God's Spirit, enables the practical theologian to discern which of the *teloi* should govern their praxis in a given situation. This discernment, by virtue of being articulated and defended, enables a more open and critical dialogue between theologians than when such selections are unwitting, or the multiplicity of *teloi* are inaccurately conflated.

In chapter four, Helen Morris assesses Pete Ward's analysis of the evangelical church's espoused and lived (operant)[40] expressions of the gospel. Ward contends that the contextualisation of sung worship into the popular music genre has led to a preponderance of song lyrics that aim to facilitate experiential encounter with God, in contrast to those that convey truths about God's nature and works or the implications of God's acts for the believer. This contextualisation has impacted Christians' operant understanding of the gospel—that which is revealed through believers' actions and words—which focuses on the experience of God's love and the assurance that God has a good plan for the believer's life. This operant understanding contrasts with the evangelical church's espoused presentation of the gospel—what the church says it believes—which is focused on the forgiveness that comes through Jesus' sacrifice. Morris agrees that the contextualisation of sung worship into the popular music genre has been impactful in this regard but contends that the cultural analysis of Charles Taylor provides a larger framework for understanding the discrepancy that Ward observes. A hallmark of secularism is the *telos*, or goal, of human flourishing without allegiance to anything external. Ward's observations suggest that this *telos* has unhealthily impacted the evangelical church's operant conception of the gospel, with the risk that believers see their relationship with God as an aid to the project of 'self' rather than submitting their lives to God in worship and service. Ward's proposed solution is that the church conveys a richer and fuller expression of the gospel that is more firmly rooted in the Gospels' account of Jesus and the grand narrative of Scripture. Morris affirms this proposal. However, she also maintains that evangelicalism's commitment to evangelism means that evangelical believers need to be equipped to share the gospel in ways that are faithful and succinct. Providing the Apostle Paul as an example, she argues that gospel presentations should invite people into the wider narrative of Scripture rather than imply that what can be said in one or two minutes is all that there is to be said. Morris also encourages gospel presenters to include the topic of human flourishing, both to bring awareness of the differences between biblical conceptions and secular counterparts and because human flourishing provides a pertinent point of connection within contemporary culture.

*Part II—Engaging with education*

In chapter five, Helen Cameron provides an edited version of her keynote address delivered to a conference celebrating the 70th Anniversary of Moorlands College. Utilising the pedagogical technique of chiasmus,[41] Cameron tops and tails her chapter by engaging with two narratives in Luke's Gospel: the boy

Jesus in the temple (Luke 2:41–52) and Jesus' encounter with two disciples on the road to Emmaus (Luke 24:13–35). The centre of her chiastic structure is drawn from the language of 'these/the things', which refers in both accounts to the works of Jesus. In context, the things of Jesus are not immediately understood and so invite both personal contemplation (Luke 2:51) and conversation with others (Luke 24:17–18). Calling this central section 'What things?', Cameron invites the reader to reflect on the things that matter most to people through listening to others' questions, with Scripture as the shared text around which conversation develops. Within this, she argues, there is a need to reflect on how the authority of Scripture is received and engaged with, raising questions about the extent to which normativity should be ascribed to particular traditions of interpretation. The other two layers of her chiastic structure consist of reflections on recent developments within practical theology and theological education. Demonstrating a contextual approach, she explores how the College's approach to theological education has developed during its 70-year history, from its inception through to the 70th Anniversary conference. Having reflected on the College's history, Cameron makes proposals regarding the College's future practice. At the heart of these proposals is her contention that students' own questions and concerns ('these things' that they are pondering) should take a more central place within the curriculum. For instance, students could engage in action research to investigate their own questions and they could contribute to co-designed assessments. Bringing students' own questions into greater focus would not diminish the importance of learning about Scripture, church tradition, and church doctrine in the classroom environment. However, allowing students' questions to be triggers for further exploration in these areas would better equip them for service in the church and world. The questions asked and answered in the classroom need to be accompanied by a willingness to travel alongside others on the road.

In chapter six, Andrew Rogers draws on his extensive experience in learning, teaching, and researching practical theology to reflect on evangelical engagement with the discipline. He demonstrates how, over the last two decades, there has been a marked increase in evangelical engagement to the mutual enrichment of both evangelicalism and practical theology. Utilising an autobiographical approach, Rogers reflects on five learning contexts: his earlier formation in churches and Christian organisations, his formal theological education, his experience of research, his participation in the British and Irish Association for Practical Theology, and teaching Pentecostals practical theology. He notes both the tensions that he has experienced as an evangelical engaged in practical theology and the benefits that such study has brought. Areas of tension include the use of the Bible in practical theology, within which it is not always granted the normative and authoritative role that Scripture has within evangelicalism. Rogers also reflects on the 'methodological atheism' within the qualitative research methods developed within the social sciences and adopted, sometimes uncritically, by practical theologians. He refers to the 2006 publication of *Practical Theology and Qualitative Research* by John Swinton and Harriet

Mowat as a turning point in this regard. He observes that Swinton and Mowat gave voice to the issues he and others had been wrestling with and provided a fruitful way forward through proposing an asymmetric relationship between the two disciplines (practical theology and the social sciences). Rogers argues that, notwithstanding these tensions, the benefits of evangelical and Pentecostal engagement with practical theology have been significant. He has seen his own faith and practice, and that of his students, transformed by the critical awareness that practical theology encourages. In particular, he argues that practical theology—particularly theological reflection—encourages the 'So what?' reflex such that students learn to expect that their theologising will lead to action. Rogers concludes with five reflections that arise from his autobiographical account. The last of these five confirms the title of this book, that evangelical and Pentecostal engagement with practical theology impacts church and world. The habit of theological reflection leads to transformed understanding and practices, which benefits both churches and wider communities.

In chapter seven, Liz Hoare reflects on her experience of teaching theological reflection to evangelical ordinands. Drawing on her own empirical research, Hoare observes a shift in attitude to theological reflection over the last decade, with the benefits of the discipline increasingly appreciated by evangelical students. She identifies developments in her own pedagogy that have contributed to this increasingly positive approach, alongside a number of external factors. External factors include an increase in the demographic diversity of the student group, enabling students to learn from a wider variety of perspectives. She also notes how recent evangelical contributions to the discipline of theological reflection, including her own article co-authored with Benno van de Toren, have provided theological reflectors with methodologies that more robustly and explicitly maintain the authority of Scripture that is so central within evangelicalism. This contrasts with other expressions and models of theological reflection that, Hoare argues, have been rightly critiqued for being Bible-lite. A further factor identified is the more integrative approach to the curriculum that has arisen over recent years. This integrative approach has enabled students to draw from their learning across the different modules to aid their reflections. In relation to her own teaching, Hoare identifies developments resulting from her experience. These include the production of her own resources to help students better navigate the relevant textbooks. She has also changed the metaphors that she uses to frame and inspire the reflective process and put a greater emphasis on biblical examples that demonstrate the role of experience in theologising. In addition, Hoare reflects on how drawing on her students' own examples has been inspirational and informative for others. Moreover, moving from the language of 'change', which can be construed both positively and negatively, to that of 'growth' has alleviated students' fears that theological reflection might unhealthily distort their core Christian convictions. Finally, Hoare reflects on how embedding theological reflection in the topic of discipleship has enabled evangelical students to better grasp the fruitfulness of this important and transformative discipline.

*Part III—Engaging with practice*

In chapter eight, Olwyn Mark proposes that Christians engage actively in public discourse around Relationships and Sex Education (RSE), rather than withdraw from the policy discussions or the teaching and learning that accompanies such culturally sensitive and contentious subjects. Focusing specifically on government guidance and legislation in England, Mark argues that there is the opportunity for Christians to present their particular perspective on sex and relationships. She contends that the Christian conception of human flourishing should be the guiding motif for such engagement, noting that anything other than the most minimalistic risk-reduction approach to sex education (reducing unintended pregnancies and cases of STIs) requires an undergirding narrative that elucidates what healthy relationships consist of, including those of a sexual nature. The Christian faith, she contends, presents a better story than secular humanist counterparts in this regard, despite the latter's erroneous claims to normative neutrality. The Christian narrative clashes with aspects of current RSE guidance, such as the removal of 'self-control' and 'self-sacrifice' from the lists of personal attributes in this guidance despite the centrality of these virtues within the Christian faith. Such a move reflects wider culture's esteeming of sexual pleasure as central to human flourishing and fulfilment. Mark observes that the emphasis on sexual fulfilment within contemporary culture provides little rationale or motivation for a young person to say 'no' to or delay first sex. However, research amongst young people indicates that significant percentages do not think that they had sex at the right time, and there is further evidence that sex in contexts that most closely align with the steadfast love and commitment of Christian marriage are healthier and less damaging than those such as hook-ups and one-night stands. Christianity's emphasis on freedom of choice means that Christians should not seek to restrict or coerce others' autonomous decision making. However, neither should Christians simply retreat from engagement with this important topic. Rather, the Christian account of human flourishing is richer and more robust than the current cultural narrative. Whilst not impelling young people to make choices that align with Christian values, presenting Christianity's 'better story' provides a compelling reason why someone would choose to wait until marriage to engage in a sexual relationship, and indeed gives an account for why someone would choose to never have sex at all.

In chapter nine, Matt Spencer reflects on his experience leading a community choir in reference to the five missional Ways of Being. These are: the facilitation and nurture of community; empowerment for and engagement in ministry; the integration of internal structures with external action; the authentic communication of the truth; and the embodiment and enactment of Christian hope. Drawing on his doctoral studies, particularly the qualitative research gathered for this thesis, he contends that the community choir can be seen to play an important role in God's mission (the *missio Dei*). In relation to the five Ways of Being, the community choir contributes to God's mission by, first, facilitating community building that is both inclusive and outward focused. Second, the

16  *Helen Morris and Helen Cameron*

choir empowers its participants for and ministry. This is the case even for those who are not Christians, Spencer argues, since all members participate in singing of, and therefore bearing witness to, the truths of the gospel through the lyrics that are sung. Third, the choir integrates internal structures with external action through benefitting the participants' spiritual, mental, and emotional health in ways that motivate and equip them to benefit their wider community. Fourth, songs are capable of making biblical truths more accessible, enabling the conveyance of biblical truth both to the singers and those who listen. Last, Spencer argues, the community choir contributes to the embodiment and enactment of hope through the creation of experiential spaces in which the act of singing produces physical, psychological, social, and spiritual benefits which overwhelm those things that stifle hope. In singing with the choir, participants are temporarily distanced from the problems of their life. They experience momentarily a hint of that for which Christians hope eternally.

*Part IV—Engagement by students*

In chapter ten, Isaac McNish utilises Alistair McKitterick's Theological Imperative Model to reflect upon his experience leading a Bible study group. He focuses on a moment of disequilibrium experienced by one member of the group when their concept of 'heaven' was challenged by his description of heaven and earth coming together, in contrast to heaven being a place people escape earth to reach. McNish observes that his impulse was to resolve the situation by minimising the differences between the two views and questions whether this was the best approach. Utilising tools from social psychology, educational psychology, and theology to 'complexify' his understanding of the event, he explores the influence of group dynamics on his own and others' behaviour and examines the role of disequilibrium within learning. In line with McKitterick's model, he identifies a theological imperative to move his thinking and practice forwards. McNish concludes that in future Bible study leading he will utilise the 'shared journey of faith' as a guiding metaphor to encourage the group to be open to challenge and change. In addition, when providing a dissenting voice, he will try to resist the temptation to minimise differences to avoid discomfort. Last, he will invite the group to engage with the content of their discussions, and any ongoing disequilibrium or tension, within corporate prayer at the end of each meeting.

In chapter eleven, Sam Norman explores how a theodramatic approach[42] could help Christians address the topic of relativism. Norman acknowledges that relativism can be defined as seeing everything else as relative in relation to one thing that is fixed. However, he maintains that, in common parlance, relativism refers to claims that lack an anchor in anything absolute. He identifies two types of relativism: the explicit relativism that a person might espouse and the implicit relativism that is revealed when a person's actions are not in line with the more objective beliefs that they claim to hold. Whilst noting the overlap, Norman contends that explicit relativism is more prevalent outside the church but that implicit relativism—revealed in contradictions between what people say they believe and how they live—is common within the church. He maintains that theodrama is an effective approach to addressing both types of relativism. As regards discrepancies between Christians' beliefs and actions, presenting the Bible as a grand narrative encourages Christians to live out its truths, much like an actor acts out the words of a play. Improvisation is essential, but the 'script' of Scripture enables Christians to locate their lives and identity in a story that is moving towards a definitive end. In relation to the explicit relativism that a person might espouse, Norman observes that such a philosophy can result in a life that lacks an anchor in anything solid. He argues that, for those struggling to find identity and meaning as a result, theodrama provides a mooring in the grand narrative of God's revelation through Scripture and can therefore be an effective approach in evangelism.

In chapter twelve, Fiona Moore reflects on her college placement in the context of hospice chaplaincy. She recalls an occasion when a time of silence created space for a movement of God's Spirit in a patient's life. This experience prompts Moore to reflect on the role of stillness and silence within evangelical spirituality. She notes how, in her own life, the pursuit of silence can sit in uncomfortable tension with her evangelical activism. For others, silence is something to be feared and avoided as it can open up space for sad and anxious thoughts. Therefore, in looking beyond this singular incident, Moore explores how silence can be responsibly integrated into hospice chaplaincy work, noting the importance of the Spirit's guidance within this.

In chapter thirteen, Sheryl Arthur reflects on what a pneumatological approach to corporate theological reflection could consist of from a classical Pentecostal perspective. Drawing on her own fieldwork conducted within an Elim Pentecostal church, and engaging with contemporary Pentecostal scholarship, Arthur explores how intentionally creating space for congregants (and the researcher) to wait upon and respond to the leading of the Spirit can result in meaningful connections between Scripture and personal Holy Spirit encounter. In evaluating this research, she offers three caveats for anyone considering a similar approach to research design. First, she notes the tendency of the participants to employ a 'this is that' hermeneutic in interpreting the texts selected. Such an approach is in line with Peter's interpretation in Acts 2, when he explains the Pentecostal event (this) as a fulfilment of Joel's prophecy (that). On this occasion, for the participants in her research, the 'this is that' approach produced fruitful insights. Arthur warns, however, that such a hermeneutical approach might not be appropriate for all biblical texts, such as certain Old Testament passages. Second, she observes that the particular group's familiarity and ease with 'waiting on the Spirit' could not be assumed in other contexts. Last, Arthur notes the unpredictability inherent in the approach she adopted, and warns that not all researchers will feel comfortable with the flexibility that is required within this sort of process. She concludes by recognising the benefit of giving consideration to the theological starting point of a congregation, so that congregants are empowered to work in collaboration with the researcher in authentically representing their faith and praxis.

18  *Helen Morris and Helen Cameron*

*Part V—Theology that impacts church and world*

In chapter fourteen, Mark Cartledge reviews the past and present shape of evangelical practical theology in order to address issues raised by and within the discipline and plot a possible way forward. In his review of evangelical practical theology, Cartledge identifies at least three different levels of practical theology within the academy: skill-based training, reflective practice, and research (both theoretical and empirical). He observes that most evangelical practical theology is skills-based, with some reflective practice incorporated within undergraduate and postgraduate programmes. In contrast, most non-evangelical practical theology consists of research. This, he contends, explains some of the distance that exists between evangelicals and the rest of the practical theology academy. A further source of distance, and the most significant for evangelicals, regards the limited engagement with sources of theology within non-evangelical practical theology. In particular, he and others have found the use of Scripture within practical theology to lack depth—either a 'proof-text' approach is used or a thin thematic treatment. The response by evangelicals has been to prioritise a starting point in Scripture, in contrast to practical theology's emphasis on starting with experience. However, contesting the starting point misses the point, Cartledge contends, since all experiences are shaped by confessional commitments and every engagement with Scripture is shaped by the interpreter's context. The real issue is weight, not chronology. Acknowledging this would encourage evangelical practical theologians to draw more explicitly and intentionally from their own traditions and sources and from other theological sub-disciplines, such as biblical studies and systematic theology. Having assessed the past and present shape of evangelical practical theology, to develop this discipline in the future Cartledge proposes a collaborative approach between evangelicalism and practical theology that focuses on seven main areas: (1) engagement with the evangelical tradition; (2) the crossing of theological sub-disciplinary boundaries; (3) engagement with the social sciences; (4) empirical research; (5) attention to intercultural and non-western voices; (6) concern for and an ability to address issues in public life; and (7) engagement with digitally mediated Christianity.

## Notes

1 John Swinton, and Harriet Mowat, *Practical Theology and Qualitative Research*, 2nd ed. (London, SCM Press, 2016), 7.
2 Bonnie J. Miller-McLemore, ed., *The Wiley-Blackwell Companion to Practical Theology* (Chichester: Wiley-Blackwell, 2012), 5.
3 Pete Ward, *Introducing Practical Theology: Mission, Ministry and the Life of the Church* (Grand Rapids, Baker Academic, 2017), 5.
4 Pete Ward, *Participation and Mediation: A Practical Theology for the Liquid Church* (London, SCM, 2008).
5 Ward, *Introducing Practical Theology*, 6.
6 As Atherstone and Ceri Jones observe, debate over the definition of evangelicalism is not unusual. They note, 'In every generation, from the eighteenth century to the

present, evangelical identity has been contested.' Andrew Atherstone and David Ceri Jones, "Evangelicals and Evangelicalisms: Contested Identities," in *The Routledge Research Companion to the History of Evangelicalism*, eds. Andrew Atherstone and David Ceri Jones (Milton: Taylor & Francis Group, 2018), 3.
7 Michael F. Bird, *Evangelical Theology: A Biblical and Systematic Introduction*, 2nd ed. (Grand Rapids: Zondervan Academic, 2020), xvi.
8 Mark Smith, "British Evangelical Identities: Locating the Discussion," in *British Evangelical Identities Past and Present: Aspects of the History and Sociology of Evangelicalism in Britain and Ireland*, ed. Mark Smith (Milton Keynes: Paternoster, 2008), 1–2; cf. Atherstone and Ceri Jones, "Contested Identities," 8.
9 David Hilborn, "Evangelical Theology," in *New Dictionary of Theology: Historical and Systematic*, 2nd ed., eds. Martin Davie et al. (London: IVP, 2012), 309.
10 Bird, *Evangelical Theology*, xxv.
11 Timothy Larsen, "Defining and Locating Evangelicalism," in *The Cambridge Companion to Evangelical Theology*, eds. Timothy Larsen and Daniel J. Treier (Cambridge: Cambridge University Press, 2007), 9.
12 Stanley J. Grenz, *Renewing the Center: Evangelical Theology in a Post-Theological Era*, 2nd ed. (Grand Rapids: Baker Academic, 2006), 345.
13 John G. Stackhouse, *Evangelical Landscapes: Facing Critical Issues of the Day* (Grand Rapids: Baker Academic, 2002), 166.
14 David W. Bebbington, *Evangelicalism in Modern Britain: A History from the 1730s to the 1980s* (London: Unwin Hyman, 1989), 3.
15 Contra those who locate the earliest roots of evangelicalism in the Reformation, Bebbington contends that, whilst the word 'Evaungelicalles' was used to describe Reformation advocates, its meaning was '"of the gospel" in a non-partisan sense.' He argues that it was only used to define certain groups (namely revivalists and revivalist doctrines) in contrast to others in the 1730s onwards. (Bebbington, *Evangelicalism in Modern Britain*, 1).
16 Garry J. Williams, "Was Evangelicalism Created by the Enlightenment?" *Tyndale Bulletin* 53, no. 2 (2002) 283–314, 311–313 and Bebbington, *Evangelicalism in Modern Britain*, 42 and 48.
17 As Larsen notes, 'no other definition comes close to rivalling its level of general acceptance' (Larsen, "Defining," 1). For example, although Williams argues that the roots of evangelicalism lie in the Reformation, this is because he maintains that the quadrilateral of priorities Bebbington identifies derived from this movement. It is not because he thinks that Bebbington's identification of evangelical priorities is inaccurate. (Although at the end of the article it becomes apparent that Williams' concern is doctrinal and not just historical in that he intends to establish Calvinism as foundational to evangelicalism and Arminian theology as deviant.) (Williams, "Evangelicalism," 314).
18 Stackhouse, *Evangelical Landscapes*, 164–165.
19 Rob Warner, *Reinventing English Evangelicalism 1966–2001: A Theological and Sociological Study* (Milton Keynes: Paternoster, 2007), 15, 20, 235.
20 Atherstone and Ceri Jones, "Contested Identities," 4.
21 Alistair E. McGrath, "Evangelical Theological Method: The State of the Art," in *Evangelical Futures: A Conversation on Theological Method*, ed. John G. Stackhouse (Grand Rapids: Baker Books, 2000), 31.
22 In his chapter in this book, Mark Cartledge notes that the relationship between evangelicalism and Pentecostalism is construed differently around the world, with the two very distinct in the USA but almost synonymous in Vietnam. Therefore, in line with Cartledge's analysis of the UK context, we have included Pentecostal perspectives as a key subset within UK evangelicalism.
23 Larsen, "Defining," 10.
24 Larsen, "Defining," 8.

25 McFarlane's quintilateral is based on the Wesleyan Quadrilateral, with the addition of 'community' as a fifth key component within evangelical theology (Graham McFarlane, *A Model for Evangelical Theology: Integrating Scripture, Tradition, Reason, Experience, and Community* [Grand Rapids: Baker Academic, 2020], 66–67).
26 McFarlane, *Evangelical Theology*, 67.
27 Noll, "Evangelicals and the Bible," 22–23, 31.
28 Liz Hoare and Benno van den Toren, "Evangelicals and Contextual Theology: Lessons from Missiology for Theological Reflection," *Practical Theology* 8, no, 2 (2015): 1–22, 1–2. On the emphasis within evangelicalism on the Bible's redemptive truth, see Mark A. Noll, "Evangelicals and the Bible" in *The Routledge Research Companion to the History of Evangelicalism*, eds. Andrew Atherstone and Jones, David Ceri (Milton: Taylor & Francis Group, 2018), 23.
29 Helen Collins, *Reordering Theological Reflection: Starting with Scripture* (London: SCM, 2020), 35–36.
30 Collins, *Reordering Theological Reflection*, 35. It is not my intention to assess Collins' arguments on this point, but simply to note her work as one recent example of evangelical reservations about the methodologies developed within practical theology.
31 Mark J. Cartledge, *The Mediation of the Spirit: Interventions in Practical Theology* (Grand Rapids: William B. Eerdmans, 2015), 43 cf. Collins, *Reordering*, 48.
32 Cartledge, *Mediation of the Spirit*, 43.
33 Cartledge, *Mediation of the Spirit*, 45.
34 McGrath, "Evangelical Theological Method," 15.
35 McFarlane, *Evangelical Theology*. 8.
36 Vanhoozer and Treier write, 'The canon [of Scripture] trains us to think evangelically, *tuning* each string in our soul so that we vibrate in harmony with what God is doing in Christ. Taken together, the stories, songs, teachings, apocalyptic visions and so forth orient desires, form beliefs, shape imagination and prompt action—in a word, they cultivate *wisdom*: knowledge that gets lived out. Scripture's role, therefore, in the economy of light is to radiate the multicoloured truth of what is in Christ into ready hearts and minds, and thus to form new habits of right thinking and desiring—in a word, the mind of Christ' (Kevin J. Vanhoozer and Daniel J. Treier, *Theology and the Mirror of Scripture: A Mere Evangelical Account* [London: IVP, 2016], 99–100).
37 Miller-McLemore, *Companion to Practical Theology*, 5.
38 This is an area I have endeavoured to contribute to through my doctoral studies, within which I included the methodology of biblical exegesis to explore what the outcome might be if Paul's body of Christ texts were brought more to the fore within the ecclesiology of those seeking to re-contextualise church in light of cultural change (see Helen Morris, *Flexible Church: Being the Church in the Contemporary World* [London: SCM, 2019]).
39 Teleology is examination in reference to a goal or purpose.
40 The language of 'espoused' and 'operant' is derived from the 'four voices of theology' identified by the Action Research: Church and Society (ARCS) project. In this schema, espoused theology refers to an individual or group's articulated beliefs (what people say they believe). Operant, or lived, theology, refers to the theology evident in an individual or group's practice (how people live). Normative theology refers to the authoritative theology derived from Scripture, church tradition, and/or officially pronounced as the formal doctrine of any one church or group of churches. Formal theology is the contribution of academia (Helen Cameron, Deborah Bhatti, Catherine Duce, James Sweeney, and Clare Watkins, *Talking about God in Practice: Theological Action Research and Practical Theology* [London: SCM, 2010], 49–56).
41 Chiasmus is a rhetorical technique wherein texts are structured in some sort of A B A' pattern (or multiple layers such as A B C D C' B' A'), such as 1 Corinthians 13,

which has the pattern A: love and spiritual gifts (13:1–3), B: love (13:4–7), A': love and spiritual gifts (13:8–12) (Roy E. Ciampa and Brian S. Rosner, *The First Letter to the Corinthians* [Grand Rapids: Eerdmans, 2010], 620).

42 Wesley Vander Lugt notes that there is affinity between a theodramatic approach and narrative theology. He argues, however, that theodrama places greater emphasis on performance and participation than narrative theology, contending that 'while a narrative framework emphasizes understanding a story from the past, a theodramatic framework highlights our present participation in a drama extending from the past into the future' (Wesley Vander Lugt, *Living Theodrama: Reimagining Theological Ethics* [Farnham: Ashgate, 2014], 7). In his chapter, Norman explores Kevin Vanhoozer and N. T. Wright's descriptions of Scripture as a five-act play, noting that although their delineation of the five acts differs, both promote the concept of improvising from the 'script' of Scripture.

# Part I
# Engaging with the discipline

# 1 Practical theology and evangelicalism
## Methodological considerations[1]

*Andrew Thomas*

## Introduction

Ever since I came to faith in an independent church in Surrey in 1990, I have identified myself as an evangelical Christian. Over the past 30 years I have been exposed to varied forms of evangelical Christianity and theological questions have been posed by the practices of others, none more so than in my time as a doctoral student in the department of Practical Theology at the University of South Africa (UNISA). The issues raised at UNISA have continued to challenge me, initially as a someone involved in church leadership, and more recently as a theological educator with Moorlands College.

Many of the challenges I have faced as an evangelical practical theologian have focused around methodology. In this chapter, I will be using a definition provided by Swinton and Mowat who note that methodology, 'has to do with an overall approach to a particular field. It implies a family of methods that have in common particular philosophical and epistemological assumptions.'[2] Different forms of theology can adopt divergent methodologies and it is the interaction between some of the methodologies of evangelical theology and those utilised within areas of practical theology that will be my focus here. Definitions for practical theology and evangelicalism will be offered before definitive aspects of evangelical theology are considered alongside methodological issues that can exist in theological practice. The chapter will conclude with proposals encouraging evangelicals to broader engagement with practical theology. Evangelicalism is a global phenomenon and I have been impacted by this diversity of thinking during my studies and ministry. I have therefore included sources and material that reflect this interaction.

## What is practical theology?

Attempts to define practical theology have often led to two extremes: some have felt it to be undefinable, whilst others have offered overly simplified suggestions that have failed to capture the complexity of the discipline.[3] A suitably broad definition is offered by Miller-McLemore who states:

DOI: 10.4324/9781003094975-3

practical theology refers to an *activity* of believers seeking to sustain a life of reflective faith in the everyday, a *method* or way of analyzing theology in practice used by religious leaders and by teachers and students across the theological curriculum, a *curricular area* in theological education focused on ministerial practice and subspecialties, and, finally, an *academic discipline* pursued by a smaller subset of scholars to support and sustain these first three enterprises.[4]

The breadth of this definition is significant for several reasons. First, in seeing the active faith of believers as practical theology it embraces the significance of the 'ordinary theology' of the global church.[5] Second, the identification of method recognises the important role that methods play in any practical theological process. Third, the recognition of ministerial training allows for the integration of the applied aspect of practical theology. Finally, the inclusion of academia acknowledges the role of thinkers in this field of activity.

## What does it mean to be evangelical?

Those attempting to identify the distinctive features of evangelicalism often gravitate towards the work of Bebbington[6] who outlines four key evangelical distinctives:

1 Biblicism: through history, evangelicals have used a mix of tradition, experience, and reason. However, the Bible is always seen to have ultimate authority in all aspects of faith and practice.
2 Crucicentrism: the death of Christ on the cross, and his resurrection from the grave, are held as centrally important by evangelicals.
3 Conversionism: evangelicals believe that there needs to be a definite turning away from a sinful life to living in the way of Jesus Christ.
4 Activism: evangelical faith moves its adherents to spread the good news of Jesus Christ.

Bebbington's work was published over 30 years ago, and scholars have since suggested additions to his original quadrilateral.[7] I have considered many of the arguments but remain to be convinced that areas like the work of the Holy Spirit or fellowship, that can be found 'folded in' to Bebbington's original distinctives,[8] are evidenced 'everywhere, always, and by all.'[9] So, whilst aware that other distinctives have been offered, I will structure the considerations in this chapter around the four areas listed above.

## Biblicism and initiation

I start my methodological considerations by looking at the role the Bible plays in practical theology. Specifically, I will focus on the interpretive paradigm and the issues that surround what I have termed here 'initiation': the point of departure in any practical theological study. As noted earlier, practical theology is a discipline with many approaches or 'orientations',[10] and tensions exist between forms of practical theology and evangelicalism. Evangelicals would have no problems with what Pieterse would see as the 'Scripture and context' form of practical theology evident in some South African colleges as this approach sees the biblical message deduced for the context in a dogmatic way.[11] Conversely, evangelicals would reject what Cartledge sees as the 'excluded approach'; practical theology that doesn't engage with the Bible in any obvious way.[12] However, between these black and white extremes lie grey areas where practical theologians engage with Scripture but differ as to when it should be used in the process.

The problem regarding initiation lies in the pre-eminence that is given to 'going first' in the practical theological task. This is highlighted in the work of the liberal practical theologian Zoë Bennett who, whilst considering what she sees as three broad ways of approaching the theory to practice relationship, asks two questions: 'Where do you start?' and 'What do you trust?'[13] Continuing on with her work it is clear that she believes that you will always start with what you trust most. When she writes, 'Behind starting with and giving precedence to,'[14] it is evident that Bennett believes there to be a clear link between precedence and initiation. In her case precedence, and the point of initiation, goes to the idiographic method that starts with lived experience. Evangelicals who follow a 'Scripture and Context' course would disagree and would argue for a point of initiation in Scripture.

So, where can one go with this area that is given such significance by evangelicals and practical theologians? A way forward would be to stop giving precedence to the point of initiation. Reasoning for this view can be built through a progression of points. First, I believe Bennett is correct when she sees pre-understanding being used to interpret Scripture because this is evident in the biblical narrative itself. This is supported by the evangelical theologian John Stott who highlights the significance of lived experience in his consideration of the Cornelius episode in Acts 10. He writes:

> Peter's order of events is important because it helps us to live through his experience with him, and so to learn just how God has shown him that he should not call anybody impure or unclean (10:28). *It took four successive hammer-blows of divine revelation before his racial and religious prejudice was overcome*, as he explains to the Jerusalem church.[15]

By using this language Stott clarifies that divine revelation for Peter came through a lived experience of the Holy Spirit and that prejudices, undoubtably formed through an interpretation of Scripture, were removed.

This noted, just because an interpretive process *can* start with life experience does not mean it *always* starts with life experience. Cartledge recognises that the reality for many Christians is that the Bible permeates their daily activities and scriptures will 'provide points of departure for theological thinking and practice.'[16] One can also argue that it is impossible to completely filter out the influence that doctrine and experience have on our approaches to theological thinking and action. Ward notes that identifying clear starting points is methodologically problematic because whatever the angle proposed 'the experience of the Christian community and the doctrine of the community are in us and have formed us.'[17] Approaches that seem straightforward when explained in a classroom can become blurred in practice when influenced by this 'affective gravitational pull of the church.'[18]

The discussion in this section so far does not appear to have been helpful in that is has led to what appears to be an impasse. This can, however, be an opportunity to explore other approaches that move towards a more complementary methodology for undertaking evangelical practical theology. One way that is worth exploring is a pneumatological appreciation of the language of inspiration and illumination in the process of interpretation. Evangelical scholar Stanley Grenz explores this area by focusing on the work of the Spirit in the community of God's people in both the compilation, comprehension, and communication of Scripture. He notes that, when one looks at the biblical accounts of the life of the community of Israel and the early church, God was often present with his people in ways beyond their ability to comprehend.[19] Grenz continues by saying, 'Our bibliology, therefore, must develop a deepened appreciation for the role of the community in the process that led to the composition, compilation and canonization of the Bible.'[20]

In focusing on the work of the Spirit in the community of God's people Grenz is making a significant point. He is saying that evangelicals must extend beyond a view of the Spirit moving individuals to form Scripture (inspiration) to one that recognises an on-going process of illumination in the people of God. Specifically, Grenz says:

> Critical to and lying behind the production of the biblical documents and the coming together of the Bible into a single canon was the illuminating work of the Spirit. The community found these books to be the vehicle through which God addressed them. But his illuminating task continues beyond the closing of the canon. Even now the Spirit attunes contemporary believers within the context of the faith community to understand Scripture and apply it to their situation.[21]

Whilst recognising that Grenz stops at application, I argue that this activity of pneumatic illumination can be extended to other forms of practical theology that do not start the interpretive process with Scripture.

Ironically, I am going to attempt to do this by starting with Scripture, drawing on imagery from Psalm 119. Zenger sees Psalm 119 as a prayer directed towards YHWH for 'a life according to Torah.'[22] Waltner, focusing on Psalm 119:105, notes that this is about a 'pilgrim passing through a world of darkness in which it would be easy to lose one's way.'[23] Drawing these thoughts together, I see a person attempting to walk worthy of the way of God but struggling to do so because the world is in darkness. To follow God's way in this darkness they need divine illumination, which is provided by God's word that is 'a lamp to my feet, and a light to my path' (Ps 119:105). Turning back to the teaching of Grenz, I see this as a combination of the divinely inspired guidance of 'God-breathed' Scripture (2 Tim 3:16)[24] and the illumination of the Paraclete Spirit who walks alongside and points to the way of Jesus.[25]

When this imagery is transposed to the interpretive paradigm, I see a process of practical theological interpretation that demands engagement with Scripture because without illumination the interpreter will easily lose their way. That said, the 'pilgrimage' is one of lived experience where there will be constant interaction between the illuminating light and the senses of the one seeking a way forward; after all, sight is not the only sense one uses on a journey in darkness. This interaction can happen at the start of the journey but, for a successful arrival at the destination, it must continue to happen throughout the duration of travel with both aspects performing complementary roles. Drawing on Grenz, this interpretive journey is best undertaken in community; shared experience can often bring fresh perspectives to Scripture and life.

An example of shared communal interpretation comes from my research in South Africa.[26] A Pentecostal church was divided over deliverance ministry to Christians. Some were supportive of deliverance events where professionals would exorcise demons, others could not accept that Christians could be possessed by evil. Progress was made when small groups gathered to consider relevant biblical material together. People came to see that *daimonizomai* did not necessarily mean 'demon possessed' but could mean 'to be influenced by an evil spirit.'[27] Although 'temples of the Holy Spirit' (1 Cor 6:19), they saw that idols linked to evil had desecrated the temple in Scripture (2 Kgs 23).[28] Allied to these studies, individuals shared stories about how oppression of this kind had been lifted through confession, repentance, and prayer. This sharing of scriptural understanding and lived experience saw the church move away from deliverance events to an 'in house' approach that recognised demonic influence on believers but ministered with a model that utilised the normal pastoral structure of the church.

## Crucicentrism and authority

My second distinctive for methodological consideration is that of crucicentrism. Here, I will not find a methodological issue in crucicentrism itself. Instead, I will bring some crucicentric theology into consideration of another methodological issue related to the use of the biblical text by evangelicals: the use of the word 'authority'. A look through evangelical statements of faith will see Scripture seen as authoritative in matters of faith and belief. This claim to authority automatically causes problems for some practical theologians, many of whom have been influenced by liberation theology and the postmodern shift in Western society.[29] This has seen a general shift in practical theology from a focus on orthodoxy (right belief) to orthopraxy (right action). Any structure that takes an authoritative stance to theology can come into conflict with forms of practical theology that centre on praxis that liberates groups, for example women, that are perceived to have been oppressed by those in authority.[30]

An example of how an authoritative claim by evangelicals can lead to tension with practical theologians can be seen in the language used regarding a reader's position to Scripture. Bennett notes that whilst evangelicals may see being 'under the text' as a position that gives due reverence to the authoritative position with which they hold the Bible, she highlights that what this stance ultimately means is that people are 'under the authority of the interpreters of the text'[31] which can lead to manipulation and domination. This unfiltered understanding of authority by some evangelicals has led to unfortunate instances of damaging practice.[32]

My transformed methodology regarding authority can be approached in four stages. First, I will acknowledge how evangelicals can be viewed. Second, I will consider theology that can explain why some evangelicals are labelled in this way. Third, I will explore how crucicentric theology can inform our approach to authority and, fourth, I will address how a crucicentric theology can lead to transformed practice relating to taking an authoritative stance on Scripture.

Regarding how others view evangelicals, Briggs notes that, 'evangelical approaches to faith and to Scripture can be naïve, literalistic, harsh, given to excessive certainty, and that there is no reasoning either in them or with them.'[33] Stott adds to this picture as he points out that, 'Evangelical people are often regarded as proud, vain, arrogant and cocksure.'[34] Whilst these are not labels that any evangelical believer would associate with themselves, it is clear that the communicative praxis of some evangelicals has not led to an accurate representation of their beliefs and practices.

Why may some view evangelicals in such a negative way? One factor that can be considered links the views expressed with how evangelical theology relates to power and control. As seen above, claims of authority for biblical texts have been used to erroneously dominate. An abuse of power like this was not uncommon amongst 'the rulers of the Gentiles' (Matt 20:25) but it was certainly not expected to be common practice amongst followers of Jesus Christ.[35] This is what Walker has termed 'the love of power' that dominates the ways of our fallen world.[36] By claiming authority for the text, but failing to recognise the self-serving 'love of power' that uses the text in positions of control over others, some evangelicals have given validity to the harsh labelling noted above.

How can evangelicals move forward in relation to this question of authority and power? The text already covered in Matthew 20:25 is a useful guide because, as noted by Witherington, it contrasts the fallen human approach to power with the approach modelled by Jesus: the way of the cross.[37] The differences here are outlined by Smail who notes:

> When we take our bearings from the cross, we can see that the only power with which Jesus works is the power of that utterly self-giving love that was itself weak and helpless on Calvary. He overcame all the violent force

and energy of evil that fell upon him there, not by exercising greater force and violence, but by renouncing them altogether. The power of Jesus, and therefore the power of the Spirit that Jesus imparts from the cross, is the power of Calvary love.[38]

When seen in this way, a crucicentric approach must have at its heart what Smail has termed 'Calvary love'. This love can transform attitudes towards power, not just in 'the world' but in the church that has, in its historical forms, all too often used power to maintain control and influence. Evangelicals, formed by this Calvary love, should not be identified with many of the tags earlier offered by Briggs and Stott. Rather, evidence should be seen of the 'quality of humility' that Stott holds as an evangelical essential.[39]

With this crucicentric filter in place, I return to considering the methodology of how one can approach the text of Scripture. I believe that Scripture can be approached with a view that sees us 'under the text', but also as on-going participants 'in the text'. To do this, I will draw from an approach offered by N. T. Wright.[40] For Wright, the grand narrative of Scripture holds authority over all cultures. This authority comes through his people telling and re-telling the narratives of Scripture—narratives that demand an appropriate response to be made. Wright helps to explain the nature of this authoritative narrative by drawing on a model of a Shakespearean play with a lost act. He notes that if you wanted to perform the play you would use actors who were immersed in the first four acts of the play, with these original acts being seen as the 'authority' for the production. From this base they would go on to perform the 'lost' final act in a way that was consistent with the four original acts, but with innovation for the time and place of performance. The four original acts could be: (1) Creation, (2) Fall, (3) Israel, and (4) Jesus with the New Testament being the initial scene for the fifth 'lost' act. As Wright concludes: 'The church would then live under the "authority" of the extant story, being required to offer something between an improvisation and an actual performance of the final act.'[41]

When Wright's model is considered, it is possible to see Scripture as authoritative and something that the church should be 'under' in humility. However, as the players, living out the lost fifth act, the church can also be seen to be 'in the text' seeking to faithfully communicate this authoritative grand narrative of God with 'Calvary love' in their own context and time. This does not mean evangelicals should affirm interpretations they do not agree with, but it does require them to be sensitive to potential abuses of power as they welcome engagement with views that challenge their own.

## Conversionism and gospel

The focus on faithful communication of God's metanarrative leads to the third distinctive for consideration: conversionism. Conversion can be seen as an appeal to respond to the good news of the gospel or evangelism. It is evangelistic methods, and underlying methodological issues, that I will be considering in this section. Here the issue will not be a specific tension between practical theology and evangelicalism but, rather, an example of how a practical theological appreciation of methodology can highlight issues that limit gospel communication.

In seeking to identify a specific methodological problem in evangelistic practice, I will draw on my own experiences from a tent crusade in Brazil in the mid 1990s. Every night we held meetings, a message was preached, and a call was made for people to 'make a decision for Jesus.' After three months in the area over 400 people had 'made decisions', a church was planted, and we moved on to a new location. When I revisited the church just over a year later numbers were down to around 30. A visit to the second site where we had ministered told a similar story. The leaders of the project concluded that this was explicable and acceptable because only some seed would fall on good, fruitful soil with other 'growth' falling away (Mark 4:1–20).

I have since witnessed similar practice in other evangelical churches and organisations, namely that a disappointing experience in relation to evangelism can be explained away using an interpretation of Scripture. In contrast to this, practical theological reflection would encourage a broader consideration of other factors like context and tradition to identify issues, possibly methodological, that may be involved. I will do this here by drawing on the work of Gordon Smith and Darrell Guder before considering a different approach to theological praxis.

In Smith's book *Transforming Conversion*, he identifies issues with the language of Christian initiation that he links to the revivalist tradition within evangelicalism.[42] He writes:

> Older revivalism assumed that conversion was punctiliar, that the focus of the religious life was religious activities, in anticipation of a life "in heaven" that would come after death, and that this "conversion" was essentially an interior, personal, and subjective transaction ... For the revivalist, the church has only one agenda: to obtain conversions; to be successful congregations should have plenty of growth by conversions.[43]

Smith does follow this by noting that revivalists performed an important role in making people recognise the need for them to take personal responsibility for their position before God but he raises the important issue that the response to the gospel message has been narrowed to a neat and controlled process that can be quantified.

The process by which this particular approach to conversion has been formed can be seen more broadly in the form of what some scholars have termed gospel reductionism.[44] Guder starts explaining reductionism by noting that God's mission is good news and that the mission of the church is to witness to this good news.[45] He continues by saying that, when anyone attempts to witness to the good news in their local context, a process of translation takes place where some reduction in the truth of the gospel message will inevitably take place.[46] Whilst noting that the reduction of the gospel is unavoidable, Guder is not so positive when considering what he calls reductionism. This moves beyond reduction and, with a desire to bring control to the process, some reductions are made 'validated absolutes.'[47] Guder explains:

> We are constantly tempted to assert that our way of understanding the Christian faith is a final version of Christian truth. We tend to enshrine one cultural articulation of the gospel as the normative statement for all cultures ... However it happens, we cut, shape, and fit the gospel into a cultural setting to serve all kinds of alien purposes. When such reductions, which inevitably occur, are made absolute and then defended as normative truth, then we confront the problem I call "reductionism."[48]

He continues by showing how reductionism of the gospel started early on in the history of the church. Using Bosch,[49] Guder explains how the church gradually became separated from its initial calling as a community of God's people (Israel) who were to challenge others by obediently modelling the way of Jesus thereby pointing to the reign of God. Instead, he writes of a group who became institutionalised and alienated from the 'Jewishness of Jesus.'[50] Under the influence of Hellenistic philosophy cultural translations of the gospel became more focused on the individual over the community, and heaven rather than this world and God's involvement in it. Whilst the Reformation may have corrected some sacramental errors in soteriology it did not alter the Christendom focus on 'the management of each soul's salvation on earth in preparation for heaven.'[51]

When Smith and Guder's thinking on revivalism and reductionism is brought together, one can see a great deal of what lies behind the issues outlined in my example of evangelistic practice from Brazil. A professional approach to gospel presentation has been formed that is neat and simple to deliver in an intelligible form. With its focus on quick, simple decisions with benefits for the individual it is attractive and easy to quantify. But one must question the methodological validity of this approach to gospel presentation when considering the nature of the reductionist theory that is driving the evangelistic method. God may have worked in incredible ways through this form of reductionist revivalism, but this is only testament to the on-going power of the gospel to work through fallen and limited means. Evangelicals and practical theologians should be asking if there is a better way.

The identification of the methodological issue above (a reductionist gospel) points to a way forward for improved evangelistic practice. If a reductionist gospel is seen to drive our evangelistic methods then it stands that a reconsideration of the gospel, as seen in the early accounts in Scripture, could lead to improved practice. The form of this gospel has been a source of much discussion. Personally, I have been persuaded by the arguments of Scot McKnight in his book *The King Jesus Gospel*.[52] McKnight carefully considers the biblical evidence before offering what he sees as 'a gospel for gospeling' today. He splits this down into four areas:

1. The gospel that was preached by the apostles in Acts is framed by Israel's story. Here, 'the saving Story of Jesus—his life, his death, his resurrection, his exaltation, and his coming again [are seen] as the completion of the Story of Israel.'[53]
2. This centres on the lordship of Jesus. Jesus is seen as Messiah and Davidic Saviour.
3. It involves summoning people to repentance, faith in Jesus Christ, and baptism.
4. The gospel saves and redeems. McKnight notes: 'The apostolic gospel promises forgiveness, the gift of God's Holy Spirit, and justification.'[54]

When McKnight's 'gospel for gospeling' is brought alongside the work of Guder, one can see how a key element that has been 'reduced' from this gospel is the involvement of Israel, the people of God, and the place of Jesus as Lord and Messiah. It is these aspects that Guder sees as essential for engaging with what he terms 'evangelization.'[55] Guder's 'evangelization' is what McKnight would term 'gospeling the gospel'. Both scholars seek to move away from an understanding of evangelism as a method or program that wins souls for eternity rather seeing 'evangelism' as the way in which the gospel becomes reality in the lives of people who believe in Jesus as Lord.[56]

What this theory can lead to in practice is what Newbigin terms 'the congregation as Hermeneutic of the Gospel.'[57] These local gatherings of God's people regularly hear and respond to the gospel message. As faithful followers of the Lord Jesus Christ, immersed in the gospel story from Scripture, they obey his call to be witnesses to King Jesus and his reign. These local translations of the gospel will lead to some reductions but, due to the accountability afforded by 'gospeling the gospel', should not veer into the reductionism that has been a feature of evangelistic practice.

## Activism and time

My final distinctive for consideration is activism. A significant feature of this activism is the urgency and drive that emanates from the language of activists. In the *Evangelical Dictionary of World Missions* it is noted that in the 1880s and 1890s Pierson was pressing for the completion of world evangelization by the year 1900 'in obedience to the Great Commission.'[58] More recently, Todd wrote, 'The ideas in this book will move you to expect that Christians, by God's grace and power, will bring an end to extreme global poverty in the next twenty-five years.'[59] These views are over a century apart, and focus on differing aspects of activism, yet the language shows similar drive and urgency.

I have no issue with this passionate call for action. After all, where would this world be today without the drive and persistence of activists like William

Wilberforce in the fight against the slave trade or Martin Luther King Jr in the battle for civil rights in the United States? Interestingly, I note that practical theologians, many of whom would be influenced by the call for *orthopraxy* or 'right-action' in liberation theology, would have little problem with this urgent push for activity. I must, however, be aware that the rush for a resolution to a challenge can lead to methodological problems in practice, especially in how Christians understand and approach time.

Problems generally surface in two forms. The first relates to how a cultural appreciation of time dominates our Christian understanding and practice. In their call for 'Slow Church' Smith and Pattison highlight how Western industrial culture has adopted many of the dimensions of the fast-food industry with efficiency, predictability, calculability, and control seen as paramount virtues. They continue by noting that many churches have unconsciously adopted this approach in their drive for growth and cultural relevance. The results, they say, have seen the church busy but they question what they see as a reduction of Christianity 'to a commodity that can be packaged, marketed and sold.'[60] When the analysis of John Swinton is also considered, one can see that this way of 'doing church' has a focus on 'time driven events': the clock dominating theological praxis.[61] Contrast this with the Benedictine approach of 'event driven time', wherein the clock did not dominate time but, rather, 'the events of the day served as constant reminders that time belongs to God.'[62] This contrast challenges the time-driven busyness that dominates many modern churches.

What is the 'driven busyness' mentioned above? In attempting to push for change and action many activists have tried to force time and, when one remembers that time belongs to God, this can alienate the activists' purposes from those of God. As Swinton says, 'When we try to master time, violence becomes inevitable.'[63] One has only to look at the evangelical political activism of the Democratic Unionist Party (DUP) in Northern Ireland to see how attempts to drive through a faith-related agenda can be linked to sectarian violence during the Troubles.[64]

A response to these issues can be found in Swinton's 'brief theology of time.'[65] He constructs this theology by drawing on the thinking of Augustine, Yoder, and Barth in relation to the problem of the eternal timeless God being found in incarnate form in created time. Swinton concludes from this interaction that:

> God is able to participate in time without being determined by time. We might conceive of the point in Trinitarian terms: God the Father participates in time through God the incarnate Son in the power of the Holy Spirit. God is both time*full* and timeless.[66]

He then considers the simultaneity of God's time by focusing on the incarnation of Christ. Drawing on Shulevitz, Swinton explains that Jesus is the Lord of time who steps into time to redeem time, and those who dwell in fallen time, to make us ready for eternity. He continues by saying, 'In Jesus, fallen time begins to encounter its redemption. In Jesus the time*fullness* of God is revealed ... In Jesus we have the opportunity truly to become timefull people.'[67] Swinton concludes his arguments by noting that if Jesus is our timefull model then we must follow his example and allow God's time to come upon us.

How could this impact some of the methodological issues we have encountered with a 'fast' attitude towards time? Drawing again on the work of Swinton, I focus on the speed of love. Using the theology of Koyama's *Three Mile an Hour God*, Swinton highlights the significance of Jesus' slow walking pace of ministry. For Swinton, if Jesus, who is God, who is love, chose to walk during his ministry then love has a speed; a three-mile-an-hour walking speed. He explains this well in relation to attitudes people can take towards disability when he writes:

> We may choose to stigmatize, alienate, downgrade, and exclude people for taking up too much of our time—for being slow in pace, speech, wit, or intellect—but in the face of the three-mile-an-hour God, such ways of being in the world become revelatory of what it means to love and to be fully human. The reality is that, when time is love, speed equals *less* of it. The love of God is inexorably slow. Jesus walked slowly: Love takes time.[68]

Broadening this out to consider the methodological problems it is easy to see that 'fast' church, and the driven busyness of some ministry, is missing the mark of a faithful, timefull ministry because it has limited, if not excluded, the love of God. Many evangelical activists would do well to look at their methods of ministry in the light of the timefull practical theology of Swinton.

## Drawing together the threads

Having considered the four distinctives, and the methodological issues identified above, I can say that the proposals made at the end of each section do highlight overlapping themes that present options for evangelicals involved in practical theology. First, it must be acknowledged that the practical theological task takes place in a dark and confusing world where Scripture and the presence of the illuminating Spirit in the lived experience are essential companions at all stages of the journey into a deeper knowledge of God. Precedence should not be bound to a point of initiation but with how the interpretive communicative actions are balanced throughout the process.

Second, the task is best undertaken as a communal response by the people of God. Situations are open to interpretation and therefore groups and teams can provide accountability and insights for renewed praxis. A 'body' approach to practical theology, whether it be church leadership, small group discipleship, or academic research, has much to offer.

Finally, evangelical practical theology must be overarched by love—a love that emanates from the cross of Calvary. There is a humility about this love and it cannot be forced or rushed. The academic researcher should consider whether their approach to fieldwork has lovingly given time for the situation under study to reveal its theological bounty; the pastor must reflect on how timefull love challenges their ecclesial practice.

These methodological considerations have only grazed the surface of what can be a complex and conflicted topic. It is my belief, however, that any evangelical who considers the points raised above can effectively engage in a broad array of theological praxis confident that they remain faithful to their evangelical heritage.

## Notes

1 This chapter was originally delivered as a paper to academics, students, and practitioners at a conference at Moorlands College in April 2019.
2 John Swinton and Harriet Mowat, *Practical Theology and Qualitative Research*, 2nd ed. (London: SCM, 2016), 69.
3 Bonnie J. Miller-McLemore, "Five Misunderstandings about Practical Theology," *International Journal for Practical Theology* 16, no. 1 (2012): 18–23.
4 Miller-McLemore, "Five Misunderstandings," 20.
5 Jeff Astley, *Ordinary Theology: Looking, Listening and Learning in Theology* (Aldershot: Ashgate, 2002).
6 David W. Bebbington, *Evangelicalism in Modern Britain: A History from the 1730s to the 1980s* (London: Unwin Hyman, 1989), 2–17.
7 See Darren Dochuk, "Revisiting Bebbington's Classic Rendering of Modern Evangelicalism at Points of New Departure," *Fides et Historia* 47, no. 1 (2015): 63–72.
8 Dochuk, "Revisiting," 65.
9 David W. Bebbington, "The Evangelical Quadrilateral: A Response," *Fides et Historia* 47, no. 1 (2015): 96.
10 Hendrik J. Pieterse, "Practical Theology in South Africa," *International Journal of Practical Theology* 2 (1998): 155–165; Johannes A. van der Ven, *Practical Theology: An Empirical Approach* (Kampen: Kok Pharos, 1993), 34–41.
11 Pieterse, "Practical Theology in South Africa," 159.
12 Mark J. Cartledge, "The Use of Scripture in Practical Theology: A Study of Academic Practice," *Practical Theology* 6, no. 3 (2013): 271–283, 277.
13 Zoë Bennett, *Using the Bible in Practical Theology: Historical and Contemporary Perspectives* (Farnham: Ashgate, 2013), 42.
14 Bennett, *Using the Bible in Practical Theology*, 42.
15 John Stott, *The Message of Acts* (Leicester: IVP, 1990), 194 (emphasis mine).
16 Cartledge, "The Use of Scripture in Practical Theology," 280.
17 Pete Ward, *Introducing Practical Theology: Mission, Ministry, and the Life of the Church* (Grand Rapids: Baker Academic, 2017), 4.
18 Ward, *Introducing Practical Theology*, 4.
19 Stanley J. Grenz, *Revisioning Evangelical Theology: A Fresh Agenda for the 21st Century* (Downers Grove: IVP, 1993), 122.
20 Grenz, *Revisioning Evangelical Theology*, 122.
21 Grenz, *Revisioning Evangelical Theology*, 123.
22 Erich Zenger, "The Composition and Theology of the Fifth Book of Psalms, Psalms 107–145," *Journal for the Study of the Old Testament* 80 (1998): 97–98.
23 James H. Waltner, *Psalms: Believers Church Bible Commentary* (Scottdale: Herald, 2006), 583.
24 Paul M. Zehr, *1 and 2 Timothy, Titus: Believers Church Bible Commentary* (Scottdale: Herald, 2010), 208.

25 George R. Beasley-Murray, *John: Word Biblical Commentary 36* (Dallas: Word, 1987), 261.
26 Andrew J. Thomas, "Pathways to Healing: An Empirical Theological Study of the Healing Praxis of 'the Group' Assemblies of God in Kwa-Zulu-Natal, South Africa" (DTh diss., UNISA, 2010).
27 Clinton E. Arnold, *3 Crucial Questions about Spiritual Warfare* (Grand Rapids: Baker, 1997), 80.
28 Arnold, *3 Crucial Questions*, 82.
29 Mark J. Cartledge, *Practical Theology: Charismatic and Empirical Perspectives* (Carlisle: Paternoster, 2003), 17.
30 See Denise M. Ackermann, "Engaging Freedom: A Contextual Feminist Theology of Praxis," *Journal of Theology for Southern Africa* 94 (1996): 32–49.
31 Bennett, *Using the Bible in Practical Theology*, 27.
32 Jeremy Punt, "Post Apartheid Racism in South Africa: The Bible, Social Identity and Stereotyping," *Religion & Theology* 16 (2009): 246–272.
33 Richard S. Briggs, "Election and Evangelical Thinking: Challenges to Our Way of Conceiving the Doctrine of God," in *New Perspectives for Evangelical Theology: Engaging with God, Scripture and the World*, ed. Tom Greggs (London: Routledge, 2010), 14.
34 John Stott, *Evangelical Truth: A Personal Plea for Unity, Integrity and Faithfulness* (Leicester: IVP, 2003), 145.
35 Ben Witherington, *Matthew* (Macon: Smyth & Helwys, 2006), 376–379.
36 Andrew Walker, "The Devil You Think You Know: Demonology and the Charismatic Movement," in *Charismatic Renewal*, eds. Tom Smail, Andrew Walker, and Nigel Wright (London: SPCK, 1995), 105.
37 Witherington, *Matthew*, 278.
38 Tom Smail, "The Cross and the Spirit," in *Charismatic Renewal*, eds. Tom Smail, Andrew Walker, and Nigel Wright (London: SPCK, 1995), 62.
39 Stott, *Evangelical Truth*, 145.
40 N. T. Wright, "How can the Bible be Authoritative?", *Vox Evangelica* 21 (1991): 16–19. Also in N. T. Wright, *The New Testament and the People of God* (London: SPCK, 1992), 139–143. This was first brought to my attention by Mark Cartledge's "Empirical Theology: Towards an Evangelical-Charismatic Hermeneutic," *Journal of Pentecostal Theology* 9 (1996): 115–126.
41 Wright, "How can the Bible be Authoritative?" 19.
42 Gordon T. Smith, *Transforming Conversion: Rethinking the Language and Contours of Christian Initiation* (Grand Rapids, MI: Baker, 2010), 1–19.
43 Smith, *Transforming Conversion*, ix.
44 Darrell L. Guder, *The Continuing Conversion of the Church* (Grand Rapids: Eerdmans, 2000), 97–119.
45 Guder, *The Continuing Conversion of the Church*, 28–72.
46 Guder, *The Continuing Conversion of the Church*, 97–100.
47 Guder, *The Continuing Conversion of the Church*, 100.
48 Guder, *The Continuing Conversion of the Church*, 100–101.
49 David Bosch, *Transforming Mission: Paradigm Shifts in the Theology of Mission* (Maryknoll: Orbis, 1991), 50–52.
50 Guder, *The Continuing Conversion of the Church*, 105.
51 Guder, *The Continuing Conversion of the Church*, 114.
52 Scot McKnight, *The King Jesus Gospel: The Original Good News Revisited* (Grand Rapids: Zondervan, 2011).
53 McKnight, *The King Jesus Gospel*, 132.
54 McKnight, *The King Jesus Gospel*, 133.
55 Guder, *The Continuing Conversion of the Church*, 150.
56 Guder, *The Continuing Conversion of the Church*, 24.

57 Lesslie Newbigin, *The Gospel in a Pluralist Society* (London: SPCK, 1989), 222–233.
58 *Evangelical Dictionary of World Missions*, ed. A. Scott Moreau (Grand Rapids: Baker, 2000), 413.
59 Scott C. Todd, *Fast Living: How the Church will End Extreme Poverty* (Grand Rapids: Somersault, 2011), 23.
60 C. Christopher Smith and John Pattison, *Slow Church: Cultivating Community in the Patient way of Jesus* (Downers Grove: IVP, 2014), 14.
61 John Swinton, *Becoming Friends of Time: Disability, Timefullness, and Gentle Discipleship* (London: SCM, 2017), 27.
62 Swinton, *Becoming Friends of Time*, 27.
63 Swinton, *Becoming Friends of Time*, 64.
64 Gladys Ganiel, "Explaining New Forms of Evangelical Activism in Northern Ireland: Comparative Perspectives from the USA and Canada," *Journal of Church and State* 50, no. 3 (2008): 475–476.
65 Swinton, *Becoming Friends of Time*, 57–65.
66 Swinton, *Becoming Friends of Time*, 62.
67 Swinton, *Becoming Friends of Time*, 63.
68 Swinton, *Becoming Friends of Time*, 68–69.

# 2 Prophetic imagination as a mode of practical theology

*Chloe Lynch*

Is it presumptuous to suggest that practical theology can be undertaken in the mode of prophetic imagination? I worry about this. For it sounds like I am claiming prophetic inspiration for the practical theology I produce. Yet, in fact, my claim is simpler. I argue that practical theology can be pursued in a mode[1] similar to the way in which the biblical prophetic tradition engaged the world and, further, that Walter Brueggemann's work on the prophetic imagination aids such an endeavour. Whether the output of such a mode is itself prophetic, however, is for others to judge, as I shall explore in the chapter's closing section.

In suggesting particular modes of doing practical theology, I focus primarily upon practical theology as scholarly discipline. Admittedly, this conversation might overflow outwards into Bonnie Miller-McLemore's other three locales of practical theology.[2] Indeed, I hope that will happen. Still, I affirm that because it is centrally the job of those who identify as scholarly practical theologians 'to attend to … concrete experiences [of divine action], giving theological shape to them,'[3] ours also is to determine how we might give such shape. It is for scholarly practical theology to support the practical theology going on in the other locales.[4] To propose scholarly methods of doing practical theology that might help others faithfully discern what is divine action within our concrete contexts is important. It is important because doing practical theology well will eventually bear fruit for ecclesial practice. Or, at least, it should if we, as academics, are doing it right.

I develop the following discussion in two parts. First, I present in brief my proposal: the prophetic imagination as a mode of practical theology.[5] Second, I explore potential contributions of the proposal, with particular (albeit not exclusive) reference to its value for evangelical practical theologians.

## Practical theology in the mode of prophetic imagination

The prophetic imagination is a concept first presented by Walter Brueggemann.[6] His hypothesis is that the biblical prophets represent a reality alternative to what he calls the dominant consciousness, with a view to critiquing and dismantling the latter reality as well as energising the community of faith towards

DOI: 10.4324/9781003094975-4

a future promise of God-given hope.[7] The prophetic imagination engages the dominant consciousness with critical questions regarding whether our wealth numbs our pain until we can consume our way past it, whether the cries of the poor are disregarded, and whether our religion is one 'of immanence and accessibility, in which God is so present to us that his abrasiveness, his absence, his banishment are not noticed.'[8] It calls us to identify our sins against the environment and our neighbour, and sins such as 'long-term racism, [and] self-indulgent consumerism.'[9]

Yet because we are often beneficiaries of the dominant consciousness that we criticise,[10] mere identification is not enough. We must learn to enter, also, into sorrow regarding our captivity to it, embracing its pathos, before we can begin its dismantling.[11] Grief is the first step in turning from our own attempts to avoid the world's brokenness and contingent nature: it pierces our denial and numbness. It calls for repentance regarding our embrace of a consciousness which seeks to manage the experience of fragility out of existence.[12] Thus, the prophet's task is to construct and speak or enact a rhetoric of grief, 'through the language of lament and the symbolic creation of a death scene,' that the community may be forced to see what they do not naturally see. Yet the prophet does not invent new language and symbols of grief for this task. Rather, these come from the community's past, reactivated not as a language not of 'analytic speech' but of metaphor—so that the community as a whole might participate in their meaning.[13]

The second prophetic task Brueggemann identifies is that of energising. The prophet energises the community of faith to engage the promise of God-given newness, the hope of a future that will annul this brokenness of the world.[14] Such hope is grounded in YHWH's agency, an assurance that what he promises he will enact.[15] The prophet again engages this task by offering symbols: these symbols contradict the dominant consciousness and, finding their roots in the community's deepest memories of a God who is living and active, give confidence to the community of faith for an embrace of the world's brokenness and contingency. For such symbols declare the hope that, in YHWH, death is swallowed up in life. Thus, having led the community to embrace the pathos of its barrenness, its impossibility, and—ultimately—its captivity to death, the prophet's second act is to speak of the grace of God which is his creative word bringing (resurrection) life out of barrenness. This attempt to express publicly the hope that has been so long silenced is no simple demand. Rather, it is the task of those who are prepared to wrestle with the awareness that 'the closed world of managed reality is false.'[16]

Participating in the prophetic imagination is, accordingly, no minor task. The dominant community is not a hospitable place for the prophets who, instead, are often found within subcommunities where they, and their imagination, are shaped. Brueggemann identifies four characteristics of such subcommunities, characteristics which are, I suggest, also the four pillars by which prophetic imagination's two major dynamics of criticism and energising might best be given form. In summary, these pillars (slightly reordered for my purposes) are,

42  Chloe Lynch

first, that the prophet will experience in relation to the status quo an 'expressed *sense of pain* ... understood as unbearable for the long term.' Second, the prophet will have access to '*a long and available memory* [of] ... an identifiable past.' The third pillar on which the prophetic imagination rests is the construction of a 'richly coded' and identifiable '*mode of discourse*.' Finally, the prophetic imagination calls for '*an active practice of hope* ... [in] promises yet to be kept.'[17] These pillars, as the form of the dynamics of criticism and energising, frame what I am calling the prophetic-imaginative mode.

As I will discuss below, I am convinced that practical theology, generally, seeks to discern divine action in the concreteness of human historical contexts and practices, reaching for that divine inbreaking which is itself eschatological. Practical theology undertaken more specifically in the prophetic-imaginative mode also honours both human and divine action. In its first aspect of *expressing the pain*, it begins with human action in the concrete now. This means practical theologians naming what truly is, in a dismantling of our numbness and denial of the way things are. For the work of naming precedes the capacity for grief. The second movement of this mode, a *deep remembering* of the tradition by which God's people have understood themselves, has a twofold purpose. The first purpose of reading the texts of the Christian tradition[18] is also an attention to human action: the practical theologian draws on the symbols of the Christian community's historical tradition, reactivating them in order to bring to fuller expression this grief over the status quo.[19]

Yet, alongside this, there is a second reason for engaging the deep remembering central to this second pillar. The practical theologian is trawling these deep memories of divine revelation—and of the community's engagement with that revelation—in hope of finding a God-given promise of newness. They are seeking the traces of divine action by which God's people may be re-energised towards hope that the hegemony of cosmic brokenness will come to an end.[20] When the movement of deep remembering yields that divine promise, the third phase of practical theology in this mode becomes possible. The practical theologian can draw upon the same traditioned memories of the faith community for their images and metaphors of hope, *coding a rich discourse* by which the particularities of this promise of divine action might be named. For giving linguistic form, and then public expression, to the promise permits the community's appropriation of it, moving divine action from unseen to seen and eschatological to present.[21] Once the discourse of hope is framed, human action can return to centre stage. Now that divine action has been named, the community can begin to name also the kinds of human actions that might constitute a participation in divine action as it has so far been discerned. These are referenced in Brueggemann's fourth pillar of the prophetic imagination: *active practices of hope*.

## Prophetic-imaginative practical theology: an assessment

Having outlined practical theology in the mode of prophetic imagination, it is time to explore its potential contribution. Because the prophetic imagination overflows from within the particular subcommunity in which the would-be prophet finds themselves, the first matter must be consideration of my own starting points in conceiving this mode of doing practical theology. Second, I will develop the claim, implicit in my proposal, that imagination is foundational to practical theology. I will assert, third, that this mode affords a renewed place for focus on divine action, albeit without undermining the study of human practice and, fourth, that the emphasis on the would-be prophet's context within a specific subcommunity constitutes potentially a corrective effect upon Western individualism. The final discussion relates to the place of power and also of affect in our theologising.

## Naming my starting points

As already indicated, the experiences, traditions, and presuppositions of the would-be prophet's subcommunity influence them as much as, and sometimes more than, their individual context. Such starting points are not necessarily problematic. All theology comes from somewhere.[22] Indeed, in the incarnation divine action, though not losing its unique ontological character, became forever intertwined with human action. Accordingly, human experience and reason, together with the traditioned understanding of the faith community, are not automatically profane. Human action can constitute a faithful participation in divine action, in the ongoing ministry of Christ to the Father and to the world, and thus these sources can indeed shape the construction of our theology, even if they are not afforded the same role as Scripture.

Yet there is need for openness regarding such starting points. Practical theology in the mode of prophetic imagination recognises that my starting points determine my theological capacity for apprehending particular realities more readily than others. The questions I ask and the sources that ground and give authority to acts of would-be prophetic imagination are unavoidably influenced by these starting points. What is more, my starting points may also blind me to the untruth of certain aspects of my worldview or my theological presuppositions. It is possible, furthermore, that I may be standing upon some of these errors even as I begin my theological acts of imagination. As a minimum, then, some theobiographical engagement with my starting points, at least as far as I can discern them, is demanded by the very nature of the mode proposed.[23] In such openness, readers—and perhaps I also—will be freer to interrogate my proposal and my interpretation of its potential contributions.

First, one of the subcommunities that I inhabit is evangelicalism: my conversion in the context of the CICCU,[24] together with subsequent immersion in British evangelical churches and the London School of Theology, has formed me in an irrevocable Christocentrism. Inevitably, the practices of evangelicalism relating to worship and to theologising have formed me deeply. Thus, whilst I engage interdisciplinarily in my theological work, and whilst I value each of tradition, reason, and experience as sources supporting theological understanding, I honour Scripture as theologically normative.[25] I am also, loosely, a 'charismatic' and the prophetic has been of interest to me for half my lifetime. In my first year of faith, I heard a young man prophesy and, from then on, I was desperate that I, too, might prophesy. I read all I could on the subject and came to understand that the prophetic can be more than the occasional gift, being, instead, a dynamic framing a person's whole way of perceiving the world. As the years went by, I sensed a calling to the prophetic which shaped everything else I was and did and, in the charismatic subcommunities that I inhabited, I heard others name the same reality regarding me. Doubtless, this fascination predisposes me to be drawn to what I propose here.

Of course, in articulating the contexts of my gathered worship I must not omit another significant context that forms me: the slightly fluid space called 'the academy'. Though I interact with theologians across the confessional spectrum, as well as scholars who claim no Christian faith, my immediate academic subcommunity is evangelical. Academic evangelicalism is often different from local church evangelicalism, even if most inhabitants of the former subcommunity also inhabit the latter. At risk of generalising overly, whereas local church tends to focus primarily on practice, the academic evangelical subcommunity can tend to prioritise theory. Evangelical practical theologians may seek to bridge this gap more intentionally than other evangelical academics, wrestling to construct and then embody theology-as-praxis.

Nevertheless, we do so in the context of sometimes painful tensions. For evangelical practical theologians, the position is complexified: more than many in the subcommunity that is our local church we may seek to think *theologically* and, simultaneously, more than many in our academic evangelical subcommunity we may seek to ground our theology *practically*. This can be a source of great loneliness and sometimes we may choose to defuse the tensive pain by prioritising the voice of one subcommunity over the other. Nevertheless, having spent a decade in local church leadership alongside another decade in the academy, and knowing well the pain of never fully belonging in either, I remain convinced that inhabiting the tension is necessary. Thus, in speaking later of the 'ecclesial' imagination and its formative influence on the prophet, I am thinking, in my own context, of both these subcommunities: those with whom I participate in local church and those engaged in confessional (usually evangelical) theology.[26]

Another starting point is more personal. I have already published work that self-identifies as practical theology in the mode of prophetic imagination. What had been merely a doctoral thesis footnote crystallised for me shortly after the viva in what felt very much like a moment of divine encounter—admittedly in the unlikely surroundings of a wet Saturday in Costa Coffee!—when I saw the possibility of Brueggemann's proposals for framing my own. The prophetic imagination became the central clarifying structure for the publication that followed: *Ecclesial Leadership as Friendship*. Admittedly, this may, with my other starting points, be perceived by some as obvious bias. Yet these realities are not necessarily problematic. In many ways, they are why I am even able to think these thoughts and offer these reflections. My imagination truly has depended on these starting points and I value them. Still, this does not mean embracing them uncritically: thus, I am continuing both to develop my proposal and to invite rigorous engagement with it by inhabitants of subcommunities similar to or other than my own.

## Practical theology as imaginative endeavour

Imagination is a category that has not gone unnoticed by practical theologians. Stephen Pattison, for example, claims that exploring, enriching, and nurturing imagination is one of practical theology's main functions.[27] Craig Dykstra agrees, adding that practical theology is to discipline imagination.[28] Yet despite this initial interest, efforts have not yet been made to mark fully the contours of a way of doing practical theology that gives significant place to the imagination. Thus, the contribution of the mode proposed here is evident: it develops the connection between practical theology and imagination.

For some who share my evangelical starting points, there may be concerns around giving place to imagination in the work of practical theology. This may include fear that theology in the mode of imagination is without moorings, especially in reason and revelation. This, however, is not so. Imagination operates in two significant and interrelated ways. First, it makes present that which is otherwise not accessible to us. It also acts as the source of sense-making, a reordering of the subject(s) of study within a wider set of perspectives upon reality such that new meaning issues from a 'shift of perspective'.[29] Accordingly, though imagination surpasses what is present, it begins there, from an understanding of what is. In Trevor Hart's words, it:

> cannot be wholly lacking in analogy to the here-and-now, otherwise we are driven to silence, and can have no hope precisely because we can expect nothing, look forward to nothing, fashion for ourselves no imaginative horizon towards which to move.[30]

Imagination, therefore, is not opposed to reason or to tradition, to revelation or to experience, insofar as these have revealed the reality of the here-and-now to us. Yet, as humanity's God-given capacity to reach for what is as yet unseen, imagination may operate to reframe knowledge through creative (and, ideally, Spirit-directed) reintegration of theological sources such as reason and tradition, revelation, and experience. Theology in this mode may be *more* than rational, transcending what has been available to reason through what appear to be epistemic leaps.[31] Yet even these so-called leaps are, in fact, based upon a reason-enabled 'scanning' of known data before a transformed view of reality is made available to the knower.[32] Imagination is thus not *less* than rational.[33] Perhaps it could even be construed as 'reason in her most exalted mood.'[34]

Imagination also does not undermine the centrality for evangelical theologians of the category of revelation.[35] Garrett Green argues that imagination, rather, is the locus in human experience of divine revelation.[36] It is 'the way in which [revelation] ... happens,'[37] the anthropological form of revelation the material content of which depends, for Christians, upon 'the paradigmatic image of God embodied in Jesus Christ'[38] and, therefore, upon Scripture as normative vision of that paradigm. Scripture is authoritative precisely because only it presents 'Christ, the image of God, fully and coherently to the imagination,' enabling the church to imagine both God and, thereby, the world in its relation to God.[39] Amos Yong's pneumatological imagination operates similarly. Arising from pneumatic encounters and rooted in images and metaphors from Scripture, it synthesises 'passive perception and active worldmaking' such that simply human imagination is transformed to be fundamentally Christological.[40]

Imagination as a mode of theologising, then, need not concern evangelicals. Rather, when participated in the Spirit, we might better perceive it as a highpoint of theological method. For our theology is deep reflection on realities both seen and unseen—and it is imagination that both makes things unseen to become seen and also reframes things seen so that we might now see them in new ways.

### Divine action in the midst of an empirical turn

The second contribution of prophetic-imaginative practical theology is a focus on divine action: Brueggemann's formulation of prophetic imagination emphasises, with Green, imagination as the locus in human experience of revelation of divine being and action. This contribution is significant because of a recent tendency in practical theology to foreground the descriptive-empirical and interpretative tasks.[41] Such work is important and the prophetic mode of practical theology affirms it. After all, it is only in reading reality carefully that we see the degree to which the dominant consciousness operates as a denial of divine agency in favour of pronouncing human monarchy. In this respect, the economics and politics of current human practice must be thoroughly examined, as I will explore below. The empirical task is indeed central to practical theology and the mode proposed does not undermine this.

Nevertheless, the prophetic imagination does challenge the marginalisation of another of practical theology's tasks. The normative task, discerning what human praxis 'ought to be', requires first that we discern divine praxis. The question becomes not 'what would Jesus do?' but 'what is Jesus doing?' For God is active in the world by his Spirit, even if practical theology has often shied away from talking about this.[42] Such divine action can be described as Christopraxis, with human praxis which is participation therein constituting genuine encounter with the reality and revelation of God.[43] The normative task, then, is essential: practical theology at its best entails a critical reflection on praxis, an effort to discern what of believers' praxis is faithful participation in divine action, the ongoing ministry of Christ, and—additionally—how to transform that of our praxis which is not.

In suggesting that aspects of human practice must be subject to a dismantling, and in energising the community of faith towards a hope rooted in the God-given word of grace, Brueggemann draws attention to this same task of prophetically discerning divine action. For prophetic imagination displays a strong concern for divine praxis by emphasising the agency of YHWH both in having spoken of future hope and in being, even now, 'a living, decisive agent in a world that largely assumed that YHWH was an irrelevant memory.'[44] Furthermore, it does so in a way that coheres with the death-to-life paradigm already articulated by certain voices within practical theology.

Specifically, Ray Anderson indicates that the hermeneutical criterion by which divine action may be discerned is that it transforms human impossibility by incorporating humanity into divine possibility, through a 'word of grace.'[45] Prophetic imagination recognises something comparable. For Brueggemann, it is in the context of bringing to public expression the pain evoked by the status quo that God speaks and then acts: even as the Israelites are crying out in their slavery to imperial oppression, God declares to Moses that he has seen and he has heard and now he will rescue (Exodus 3:7–8).[46] Human impossibility is real in Israel's experience of subjugation by the empire and yet this God, in Brueggemann's words, 'is unco-opted and uncontained by the empire.'[47] That is, it is in the very midst of the *ex nihilo* of this impossibility that the divine word of grace sounds the promise of liberation and, as Israel receives and participates in it, enacts that freedom notwithstanding the empire.[48]

In the mode of prophetic imagination, then, the practical theologian's task is like that of the prophets, who identify the divine word of grace by 'bring[ing] contemporary life under the aegis of the old tradition and the God of that tradition,' so as 'to offer ... hope for a new ... possibility.'[49] Though the move from the old tradition, these memories of divine praxis, to questions regarding divine action in the contemporary context is not a simple one, Brueggemann does present the 'history of God' as a frame for this work,[50] with Scripture as revelation foundational to that frame.[51] For him, it is only as a result of this prophetic discerning, itself a pneumatic activity,[52] that the subcommunity can articulate and then enact the active practices of hope by which the alternative kingdom is brought from future into present. Thus, for practical theology in the mode of prophetic imagination it is *only* after discernment of divine praxis that the pragmatic task of articulating faithful human praxis is possible. This corrective movement which reinstates the normative task as central is, I think, a helpful one within practical theology and of especial importance to those who understand their work from a confessional, evangelical perspective.

### Bringing community to the foreground in theological method

Practical theology in the mode of prophetic imagination brings another balancing emphasis in the form of references to the prophet's subcommunity. Brueggemann says that though God may '"raise up prophets" ... anywhere, anytime,' certain communities are more hospitable to the prophetic impulse than others.[53] This contention is not developed in significant detail but remains implicit throughout Brueggemann's proposals. For example, in considering preaching as the practice of prophetic imagination, he comments that the act of imagining is 'interactive between preacher and congregation.'[54] That is, the work of coding the discourse and actively practising hope is one done in a subcommunity that already treasures the memories of its tradition and shares deeply in the pain of the status quo. The prophet's work comes out of this subcommunity's reading of present and past and enters back into this subcommunity as a catalyst of new practices of 'future-opening possibility.'[55]

Whilst Brueggemann does not foreground this aspect, I think it very relevant. Whereas in the West, especially, individualism can tend to prevail, even in our theological method, the place of community is an important corrective. To affirm a community element in theological method is to speak of more than simply tradition, the reading by the historical Christian community of the texts and practices of Israel and the early church. That would be perhaps easier, for time has a way of sanctifying and authorising the interpretations of our brother or sister who reads this text in that way. Easier to quote Augustine or Thomas Aquinas or the Nicene Creed than to permit my hermeneutic to be shaped by the person who sits three rows behind me and sings off-key and out of time![56] Yet whilst the prophetic imagination may still render more weight to tradition, in honour of its longevity of testing and embrace by subsequent ecclesial generations, it does celebrate, too, the prophet's *contemporary* subcommunity and its readings of the Scriptures and of divine activity together with its experience of pain in the midst of the status quo.[57]

Dykstra writes helpfully about this. He claims that the 'many' of an ecclesial community can, in their exercise of imagination, shape the imagination of the 'one', the pastor who serves them. Believers can, in practising Christian faith, discover 'a way of seeing the world through eyes of faith.' They begin to be formed in what Dykstra calls an 'ecclesial imagination.' This ecclesial imagination exists in mutual relationship with the 'pastoral imagination,' the way of seeing and interpreting unique to the pastor and formed in the midst of pastoral work. The one feeds the other in a 'spiral of mutual influence' and thus, importantly for current discussion, the ecclesial imagination of the many becomes the context within which God gives to the one the gift of a pastoral imagination.[58] In parallel, we might perhaps say, the subcommunity births the prophet whilst its hermeneutic for reading its deeply rooted memories frames and forms the hermeneutic of the prophet's imagination. For the prophet—or, here, the practical theologian—to refuse this ecclesial forming is to refuse the spiral of mutual influence and the means by which God is giving this gift of imagination. The practice of listening to believing voices in local church and academy, becoming deliberately immersed in the ecclesial imagination, is, then, foundational to practical theology in the mode of prophetic imagination, which recognises its interdependence with the ecclesial imagination.

## *Power and affect in practical theology*

Having so far evaluated my proposal through the lenses of imagination, divine action, and the ecclesial community, I turn now to the final aspects for consideration: power and affect. That the prophetic imagination not only delineates the status quo but also recognises the politics that undergird it is important to note. Specifically, the prophetic imagination asks questions concerning affluence, oppression, and religion, for the prophetic subcommunity knows that an 'economics of affluence' and a 'politics of oppression' are characteristic of the dominant consciousness. What is more, these dynamics tend to be underpinned by a third: *'the establishment of a controlled, static religion* in which God and his temple have become part of the royal landscape.'[59]

Accordingly, as I have said, to engage practical theology in this mode means not only to name the status quo but to consider the ways in which its economics and politics operate, and to ask whether their effect has been to subordinate God's sovereignty to the powers-that-be.[60] The outcome of such reflection is a deeper understanding of reality as it is, perhaps especially for those who are beneficiaries of the dominant consciousness. For practical theologians such as myself—white, middle-class Westerner—it may force us to ask the power questions that it is the privilege only of the powerful not to see.[61] Thus, naming the status quo and entering fully into the pain of it may mean facing the ways in which reality has encouraged our attempts at self-sufficiency. It may mean admitting our implicit efforts to wrest power from God so that we may be kings over our own lives and over those around us. It may mean naming the ways in which our mode of living does violence against our neighbour and against creation.

The dominant narrative works against such truth-telling, 'disenfranchis[ing] … grief because it cannot afford to be honest.'[62] Yet if practical theology is to find the hope that will energise the community of faith to recognise and participate in divine action towards newness of life, the full reality of the status quo must be named and grieved. Indeed, according to Brueggemann, the prophets not only observed and named the pain and loss of current reality for Israel but also imagined YHWH's grief, declaring it in first-person speech.[63] In the same way, as practical theology in this mode moves towards the acts of deep remembering, of mining the subcommunity's tradition regarding God, it will begin to recognise that a full expression of pain regarding the status quo involves not only a wrestling with unjust economics and politics as they affect our neighbour negatively but also an admission, in humility, of the divine response to such things.

This centrality of pathos demands its own discussion. For Brueggemann, prophecy is disciplined by the Torah yet also 'erupts in emotive possibility that is not constrained by … reasonableness.'[64] Indeed, 'passion,' he says, 'is a primary prophetic agenda,' a loving, suffering and feeling consistent with God's own capacity.[65] Pathos is core to prophetic imagination: the focus on prophetic criticising and prophetic energising in the context of the Exodus account is a 'movement from the articulation of agony to the articulation of ecstasy,' themselves 'wellsprings of the prophetic imagination.'[66]

In affirming prophetic imagination's affective dimension,[67] I want, however, to highlight the affections in the traditional sense rather than only the passions. The one who would engage in prophetic imagination does so from a place of affections deliberately directed toward God, with prophetic pathos being grounded in this prior relational or, better, covenantal reality. The default state of those whose affections are not so directed is numbness: Brueggemann proposes that only 'the *ache* of God could penetrate the numbness of history' and that it is 'the grief of God that Israel must finally share.'[68] From this we must elicit that the emotive possibility that Brueggemann describes as erupting is no mere passion in the sense of some involuntary and non-cognitive impulse[69] that comes as if from nowhere. Rather, this passion is the overflow of a heart trained deliberately upon God and now participating in the *divine* pathos.[70] Just as divine pathos 'is not a passion, an unreasoned emotion' and is yet still emotion*al*, neither is prophetic pathos simply involuntary emotion, although it may overflow into emotion.[71]

Where the prophet is centred continually and deliberately upon God, their will directed to love of God and to discernment of his activity in Christ in the world, feelings of agony or ecstasy may well be part of doing prophetic-imaginative practical theology, especially in the work of criticising and re-energising.[72] Such feelings may even be trusted, 'passional reason' being reliable in the context of orthopathy (affections rightly directed).[73] Nevertheless, whilst constancy of the affections in terms of an inclination towards God is always fundamental, a constancy of agonistic or ecstatic emotion is not necessary to faithful engagement of this mode. Emotion is not the acid test of pathos: action, involvement, 'in history, as living care' is.[74]

For those identifying as confessional practical theologians, surely any mode of working that faces us with questions regarding the focus of our affections and the kind of lifestyle thereby mandated is helpful. Though we may not always feel the pathos of the dominant consciousness as deeply as its reality might properly indicate, it is appropriate to be reminded that our affections should progressively tend towards a desire for deeper participation in divine action, if we would hope also to be faithful in our theologising. Furthermore, practical theology as imagination calls us to 'a theology of the heart,'[75] a theology that does justice to the Hebraic understanding of knowing and of heart as the integrating centre of cognition *together with* the affections.[76] For those from theological traditions that tend to see 'head' as superordinate to 'heart' (as narrowly conceived) and logic as preferable to emotion, such a gentle challenge to explore integration of the two can only be a good thing.[77]

## Welcoming the ecclesial imagination

If prophetic imagination is to prove faithful in what it declares, we have seen that it must have been shaped also by the prophet's subcommunity, being formed by an ecclesial imagination. It is therefore for others to judge whether my act of imagination in this chapter proves prophetic or not: the arc here inscribed needs not only my critique but also the mutually formative response of ecclesial imagination. I envisage that this might come in two particular ways. One will be through primarily theoretical engagements, critiquing and developing from a methodological perspective the validity of this prophetic-imaginative mode of doing practical theology.[78]

The second kind of engagement by which I hope to benefit from the spiral of mutual influence is more practical. Sometimes it is only by employing a method, or mode, in the context of doing real-life practical theology that we discover its strengths and weaknesses. My work in ecclesial leadership represents this second type of interaction: it formed my understanding of how the prophetic-imaginative mode might operate. Particularly, the mode gave me permission to sit with my grief as a church leader, emphasising for me that lament is a step not to be omitted in prophetic-imaginative practical theology.

Specifically, in Western evangelicalism, our leadership activism tends to drive local churches ever onwards to greater productivity, often without asking whether increasing 'ministry output' and optimising efficiency in terms of ministry-per-pound—or ministry-per-minute—is really the true end towards which Christ calls us. Mentored fully into this narrative by popular-level church leadership literature, conferences and podcasts, and yet torn by a deep sense of unease regarding it, I felt uncomfortable throughout much of the doctoral process with the idea that I might simply sit with that pain for long periods, deepening my identification with it. Yet this is exactly what prophetic-imaginative practical theology encourages. My urgency to 'discover what God was saying'—an urgency both product of my charismatic evangelicalism and, I confess, of the pressure every doctoral student feels to 'find their original contribution'!—had to be counterbalanced by the reminder that God invites us to enter fully into his pathos, an experience of human impossibility, before we can receive the divine word of grace.

Though employing the prophetic-imaginative mode in that project formed my understanding and development of its contours, especially regarding the importance of lamenting without seeking to manage the pain out of existence, with greater distance from the project I now realise that perhaps I did not allow prophetic imagination to ask all the questions it might have posed regarding leadership power dynamics. Such is the iterative reality of working in this mode: the more I engage it, the more it forms my work but, also, the more I realise how much more it could be engaged next time. My hope, then, is for that iterative, spiralling dynamic to become mutual. What critical development of this mode might follow if others were to engage it, from the perspectives of their own subcommunities, in the context of forming theological responses to the questions of our time?

And, indeed, what differences might it make to those responses themselves if we were to listen for the 'expressed *sense of pain*' and draw on the '*long and available memory* [of] ... an identifiable past' in order to identify the promise of a God who is living and active, before coding the '*mode of discourse*' that can ground '*active practice[s]of hope*'?[79] For, in days repeatedly being called unprecedented, there is without doubt a dominant consciousness that holds us now captive but there is also—and equally without doubt—future hope of death-swallowed-up-in-life.

Of this we must prophesy.

## Notes

1 This is not quite the proposal of a method *per se*, being still insufficiently tested to ground such a scholarly self-claim.
2 These are: curricular area; methods studying (and potentially transforming) embodied theologies and experiences; and activity of faith done by ordinary believers (Bonnie J. Miller-McLemore, "Five Misunderstandings about Practical Theology," *International Journal of Practical Theology* 16, no. 1 [2012]: 20).
3 Andrew Root, *Christopraxis: A Practical Theology of the Cross* (Minneapolis: Fortress, 2014), 29.
4 Miller-McLemore, "Misunderstandings," 20.
5 I am aware of no other work on this, though Courtney T. Goto comes closest to my proposals: *Taking on Practical Theology: The Idolization of Context and the Hope of Community* (Leiden: Brill, 2018). Practical theology engages the prophetic in: Stephen B. Bevans and Roger P. Schroeder, *Prophetic Dialogue: Reflections on Christian Mission Today* (Maryknoll: Orbis, 2011); Gerard Hall, "Prophetic Dialogue: A Foundational Category for Practical Theology," *International Journal of Practical Theology* 14 (2010): 34–46; Richard R. Osmer, *Practical Theology* (Grand Rapids: Eerdmans, 2008), ch.3.
6 Walter Brueggemann, *The Prophetic Imagination*, 2nd ed. (Minneapolis: Fortress, 2001). A more recent '40th anniversary edition' exists (Fortress, 2018) but it is the preface to this second edition that catalysed my proposal and I refer to that edition throughout. Further: Walter Brueggemann, *The Practice of Prophetic Imagination: Preaching an Emancipating Word* (Minneapolis: Fortress, 2012).
7 Brueggemann, *Prophetic*, 3.
8 Brueggemann, *Prophetic*, 36.
9 Brueggemann, *Practice*, 68–69.
10 Brueggemann, *Prophetic*, 39.
11 Brueggemann, *Prophetic*, 57. Abraham J. Heschel also describes the prophet as sharing in what he calls the divine pathos and communicating it to humanity, framing this as the prophet's 'fundamental experience'. This divine pathos follows from the reality that 'God is involved in the life of man' and the divine word given to the prophet is 'aglow with pathos' (*The Prophets vol.1* [New York: Harper Torchbooks, 1969], 26, 241).
12 Brueggemann, *Prophetic*, 41, 45.
13 Brueggemann, *Prophetic*, 45–46.
14 Brueggemann, *Prophetic*, 59–60.
15 Walter Brueggemann, "Prophetic Leadership: Engagement in Counter Imagination," *Journal of Religious Leadership* 10, no. 1 (2011): 20–21.
16 Brueggemann, *Prophetic*, 64–65.
17 Brueggemann, *Prophetic*, xvi.
18 I mean 'texts' in the widest sense: not only Scripture but also ecclesial tradition, reasoned theological reflections, and the historical praxis of God's people.
19 As discussed below, this grieving may be understood also as participation in divine action, namely a sharing in God's pathos regarding aspects of human action in the concrete now.
20 The twofold purpose for sinking deep into the memories of the community's tradition—both to provide the symbols which can dismantle a numbness to, and denial of, the dominant consciousness and also to identify the promise by which a prophetic re-energising is rendered possible—makes clear that the four pillars (or 'movements') proposed do not exist as entirely separate. For this second movement of deep remembering influences both the expression of pain and the coding of a discourse. So, also, to begin coding the discourse of hope may well exacerbate the pain of the status quo as denial is broken down more completely. Such interpenetration of 'phases' in practical theological method is entirely normal.

21 Brueggemann, *Prophetic*, 65.
22 See John Swinton and Harriet Mowat, *Practical Theology and Qualitative Research*, 2nd ed. (London: SCM, 2016), 57–58.
23 Theobiography is Pete Ward's language (*Participation and Mediation: A Practical Theology for the Liquid Church* [London: SCM, 2008], 4).
24 Cambridge Inter-Collegiate Christian Union.
25 For how evangelicalism influences my metatheoretical assumptions relating to theology's sources, Scripture's priority, and interdisciplinarity, see Chloe Lynch, *Ecclesial Leadership as Friendship* (Abingdon: Routledge, 2019), appendix. My evangelicalism may also lead me to favour, more than Brueggemann might, theology informed by historico-grammatical exegesis: see Tim Meadowcroft, "Method and Old Testament Theology: Barr, Brueggemann and Goldingay Considered," *Tyndale Bulletin* 57, no. 1 (2006): 35–56.
26 The ecclesial imagination of each, of course, remains influenced also by its outsiders: the local church by unbelieving local neighbours, the confessional theological academy by non-confessional theologians, and by academics of other disciplines. Practical theology is inevitably interdisciplinary.
27 Stephen Pattison, *The Challenge of Practical Theology: Selected Essays* (London: Jessica Kingsley, 2007), 284.
28 Craig Dykstra, "Pastoral and Ecclesial Imagination," in *For Life Abundant: Practical Theology, Theological Education, and Christian Ministry*, eds. Dorothy C. Bass and Craig Dykstra (Grand Rapids: Eerdmans, 2008), 41–61.
29 Trevor Hart, "Imagination for the Kingdom of God? Hope, Promise, and the Transformative Power of an Imagined Future," in *God Will Be All In All: The Eschatology of Jürgen Moltmann*, ed. Richard Bauckham (Edinburgh: T&T Clark, 1999), 54–55.
30 Hart, "Imagination," 75.
31 Existing epistemological categories are necessarily framed by what is familiar and thus cannot go beyond this (Hart, "Imagination," 76). Leaps of imagination are what might enable new seeing of what we have never before seen.
32 James E. Loder discusses constructive acts of the imagination—epistemic leaps—in his account of knowing (*The Transforming Moment*, 2nd ed. [Colorado Springs: Helmers & Howard, 1989], 37–40). Even so, the imagination also 'stand[s] alone as the vehicle ... of a truth that all the resources of rational and empirical method can neither reach nor explain' (Hart, "Imagination," 195).
33 Trygve David Johnson blames Feuerbach for the assumption that reason and imagination must exist in opposition to one another (*The Preacher as Liturgical Artist: Metaphor, Identity, and the Vicarious Humanity of Christ* [Eugene, OR: Cascade, 2014], 11). Yet this is not necessarily a binary relationship. Indeed, Kieran Egan counterclaims that imagination 'greatly enriches rational thinking' (*Imagination in Teaching and Learning: Ages 8 to 15* [London: Routledge, 1992], 43). More succinctly: '[t]he intellect is not an imagination-free zone' (Hart, "Imagination," 193).
34 Egan, *Imagination*, 42.
35 For Paul D. Avis, 'divine revelation is given above all (though certainly not exclusively) in modes that are addressed to the human imagination' (*God and the Creative Imagination: Metaphor, Symbol and Myth in Religion and Theology* [London: Routledge, 1999], 3).
36 Garrett Green, *Imagining God: Theology and the Religious Imagination* (Grand Rapids: Eerdmans, 1998), 43. In homage to Brunner and his ensuing debate with Barth, Green calls it the *Anknüpfungspunkt*, 'the anthropological point of contact for revelation' (*Imagining*, 29).
37 Green, *Imagining*, 40.
38 Green, *Imagining*, 84, 104.
39 Green, *Imagining*, 106, 123, 125.

40 Amos Yong, *Spirit-Word-Community: Theological Hermeneutics in Trinitarian Perspective* (Farnham: Ashgate, 2002), 133–141. Cf. Yong's discussion of Green's proposals at 143–144: Yong argues for imagination as more active in its worldmaking than he reads Green as indicating.
41 Miller-McLemore, "Misunderstandings," 23–25.
42 Root, *Christopraxis*, 13.
43 Ray S. Anderson, *The Shape of Practical Theology: Empowering Ministry with Theological Praxis* (Downers Grove: IVP Academic, 2001), 54; Ray S. Anderson, *The Soul of Ministry: Forming Leaders for God's People* (Louisville, KY: Westminster John Knox, 1997), 28–29.
44 Brueggemann, "Prophetic," 3.
45 Ray S. Anderson, "A Theology for Ministry," in *Theological Foundations for Ministry*, ed. Ray S. Anderson (Edinburgh: T&T Clark, 1979), 14; Anderson, *Shape*, 69.
46 Brueggemann, *Prophetic*, 12.
47 Brueggemann, *Prophetic*, 19.
48 Ultimately, of course, the final and complete divine word of grace is Jesus, whose entire life, death and resurrection 'bears the paradigm of the ex nihilo': he is divine possibility entering human impossibility (Root, *Christopraxis*, 110). Brueggemann echoes this to some degree with his presentation of Jesus' actions as his 'capacity for God's impossibilities that make all things new' (*Practice*, 127).
49 Brueggemann, *Practice*, 36–37.
50 Brueggemann, *Practice*, 38–39.
51 The church 'must be formed and ordered from the inside of its experience and confession and not by borrowing from sources external to its own life' (Brueggemann, *Prophetic*, 5).
52 Brueggemann notes that what he 'parsed as "imagination" … is … "the guidance of the Spirit",' although admitting this perspective was largely inchoate in *The Prophetic Imagination* (Walter Brueggemann, "Response to Symposium on *The Prophetic Imagination*," *Journal of Pentecostal Theology* 23 [2014]: 16).
53 Brueggemann, *Prophetic*, xvi.
54 Brueggemann, *Practice*, 41.
55 Brueggemann, *Practice*, 126.
56 Or, of course, than by the academic colleague who might filibuster their way through faculty meetings. For, as noted earlier, our ecclesial subcommunities may, for practical theologians, comprise not only local church but also confessional academic communities, each with their own formative challenges!
57 Further on the ecclesial dynamic in hermeneutics: Daniel J. Treier, *Introducing Theological Interpretation of Scripture: Recovering a Christian Practice* (Nottingham: Apollos, 2008), ch.3.
58 Dykstra, "Imagination," 42–43, 49.
59 Brueggemann, *Prophetic*, 28.
60 Brueggemann, *Prophetic*, 28. My focus here is naming the politics and economics of the subject being engaged from time to time by the practical theologian. Goto, however, points to a meta-reality of potentially oppressive politics and economics: namely those injustices inherent in the paradigm that determines who is authorised to produce knowledge in the field of practical theology itself (Goto, *Taking*).
61 Roy Kearsley, *Church, Community and Power* (Farnham: Ashgate, 2008), 109. Western practical theologians, especially, should be intentional in listening to a wider range of voices, including more from the majority world.
62 Brueggemann, *Practice*, 69. See Jon Sobrino's discussion of human 'dishonesty about the real' (*Spirituality of Liberation: Toward Political Holiness*, trans. Robert R. Barr [Maryknoll: Orbis, 1988], 14–19).
63 Brueggemann, *Practice*, 72.
64 Brueggemann, *Practice*, 25.

65 Brueggemann, *Prophetic*, 35–37.
66 Rickie D. Moore, "Walter Brueggemann's *Prophetic Imagination*: Not without Honor," *Journal of Pentecostal Theology* 23 (2014): 4.
67 Lee Roy Martin, "'Your sons and daughters will prophesy': A Pentecostal Review of Walter Brueggemann's *The Practice of Prophetic Imagination*," *Journal of Pentecostal Theology* 22 (2013): 160; cf. Mark J. Cartledge, "Affective Theological Praxis: Understanding the Direct Object of Practical Theology," *International Journal of Practical Theology* 8 (2004): 38.
68 Brueggemann, *Prophetic*, 55–56.
69 See Gregory S. Clapper's definition of affections: "Orthokardia: John Wesley's Grammar of the Holy Spirit," in *The Spirit, The Affections, and the Christian Tradition*, eds. Dale M. Coulter and Amos Yong (Notre Dame: University of Notre Dame Press, 2016), 263.
70 'The characteristic of the prophets is not foreknowledge of the future but insight into the present pathos of God' (Abraham J. Heschel, *The Prophets vol.2* [New York: Harper Torchbooks, 1975], 11).
71 Heschel, *Prophets vol.2*, 10–11.
72 '[T]he affections function as ways to avoid fanaticism while advocating a place for emotional correspondence to religious experience' (Daniel Castelo, "Tarrying on the Lord: Affections, Virtues and Theological Ethics in Pentecostal Perspective," *Journal of Pentecostal Theology* 13, no. 1 [2004]: 38).
73 William J. Wainwright, *Reason and the Heart: A Prolegomenon to a Critique of Passional Reason* (Ithaca: Cornell University Press, 1995), 5. Cf. Wolfgang Vondey, *Beyond Pentecostalism: The Crisis of Global Christianity and the Renewal of the Theological Agenda* (Cambridge: Eerdmans, 2010), 45–46; Heschel, *Prophets vol.2*, 36: 'emotion can be reasonable just as reason can be emotional.'
74 Heschel, *Prophets vol.2*, 11.
75 Vondey, *Beyond*, 46.
76 Heschel, *Prophets vol.2*, 37.
77 Don E. Saliers, *The Soul in Paraphrase: Prayer and the Religious Affections* (Ashland City: OSL, 2011), 10. Note Stephen J. Land's comments on integrating orthodoxy, orthopraxy, and orthopathy (*Pentecostal Spirituality: A Passion for the Kingdom* [Sheffield: Sheffield Academic Press, 1993], 41, 133).
78 In this regard, I am grateful to Moorlands College conference participants and the Rosina Parker Senior Seminar (London School of Theology) for formative reflections on an earlier version of this chapter. Whilst there is, for confessional practical theologians, interplay of local church and academy subcommunities, I envisage that the engagement described here will come mostly from the latter because of the specific skills involved. As to the former, work remains to adapt this mode for accessibility to ordinary theologians.
79 Brueggemann, *Prophetic*, xvi.

# 3 The role of teleology in practical theology

*Alistair J. McKitterick*

What is the role of teleology in practical theology? Teleology has been understood in various ways, so it is worth just spelling out what I mean by the term. *Telos* as a Greek term can mean goal or end, and it is often used to describe the purpose behind everything from a statue to a universe. In Scripture we read that Christ is the *telos* of the law (Rom 10:4), and whereas it can be understood to mean the end of the law, it can just as well be read as the goal or perhaps the purpose of the law. The term *telos* is sometimes used in apologetic design arguments.[1] The concepts of teleology that are the focus of this paper are the flourishing of human beings and the goals of God. How can such theological goals be used in practical theology?

## What is practical theology?

Practical theology is a reflective discipline as well as an activity within ministry.[2] It is associated with reflecting upon actions and beliefs, often in some form of critical correlation with other disciplines. I am interested in the interdisciplinary engagement that practical theology has with the social sciences because they share a common interest in the human condition. Swinton and Mowat argue that practical theology should critically engage with the social sciences. They use the metaphor of conversion for such theological engagement with secular insights, believing that it produces a fresh vision of creation, closer communion with God, and greater wonder and praise.[3] Swinton and Mowat describe the social sciences as being 'baptized' or 'converted' tools when 'drafted into the service of God'[4] to enable more faithful Christian practice. This faithful Christian practice is described in teleological terms.

> Practical Theology has a particular goal: to enable faithful living and authentic Christian practice. This is an important point to reflect on. Practical Theology has a telos and a goal that transcends the boundaries of human experience and expectation.[5]

## Dialogue with social sciences

Dialogue between theology and the social sciences is usually descriptive and done in the indicative mood in that it does not judge the practices or situations

DOI: 10.4324/9781003094975-5

under discussion but rather recounts and locates them within believing communities. Such dialogical engagement is non-directive because science by nature is a descriptive discipline based upon empirical observation. Science, in theory at least, is sceptical about tradition and authority and takes nobody's word for it (as the motto of the Royal Society has it).[6] Its task is to explain observations, rather than to adjudicate whether what is observed is good or bad.[7] 'Social science can only describe and seek to explain the natural world and must remain mute regarding the supernatural context that surrounds the world as we know it.'[8] Science has increasingly adopted a materialist methodology, one where no god directs the paths of the planets or provides food for the raven when its young cries out (Job 38:41). Any reference to a sense of purpose or goal in nature would be to appeal to an external mind that gave it that purpose.[9] As Simon Oliver puts it, 'The rise of modern natural science and philosophy is often narrated in terms of the demise of teleological accounts of causation.'[10] Modern thought is said to have a 'general antipathy towards the concept of final causation or *telos*.'[11] Speaking of psychologists, Browning argues that the modern psychologies cannot contribute to 'ultimate metaphysical goals' because they 'disdain metaphysics and questions of ultimate concern.'[12]

## Theology and social science

Given that this is the situation that evangelical Christian practical theologians find themselves in, how might they respond? An unhelpful response would be to retreat from a rather unwelcoming academy back into the security of their own domain, namely the church. But that would be to reinforce the divide between these different disciplines, rather than seeking how it might be bridged. Rather than framing this scientific rejection of teleology in terms of opposition, Nancey Murphy sees it as an opportunity for theology because of the area of purpose vacated by the sciences. Reflecting on the interaction between theology and psychology, she suggests that it highlights the unique role that theology must take in such interdisciplinary dialogues.

> My question for the psychologists is this: If the secular academy has indeed turned away from any theological account of the telos of human life, is it not necessarily the case that secular psychologists will have confused ideas about what they are supposed to be doing?[13]

So long as psychology focuses upon phobias or neuroses, anxieties or compulsions it seemed obvious that the role of psychology was to restore the person back to normal or to give them new skills to cope in society. Such an approach takes for granted that these are problems to be solved, and to that extent psychology has an intrinsic goal, namely, to undo the negative effects of problematic symptoms and revert to the norm. But psychology has little to say to the person who is well but who asks, 'what does psychology say would make me a better person?' To be able to answer that, psychology would have to answer the prior questions 'what does the good psyche look like and what is it for?' To the extent that social science theories do carry moral implications (what Browning calls 'premoral goods'),[14] they are participating in theological discourse, and this needs to be recognised and articulated, as they are usually made unconsciously and unwittingly.[15] Practical theology must critically engage these disciplines theologically. As Weber put it when reflecting upon the limits of sociology, science is unable to answer the simple questions of 'What shall we do and how shall we live?'[16] To do so, the social sciences would first have to say what humanity and human society is 'for'.[17]

## Aristotelian ethics and causation

The question 'what is something for?' is associated with Aristotle's ethics in contemplating nature.[18] Aristotle articulated four interconnecting causes needed to account for a thing's existence and to answer the 'why' question. We could look at a marble statue of an emperor and ask, 'why does this statue exist?' or 'what caused it to come into being?' Aristotle gives four causes: 'the matter, the form, the mover, and "that for the sake of which".'[19] First of all, a marble statue of an emperor has a material cause, the matter of which it is composed, in this case the block of marble. Without the marble you get no statue, so the marble must be part of the cause of the statue. Second, the statue has a formal cause, a blueprint that prescribes its precise shape (in this case the image of the emperor). The statue also needs an efficient cause (the mover), namely the sculptor without whom the material and formal causes would not have been actualised. We now have a statue, made from marble, made in the likeness of the emperor, and made by the sculptor. But we need one more causal explanation: the 'for' explanation. Aristotle's final cause is the cause 'for the sake of which' it was made in the first place. It is the answer to the 'why' question. The final cause of the statue would be to stand in the space set for it in the temple or stadium to represent the emperor to the people. The first three causes are essential to the statue (its material, its process of construction, its actual shape and function) because without any one of them there can be no statue. The final cause is 'extrinsic' to the statue and is given to it as its purpose. There is nothing in the first three causes of the statue that necessitates its final cause, which instead comes from an external mind (in this case the person commissioning the statue to be made).

Purpose is present in nature as it is in art, and nature is 'a cause that operates for a purpose.'[20] Purpose in nature was important to Aristotle who argued that all nature had some sense of itself, some internal motivating power that meant objects like the planets could desire God as the object of love. Dudley writes:

> Aristotle supposed that the spheres in which the heavenly bodies travelled must all have souls and be intelligent ... The intelligences of the spheres made the spheres rotate in a perfect circle around the earth because the

spheres desire to come as close as possible to the Unmoved Mover, Aristotle's God. The spheres cannot come any closer to God, but attempt to do so by perfect circular movement. The intelligences of the spheres wished to come as close to God as possible because God is perfectly good and the spheres are attracted out of love for God's goodness.[21]

Since the love of God's goodness is the *telos* of the inanimate world, it follows that we can extend that logic to humanity. Aristotle argues that whatever choice or possession for humanity 'will most produce the contemplation of God, this is the best and this standard is the finest.'[22] Dudley concludes his argument saying that 'the Unmoved Mover is the final cause of the best life and supreme happiness of man and that Aristotle's moral ideal is the love and contemplation of God.'[23]

## Newtonian mechanics and materialism

This kind of argumentation has failed to find purchase in the academy. Aristotle's view of the intrinsic *telos* of the planets as being the contemplation of God was replaced by Newtonian mechanics. Newton's law of physics replaced the Aristotelian vision of the spheres having internal affection to travel in circles as their expression of the love of God. These heavy bodies orbited the larger mass of the sun as a result of gravity, not desire. Gravitational attraction replaced the attraction of love. Newton's laws of motion fully described the movement of planetary objects and left no room for any 'intention' within matter.[24] Since there is no intrinsic purpose within inert matter, any goal that matter serves would have to be imposed upon it externally by a mind, and nature, to use Oliver's phrase, 'does not deliberate.'[25] The only source for purposefulness would have to be externally imposed (by God) as a final cause, and Oliver (writing in *Studies in Christian Ethics*) thinks this concept to be 'arbitrary.'[26] In Bertrand Russell's famous phrase, 'the universe is just there, and that's all.'[27] Nature has no final cause, and so despite the abundance of purposeful, teleological thinking in human culture we should not impose this 'unnatural' way of thinking into a purely scientific explanation of the world and our place in it.

> Against the background of the modern separation of nature and culture, and mind and matter, the intentional teleology which belongs to humanity and its artefacts is profoundly unnatural, belonging to culture rather than nature. Insofar as teleology belongs to the natural, it is understood as a mere projection onto an essentially material realm of efficient causes.[28]

Ever since Darwin, Oliver argues, humans have been thought of as belonging to base nature, and nature is mindless and cannot intend anything ahead of time. He argues that we need to reframe human teleological thinking in terms of material and efficient causes alone. But Oliver's reductive argument is weak.

He challenges the Aristotelian 'statue' illustration of final cause by suggesting that marble blocks are naturally 'orientated towards' becoming a statue as if they contained statue-like potentiality just waiting to express itself. This argument is especially revealing. Oliver wants to locate the form of an emperor in the marble block itself, as if all the sculptor did (and in this analogy the sculptor would be 'mother nature') was to remove the pieces that were in the way of the statue to allow it to emerge by itself.[29] As philosopher Henry Wang puts it,

> the dominance of mechanical explanation in modern thought stems from the breakup of the unity of four causes in the Aristotelian teleology, as a result of which efficient cause is singled out as the only effective or "real" cause.[30]

Oliver's attempts at denying external forms and excluding final causes is not an explanation but rather a dogmatic denial of purpose in order to fit *a priori* a materialist philosophy.

## The role of theology

The point of rehearsing these teleological arguments is not simply to sketch the intellectual context of the academy and its antipathy to purposeful thinking. It is to highlight the unique and necessary role that theology can and must play in thinking about the purpose of humanity and our place in the universe. Only theology (for Aristotle's *Physics* was really a natural theology) can provide a sufficient basis for thinking about final cause in the universe. This, I think, points to two ways of 'doing theology'.

### Theology in dialogue

The first way of doing theology is to join in with the descriptive discussion of the social sciences. The social sciences describe a situation, action, context, relationship, or process using concepts that help us understand what is going on. Swinton and Mowat refer to deepening understanding 'by entering into dialogue with other sources of knowledge that will help us develop a deeper understanding of the situation.'[31] Sociology will describe the environment, the political context, the power-relationships, the insider-outsider groups, routines, and revolutions. Psychology will reflect on the perceptions and biases, conditioning and development, needs and neurology of those involved. And theology too can participate within a descriptive trialogue.

Theologians can describe the beliefs and spiritual realities of participants and the society of which they are a part, the fallenness of the cosmos, the influence of spiritual beings, the doctrines and religious traditions that inform such insights. They can contribute the importance of beliefs and faith, and the influence of the church in people's lives. Theology's first contribution, in short, is to account for the reality of God through the power of the Holy Spirit in describing what is going on, a reality which the social sciences all too often choose to ignore.[32] Practical theology has revived a theological engagement with such contemporary issues by taking a more public theology approach and engaging with other disciplines.[33] It is what I have called the critical descriptive phase of practical theology.[34] This interplay of different perspectives, this open discussion between those who see the same thing but through different lenses, is how I understand the term 'critical correlation'. This relationship between theology and the other disciplines does not assert priority of theology at this stage. It encourages a humbler attitude, an openness towards the insights of others, and an awareness that our theological perceptions are as likely to need critique as those of the other disciplines in the discussion. It shows what Swinton and Mowat describe as 'hospitality' towards the perspectives of others whilst not at all denying our own Christian perspective.[35]

## Theology as normative (theological imperative)

But this descriptive activity is only the first way of doing theology. The unique contribution of theology to interdisciplinary dialogue is to provide the possibility of a final cause, a goal and purpose for any given situation. And this second way is where theology becomes entirely asymmetric in its relationship with the other disciplines. At some point, the indicative or descriptive nature of the discussion gives way to the imperative mood and the theologian puts forward a theological norm or teleological claim which changes the language mood from 'is' to 'ought', from indicative to imperative.[36] Teleological language is of necessity from outside of a situation and is a voice of revelation and authority. It is a discernment of the will of God mediated through Scripture by the Holy Spirit to the situation under consideration. Teleological thinking is therefore fundamentally a hermeneutical activity, seeking to interpret the Word of God appropriately for a sense of direction appropriate for each encounter. Teleology provides moral impetus for practical theology. It is the rationale behind Christian praxis that makes praxis theological. It is seeking the mind of Christ.

What is the *telos* of humanity and human society? To put the question this way is to highlight the massive nature of the topic and engages philosophy and theology with anthropology and politics. I will attempt to do nothing more than sketch the main arguments that I have found convincing when teaching practical theology at Moorlands College for the last few years. The more important point to note is how theology is being used in two different ways: descriptively and normatively. Students have found this distinction empowering as they realise the capacity of theology in general (and Scripture in particular) to inspire and direct a vision for ministry.

Aristotle's natural theology implied that the goal for humanity was the unhindered contemplation of God, a pre-Christian form of the beatific vision.[37] The activity of God is to contemplate himself, as there is nothing higher for him to contemplate, and therefore the *summum bonum* of humanity is to engage in *theoria*, the contemplation on the essence of God. (It has to be said that Aristotle's god had no interest in contemplating us, and the idea that he might become the incarnate son of Mary would have been incomprehensible to him.) Nonetheless, Aquinas follows this way of thinking: the contemplation of divine truth is 'the end of the whole human life.'[38] Aquinas himself cites Augustine in support saying 'the contemplation of God is promised us as being the goal of all our actions and the everlasting perfection of our joys' (*De Trin.* I,8). Other statements along the same lines might include the Westminster Shorter Catechism's classic doctrine that our 'chief end is to glorify God and enjoy him forever.'

What Aristotle recognised in all this, and what is clear to the practical theologian, is that no single doctrine, ethical theory, or moral principle can determine the goals for the various practical situations in which we find ourselves. Nor is there is a complete list of doctrines or commands that suffice to cover the complex issues that practical theology routinely faces. Aristotle describes an additional virtue, that of practical wisdom or *phronêsis*, associated with deliberation, that enables the wise person to discern purposes and make wise decisions.[39]

## Haphazard teleology

The concept of teleology is often used quite haphazardly in practical theology. In a paper by King and Whitney entitled 'What's the "Positive" in Positive Psychology? Teleological Considerations Based on Creation and *Imago* Doctrines', the authors recognise that 'few social scientists have explicitly addressed these teleological issues.'[40] The fact that God demonstrates purpose in the creation of human beings will have implications for them as psychologists. Drawing on the concept of flourishing, or thriving, they say that 'human thriving can only be evaluated in terms of what a given human is supposed to be.'[41] They argue that 'creation provides the context for thriving,'[42] and that the Spirit enables it, and that we might have different *teloi* depending on whether we are Christians or not. They conclude with Stanley Grenz that '[t]he divine image is the goal or destiny that God intends for his creatures,'[43] although they note that such a *telos* presents difficulties in that we usually argue that humanity is, by virtue of being human, already made in the image of God, and that perhaps being transformed into the likeness of Christ would be a more appropriate Christian *telos* (2 Cor 3:18; cf Jas 3:9). What is encouraging, however, is their use of teleology to engage with psychology at all. 'We are careful to note that thriving towards this particular *telos* found in and through Christ is something that secular positive psychology does not recognize.'[44]

Graham Tomlin argues that 'the *telos* of theological education is to enable the *teleiōsis*, or maturity of the church.'[45] He later redefines that sense of maturity as 'the reconciliation of all things in Christ.'[46] It is not that I disagree particularly with either statement, but rather that they are just not the same and he is trying to ride two teleological horses at once. He compounds the sense of ambiguity restating that:

the goal of theological education is not knowledge, understanding, skills, or professional competence, but rather the development of people steeped in Christian wisdom, defined as knowing what to do and how to do it to enable the church to come to full maturity in Christ.[47]

And that may be right for all I know, namely that the *telos* of a place like Moorlands College is to teach Christian wisdom, which I might expound along the lines of learning practical theology. But the point I am making is that very often Christian writers will make totalising claims about 'the point of it all is…' or 'at the end of the day it is all about…' yet these descriptions of ultimate purpose are often at odds with each other. Teaching Christian wisdom is simply not the same as the reconciliation of all things in Christ, although the one may well imply the other. Elsewhere Woodward writes that 'the telos of theological education [is] immersing candidates for ministry within an intense experience of the Christian way of life that moves them toward ever greater discipleship.'[48] Is that right, and how would Tomlin respond to that competing claim? Stanley Grenz expresses a different *telos* for humanity, more in line with the Westminster Shorter Catechism: 'Glorifying the Father in the Son … marks the *telos* for which humans were created in the beginning.'[49] Greenway, Barrett, and Furrow argue that '*shalom* is "the way things ought to be" and in this sense represents another candidate for a brief definition of humanity's *telos*.'[50] Since so many competing *teloi* are proposed by different authors, how useful is the concept of *telos* for practical theology? Might they in fact all be wrong, or at least not be of any practical use?

## Kelsey and God's three irreducible *teloi*

David Kelsey has argued that God, in fact, has a plurality of *teloi*, and that none can be reduced to the other. I will argue that God's having a plurality of *teloi* enables us to use the concept of teleology more intentionally in practical theology. Kelsey argues against the traditional view that all of God's activities ultimately resolve into 'a single *ultimate* divine purpose.'[51] The creation, fall, reconciliation, and new creation, he argues, are four movements of the economy of God that different traditions frame as either all about maturation (Irenaeus), or cosmological reintegration (Aquinas), or salvation history revealing God's eternal decree (Reformed tradition). Kelsey challenges 'the necessity of ascribing to God only a single *telos*' in light of the 'serious systematic problems' it presents for Christian theology.[52]

Of these four movements, the fall seems most obviously not a goal of God. This, says Kelsey, leaves three different ways that God relates to all else: a) to relate to realities genuinely other than God that are, in their finite ways, good, true, and beautiful manifestations of God's glory; b) to reconcile creatures to God when they are estranged; c) to glorify creatures eschatologically.[53] These movements are creation, reconciliation, and eschatological consummation. If one of these is God's real, single goal, then the other two must be framed as

64  *Alistair J. McKitterick*

being reducible in some way to it, or instrumentalised by it. But this, Kelsey argues, 'inevitably leads systemically to distortions of doctrine about the Triune God who pursues those goals.'[54]

If, for example, we make reconciliation God's single *telos*, then God only created creatures to reconcile them, rather than for creation's own sake. Such a doctrine 'implicitly legitimates exploitative attitudes toward creatures as instruments,'[55] something that environmentally concerned Christians will want to oppose strongly. New creation would be seen as a 'postscript' or 'bonus' to reconciliation, discontinuous with it and nothing to do with what God is doing today in this world: there can be no eschatological 'now'; only 'not yet'. But if we make eschatological consummation the single *telos* of God, then both creation and reconciliation are necessary phases to be endured before the real purpose of God is fulfilled. And this would make the fall 'itself one of God's subordinate goals,' something which at the very least brings into question God's goodness.[56] It makes creation a 'botched job' on the way to doing it properly.[57] And finally, if we were to make creation God's single *telos* then reconciliation is part of the natural order of things, like the skin healing naturally from a cut, and there is nothing 'not yet' to hope for because everything is already 'now'.

Kelsey argues that these three goals of God are inseparable and irreducible. By choosing to orientate ourselves to one, we do not deny the others, but recognise that we cannot orientate our lives and actions to all three simultaneously. We need the virtue of practical wisdom and the gift of discernment to decide which theological *telos* to aim for in each situation and personal encounter we face.

## Transgenderism and *teloi*

If we take Kelsey's threefold *teloi* as a provisional guide for doing practical theology, we can illustrate what difference the choice of *telos* makes to our praxis in a particular personal encounter. My view of practical theology is that it must be able to address the difficult topics if it is to be of value to theologians and Christian ministers. Let us take the issue of transgenderism and imagine that we have encountered a young man seeking our Christian input in responding to a crisis of sexual identity. We encounter him perhaps as his youth leader or family worker. We listen to his story, we critically correlate the different disciplines of social science and descriptive theology, and at some point in our reflection we get a sense of discernment, a moment of clarity, about the theological imperative or teleological goal to use in this situation. What this illustration will show is the profound differences in our Christian praxis depending on which of Kelsey's three *teloi* we adopt.

From Kelsey's typology, if we discern that we should adopt the *telos* of creation, then we might take as our theological imperative the goal to be made in the image of God as originally created:

So God created mankind in his own image, in the image of God he created them; male and female he created them.

(Gen 1:27)

Our praxis might be towards harmonising the young man's maleness and masculinity (on the assumption that in creation there was no divergence between sex and gender identity). Such a teleological approach would emphasise the binary nature of human sexuality in the creation narrative.

If we were instead to opt for the *telos* of reconciliation, then our aim for our friend is different. We might highlight the disrupting effects of the fall on our psyches as well as our bodies. We might perceive the problem in terms of the distorting values of society and gendered expectations more generally. The *telos* of reconciliation would point us towards a Christian praxis of acceptance, of welcoming back and welcoming in however broken someone is, paradigmatically seen in Jesus' parable of the prodigal son (Luke 15). Our theological imperative for our young friend might be based on God's acceptance of the Ethiopian eunuch, received into the communion of the holy people even though he would not have been permitted into Israel's temple grounds because of his imperfect sexual identity (Acts 8).[58] Or we might emphasise the reconciliation and unity over diversity seen in verses like Galatians 3:28:

There is neither Jew nor Gentile, neither slave nor free, nor is there male and female, for you are all one in Christ Jesus.

And finally, if we were to adopt Kelsey's third *telos* of new creation then our theological imperative might be to see ourselves as the glorified bride of Christ (Rev 21). This is not to sexualise the corporate relationship with Christ, but rather to recognise that the categories of our eternal relationship in Christ use gendered language in a way that shows a certain ambivalence towards a strict binary scheme.[59] Men are every bit as much the bride of Christ (2 Cor 11:2) as women are all sons of God through faith (Gal 3:26) or sons of the resurrection (Luke 20:36). The present gender ambiguity experienced now by our friend might find a theological fulfilment in the angelic life Christians anticipate in the new creation (Matt 22:30).[60]

Kelsey's teleological typology provides, I think, a more biblical framework than, for example, the 'integrity', 'disability' and 'diversity' categories that Yarhouse uses.[61] This same typology can be applied to any complex issue for practical theology to consider. Each of the three *teloi* provides motivation for distinctive Christian praxis, in that they do not just describe the situation but provide theological imperatives for goal-oriented actions. Which one to choose in each personal encounter will depend upon the reflection and correlation of the complex issues in the critical descriptive phase. In the above example it is not obvious which *telos* should be adopted, and any decision would need to be justified and defended theologically. Ultimately it is a matter of prayer and spiritual discernment. Discerning which *telos* to follow aligns us with a specific, irreducible (and biblical) goal of God. The use of teleology to motivate and guide our Christian praxis prevents practical theology from being mere subjective opinion insulated from criticism. The choosing of a theological imperative to act upon is not simply a matter of private revelation. It is an open, critical process whereby we offer a theological critique and biblical defence of our choice of *telos* and the subsequent Christian praxis we adopt in the name of the Lord.

## Conclusion and critique

I conclude this discussion on the use of teleology and practical theology with a reflection, a critique, and one suggestion.

My reflection is that recognising the use of different *teloi* in practical theology helps to explain misunderstandings between different evangelical groups advocating different Christian praxes to the same situation. Each group believes itself to be just as 'biblical' as the others (with each holding a high view of Scripture). It behoves Christians to be explicit in articulating what theological goal (what *telos*) is motivating their Christian praxis, and to defend why they think their theological imperative fits better the complex details of the situation compared with the alternatives. Having differences of opinion is not a theological stopper: each theological position is open to critical evaluation as to how it integrates the prior interdisciplinary dialogue. Criteria for evaluating a good theological imperative would be that it is specific to the personal encounter, integrates insights from the critical correlation, is goal-oriented, shows creativity, and is specifically drawn from our shared Christian tradition.[62]

The critique of Kelsey's argument would be that the incarnation of God is a missing *telos*. I suppose that it could be a subsidiary goal to one of the other *teloi*, but Christ's incarnation endures even into the new creation, bearing the marks of redemption, and it enables us to 'follow Jesus' as a teleological goal in itself, rather than a means to an end.[63] So much good theological praxis has been motivated by the theology of incarnation that it seems a reasonable suggestion to include it into the list of irreducible *teloi*.[64]

My suggestion is to offer a way of holding these three (or four) irreducible *teloi* together. As Kelsey already indicated, creation, (incarnation), redemption, and new creation are movements in the one story of God, and narrative is the right kind of genre for holding different themes in dramatic tension. Holding God's irreducible *teloi* in narrative tension would locate the practice of practical theology within the ongoing story of the people of God. Swinton and Mowat say that the 'goal and endpoint of Practical Theology is to ensure, encourage and enable faithful participation in the continuing gospel narrative.'[65] Discerning which of these different *teloi* should govern our praxis for a given situation becomes a matter of recognising where we find ourselves in the narrative of God, a combination of conscientisation and revelation.[66] Are we being called in this or that encounter to faithfully follow Christ along dusty

Galilean roads (incarnation), to stand before his cross in darkness and silence (reconciliation), or to declare the transformative power of the risen king to the ends of the Earth (eschaton)? Christians live in the overlap of ages, but the giving of the promised Paraclete at Pentecost might suggest the church's default setting to be the *telos* of the eschaton as we live in the light of the risen and ascended Christ and anticipate his return.

Teleological practical theology, as I have described it, is dependent on both biblical theology and pneumatology. We need not take on our shoulders the burden of ensuring that the story ends correctly, for God alone is responsible for fulfilling the already inaugurated eschaton. As practical theologians we seek to live faithfully within the biblical narrative and to discern which of the *teloi* of God should motivate our Christian praxis in the world at any given time. Our role, to use Wells' concept, is to improvise in the unfolding drama of Scripture and the revelation of God's *teloi*.[67]

## Notes

1 See, for instance, John M. DePoe, "The Heavens Are Declaring the Glory of God: Contemporary Teleological Arguments," *Review & Expositor* 111, no. 3 (2014): 244–258; this is not my focus for this discussion.
2 For a fuller definition of practical theology, see Bonnie J. Miller-McLemore, "Introduction: The Contributions of Practical Theology," in *The Wiley-Blackwell Companion to Practical Theology*, ed. Bonnie J. Miller-McLemore (Chichester: Wiley-Blackwell, 2012), 5.
3 John Swinton and Harriet Mowat, *Practical Theology and Qualitative Research*, 2nd ed. (London: SCM, 2016), 264.
4 Swinton and Mowat, *Practical Theology and Qualitative Research*, 264.
5 Swinton and Mowat, *Practical Theology and Qualitative Research*, 9–10.
6 'Nullius in verba'. Modern science has often set itself up in opposition to the authority of Scripture on topics such as the origin of life or the place of humanity in the world.
7 For what counts as a scientific theory, see Peter Lipton, "What Good Is an Explanation?" in *Explanation*, eds. Giora Hon and Sam S. Rakover, Synthese Library 302 (Dordrecht: Springer, 2001), 43–60.
8 James R. Beck and Bruce A. Demarest, *The Human Person in Theology and Psychology: A Biblical Anthropology for the Twenty-First Century* (Grand Rapids: Kregel, 2005), 68.
9 For an illustration of the problem, see Doug Bolton, "The Scientific Community Isn't Happy about a Paper Mentioning a 'Creator'," *The Independent*, March 3, 2016, www.independent.co.uk/news/science/scientific-study-paper-creator-intelligent-design-plos-one-creatorgate-a6910171.html.
10 Simon Oliver, "Teleology Revived? Cooperation and the Ends of Nature," *Studies in Christian Ethics* 26, no. 2 (May 2013): 158.
11 Henry Wang, "Rethinking the Validity and Significance of Final Causation: From the Aristotelian to the Peircean Teleology," *Transactions of the Charles S. Peirce Society* 41, no. 3 (2005): 603.
12 Don S. Browning, *Christian Ethics and the Moral Psychologies. Religion, Marriage, and Family* (Grand Rapids: Eerdmans, 2006), 11; he does allow a more limited engagement with teleology insofar as they dialogue with the moral traditions of the West, in particular Christianity.

13 Nancey Murphy, "Constructing a Radical-Reformation Research Program in Psychology," in *Why Psychology Needs Theology: A Radical-Reformation Perspective*, eds. Alvin C. Dueck and Cameron Lee (Grand Rapids: Eerdmans, 2005), 56.
14 Browning, *Christian Ethics and the Moral Psychologies*, 12.
15 Browning, *Christian Ethics and the Moral Psychologies*, 13.
16 Cited in Michele Dillon, *Introduction to Sociological Theory: Theorists, Concepts, and Their Applicability to the Twenty-First Century*, 2nd ed. (Chichester: Wiley Blackwell, 2014), 147.
17 For further discussion, see Peter Medawar, *The Limits of Science* (Oxford: Oxford University Press, 1984).
18 For an online version, see Aristotle, "Physics," The Internet Classics Archive, accessed May 1, 2020, Book 2, Part 3, http://classics.mit.edu/Aristotle/physics.2.ii.html.
19 Aristotle, "Physics," Book 2, Part 7.
20 Aristotle, "Physics," Book 2, Part 8.
21 J. A. J. Dudley, "The Love of God in Aristotle's Ethics," *Neue Zeitschrift Für Systematische Theologie Und Religionsphilosophie* 25, no. 1–3 (2009): 126.
22 Aristotle, *Eudemian Ethics* VIII, iii, 15–16, 1249 b 13–21; cited in Dudley, "The Love of God," 131.
23 Dudley, "The Love of God," 137.
24 And matter was resolutely inert in light of Descartes' division of the cosmos into matter and mind.
25 Oliver, "Teleology Revived?" 160.
26 Oliver, "Teleology Revived?" 163.
27 Taken from a transcript of the Fr. Copleston vs. Bertrand Russell Debate on the Existence of God, 1948 BBC Radio; www.biblicalcatholic.com/apologetics/p20.htm.
28 Oliver, "Teleology Revived?" 165.
29 Oliver, "Teleology Revived?" 162.
30 Wang, "Rethinking the Validity and Significance of Final Causation," 611.
31 Swinton and Mowat, *Practical Theology and Qualitative Research*, 91.
32 Browning, *Christian Ethics and the Moral Psychologies*, 11.
33 Elaine Graham, "Why Practical Theology Must Go Public," *Practical Theology* 1, no. 1 (2008): 11–17.
34 For a description of how I use the terms personal encounter, critical description, theological imperative, and Christian praxis, see Alistair J. McKitterick, "The Theological Imperative Model for Practical Theology," *Journal of European Baptist Studies* 16, no. 4 (2016): 9–13.
35 Swinton and Mowat, *Practical Theology and Qualitative Research*, 86–87.
36 For a fascinating discussion on this topic, see C. S. Lewis, *The Abolition of Man: Or, Reflections on Education with Special Reference to the Teaching of English in the Upper Forms of Schools* (London: HarperCollins, 1944), 32.
37 For a good introduction to the topic, see Hans Boersma, "Thomas Aquinas on the Beatific Vision: A Christological Deficit," *TheoLogica* 2, no. 2 (2018): 129–147.
38 Thomas Aquinas, "SUMMA THEOLOGIAE: The Contemplative Life (Secunda Secundae Partis, Q. 180)," New Advent, Article 4, accessed May 2, 2020, www.newadvent.org/summa/3180.htm.
39 Aristotle, "Nicomachean Ethics," The Internet Classics Archive, Book VI: 1140a, 1141b, 1142b, accessed May 2, 2020, http://classics.mit.edu/Aristotle/nicomachaen.6.vi.html.
40 Pamela Ebstyne King and William B. Whitney, "What's the "Positive" in Positive Psychology? Teleological Considerations Based on Creation and *Imago* Doctrines," *Journal of Psychology and Theology* 43, no. 1 (2015): 47–59, 48.
41 King and Whitney, "What's the "Positive" in Positive Psychology?" 48.
42 King and Whitney, "What's the "Positive" in Positive Psychology?" 48.

43 Stanley Grenz, *Theology For The Community of God* (Grand Rapids: Eerdmans, 2000), 173 cited in King and Whitney, "What's the "Positive" in Positive Psychology?" 51.
44 King and Whitney, "What's the "Positive" in Positive Psychology?" 52.
45 Graham Tomlin, "The Telos of Theological Education," *Theological Education* 51, no. 2 (2018): 113–125, 115.
46 Tomlin, "The Telos of Theological Education," 116.
47 Tomlin, "The Telos of Theological Education," 117.
48 Scott Woodward, "The Telos of Theological Education: A Theological Reflection," *CrossCurrents* 69, no. 1 (2019): 39–44, 42.
49 Stanley Grenz, *The Social God and the Relational Self: A Trinitarian Theology of the Imago Dei* (Louisville: Westminster John Knox Press, 2001), 327; cited in King and Whitney, "What's the "Positive" in Positive Psychology?" 55.
50 Tyler S. Greenway, Justin L. Barrett, and James L. Furrow, "Theology and Thriving: Teleological Considerations Based on the Doctrines of Christology and Soteriology," *Journal of Psychology and Theology* 44, no. 3 (2016): 179–189, 185, citing Cornelius Plantinga, 1995, 10.
51 David H. Kelsey, "God and Teleology: Must God Have Only One 'Eternal Purpose'?" *Neue Zeitschrift Für Systematische Theologie Und Religionsphilosphie* 54, no. 4 (2012): 361–376, 362.
52 Kelsey, "God and Teleology," 364.
53 Kelsey, "God and Teleology," 367.
54 Kelsey, "God and Teleology," 368.
55 Kelsey, "God and Teleology," 368.
56 Kelsey, "God and Teleology," 370.
57 Kelsey, "God and Teleology," 370.
58 Emma Percy, "Can a Eunuch Be Baptized?: Insights for Gender Inclusion from Acts 8," *Theology* 119, no. 5 (2016): 327–334.
59 For a historical perspective, see Hans Boersma, "Putting on Clothes: Body, Sex and Gender in Gregory of Nyssa," *Crux* 54, no. 2 (2018): 27–34; for a contrary view, see James M. Childs, "Eschatology, Anthropology, and Sexuality: Helmut Thielicke and the Orders of Creation Revisited," *Journal of the Society of Christian Ethics* 30, no. 1 (2010): 3–20.
60 Dyan Elliott, "Tertullian, the Angelic Life, and the Bride of Christ," in *Gender and Christianity in Medieval Europe: New Perspectives*, eds. Lisa M. Bitel and Felice Lifshitz (Philadelphia: University of Pennsylvania Press, 2008), 16–19.
61 Mark A. Yarhouse, *Understanding Gender Dysphoria: Navigating Transgender Issues in a Changing Culture* (Downers Grove: IVP Academic, 2015).
62 McKitterick, "The Theological Imperative Model for Practical Theology," 16–17.
63 Rowan Williams, "To Stand Where Christ Stands," in *An Introduction to Christian Spirituality*, eds. Ralph Waller and Benedicta Ward (London: SPCK, 1999), 1–13.
64 Samuel Wells, *Incarnational Ministry: Being with the Church.* (Grand Rapids: Eerdmans, 2017).
65 Swinton and Mowat, *Practical Theology and Qualitative Research*, 10.
66 Keith Clements, "Theology Now," in *Companion Encyclopedia of Theology*, eds. Peter Byrne and J. L. Houlden (London: Routledge, 1995), 284.
67 Samuel Wells, *Improvisation: The Drama of Christian Ethics* (London: SPCK, 2004).

# 4 A wonderful plan for my life? Pete Ward's "the Gospel and Change" in dialogue with Charles Taylor

*Helen Morris*

## Introduction

The vision statement of Moorlands College is 'to equip people passionate about Jesus Christ to impact the Church and the world.' Alongside equipping others, I hope to make an impact myself. As an evangelical, I believe that faithful articulation of the good news of Jesus Christ, the gospel, is central to this aim. An invitation to preach at the 2020 Christchurch churches joint Good Friday service provided such an opportunity. The invitation excited me, but I also felt a weight of responsibility. Twelve months prior, I had researched the UK evangelical church's relationship to the gospel for a conference paper that forms the basis of this chapter. Having made proposals about how the gospel can best be communicated in contemporary UK culture, I knew it was important to respond to my own advice! In what follows, I will outline and develop the arguments that I made at the conference. I shall then conclude by noting how my analysis of the evangelical church's articulation of the gospel informed my approach to the Good Friday sermon.

## A clash of narratives

1 Kings 21 recounts a dispute between King Ahab and his wife Jezebel over a vineyard belonging to a man named Naboth. Ahab wants to buy Naboth's vineyard but Naboth will not sell it to him. Ahab is despondent over Naboth's refusal to give him what he wants and, when Jezebel finds out, she is not impressed. 'Is this how you act as Israel's king?' She berates him. 'Cheer up! I'll get you the vineyard.' As the narrative continues, the reader is informed that, through Jezebel's deceitful scheming, two scoundrels falsely accuse Naboth of cursing God and the king. Naboth is stoned to death and Ahab takes possession of his vineyard.

In his assessment of this narrative, Waldemar Janzen contends that the conflict over the vineyard arises because of a clash of stories. Had Naboth and Ahab been equally shaped by the narrative of Israel's history, specifically God's intervention, acts, and revelation in this history, Ahab would not have made his request. He would have been embedded in a worldview that maintained that

DOI: 10.4324/9781003094975-6

the whole land is God's. God is the creator and unopposed sovereign of his creation. Moreover, in his grace, God has apportioned plots of land to his people to steward: the land of Canaan to Israel and, within Israel, particular bounded sections to each tribe, clan, and family. According to this worldview, the land is Naboth's as given to him by God and no-one, not even a king, has the right to remove it from him. Equally, Janzen notes, had both Ahab and Naboth been shaped by the narrative of Canaan, no conflict would have occurred. In this way of seeing, the king's power and rights are absolute. If the king lays claim to a plot of land, that land is his. This is how Jezebel sees things. If Naboth was also immersed in this narrative, presumably he would not have liked it, but he would have ceded ownership of his vineyard to Ahab anyway. He would have been persuaded that, as much as he disliked it, it was the right thing to do. However, Naboth and Ahab have not been shaped by the same story. Naboth is a faithful Israelite, seeing the world in accordance with God's revelation in history. Ahab, as Janzen puts it, 'hovers at the edges' of this story and is vulnerable to the corrupting influence of his wife. She provokes him to move further from the God-ordained way of seeing and acting and he ends up responsible for murder and theft.[1]

Janzen draws on Stanley Hauerwas to note that ethical decisions do not arise because of isolated quandary situations. Rather, quandary situations, and so ethical decisions, arise because people's values and character have been shaped by different stories.[2] Alasdair McIntyre affirms such sentiments, observing, 'People cannot answer the question "What am I to do?" unless they have first answered the question "Of what story or stories do I find myself a part?"'[3] In noting this connection between the narratives that people live by and their conduct it is not Janzen's intention, nor mine, to simply observe difference. The stories that Naboth and Jezebel live by are not just two alternative or morally neutral options. For the author of 1 Kings, Naboth is right, Jezebel and Ahab are wrong. There is, Scripture affirms, a givenness to the world; it is as God made it and therefore character, behaviour, attitude, and vision that aligns with this reality is good and right; that which is against God's character and design is distorted and corrupt.

Why start an assessment of Pete Ward's arguments about the gospel with an analysis of the story of Naboth's vineyard? There are two reasons. First, the notion of living out of a narrative is central to practical theology and, more specifically, the issues that I wish to address in this chapter. Second, the importance of being immersed in the Bible's narrative is the solution that Pete Ward proposes to a problem that he identifies regarding the evangelical church's presentation of the gospel.

## Practical theology and the power of narrative

Swinton and Mowat define practical theology as 'critical, theological reflection on the practices of the Church as they interact with the practices of the world, with a view to ensuring and enabling faithful participation in God's redemptive practices in, to and for the world.'[4] A key distinctive of practical theology is its focus on human experience. The practical theologian aims to reflect deeply on a situation as it *is* in order to propel that situation towards the *ought*, as defined in reference to God's revelation of his character and purposes for creation. For Swinton and Mowat, experience is the starting point for practical theology in that its goal is to reflect on and respond to situation A, practice B, or crisis C. However, they qualify that experience arises in response to God's acts and can only be properly understood and modified in light of God's revelation. They note,

> While we have suggested that the starting point for Practical Theology is human experience, in fact this is not strictly the case. God and the revelation that God has given to human beings in Christ is the true starting point for all Practical Theology. The discipline of Practical Theology emerges as a response to and recognition of the redemptive actions of God-in-the-world and the human experience which emerges in response to those actions. It is in taking seriously those responses that Practical Theology finds its vital initial reflective position and an important position within the wider theological enterprise.[5]

In their assessment of how this revelation is received and responded to, Swinton and Mowat, like Janzen, turn to Hauerwas. Hauerwas' focus on narrative theology and ethics finds practical expression in the metaphor of performance. Just as Shakespeare's *King Lear* consists of not only a script but also the performance of that script, so Christianity involves not just a text but the performance of that text.[6] Swinton and Mowat note that accurate reception of the 'script' is vital if the performance is to be faithful to the revelation of God through Scripture, as centred on the person and work of Jesus Christ. They note that although people's interpretation of the 'script' varies, it is possible to move so far away from the 'fundamental plot, structure, storyline and outcome' that the performance becomes unrecognisable—just as, in an attempt to contemporise Shakespeare's language and context, one might move so far from the script of *King Lear* that it becomes a completely different play.[7] Therefore, immersion in Scripture is vital if practitioners are to perform in a way that is faithful to this narrative.

Such immersion is also necessary for faithful reflection. Practical theology requires reflectors who choose to reflect on an experience, be that their own or the experience of an individual or group. Therefore, as practical theologians emphasise, the worldview, presuppositions, background, context, and beliefs of the reflector inform their analysis.[8] Prior to this, the worldview and beliefs of the reflector also determine which situations they prioritise for reflection in the first place. As Bennett asserts, good practical theology involves 'seeing' connections between the Bible and contemporary experiences, rather than 'making' them.[9] The more familiar a reflector is with the Bible's grand narrative, the better placed they are to see such connections. For example, drawing again on

Janzen's analysis, Elijah sees a problem because of his self-conscious location in the Israel's story. He would have responded differently had he, like Jezebel, been immersed in the narrative of Canaan. Were this the case, Elijah would have accepted the murder of Naboth as an inevitable consequence of refusing to accede to a king's demands. However, like Naboth, Elijah is shaped by the history of God's revelation. Therefore, when God reveals the situation to him, Elijah recognises Ahab's actions as out-of-keeping with how things should be and obeys God's instruction to deliver God's warning and rebuke.[10]

## Two gospels?

The importance of being familiar with, indeed immersed in, the Bible's grand narrative is not just pertinent for practical theology more generally; it is also the solution that Pete Ward proposes to a problem relating to the evangelical church's presentation of the gospel. Ward contends that a right desire to share the good news of Jesus has prompted the evangelical tradition, specifically the 'entrepreneurial' strand,[11] to establish a 'fixed form' of the gospel message as conveyed in a series of propositional statements: in love God created the world; his people rebelled against him and became separated from God because of their sin; Jesus' death on the cross enables people to be forgiven and reconciled with God; forgiveness is received through repentance and faith. This simplified gospel presentation, Ward contends, has been cemented in tracts, such as the Bridge to Life diagram and the Four Spiritual Laws, that were developed within American youth ministry as an aid to evangelism (although, noticeably, the Four Spiritual Laws differs from the Bridge tract in its focus on God having 'a wonderful plan for your life', alongside an emphasis on sin and the cross).[12] Ward notes the influence of those such as the great evangelist Billy Graham and, before him, D. L. Moody and Charles Finney, alongside the writings of John Stott, in establishing and cementing this particular presentation of the gospel within evangelicalism. The fixed form is, however, a distilled version of such teaching, lacking the complexity and theological nuance of what these individuals actually taught.[13] Ward notes that simple presentations of the gospel have proved effective in facilitating conversion. However, such simplified conceptions have not, he contends, proved robust enough to sustain ongoing discipleship or withstand the influence of cultural pressures that have resulted in quite a different understanding of the gospel in believers' lived experience. Ward thereby observes a discrepancy within Western evangelical and charismatic Christianity between the 'espoused' gospel (the message of the gospel conveyed through tracts and propositional statements) and the 'operant' gospel (believers' lived experience of their gospel faith).[14]

In his use of the terms 'espoused' and 'operant', Ward draws on the four voices of theology identified by the ARCS team.[15] In this four voices schema, espoused theology refers to an individual or group's articulated beliefs (what people say they believe). Operant, or lived, theology, refers to the theology evident in an individual or group's practice (how people live).[16] Ward evidences and illustrates the discrepancy he observers between the operant and espoused gospel in reference to research that he and Paul Fiddes undertook at a baptismal service in Oxford. He notes that the sermon consisted of a classic evangelical account of the gospel, with a focus on sin, Jesus' crucifixion, repentance, and forgiveness. He observes, though, that these themes were noticeably absent from the testimonies of those getting baptised who spoke, not of sin, the cross, and forgiveness, but of their subjective experience of God's love and their excitement in trusting that God had a good plan for their lives.[17] Ward suspects that the more classical formulation of the gospel was accepted by those giving their testimony—if asked directly, he imagines that all would affirm that Jesus died on the cross for their sins, enabling them to be forgiven. But, Ward contends, such objective truths were not perceived to be 'the primary or even necessary part of the explanation of what it means to be a Christian.'[18]

Ward argues that this disjunction between operant and espoused gospel is the result of a failure to take account of the inherent relationship between medium and message.[19] Western evangelicalism, Ward argues, has overlooked the meaning that cultural forms convey through the various associations that they carry. He gives the example of the acoustic guitar and the association between this instrument and the myriad of singer-songwriters who use it as a vehicle to express their inner worlds, often with a focus on romance and intimacy. The evangelical church's under-appreciation of the meaning-laden nature of cultural forms has led to the erroneous belief that a fixed and unchanging message, the gospel, can be transplanted from one form to another, specifically one worship style to another, with no change in meaning. However, medium and message cannot be so neatly demarcated, Ward contends, and therefore, as the medium changes, so too does the meaning. Changes in worship style have altered how the gospel is perceived in believers' everyday experience.[20]

The medium Ward concentrates on is the contextualisation of sung worship into the pop music genre. He analyses the lyrics of popular worship songs from the 1960s onwards when, he argues, the contextualisation of sung worship into the pop music genre became prominent in the evangelical church's life. Drawing on Lionel Adey's classification of Christian hymnology, Ward divides worship songs into three categories: 'objective' accounts of biblical themes and events; 'subjective' hymns, which focus on the implications of God's revelation and acts for the worshipper; and 'reflexive' songs, which focus predominantly on the experience of worship itself, wherein encounter with God is the primary aim.[21] The popular music genre, Ward notes, is primarily associated with intimate love songs and so it is unsurprising that the contextualisation of sung worship into this genre has been accompanied by a decrease in the quantity of objective hymns and a large increase in the proportion of subjective and reflexive lyrics. All three genres have biblical warrant and should be part of the church's corporate praise. However, Ward warns that an imbalance towards reflexive songs is of concern; if the objective truth of who God is, as Father, Son and Holy Spirit, and his acts in history is not maintained amongst a predominance of songs sung to a less clearly defined 'you', there is a danger that the experience of worship displaces the object of worship.[22]

This change in sung worship style, Ward contends, has influenced believers' operant understanding of the gospel—what they experience the gospel to be, or expect to experience. Contemporary sung worship promotes an understanding of the gospel that is focused on intimate, highly personalised, and experiential encounters with God.[23] This influence, Ward maintains, was evident at the baptismal service that he observed, wherein the content of testimonies accorded with the predominant themes within contemporary sung worship: the believers' experience of God's love and an expression of trust in his plans for their lives. This, he argues, contrasted with the more objective content of the sermon.[24] But is this discrepancy as problematic as Ward suggests? Ward notes that the objective aspects of the evangelical presentation of the gospel exist in contemporary worship as the assumed foundation of those elements that emphasise personal relationship. He observes that core Christian doctrines are included in contemporary worship songs, although usually just 'hinted at or referred to in passing.'[25] Ward emphasises the relationship that exists between medium and message. Sermon, song, and testimony are distinct genres. Perhaps it could be argued that a sermon, as an exhortatory exposition of biblical truth, will rightly focus on the objective truths of Christ's death on the cross, forgiveness and repentance, while testimony, being a personal account of conversion and salvation, and song, as poetic expression of praise to God, more naturally focus on the subjective experience of these same truths?

In order to answer this question, I shall heed the call of practical theology to look at situations from different angles. As Alistair McKitterick argues, engaging with different disciplines can help generate the 'thick description' of a given situation that is so important for any critical and proper response.[26] In what follows, I will bring Ward's analysis into dialogue with the Catholic philosopher Charles Taylor. I will argue that Taylor's assessment of contemporary secularism sheds further light on Ward's findings and should be taken into account in any proposal offered in response to Ward's analysis.[27]

## The inward turn

Taylor notes that the word 'secular' can be used in different ways. In meaning one, as he labels it, 'secular' describes the barring of faith claims in the political and public spheres. In meaning two, 'secular' describes diminishing religious adherence within the Western world, particularly the decline of the church. Taylor is most interested in the third way in which 'secular' is used, which is to describe the shift from a time when belief in God, or gods, was the norm, such that disbelief was not countenanced, to the current time, where belief in God is one option among many and disbelief in God is not just plausible but perceived as the default.[28] In this third sense, secularism is presented as a 'subtraction story'. In former years, the narrative asserts, blinded by ignorance and superstition, people believed in all kinds of gods, spirits, versions of the supernatural and so on. When such superstition and naivety is cleared away, secularism is what remains—like clearing the dirt from your car to see, as if for the first time, the colour underneath.[29] As Taylor notes, this subtraction story is a myth. Rather than being a default option that everyone would arrive at if only they got rid of their naïve superstition, secularism has a positive story of its own.[30] Ironically, Taylor argues, this positive story is founded on the very Christianity that secularism has been so determined to reject. Via the midway point of providential deism, Taylor argues, secularism has built itself on Christian values and beliefs, and then lopped off the transcendent, removing the notion of 'God' to create a purely human-centred version. More specifically, secularism has adopted a Christian belief in human flourishing but detached this from God such that now the 'ultimate good', as Taylor describes it, is perceived as human flourishing without the allegiance to anything external.[31]

As Taylor stresses, it is the 'without allegiance to anything external' that is unique to contemporary secularism. Although human flourishing has been a consistent emphasis through history, there are rare examples of this flourishing being defined so autonomously.[32] Rather, Taylor observes, in ancient societies, people's sense of identity was primarily determined by that which was external to them: their lineage, family, role in society, deeds, and so on. He tracks a gradual shift through Plato, Paul, Augustine, Descartes, Freud, and Jung culminating in a markedly different situation today, wherein people's identity is determined far more than in yesteryear by that which is internal to them: their desires, emotions, opinions, attractions, values, and so on.[33] He labels this the 'inward turn', noting that this shift in identity is manifest in expressive individualism, wherein the ultimate *telos*, or goal, is to express the fullness of who you are, as identified by looking inside yourself to figure out what exactly that might be.[34] This 'ultimate good' is evidenced in the current emphasis on authenticity, wherein, living according to external demands is perceived as inauthentic, and so bad, whereas living according to one's own desires and feelings is perceived as authentic, and so good. It is also evidenced in the popular, but seemingly self-contradictory, mantras that call people to find, make, and be themselves.[35]

## A wonderful plan for my life?

Taylor's contentions regarding the *telos* of human flourishing within wider culture indicate that the contextualisation of sung worship into the popular music genre is not the only, or even main, reason why human flourishing—expressed in terms of experience of God's love and excitement regarding his plan for the believer's life—plays such a central role in believers' lived experience of the gospel. Taylor's analysis also suggests that it is not the emphasis on human flourishing within the evangelical church's operant understanding of the gospel *per se* that is problematic, but the danger that secular conceptions of such flourishing are unwittingly adopted. There is *a clash of narratives* between Christian and secular notions of human flourishing. The ultimate good, according to the Christian faith, is not that I as an individual reach my full potential in any secular sense, but that I love and worship God with a willingness to put aside my own goals for the sake of faithfulness to Christ and a commitment to others. As Taylor asserts, 'The injunction "Thy will be done" isn't equivalent to "Let humans flourish", even though we know that God wills human flourishing.'[36] In addition, as Volf and Croasman highlight, Christian conceptions of human flourishing are located in a 'now' and 'not yet' eschatological framework wherein, for the believer, full restoration and peace are experienced in part now but not fully until Christ returns.[37]

Therefore, the emphasis on human flourishing within the church's operant expression of the gospel is problematic not because an emphasis on human flourishing is itself unwarranted or unbiblical. Rather, the problem is the ease with which secular notions of human flourishing, though they find their roots in Christianity, are read back into Christianity such that the Christian conception of human flourishing is distorted by its secular counterpart. Ward's empirical research warns that evangelical Christians may find themselves *hovering at the edges* of the Christian story in this regard, rather than being fully immersed and embedded within it. Volf and Croasmun note the tendency for the Christian faith to be reduced to a set of resources to help people pursue their own vision of flourishing—be that framed around emotional health, success, relational fulfilment or comfort—rather than seeing Christianity as revealing what true flourishing actually consists of.[38] Contemporary sung worship, with its focus on intimacy and experience, is liable to such distortion, particularly in a wider context in which 'the self' is seen as 'the primary concern and central project of life.'[39] Such distortion is problematic as a matter of truth versus falsehood but also, if people receive the gospel on the basis that things will go well for them in the here and now, what foundation for resilience is there when pain and grief strike? Where is the impetus to lay down one's own comfort and desires out of allegiance to Christ and love for others? What perseverance will there be when following Christ results in more hardship, not less? As Ian Paul wryly notes, in Jesus' message to the church in Smyrna (Rev 2:8–11), which consisted of believers who were suffering as a result of their faith, 'There is no sense here of "Jesus has a wonderful plan for your life."'[40]

Ward observes a similar danger, though through engagement with Christian Smith, Melinda Denton, and Kenda Creasey Dean rather than Taylor. He observes a 'turn to self' as manifest in what Smith and Denton label 'Moralistic Therapeutic Deism'. Moralistic Therapeutic Deism is not a formal doctrine of any Christian church but depicts the personal beliefs of young US believers, who express faith in a god who wants people to be nice to each other and is on hand to sort out believers' problems. Such intervention is important because the ultimate goal is to be happy and fulfilled and, if you are good, go to heaven when you die.[41] Such beliefs are not identical to the operant understanding of the gospel that Ward identifies in the UK church but illustrate how cultural forces can result in conceptions of the Christian faith that are far removed from any orthodox creed or espoused doctrine. Ward's warning about unwitting changes to the 'unchanging gospel' thus need heeding.

## The gospel and narrative

By way of solution, Ward encourages the church to help believers root their understanding of the gospel more firmly in the Gospels' account of Jesus and root their understanding of the Gospels in the wider narrative of Scripture.[42] He argues that summaries of Scripture's grand narrative, such as Andrew Walker's nine-point synopsis, can help believers conceptualise and express the gospel in the framework that the church has consistently understood and witnessed to over the centuries. Such guidance is important so that the gospel is communicated truly.[43] In addition, narrative summaries do not encourage the reductionism that simplified propositional gospel presentations promote, such as the Bridge to Life tract, since story synopses encourage their readers to delve into the whole account.

Ward notes that the Spirit has worked through simplified gospel presentations to bring people to faith in Christ, arguing that these presentations have been a 'door' to faith even though they are not the 'whole house.'[44] Given the importance of conversion within evangelicalism, evangelical Christianity should hold fast to its evangelistic impulse to equip every believer to share the gospel in a succinct, accurate and engaging manner.[45] Ward therefore contends that the impulse to convey simplified gospel presentations to help people enter faith is not the problem *per se*. Rather, the problem occurs when such simplifications become 'the gospel' in its entirety. However, as Ward's contentions regarding Walker's narrative summary illustrate, it is possible to simplify the gospel either in ways that invite people into a deeper search or leave them feeling as though they already have the complete package.

1 Corinthians 15 provides an example of the first of these—a succinct gospel presentation that invites people into Scripture's larger narrative. As Scot McKnight contends, 1 Corinthians 15 reveals the early church's understanding of the gospel's core. The Apostle Paul recites the 'apostolic gospel tradition' as he reminds his readers of the gospel (*euangelion*) that he proclaimed: 'that Christ died for our sins in accordance with the scriptures, and that he was buried, and that he was raised on the third day in accordance with the scriptures' (1 Cor 15:3b-4 NRSV). Paul then progresses from Jesus' resurrection to the hope of his return and accompanying establishment of God's kingdom such that God is 'all in all' (15:28). This synopsis differs from the simplified presentations that Ward critiques since repeated reference to 'the scriptures' provides an invitation for the hearer to dig deeper into the Bible's whole revelation, and the progression from Jesus' resurrection to his future return brings into focus Scripture's grand narrative with its ending in a restored creation where all things are aligned with God's rule.[46]

## The gospel and human flourishing

Immersion in the narrative of Scripture is vital for equipping believers to know how best to share the good news of their faith in any given circumstance.

Moreover, believers should be encouraged to think through how they can best summarise the gospel in a way that focuses on the person and work of Jesus Christ while also inviting their hearers into the wider narrative of Scripture (as Paul does in 1 Corinthians 15). In addition, I propose that gospel presenters seek to include the human flourishing component that has become so significant, and yet distorted, in believers' lived experience.[47] There are two reasons for this.

First, making the topic of human flourishing explicit in simplified gospel presentations highlights the clash of narratives between biblical and secular conceptions. The gospel promotes a God-orientated perspective in contrast to contemporary culture's self-focus. The gospel invites people to join God's plans and purposes (the *missio Dei*), challenging any idolatrous notion that God is there to assist the project of the self. Highlighting this clash demonstrates the countercultural nature of the Christian faith to those unfamiliar with its tenets and equips believers to challenge those aspects of secularism that are contrary to their faith. In addition, when human flourishing is located in the New Testament's 'now' and 'not yet' eschatological tension, wherein God's kingdom is inaugurated but not yet consummated, the more painful aspects of life are not, as they are in secular understandings, unexpected and unwarranted intrusions. Rather, suffering provides an opportunity for believers to demonstrate the solidity of their hope in contrast to the transience of secular markers of a life well lived, be that wealth, success, popularity, or self-expression. Suffering out of allegiance to Christ is part of Christian flourishing this side of Christ's return and lament a central practice.[48] Demonstrating love and joy in the midst of such suffering is a powerful witness to the robustness of the Christian faith.[49] Moreover, laying down one's own preferences is not an inauthentic eschewal of personal freedom, but demonstrates commitment to the self-sacrificial path of love paved pre-eminently by Christ.

Second, including human flourishing in summarised gospel presentations can enhance the church's impact on the wider world. As Cameron, Reader, Slater, and Rowland observe, for the last decade, human flourishing has been a topic of interest and debate in the social and political arenas.[50] In reference to the contemporary wellbeing debate, these authors cite Hartley Dean's contentions regarding the need to move beyond 'thin' conceptions of human personhood, framed solely in relation to need, to 'thick' notions that convey human personhood in terms of fulfilment and potentiality.[51] As Olwyn Mark argues in this current book, Christians should not withdraw from the common life but seek to influence the wider world positively and prophetically. She cites Volf and Croasmun's contention that 'a vision of human flourishing—and the resources to realize it—is the most important contribution of the Christian faith to the common good.'[52] Human flourishing, as the Bible presents it, is full flourishing, everything else falls short of this. The church, as a community of Christ's followers, is called to model this flourishing and play a part in helping others flourish too, working against those ills, such as injustice, oppression, poverty, and spiritual blindness, that inhibit people's ability to be all that God has created them to be.[53] Therefore, making human flourishing an explicit component of the simplified gospel presentations not only encourages believers to have a proper conception of this facet of biblical truth, but also provides a pertinent point of connection with those currently seeking to fulfil their humanity in ways other than the only way found in Christ. The gospel provides the answer to a question that many are asking.

## And that rock was Christ

The following questions were in my mind as I reflected on how best to communicate the gospel at the Good Friday service I had been invited to preach at.[54] How could I best focus on Jesus' crucifixion, as remembered on Good Friday, while also inviting my hearers into the wider story of Scripture; and how could I incorporate the human flourishing component of the gospel as a point of connection for those unfamiliar with Christianity's claims while also conveying a distinctively biblical conception of such flourishing in contrast to secular counterparts? My answer was to start somewhat left-field with a quotation from 1 Corinthians 10:1–4,

> For I do not want you to be ignorant of the fact, brothers and sisters, that our ancestors were all under the cloud and that they all passed through the sea. They were all baptized into Moses in the cloud and in the sea. They all ate the same spiritual food and drank the same spiritual drink; for they drank from the spiritual rock that accompanied them, and that rock was Christ.
>
> (NIV)

By starting with 1 Corinthians 10:1–4, I sought to highlight that the events of Good Friday should be understood in light of the Bible's wider narrative. I hoped to provoke those familiar with the Christian faith to remember that there is always more to understand and learn. Conversely, and perhaps counterintuitively, I aimed to put at ease those who were less familiar with the Christian faith. Through expressing the difficulty of understanding this passage, I sought to allay any fears a listener might have that they are the only ones struggling to comprehend Christianity's claims and invite them on a journey of exploration and discovery. I then engaged with a more conventional Good Friday passage (Luke 24:32–49), elucidating the significance of Jesus' death and why it is marked by a day entitled 'good'. At the end, I came back to 1 Corinthians 10:1–4. The language of 'rock' was significant given the context of my sermon, which was delivered online during the first national lockdown brought about by the Covid-19 pandemic. It also provided a link between the events of Good Friday and the topic of human flourishing (though I did not use that term). Times of national and global crisis reveal that the foundations people tend to build on (good health, financial security and so on) are insecure. Having outlined the Exodus context of Paul's reference, and the connection that Paul makes between God's deliverance of Israel and the deliverance offered in Jesus, I encouraged my hearers that the rock of Christ is the best foundation on which to build.

## Conclusion

The good news of Jesus Christ is rich and full. To understand it more deeply, believers should be encouraged to immerse themselves in the full narrative of Scripture. The more embedded a believer is in the biblical narrative, the more easily they will discern a *clash of stories* when such occur. Such discernment is vital if believers are to proclaim the gospel with their actions as well as their words.[55] Nevertheless, the conversionist impulse of evangelicalism arises from the conviction that the gospel of Jesus is liberating and transformative and the church should seek to share this gospel succinctly in ways that are faithful and accessible. A single presentation cannot exhaust the gospel's depth.[56] However, simplified presentations can be phrased in a way that shuts down, as if what has been communicated is all that need be said, or opens up, drawing the listener into deeper exploration. In this chapter, I have encouraged the evangelical church to consider how the gospel can be communicated in a way that draws people into the Bible's wider story. In addition, I have suggested that gospel communicators include the topic of human flourishing. Highlighting this component of the gospel message provides a point of connection for those unfamiliar with the Christian faith and alerts hearers to ways in which the Bible's presentation of such flourishing differs from secular counterparts. Through the person and work of Jesus, God has a wonderful plan for his creation, and by the power of God's Spirit, believers have the privilege of playing a part in that plan.

## Notes

1 Waldemar Janzen, *Old Testament Ethics* (Louisville: Westminster John Knox, 1994), 31.
2 Janzen, *Ethics*, 31 drawing on Stanley Hauerwas, *The Peaceable Kingdom: A Primer in Christian Ethics* (Notre Dame: University of Notre Dame Press, 1983), 116f.
3 Alasdair MacIntyre, *After Virtue*, 2nd ed. (Notre Dame: University of Notre Dame Press, 1984), 216.
4 John Swinton and Harriet Mowat, *Practical Theology and Qualitative Research*, 2nd ed. (London: SCM, 2016), 7.
5 Swinton and Mowat, *Practical Theology*, 11.
6 Swinton and Mowat, *Practical Theology*, 4.
7 Swinton and Mowat, *Practical Theology*, 5.
8 For example, the inevitability of subjectivity is a strong theme in Bennett's exploration of the Bible's role in Practical Theology. Correspondingly, Bennett is overly pessimistic about the possibility of objectivity (Zoë Bennett, *Using the Bible in Practical Theology: Historical and Contemporary Perspectives* [Abingdon: Taylor & Francis, 2016], esp. chapter two).
9 Bennett, *Bible in Practical Theology*, 134–35. In this, Bennett's contrast is between methodologies that she perceives to be overly prescriptive and mechanical (making) versus approaches that are more intuitive and less systematic (seeing). However, such an argument elevates the means above the end. What is key is not how the connections are drawn but their validity and coherence; in other words whether they derive from wise discernment and prophetic insight or convoluted concoction. It is this distinction that draws me to language of 'seeing' over 'making', though I am not using it in the same way as Bennett.

10 A contemporary example of such 'seeing' is found in John Swinton's *Becoming Friends of Time* (John Swinton, *Becoming Friends of Time: Disability, Timefullness, and Gentle Discipleship* [London: SCM, 2016]). Time is considered such a given that few people stop to reflect on ways in which Western conceptions of time might be distorted and oppressive (notions of time that are clock-driven and portray time as a commodity rather than a gift). Swinton's reflection arises from his commitment to the narrative of Scripture and his insight that the biblical notion of time clashes with his experience in the world.
11 Pete Ward, *Liquid Ecclesiology: The Gospel and the Church* (Leiden: Brill, 2017), 106 drawing on Robert Warner, *Reinventing English Evangelicalism 1966–2001* (Milton Keynes: Paternoster, 2007). 15.
12 Ward, *Ecclesiology*, 110–121.
13 Ward, *Ecclesiology*, 110–113.
14 Ward, *Ecclesiology*, 134–141, 173–178.
15 The 'Action Research: Church and Society' project initiated by the Pastoral and Social Studies Department of Heythrop College in 2006 (Helen Cameron, Deborah Bhatti, Catherine Duce, James Sweeney, and Clare Watkins, *Talking about God in Practice: Theological Action Research and Practical Theology* [London: SCM, 2010], 1).
16 In addition to operant and espoused, the four voices of theology include 'normative' theology, which is the authoritative theology derived from Scripture, church tradition and/or officially pronounced as the formal doctrine of any one church or group of churches, and 'formal' theology, which is the contribution of academia (Ward, *Ecclesiology*, 95–99 drawing on Cameron, Bhatti, and Duce, *Talking about God*, 49–56).
17 Ward, *Ecclesiology*, 134–139.
18 Ward, *Ecclesiology*, 139.
19 In this he builds on his earlier work in Pete Ward, *Participation and Mediation: A Practical Theology for the Liquid Church* (London: SCM, 2008), 66–80, esp. 75–76.
20 Ward, *Ecclesiology*, 71–78, 176–178.
21 Ward, *Ecclesiology*, 146 building on his early work in Pete Ward, *Selling Worship: How What We Sing Has Changed the Church* (Milton Keynes: Paternoster, 2005), 206–207.
22 Ward, *Selling*, 206–210.
23 Ward, *Ecclesiology*, 147–163 esp. 158.
24 Ward, *Ecclesiology*, 158.
25 Ward, *Ecclesiology*, 159.
26 Alistair J. McKitterick, "The Theological Imperative Model for Practice Theology," *Journal of European Baptist Studies* 16, no. 4 (2016): 10.
27 Charles Taylor, *A Secular Age* (Cambridge, MA: Harvard University Press, 2007) and *Sources of Self: The Making of Modern Identity* (Cambridge: Harvard University Press, 1989).
28 Taylor, *Secular*, 1–3.
29 Taylor, *Secular*, 29.
30 Taylor, *Secular*, 22.
31 Taylor, *Secular*, 18 and *Sources*, 36.
32 Taylor, *Secular*, 18 and *Sources*, 36.
33 Taylor, *Sources*, Part II.
34 Taylor, *Sources*, 111.
35 Taylor, *Secular*, 475. Taylor's parlance is 'find yourself, realize yourself, release your true self.' See also Helen Morris, *Flexible Church: Being the Church in the Contemporary World* (London: SCM, 2019), 39–41 and 62–63, where I engage with Taylor's contentions.
36 Taylor, *Secular*, 17.

37 Miroslav Volf and Matthew Croasmun, *Life of the World: Theology That Makes a Difference* (Grand Rapids, MI: Brazos, 2019), esp. chapter six.
38 Volf and Croasmun, *Life of the World*, 31.
39 Pete Ward, *Celebrity Worship* (Abingdon: Routledge, 2020), 4.
40 Ian Paul, *Revelation: An Introduction and Commentary* (Nottingham: IVP, 2018), 86.
41 Ward, *Ecclesiology*, 127 engaging with Kenda Creasy Dean, *Almost Christians: What the Faith of Our Teenagers is Telling the American Church* (Oxford: Oxford University Press, 2010), 14 and Christian Smith with Melinda Lunquist Denton, *Soul Searching: The Religious and Spiritual Lives of American Teenagers* (Oxford: Oxford University Press, 2005), 292–307.
42 Ward, *Ecclesiology*, 179–180, 187–189.
43 Ward, *Ecclesiology*, 91–94 referring to Andrew Walker, *Telling the Story* (London: SPCK, 1996).
44 Ward, *Ecclesiology*, 187.
45 Conversionism is one of the components of Bebbington's quadrilateral of evangelicalism, alongside biblicism, activism, and crucicentrism. This quadrilateral is, as Larsen notes, the 'standard definition' of evangelicalism in that it is the most widely accepted (Timothy Larsen, "Defining and Locating Evangelicalism," in *The Cambridge Companion to Evangelical Theology* eds. Timothy Larsen and Daniel J. Treier [Cambridge: Cambridge University Press, 2007], 1).
46 Scot McKnight, *The King Jesus Gospel: The Original Good News Revisited* (Grand Rapids, MI: Zondervan, 2011), chapter four.
47 It is significant that crucicentrism is one of the four markers of Bebbington's quadrilateral. Without Jesus' sacrificial death that fulfils God's justice, there is no foundation or potential for true human flourishing since the world would be resigned to sin, which would remain an impenetrable barrier to such flourishing.
48 Volf and Croasmun, *Life of the World*, 178.
49 Volf and Croasmun, *Life of the World*, 168 and 179.
50 Helen Cameron, John Reader, Victoria Slater, and Chris Rowland, *Theological Reflection for Human Flourishing: Pastoral Practice and Public Theology* (London: SCM, 2012), xix–xxv.
51 Hartley Dean, *Understanding Human Need: Social Issues, Policy and Practice* (Bristol: Policy Press, 2010), 100 as cited by Cameron et al., *Flourishing*, xx.
52 Volf and Croasmun, *Life of the World*, 63 as cited by Olwyn Mark, 'Educating for our Common Life: Engaging Relational Truth in a World of Ideas.'
53 Volf and Croasmun argue that human flourishing is not just a central theme in the gospel but also the topic towards which Christian theology should be ultimately orientated. Their concept of such flourishing is opposed to the secular notions Taylor identifies and, instead, is defined in reference to God's presence and self-revelation in Christ and the Spirit and the hope (partially realised in the present and fulfilled in the future) of God's presence being on earth as it is in heaven (Volf and Croasmun, *Life of the World*, esp. 6–11, 21–26).
54 "Christchurch Joint Good Friday Service," Twynham Church Online, filmed 10 April 2020, video, 15:00, www.youtube.com/watch?v=5MMZrE561Pg&t=899s.
55 Swinton and Mowat convey the importance of proclamation through actions via the metaphor 'gospel-as-performance' (Swinton and Mowat, *Practical Theology*, 19).
56 As Ward notes, 'Preachers … are very aware of the limitations of their messages, even as they believe that they can become places where God might change those who are in the congregation' (Ward, *Ecclesiology*, 199).

Part II
# Engaging with education

# 5 From the boy in the temple to the man on the road

## The maturing role of practical theology in the life of the church

*Helen Cameron*

## Introduction

This chapter was originally the keynote lecture at a conference in April 2019 to celebrate the 70th anniversary of the founding of Moorlands College. As such it was written to be read aloud to a particular audience on a particular occasion for a particular purpose. I understood my responsibility as a keynote speaker as being to address the theme of the conference, in this case 'Theology that impacts the Church and the World'. But I also saw it as to draw together the different elements of the conference and make them accessible to the audience, stimulating their thinking about the purpose of the event and how they might respond to it. The conference was attended by those with an academic interest in practical theology, whether as staff, students, or alumni of the college, but it was also attended by practitioners in ministry who wanted to reflect. In preparing this lecture for publication, I thought about whether I should remove the particularity and performativity to make it 'more academic'. I have concluded that to do so would undermine the case I want to make about the relationship between theological education and practice. Instead, I will make use of footnotes to offer a commentary on my approach. The structure and presentation of the lecture deployed techniques I would use as a facilitator as well as the ancient pedagogical technique of chiasmus.[1] I have numbered the side-headings so you can see my use of chiasmus to structure my argument:

A1 Starting with Scripture
B1 The maturing of practical theology
C1 Where are we now?
D What things?
C2 Where next in theological Education?
B2 Maturity reborn
A2 Finishing with Scripture

## A1 Starting with Scripture

I want to start this lecture as this College started, by reading the Bible.[2]

88  *Helen Cameron*

These two narratives (Luke 2:41–52 and 24:13–35) act as brackets around Luke's account of the ministry, death, and resurrection of Jesus.[3] Both come from the material found only in Luke's Gospel. Let me give you a minute to read them before I continue.[4]

For the moment I want to draw attention to the similarities between the two stories. There are three things I would like to point out: first, both have a husband and wife on the road to and from Jerusalem.[5] The second is the central place of Scripture in both stories. The third is that they both involved challenging conversations with Jesus.

Turning to your neighbour please discuss this question: What comparisons would you make between the two passages?

## B1 The maturing of practical theology

I want to put the development of practical theology into three eras that I am calling 'Equipping', 'Relevance' and 'Enculturation'. They are not definitive but illustrate how changes in the life of the church have shaped practical theology which in turn has shaped those who minister.[6]

### *Equipping 1945–1965*

The founding vision of Moorlands in 1948 was 'to equip young people for evangelism ... with well-rounded training, not simply lectures and academic study'.[7] The word equip is still in the vision statement.[8] During the Second World War, a Church of England Commission on evangelism looked at the challenges that would face the church and recommended new approaches to evangelism in its report *Towards the Conversion of England*.[9] The need identified was to equip churchgoers with the practical and theological tools to rebuild the UK and Europe after the war. For Moorlands students that meant studying the Bible but also picking up practical skills such as building walls and delivering babies. Stephen Pattison describes this as the era of pastoral studies—the 'how to' of ministry to a population that would largely describe itself as Christian.[10] So, in this era, the emphasis was on equipping and the approach used was training young people in knowledge of the Bible and with practical skills.

### *Relevance 1965–1995*

Moorlands College was re-founded in a new location in 1968 but with assurance of the relevance of its mission. Part of the ethos of the College was to 'meet current needs.'[11] However, that search for relevance reflected a declining salience of Christian ministry as people became less religiously observant.

For evangelicals, this period was one of looking for more effective methods of evangelism, with multiple initiatives culminating in the decade of evangelism and the growth of the Alpha course.[12] This era saw pastoral studies evolve into practical theology and so open up a dialogue with other relevant disciplines such as counselling and community work.[13] I undertook my doctoral studies in the 1990s and was absorbed by the way in which different disciplines could contribute. This resulted in co-editing *Studying Local Churches* that embraced four disciplines: practical theology, sociology, anthropology, and organisational studies.[14] This era was a search for relevance as a response to secularisation.[15] The emphasis was correlation of experience and tradition, and theology and other disciplines.

*Enculturation 1995–2010*

For the College, 1995 saw a move to university validation that respected Moorlands' distinctives set out in its ethos as spiritual, practical, academic, and relational. There was rapid growth in MA degrees in practical theology.[16] This brought the university in as a key stakeholder in defining the discipline alongside the church and the world. However, it also marks the shift from evangelism to enculturation in much ministerial education. The Anglican booklets *From Maintenance to Mission* and *Building Missionary Congregations* both date from this year and call the churches to discover the seed of the gospel in secular culture.[17] In this era, it was recognised that the church was simultaneously declining and growing. Declining in mainstream denominations, but growing in Black majority churches and new churches.[18] Practical theology became a servant of missiology with its key task to shape reflective practitioners by teaching theological reflection.[19] This era also saw a resurgence in apologetics in response to science, the new atheism, and inter-faith relationships amongst other things.[20] It is marked by tensions between applied theology and practical theology.[21] My contribution to this era was the book *Resourcing Mission* in which I described the local church as existing in a number of cultural forms that can both be subverted by culture and can be subversive of culture.[22]

To summarise, this era was one of enculturation and apologetic as a response to greater social pluralism and the commodification of culture. The main approach used by the discipline was theological reflection.

## C1 Where are we now?[23]

Is further change needed to secure the impact of Moorlands College and its students on the church and the world? If more effective enculturation of the answers to life's questions provided by the Christian faith is losing effectiveness, where do we go next? We can start by asking what has changed in last 10 years:

- The Internet is reshaping every social institution both for good and ill.[24]
- The global financial crisis has led to austerity that is uneven in who is affected and invisible to those who choose not to notice it.[25]

- And then finally the Brexit referendum has revealed a society divided between socially liberal people leading cosmopolitan lives in chosen places and socially conservative people identifying with place as a given.[26]

However, rather than focusing on such apparent changes, I want to take an approach suggested by the unnamed disciple on the Road to Emmaus. I want to focus on things that we are not talking about in the church and the university. These 'unknown unknowns' are also shaping the way in which Moorlands College prepares students for the world. Here are four silences which I am hearing.

### *(i) The silent withdrawal of women's unpaid labour from the life of the church*[27]

The history of Moorlands shows the changing role of women in each of the three eras I named: from doing women's work, to being auxiliary wives, to having paid ministries.[28] The more women have participated in paid work outside the home, the less time they have given unpaid to the work of the church. This has been depicted as a failure of women in the civic generation to handover their church work to women baby boomers.[29] However, in any church with the cash to do so, unpaid work has been replaced by paid ministries whilst churches without the cash struggle. This has led to a flourishing of lay ministries and accredited training for them.[30]

### *(ii) Encounters with the unknown God*[31]

Those who attend church are increasingly baffled at how they can speak about the gospel to those who have never read Scripture and where there is no shared Christian language to build upon.[32] Let me give you an example.

I was enjoying a pub meal with a friend, let's call her Joanna, who teaches 5-year-olds. She was sharing with me that she was struggling with being asked to explain to her class how, in four months, Jesus went from being a baby in a manger to dying on a cross. I suggested that the story of Jesus as a boy in the temple might help the children make the transition. She asked me to tell her the story.

Joanna was shocked by the story. Who had organised this journey to Jerusalem? Where was the safeguarding? Why was there no dynamic risk assessment? Did Jesus' parents not care about his safety? She laughed but I could tell that this story fed into her concern that the church might not be a safe place for children. I opened my mouth to tell her what the story really meant. But closed it again. The questions this Bible passage provoked in her were genuine ones and reflected how time-consuming parenting has become now it starts from an assumption that nowhere is safe. What does Scripture have to say to a teacher and parent who experiences the world as an unsafe place?

One of the ways in which ordinary church members have tried to explain this unknown God is by increasing the social action of the local church because they know that this is a language their unchurched neighbours can understand. The foodbank, debt counselling, street pastors offer explanations free from explicitly

Christian language but with an operant message of salvation from harm. Have we reconciled this reassuring message with the questions about abuse in the church which people are more reluctant to articulate?[33]

I mentioned earlier that the university is now a stakeholder in the relationship between the church and practical theology. My final two 'silences' refer to that relationship.

### *(iii) Higher education as a positional good rather than a social good*[34]

Around half of young people in the UK go through higher education,[35] but a much higher proportion of those engaging in ministry go through higher education by way of preparation. What does this say to the other 50% about who does ministry and who the church is for? The clearest marker between those who live their lives somewhere and those who can live anywhere is that the 'anywheres' have university-level education. Higher education focuses on individual achievement, to collaborate is to cheat. To fail to send your child to university is to 'lack aspiration'. Who is church for the non-aspirational 50%?

### *(iv) Learning triggered by assessment; knowledge packaged in modules*[36]

Mass higher education depends upon streamlining learning and assessment processes. Most study for ministry is undertaken alongside other paid or unpaid work. Students focus on where their effort is going to have the greatest pay off and that is inevitably on assessment. The performance of colleges is judged by the performance of students in assessments and so it becomes a focus for teachers too. What assumptions about ministry do we learn from this model of education?

So those are four silences that I hear in the relationship between practical theology and the church. Let me give you a few moments to reflect upon what silences you hear.

## D What things?

Your silences will have been different from mine. Giving voice to the silences we are hearing can give us a sense of our potential blind spots in mission. What they have in common are that they are things that matter. Mary and Cleopas talk to Jesus about the things that really mattered to them. The phrase 'these things' is used repeatedly. Mary reflects upon her conversation with her son Jesus and treasures 'these things' in her heart. I want to move on and discuss a development in practical theology which is designed to discuss the things that really matter to people. Their questions rather than mine.

### *Re-voicing the tradition: four voices of theology*

I was privileged to be a member of the ARCS project from 2006 to 2010.[37] The project aimed to explore the nature of the church's engagement with the world by asking practitioners what questions they had about their practice and accompanying them in finding answers. In doing this we discovered a trigger that re-engaged practitioners with Scripture and tradition and generated the energy to discuss its meaning.

Practitioners in mission that engaged with the world were invited to identify questions they wished to ask. The ARCS team as outsiders to their practice worked with them to gather data and discuss it. As we supported these conversations, we became aware of four theological voices.[38]

- Operant theology: the theology embedded within their practice.
- Espoused theology: the theology in their articulation of their beliefs.
- Normative theology: the theology of whichever aspects of the Christian tradition they took to be authoritative.
- Formal theology: the theology of academic theologians and the insights of other disciplines.

The conversation between practitioners and the ARCS team contained these four voices and the interaction between them led to disclosures that were meaningful in answering their questions. We named these disclosures as gifts from the Holy Spirit and discerned them as indications of divine self-revelation. The four voices were heard like a chord—each contained the resonance of the other, both dissonance and harmony were audible. This approach is one of a number that are turning practical theology back to a conversation with the tradition.[39] It was developed by conversation for conversation.

*Including Scripture in the conversation?*

Including Scripture in the conversation wasn't and isn't easy. Let me identify three challenges.

In the temple Jesus is 'sitting among the teachers, listening to them and asking them questions'. As seasoned Christian readers we assume and insert 'about Scripture'. 'On the road' Jesus starts the theological conversation by asking Cleopas and Mary, 'what things?' which prompts them to narrate what is important to them. But when he starts to talk to them about Scripture, they don't stop him and say, 'what book?'. They have a shared text around which the conversation develops. I share with other practical theologians concerns about the Bible falling silent in the church[40] and theological education[41] let alone in everyday life. There has been a stream of work within practical theology looking at how it can better engage with the Bible.[42]

So, the first challenge is to trigger in Christians a desire to return to the temple classroom to learn about Scripture in order to include it in the conversation on the road. The second challenge is to find ways of talking about God that, as well as embracing language such as values and spirituality, enable people outside the church to directly access Scripture. The third challenge is to find ways of helping disciples hold back long enough to hear and take seriously the questions that Scripture provokes in others.

*Discussing our normativity*

To draw Scripture into the conversation we need to be aware of both why and how we give it authority and what questions we are asking that we regard as needing normative rather than pragmatic answers. Is it rational to give authority to a tradition? What do we regard as normative? Is anything else exercising an undisclosed normativity for good or ill? How do we know which parts of Scripture to consult? How is that normativity mediated (though worship, singing, preaching, sacraments, Bible reading practices)?[43]

I would see the turn to tradition in practical theology as an attempt to resist relativism and engage with the normative.[44] The approach by which we make this turn is conversation.

There is a critique of this turn to tradition from liberal practical theologians in an important book *Invitation to Research in Practical Theology* written by Zoë Bennett, Elaine Graham, Stephen Pattison and Heather Walton on two counts.[45] First is this a turn to the church and away from the world? Olwyn Mark[46] demonstrates that this is not the case and I would also point to my own work on social justice[47] and John Swinton's books on dementia and disability.[48] So, their concern is justified but not entirely. Second, how can we assume that the tradition is to be trusted when it has been used to endorse so much oppressive behaviour? I take this seriously and feel it is important to acknowledge and address the damage done by some past interpretations and their contemporary legacy. I have tried to draw attention to the un-naming of women in Scripture by way of example in this chapter.[49]

Let me now invite you to turn to your neighbour and discuss this question:

> What are 'these things' that matter deeply to you in your life and ministry and that you therefore want to reflect on personally and discuss with others?

Moorlands College has hosted GuvnaB so, as an exemplary example of fruitful dialogue, I would like to reference his conversation with Jahaziel on the BBC World Service.[50] He showed how it is possible to reference your own normativity without dismissing or undermining the questions of others, whilst at the same time talking about things that mattered to them both.

## C2 Where next in theological education?

I have been tasked with challenging the College about its future practice. My proposal is that if we, as students and teachers, take time to uncover our own assumptions, we will find it easier to engage in mission that starts with other people's questions rather than enculturating our answers. To address this, I want to suggest a three-stage educational process of regeneration, a return to the tradition and co-designed assessment.[51] The founding vision of the College was to 'equip for evangelism.' Today's vision statement uses the phrase 'impact the church and the world.' But the statement of faith says that the work of the Holy Spirit is to make people increasingly Christ-like. How is that to happen? Surely by the time people come to this College they have been converted and received a calling to ministry or be open to such a call? Different strands of Christianity understand the ongoing work of the Holy Spirit in different ways, but they all recognise its importance. The College uses the term regeneration, I would use the term sanctification, my Catholic colleagues would talk of evangelization. If students come here wanting to make an impact, how can they prepare themselves for a conversation with those who have never read Scripture?

### Regeneration through action research into my practices

My suggestion is that the curriculum needs to start with 'these things', the treasures and burdens of each heart. Only at the point at which I have questioned 'these things' am I in a position to hear the questions of others rather than offer them the answers to my questions. But this means giving students time to undertake action research into their own questions.

I realise that a validation meeting with a university that starts by saying that the curriculum cannot be specified at all will be a hard conversation. I would like to guess that there are some questions that students might identify:

- My consumption and its relationship to the environment. When I open the door of my fridge or my wardrobe what questions am I confronted with?
- My identity and who I include. When I access my social media accounts what story about myself am I telling?
- My relationships and my idea of faithfulness. Who gets time in my calendar?
- My context and my concept of community. Where are my go and no-go areas? What does my monthly google maps timeline tell me about the boundaries of my community?

### A return to the tradition

My argument is that if groups of students use action research approaches to address 'these things', they will uncover theological questions they want to bring to Scripture and tradition. This should provoke an insider (students)/outsider (teachers) conversation to disclose what the curriculum should be, where it should be taught (context or classroom) and what style of learning is appropriate (action research, reflection, or instruction). At what points do students need to be on the road and when do they need to be in the temple at the feet of their teachers?

*Co-designed assessment*

An implication of this proposal is that assessment needs to be co-designed with students, class, context, and teachers all having a stake. But this then requires designing assessments that do not trigger individualism. Assessments should capture not only what is learned, but how it is learned and why it is learned. Is this a practical proposal? It certainly has challenges. However, this multi-stakeholder approach to assessment seems to me to be a better preparation for ministry.

For this proposal to work there would be a challenge to the church to give students time to go through a process of regeneration as part of the explicit curriculum rather than as an implicit 'formation'. For this proposal to work there would be a challenge to the university to find ways of validating a curriculum that starts with students' questions and ends with co-designed assessment.

## B2 Maturity reborn

An enquiry-based curriculum with co-designed assessment does not mean ignoring what has gone before in previous eras. It continues enculturation by reflecting on a context. Having become aware of the way in which I consume culture, I am better placed to help others find God in their culture and context. It continues relevance by becoming bilingual in another epistemic community. It values rather than asks students to leave behind past world views. It would actively welcome students training for bi-vocational ministry investigating both a secular and ministry calling alongside each other.[52] It continues equipping by teaching skilful performance. The word 'equip' in the College vision statement is still important, although I have tried to stretch its meaning. We need good sermons, effective pastoral care, engaging children's ministry, creative use of digital technology. Maturity is not a restless moving with the times so we stop singing yesterday's song—it is a recapitulation of past themes skilfully woven into a new song written 'with' rather than 'for' those we teach or minister to. If practical theology is to be of service to church and world, it needs the maturity to discern when to spend time in the classroom and when to offer accompaniment on the road.

## A2 Finishing with Scripture

And as you might expect, I want to finish with Scripture by inviting you again to compare the two stories on your handout. They both contain examples of chiasmus.[53] When we look at the central idea, we see that the first story is about questions and understanding (Luke 2:47) and the second about being alive in Christ (Luke 24:23). There is a move from the dialectic of the classroom to the challenging conversation on the road. I have argued that we need to take more seriously 'these things' that trigger the challenging conversations. But I am also arguing that we need the power of those triggers to take us back into the classroom to learn Scripture and about the history of the church by which it has reached us and the systematic reflection on it that has become doctrine.

Luke like many writers of his age structured his narratives in a way that we wouldn't. He put the central point of the story in the middle with paired ideas leading to and from that central point. He would not pass a study skills module today because, as we 'know', the important material is at the beginning and the end. But my argument is that we need to learn to know what we don't know so that we can bring the tradition to those who don't already have it in their hearts on the road.

I want to offer two minute's silence for you to reflect on what is on your heart having engaged in this conversation.

I now invite you to turn to your neighbour and discuss, where do you want to take this conversation next?

There followed a plenary discussion followed by the conference dinner.[54]

## Notes

1 The Salvation Army, *Building Deeper Relationships: A Guide to Faith-Based Facilitation* (London: International Headquarters, 2010). I was involved in the development of this approach to facilitation. John W. Welch, ed. *Chiasmus in Antiquity: Structures, Analyses, Exegesis* (Maxwell Institute Publications 22: Brigham Young University Scholars Archive, 1998). Chiasmus is the practice of arranging a story in paired points that converge on the main point in the middle of the passage that gives the meaning of the story.
2 The audience had been given copies of Luke 2:41–52 and Luke 24:13–35.
3 Tom Wright, *Luke for Everyone* (London: SPCK, 2001), 29.
4 I have reservations about the lecture as a pedagogical strategy. I resist the form by engaging the audience in various forms of participation to trigger reflection.
5 In Luke 24, the disciple with Cleopas is unnamed. However, we read Mary's name into the first story, should we be reading Mary the wife of Cleopas who stood at the foot of the cross (John 19:25) into the second?
6 Historians use periodisation as a way of making sense of different emphases at different periods. In the absence of an academic history of the College, I used key Church of England reports to signal transitions. A subsequent discussion of the trajectories of the discipline can be found in Stephen B. Roberts, "Keeping Contact: Traditions and Trajectories of British and Irish Practical Theology as Evidenced in the History of BIAPT's Journal," *Practical Theology* 13, no. 1–2 (2020): 19–31.
7 Alison Notman, *Faith and Vision: The Moorlands Story* (Sopley: Moorlands College, 1998).
8 See College website, "Our Core Values," Moorlands College, accessed April 4, 2019, www.moorlands.ac.uk/our-core-values/.
9 Commission on Evangelism, *Towards the Conversion of England* (London: Church of England, 1945).
10 Stephen Pattison, "Pastoral Studies," in *The Challenge of Practical Theology*, ed. Stephen Pattison (London: Jessica Kingsley Publishers, 2007).
11 Notman, *Faith and Vision*.
12 Andrew Brookes, ed. *The Alpha Phenomenon: Theology, Praxis and Challenges for Mission and Church Today* (London: CTBI, 2007).
13 David Lyall and Paul Ballard, "Soil, Roots and Shoots: The Emergence of BIAPT," *Practical Theology* 13, no. 1–2 (2020): 8–18.

14 Helen Cameron, Philip Richter, Douglas Davies, and Frances Ward, eds. *Studying Local Churches: A Handbook* (London: SCM, 2005).
15 Following Andrew Root's account of Charles Taylor's three types of secularisation I would see this as Secularisation 2 in which the scope of religious institutions is challenged. See Andrew Root, *Faith Formation in a Secular Age: Responding to the Church's Obsession with Youthfulness* (Grand Rapids: Baker Academic, 2017).
16 See the research reported in Paul Ballard and Stephen Pattison, "Practical Theological Education—a Profile," *British Journal of Theological Education* 13, no. 2 (2003): 97.
17 Paul Simmonds, *From Maintenance to Mission* (Grove Booklets, Evangelism Series 32. London: Grove Books, 1995). Robert Warren, *Building Missionary Congregations* (London: Church House Publishing, 1995).
18 David Goodhew, ed. *Church Growth in Britain: 1980 to the Present* (Farnham: Ashgate, 2012).
19 Stephen Pattison, "Is Pastoral Care Dead in a Mission-Led Church?" *Practical Theology* 1, no. 1 (2008): 7–10.
20 Elaine Graham, *Between a Rock and a Hard Place: Public Theology in a Post-Secular Age* (London: SCM, 2013). Luke Bretherton, *Christianity and Contemporary Politics: The Conditions and Possibilities of Faithful Witness* (Oxford: Wiley-Blackwell, 2010). Alister McGrath, *Surprised by Meaning: Science, Faith, and How We Make Sense of Things* (London: Westminster John Knox Press, 2010).
21 Pete Ward, *Introducing Practical Theology: Mission, Ministry and the Life of the Church* (Grand Rapids: Baker Academic, 2017).
22 Helen Cameron, *Resourcing Mission: Practical Theology for Changing Churches* (London: SCM, 2010).
23 To each of the four points in this section I will add a further footnoted reflection drawing upon material published since the conference.
24 Heidi A. Campbell, ed. *The Distanced Church: Reflections on Doing Church Online* (Texas: Digital Religion Publications-Network for New Media, 2020). Published within a month of public worship being closed in both the USA and UK due to the Coronavirus pandemic.
25 Helen Cameron, "The Morality of the Food Parcel: Emergency Food as a Response to Austerity," *Practical Theology* 7, no. 3 (2014): 194–204. I would add to this now the impact of the pandemic which has also exposed inequality and returned many economies to recession.
26 Greg Smith and Linda Woodhead. "Religion and Brexit: Populism and the Church of England," *Religion, State and Society* 46, no. 3 (2018): 206–223; David Goodhart, *The Road to Somewhere: The Populist Revolt and the Future of Politics* (London: Hurst & Company, 2017).
27 The events of summer 2020 led to many theological colleges resolving to tackle the way in which they were blinded by whiteness. I found Willie Jennings book helpful. In this chapter I address the way in which both the missional and educational thinking of the church fails to engage with the changing reality of women's lives but assume they will adapt to prevailing expectations in order to belong. W. J. Jennings, *After Whiteness: An Education in Belonging* (Grand Rapids: Eerdmans, 2020).
28 Notman, *Faith and Vision*.
29 Abby Day, *The Religious Lives of Older Laywomen: The Last Active Anglican Generation* (Oxford: Oxford University Press, 2017).
30 Much of this work is part-time, low paid on fixed-term contracts and undertaken by young people and women. It has failed to engage with the messy reality of women's lives as they combine paid work, domestic work and unpaid care for children and parents. The form of enculturation that best recognises this reality is Messy Church. It recognises the challenges of weekly participation in any activity for women with small children and their appetite for messy play to take place outside their homes.

See Clare Watkins and Bridget Shepherd, "The Challenge of 'Fresh Expressions' to Ecclesiology," *Ecclesial Practices* 1, no. 1 (2014): 92–110.

31 In summer 2019 I listened to Courtney Goto's keynote address at the BIAPT Conference in which she spoke of the way in which the Brexit debate had exposed the habits of ignoring those from whom we differ in UK society. The repeated refrain in her talk was, 'Why do we not know what we do not know?' I wonder in this section whether theological education is guilty of ignoring people who have developed a satisfactory world view without explicit knowledge of the Christian tradition. How do we learn about what we ignore from the narratives of those who don't have our knowledge of the tradition? I realised that Joanna was telling me what the church was ignoring in her world view, her concern for the safety of children. C. T. Goto, "The Ubiquity of Ignorance: A Practical Theological Challenge of Our Time," *Practical Theology* 13, no. 1–2 (2020): 138–149.

32 See Root, *Faith Formation* for an account of Charles Taylor's Secularisation 3 in which the existence of God cannot be taken for granted in Western societies.

33 Rachel Hurcombe, *Child Sexual Abuse in the Context of Religious Institutions* (London: IICSA, 2019).

34 Higher education qualifications and particularly the experience of living away from home mainly contribute to an individual's social position and ability to relocate rather than benefit the community in which they grew up. See Goodhart, *The Road to Somewhere*. Whilst I have benefited from studying at so-called elite universities, I have worked equally hard to become proficient in participatory approaches that are regarded as inferior by those institutions. I think it is worth asking if a higher education qualification is necessary for all forms of ministry. Are the churches allowing the HE system to implicitly set the criteria for ministry? When non-traditional HE applicants access HE to train for ministry what do they learn from the hidden curriculum? Do they then import that hidden curriculum into ministry with its emphasis on individualism, credentialism, judgmentalism, and separating knowledge from practice? I valued reading David Goodhart, *Head Hand Heart: The Struggle for Dignity and Status in the 21st Century* (London: Allen Lane, 2020).

35 Paul Bolton, *Higher Education Student Numbers* (London: House of Commons Library, 2020), 13.

36 I am not alone in raising these concerns. Henk de Roest and colleagues at PThU in the Netherlands have worked creatively with ministerial students and their placements to challenge who learns what, where, and with whom. Roest, H. de, *Collaborative Practical Theology: Engaging Practitioners in Research on Christian Practices* (Leiden: Brill, 2019).

37 The approach developed by the ARCS project is described in Helen Cameron, Deborah Bhatti, Catherine Duce, James Sweeney, and Clare Watkins, *Talking About God in Practice: Theological Action Research and Practical Theology* (London: SCM, 2010). A fuller account of its theological outcomes is now available in Clare Watkins, *Disclosing Church: An Ecclesiology Learned through Conversations in Practice* (London: Routledge, 2020).

38 See Watkins, *Disclosing Church*, 46

39 Elizabeth Jordan, "Conversation as a Tool of Research in Practical Theology," *Practical Theology* 12, no. 5 (2019): 526–536. Cathy Ross and Colin Smith, eds. *Missional Conversations: A Dialogue between Theory and Praxis in World Mission* (London: SCM Press, 2018).

40 Pete Ward, *Liquid Ecclesiology: The Gospel and the Church* (Leiden: Brill, 2017).

41 Anthony J. Clarke, "Forming Ministers or Training Leaders? An Exploration of Practice and the Pastoral Imagination" (PhD Thesis, University of Chester, 2017).

42 Paul Ballard and Stephen Holmes, eds. *The Bible in Pastoral Practice: Readings in the Place and Function of Scripture in the Church* (London: Darton, Longman and Todd, 2005). Zoë Bennett, *Using the Bible in Practical Theology: Historical and*

*Contemporary Perspectives* (Farnham: Ashgate, 2013). Andrew Rogers, *Congregational Hermeneutics: How Do We Read?* (Farnham: Ashgate, 2015).
43 Is imagination involved as Chloe Lynch's chapter suggests? Is the Holy Spirit the animator of the conversation as Sheryl Arthur's chapter suggests?
44 Two of the student contributions in this volume engage with this concern, Sam Norman and Isaac McNish.
45 Zoë Bennett, Elaine Graham, Stephen Pattison, and Heather Walton, eds. *Invitation to Research in Practical Theology* (London: Routledge, 2018).
46 See her chapter in this volume.
47 Cameron, *The Morality of the Food Parcel*; Helen Cameron, *Just Mission: Practical Politics for Local Churches* (London: SCM, 2015).
48 John Swinton, *Dementia: Living in the Memories of God* (London: SCM Press, 2012). John Swinton, *Becoming Friends of Time: Disability, Timefullness and Gentle Discipleship* (London: SCM, 2016).
49 This practice has been named as problematic in feminist theology for a long time. See Elizabeth Schussler Fiorenza, *In Memory of Her: A Feminist Theological Reconstruction of Christian Origins* (London: SCM, 1983).
50 BBC World Service. *Fork in the Road—Two Journeys out of Gang Violence.* Podcast audio. Heart and Soul 05.04.19. Accessed April 6, 2019.
51 In doing this I build upon the doctoral thesis of Susy Brouard who used theological action research in a formative way see Susanna Brouard, "Using Theological Action Research to Embed Catholic Social Teaching in a Catholic Development Agency: Abseiling on the Road to Emmaus" (PhD Thesis, Anglia Ruskin University, 2015). See also Nick Shepherd, "Action Research as Professional Development," *Journal of Adult Theological Education* 9, no. 2 (2012): 121–138.
52 See Samuel L. Perry and Cyrus Schleifer, "Are Bivocational Clergy Becoming the New Normal? An Analysis of the Current Population Survey, 1996–2017," *Journal for the Scientific Study of Religion* 58, no. 2 (2019): 513–525; Hartness M. Samushonga, "A Theological Reflection of Bivocational Pastoral Ministry: A Personal Reflective Account of a Decade of Bivocational Ministry Practice Experience," *Practical Theology* 12, no. 1 (2019): 66–80 and Hartness M. Samushonga, "On Bivocational Ministry-Focused Training in British Theological Schools: Dialoguing with British Theological Educationalists," *Practical Theology* 13, no. 4 (2020): 385–399.
53 John Breck, "Biblical Chiasmus: Exploring Structure for Meaning," *Biblical Theology Bulletin: Journal of Bible and Culture* 17, no. 2 (1987): 70–74. Welch, *Chiasmus in Antiquity*.
54 It is common for people to say they learn more from the mealtime conversations at a conference than in the session. This is echoed in the Emmaus Road story and in my inclusion of conversation in the session to trigger conversations that can be continued around the table.

# 6 Evangelicals learning practical theology
## Autobiographical reflections

*Andrew Rogers*

In this chapter I will reflect on how evangelicals learn practical theology through my own experiences of learning, teaching, and researching in practical theology. This will of course be a partial account rooted in my locations and history, but practical theology is nothing if not contextual, and autobiographical accounts are not uncommon in practical theology. In particular, such an approach will allow me to consider issues arising for both evangelicals and Pentecostals, as these have been distinctive aspects of my experience. The motivation for writing such an account is ultimately because I believe evangelicals have much to gain from practical theology, and that practical theology is being enriched by the presence of evangelicals. In addition, and behind the genesis of this volume, there has been an increasing engagement by evangelicals with practical theology in the UK over the 16 years I have known of such a thing.[1]

Definitional questions could detain us for a long time, and other chapters will have tackled what is meant by evangelicalism. It will suffice for me to nod as is customary to David Bebbington's quadrilateral as well as note Rob Warner's development of this.[2] It has also become customary in many publications to include Pentecostalism under the evangelical umbrella.[3] While there are many similarities, I have found people self-designate in complicated ways using the terms evangelical, Pentecostal, and charismatic that belie this simplicity,[4] so will include the acronym EPC to reflect this variation.[5] What is important to stress is that this chapter is written out of the British evangelical context which is configured quite differently to evangelicalisms in other parts of the world, especially regarding political affiliation[6] and the supposed shibboleth of inerrancy.[7] As to what is meant by practical theology, I shall also let that unfold below.

Writing this account has been challenging, as it is my first sustained piece of autobiographical writing, requiring some self-interrogation along the way (i.e., was it really like that?). I am glad, however, that practical theology makes space for accounts of this type, arising from its own theological logic.[8] I am also aware that the traditions, communities, and institutions that have formed me (and that I have contributed to) are precious to me, even though I am also frustrated by what I see as their weaknesses. Critique therefore has needed careful steps on the reflexivity tightrope. The account that follows draws

DOI: 10.4324/9781003094975-9

selectively on my experiences in five areas given in chronological order, but with each area also reaching forward in time on the same theme, as this seemed the least confusing approach.

## Church, life, and practical theology

I cannot recall hearing of practical theology before starting my PhD at King's College, London in 2004. I was already in my mid-thirties, had been in church circles for almost all of that time, had worked for some large parachurch organisations, and had been studying in theological institutions for some years prior to this. As someone who had grown up in the evangelical tradition, with its emphasis on 'relevance for life,'[9] experiential encounter with God and missionary activism, why was practical theology so elusive?

I grew up in the open Brethren in the English Midlands, attending 'assemblies' in Northampton and Coventry. Church was a major part of family life and faith was also understood as for all of life.[10] These close and supportive Christian communities embodied the importance of the Bible, of mission (particularly global mission), and of the need for conversion made possible through Christ's work on the cross (so very many 'gospel services'). 'Jesus Christ is Lord' was written across the front of the church. We might have been Bebbington's key informants. Alongside the many gifts I received from this upbringing, I also gained the impression that this was how Christianity should be done. Such an impression shrouded other Christian traditions in mystery (such as the Anglican church thirty metres away), and not a little suspicion. While my future churches all were evangelical, they varied in emphases according to their congregational make-up, tradition, and denominational influences, and included charismatic, conservative, and open evangelical congregations.[11]

On leaving home for university to study Computer Science, there were a number of key catalysts in terms of faith development. University Christian Union turbo-charged the importance of mission, especially global mission, and this began for me a long engagement with African Christianity and culture, starting in Botswana, then leading to longer periods in Kenya and Ethiopia working with national churches and Christian cross-cultural mission agencies. As part of preparation for Kenya, I was fascinated by the anthropology we had been encouraged to read, and, when there, was given time to just 'hang out', watching and listening and learning language (badly) along the way. It was these early mission experiences in Botswana and Kenya that opened up a wider understanding of faith to me. I began to see how culture was intertwined with faith, as well as what wealth and poverty meant for mission, complexifying for me the taken-for-grantedness of my own beliefs and practices, and how biblical ideas might be perceived rather differently in Tswana or Gabbra communities. It was not just far away cultures that had this impact, but youth subcultures in Bristol and Essex, as I spent some years running church youth groups with the desire to communicate the Gospel. This too needed work in understanding their lives and contexts, which in the 1990s seemed to involve a lot of Spice Girls and Oasis.

Throughout early adulthood I had frequently encountered quite contrary intellectual perspectives on Christian faith, through the study of Philosophy as part of my first degree, as well as through teaching Philosophy of Religion and Ethics 'A' level as a Religious Education teacher in Essex. I wanted to dig deeper and being just a chapter ahead of the students got tiring, so I took up a distance learning course part-time through the Open Theological College (more of this later). On returning to teach Religious Education (RE) a few years later at a Roman Catholic Sixth Form College, I had some fantastic practical theology training in teaching 'General RE' which comprised 45 minutes with south London teenagers finding a religious perspective on the issue of the day. The lesson plan was often just three questions.

Returning to my question, the elusiveness of 'practical theology' before my formal theological education was no great surprise. The gap between church and academy in theology has often been commented upon,[12] and this was also the case for the evangelicalism I knew. Church and academy were nearly parallel worlds that rarely intersected. Therefore, it was not just 'practical theology' that was elusive, but 'theology' itself that was rarely discussed explicitly in my early years, except perhaps to dismiss it as irrelevant or even dangerous for everyday faith. There were some acceptable bridges to academic theology, however, through trusted evangelical Bible commentaries and speakers at large Christian events.[13]

The more important question, however, is whether I was learning practical theology without naming it as such? Actually, as a number of practical theologians have argued, is it not practical theology that Christian communities are engaging in everyday?[14] As a young Christian, dealing with how to behave at school and home, what subjects to choose, relationship choices, how to be 'a witness'—we were encouraged to let faith frame all of this—'Jesus Christ is Lord' after all. This would have been expressed in terms of following Jesus, of wanting to become like him, of being disciples. While these roots remained, as a young adult a more reflective faith was needed to tackle the questions posed by youth work, faith and culture, the intellectual challenges from philosophy, and the lives of friends and colleagues who seemed to manage just fine without God. I can't recall thinking about the process, and it wasn't particularly systematic, nor did I follow any particular explicit model, but it was a practical theology sensibility—looking at church and world through faith.[15] When I finally met academic practical theology, I eventually realised it could be in continuity with where and how I had been formed.[16]

## Formal theological education

The elusiveness of practical theology in my formal theological education further brings into relief evangelical engagement with practical theology sensibilities. 'Practical theology' was not a term I encountered at the Open Theological

College (OTC) or at the evangelical London School of Theology (LST) in the latter part of the 1990s.[17] The OTC was the beginning of my formal theological education journey. I recall being caught up by learning about the kingdom of God and the bigger story of salvation this implied, as well as puzzlement as to why the kingdom theme had been absent from my formation to date, given the prominence of the theme in the synoptic Gospels. To make up for lost time, for a while all my sermons were essentially about the kingdom, as an elder from my childhood church observed.

At LST, biblical studies and doctrine featured heavily, as I expected and wanted, but mission and a course on 'Today's World' particularly encouraged engagement with contemporary culture, worldview, and ethics. I did hear the Principal say, 'orthopraxis follows orthodoxy,' but the classroom reality was a little fuzzier. This sentiment would have been called 'applied theology' at the time, a term that has effectively become practical theology kryptonite, although there are now attempts to resurrect the term.[18] Interestingly, the mission class, with its emphasis on inculturation, would have agreed with some critiques of applied theology, as would my subsequent master's degree in biblical hermeneutics also taught at LST—sometimes the curriculum subverts the institution. This master's programme also introduced me to contextual theologies and interpretations, particularly from African scholars,[19] as well as to 'Theology of the Poor', bringing more radical thinking about the gospel, politics, and social justice to my attention.[20] These two years studying theology full-time were highly transformative and life-changing—as I described it at the time, it felt like 'rewiring my brain'.

Formal theological education also brought about some 'theology shock', as I have since come to call it.[21] I recall quite clearly sitting in an LST New Testament class and hearing the lecturer say something like, 'This is one of the more reliable sayings of Jesus.' Immediately I wondered what less reliable sayings there might be and what that meant about Scripture that was not being said in this class. Less of a shock, but no less formative, was the advent of post-evangelicalism and its critique of evangelical beliefs, practices, and formation.[22] This was wrapped up with a widespread desire at the time to engage with postmodernity,[23] which often appeared to start with the changing culture and ascribe to it significant authority for mission and ecclesiology. This made quite an impression on me at the time, as I recognised the critiques of evangelicalism from my own experience and agreed with some of them, yet I was not willing to abandon the tradition either.[24] It took some years to understand, evaluate, and integrate these sorts of critical perspectives into my own theological system, which led to me identifying as an 'open evangelical' when pressed.[25]

Returning to LST fifteen years later as external examiner, a lecturer in practical theology had been appointed, with practical theology part of the curriculum and students engaging in theological reflection with methodological sophistication. At two other evangelical theological colleges where I was external examiner for practical theology, I variously remarked that students 'make interesting and sometimes brave connections in their theological reflections' and 'are genuinely learning to become theologically reflective practitioners.' In 2020, LST appointed a senior practical theologian, Reverend Professor Mark Cartledge, as Principal. These developments point to changes in evangelical engagement with practical theology, alongside the growing recognition of its place within the theological curriculum.

## Research

Explicit engagement with practical theology as an academic discipline began with my PhD at King's College, London, within the Centre for Theology, Religion and Culture (CTRC). Many students had a ministry background and a fair few were evangelical or post-evangelical. Prayers were said at our research seminar (possibly without the institution knowing this). By this stage of my theological education, I was used to reading and hearing from scholars well beyond the evangelical tradition, which was just as well, since there were very few evangelical scholars to draw upon in practical theology at the time. Like many students, however, I just got on with doing what I was advised to do, without initially thinking too much about the theological implications.

Having studied formal biblical hermeneutics at master's level, I now wanted to explore through fieldwork how evangelicals in congregations did hermeneutics. Hanging out in churches to discover their 'congregational hermeneutics' seemed a very exciting prospect. CTRC was intentionally based in an education department to encourage interdisciplinary working—it felt like both students and staff were working out what practical theology and its methodology was as we went along, which brought a lot of energy to the research experience. I did worry sometimes where the theology was coming from, especially when sitting in statistics and ethnography classes with education and nursing students, wondering what I was doing there. Fieldwork was understood through the social sciences, but there was an uneasiness with these being the only methodological sources. Being apprenticed in critical realism helped to pinpoint some of this unease, especially the bracketing of divine agency required by a methodological atheism.[26] The publication of *Practical Theology and Qualitative Research* by John Swinton and Harriet Mowat in 2006 gave expression to the issues a number of us had been wrestling with. The book recognised evangelical concerns about the relation between revelation and experience and proposed an asymmetric relationship for a revised mutual critical correlation shaped around hospitality, conversion and critical faithfulness.[27] This was a significant framework that aided me and other students to develop their practical theology work as evangelicals, albeit in our own directions.[28] Some years later, the Ecclesiology and Ethnography network provided a forum for exploring further what a 'theological ethnography' might look like, which was very helpful for many, including myself, who were working out how to do fieldwork as a theologian.[29]

I had the privilege of disseminating aspects of my doctoral research in congregations around the UK through developing a hermeneutics course for congregations with Bible Society. While Bible Society works with all churches, a number of evangelical churches and institutions took part. The course built up to using a theological reflection cycle to reflect on homelessness and had a significant impact on some of the participants. Confidence to engage in theological reflection was one reported outcome;[30] others were struck by the significance of poverty and justice themes in Scripture; others commented how it was 'the beginning of starting to sort of see how we relate to the world at large'. At the same time, other responses indicated the challenges of communicating theological reflection in evangelical contexts in relation to the Bible.[31]

## BIAPT

The British and Irish Association for Practical Theology (BIAPT) has been and continues to be an important influence in my learning of practical theology. As an academic association should, it has helped me to engage critically with a wide range of theological perspectives, some of which I might not encounter otherwise, or may be outside of my comfort zone, and will interrogate, test, or deepen my own theologising. While such engagement often takes the classic academic form of keynotes and short papers, much of the hoped-for 'mutual encouragement and mature disagreement'[32] occurs in conversation with other delegates in the spaces between the formalities. As an academic association of practical theologians should, it incorporates both academics and practitioners, so as not to lose contact with its *raison d'être*. I also appreciate the framing of conference days with prayer, unusual for an academic association in my experience. Also unusual in my experience was the fairly even gender balance in practical theology, which was in welcome contrast to the mostly male scholarship I had encountered prior to doctoral studies.

My first encounter with BIAPT, while wrestling with methodological matters in my PhD, was the annual conference in 2006 in Manchester.[33] The conference focussed on the book *Theological Reflection: Methods* and the authors Elaine Graham, Heather Walton, and Frances Ward were the keynote speakers.[34] This was an instance of testing my own fledging understanding and approach to practical theology, which generated some theology shock for me, as out of the sevenfold typology of methods offered, only one appeared to give a normative role for Scripture, described as '"Telling God's Story": Canonical Narrative Theology'.[35] Being limited to one option amongst seven led to an impression of where the theological centre of gravity was within the discipline.[36] I may have missed it at the time, but Graham, Walton, and Ward recognise in the same book how 'practical theology often has an uneasy relationship with the study of the Bible.'[37]

Fortunately, I returned to the 2008 conference, and to most annual conferences since. I have found, despite different methodological approaches and theological convictions, a strong sense of welcome, and of one's contribution being valued and appreciated. Later on, as vice-chair and chair, along with the committee, we committed the importance of theological diversity to writing in a 'Five year strategy for BIAPT (2017–2022)', which included 'a broader range of

Christian traditions' alongside (importantly) 'high quality conversation ... that allows for a culture of mutual encouragement and mature disagreement.'[38] Of course, the practice is harder than the strategy, but there are signs that this is happening,[39] with friendships being key in making this work.

An important part of my formation within BIAPT has been co-convening the Bible and Practical Theology special interest group since 2011. This has been a 'learning together' of BIAPT members and guests, including some EPCs, calling for an increased and more confident engagement with Scripture in practical theology; addressing what practical theological engagement with the Bible looks like and should look like, including the vexed question of where one should 'start'.[40] The most enriching part of our meetings, one that was noted as uncommon in academic settings, was reading Scripture together. We would contend that the aforementioned relationship between the Bible and practical theology has become a more fruitful one over the past decade or so.[41]

## Teaching Pentecostals practical theology

From 2009, I took up a lecturing post at the University of Roehampton in south west London. This role provided a more sustained experience of evangelicals learning practical theology than previously encountered, so this section forms the longest in the chapter. A significant part of this experience has been convening (and teaching on) an undergraduate programme in Ministerial Theology where theological reflection has been a core feature. Comprising a two-year foundation degree and one year honours degree 'top-up', a key learning outcome of the foundation degree is that students are expected to 'have developed as theologically reflective practitioners within a ministry context.'[42] Although I say so myself, the programme is unique within the British context, given its particular history and development, and I will explain how this is not just convenor pride speaking.

From its inception in 2007, this open access programme attracted a growing number of African and Caribbean heritage students largely through word of mouth within families and congregations. The key entrance requirement has been engagement in Christian ministry (broadly defined), and while we have welcomed students from a wide range of church traditions, the majority to date have been Pentecostals. Based on an analysis of student data made at our tenth anniversary in 2017, 77% of students identified as being of African ethnicity,[43] the median age was 43 years old,[44] and 25% commuted twice weekly from the home counties and beyond.[45] The growth and demographics of the programme reflect the increasing demand for theological education amongst black majority churches,[46] many of which have now been established for decades in London and the UK, and are still growing.[47] These contextual factors are significant for how our students have engaged with practical theology, which I will expand on now aided by colleagues who have researched aspects of the same interface.[48] Mark Garner et al. and Richard Burgess' work were based on small-scale fieldwork with our students.

*Evangelicals learning practical theology* 107

My main experience of teaching practical theology with our Pentecostal students has been through core modules on theological reflection, where students write reflective journals about their ministry practice. Co-teaching a module on biblical hermeneutics, where the focus has been on making connections between contemporary issues and the voices of Scripture, has also been an important aspect of this pedagogical experience.[49] Insights into student engagement with practical theology sensibilities have been gained through classroom discussions and in assessing (a lot of) student work in these modules, but also through interactions in other areas of the curriculum. The model of theological reflection used to date has been the pastoral cycle adapted from Laurie Green and supplemented by other works, particularly the Judith Thompson et al. textbook.[50] The choice of theological reflection model was largely pragmatic—what I was aware of when setting up the modules, what resources were available and what was the most accessible for open access students.

In terms of what I have found distinctive about these Pentecostals learning practical theology over the past eleven years, I have three initial observations. First, I have heard and seen many students be transformed in their understanding of Christian faith and practice, with some resonance with my own experience. More of that shortly. Second, learning contexts are all different and this one is no exception—there are contextual factors such as cultural heritage, educational background, and a mature age profile,[51] with students often having many years of ministry experience prior to their formal theological education with us. It is better to speak of 'these' Pentecostal students and make observations subject to their contingencies. Third, a number of the issues that arise for these Pentecostals learning practical theology, and theological reflection in particular, appear to be similar to those in other ministry formation programmes across different theological traditions, as colleagues in BIAPT and in the literature testify. The difficulty of theological reflection has been a perennial theme of British practical theology from Pattison's 'making bricks without straw' through to informing the theme of the 2018 BIAPT conference.[52] At least to begin with, our students variously have found it difficult to grasp the process of theological reflection,[53] struggle to know what sort of engagement with 'the Christian tradition' is expected,[54] treat the theological reflection phase in isolation or as 'icing on the cake',[55] and can tend towards mere description of practices. I might also add that the cycle is somewhat artificial, particularly for students with existing habits of 'ordinary' theological reflection developed over many years, and there is a default tendency to fix on problems that need resolving that students absorb from the discipline.

Issues that may be more specific to our students arise with expected forms of criticality in theological reflection. Becoming a theologically reflective practitioner sometimes requires a critical appraisal of practices in a student's context of ministry with a view to revising such practices, according to models of theological reflection and definitions of practical theology.[56] One student identified a problem:

It's been difficult for me to grasp because it's not something that I was encouraged to do in church so already my mind is not really thinking like that. It's whatever the pastor says, you just accept it, you are not really taught to have that kind of mind where you think, where you reason, and where you are critical. And I think that holds so many cultural and social attachments to it as well because in another culture, it can be seen as quite normal. Its encouraged. But from my background it's not encouraged. I'm getting it more and more now, but personally it's been quite hard to grasp because that wasn't encouraged as I was growing up.[57]

While this is by no means true of all our students' experiences, there were a number that spoke of the difficulty of appearing to criticise one's elders and pastor, which may be implicit in a critique of church practices.[58] This is particularly the case for those not in leadership and for women, with the corollary that some students in leadership also take a while to develop the habit of self-critique as part and parcel of theological reflection. Some of these power dynamics also spill over into the classroom, comprised as it is of students in a wide variety of roles and ministries. I have heard that some students do not speak freely due to who else is in the class, because of a concern about appearing heterodox. Nevertheless, properly managed by the tutor and given time to build up trust, the classroom is often a liberating space for students to ask questions. On this point, the old slogan of the University appeals to many of our students: 'open spaces, open minds'.

A closely related form of expected criticality is with regard to the 'Christian tradition' (as it is often summarised in practical theology), which usually includes at least Bible, doctrine, liturgy, church history and theological writings. For most of our students, the Bible is the default sole representative of the Christian tradition in their theological reflections when they start with us. Learning to use the Bible in a critical way that takes account of context, genre, their own location and scholarly perspectives takes time and it is a while before such skills begin to inform their theological reflections.[59] In many ways this critical approach runs counter to students' inherited congregational hermeneutics. Students are often steeped in the Bible and are familiar with offering biblical exemplars and traditioned readings of texts as normative. Such readings frequently involve citing texts, often one verse, that have become traditional evidence in their congregations for a doctrine or practice.[60] Stumbling blocks arise around issues such as questions of historicity, authorship (e.g., Moses and the Pentateuch), Scripture's authority, use of the Old Testament, eschatology, healing, prosperity, and tithing. This disconnect between critical study of the Bible and the use of the Bible in the church has been explored by many, particularly in relation to evangelical theological convictions, as my colleague has recently summarised.[61] The potential for theology shock is high (as I have experienced something similar myself) but is not necessarily unhelpful pedagogically if managed appropriately. As is the case in many other ministerial formation programmes, this desired criticality of the Bible (tradition) is not taught directly in theological reflection modules, but in biblical studies and doctrine modules with a hoped-for diffusion within the curriculum. This hope benefits from doctrine and biblical studies modules that work towards practice and sometimes from it as well.[62] For example, in our co-taught Engaging Scripture module, my colleague teaches exegetical skills that primarily move from text to context, and I follow by working with students on how to listen to the voices of Scripture on a range of contemporary topics (e.g., tithing, homelessness, the environment, migration, disability). This approach is designed to strengthen the biblical hermeneutics aspect of theological reflection to then develop elsewhere in the curriculum.[63]

How have our students and staff tackled these issues in learning and teaching practical theology? There are a range of responses, although there is no magic bullet for working through the issues raised by criticality. A few students compartmentalise their learning for a time, where university and church become separate worlds that do not touch each other.[64] Related to this, students are investing time, money, and reputations in their studies, so there is often a pragmatic desire to do what is required to achieve their degree, as well as deference to academic authority. More transformative learning comes through small steps which will be familiar to theological educators. Building a relationship of trust between staff and students is vital, so they understand that critical questions are not intended to undermine faith, but can be part of 'faith seeking understanding'. Staff drawing on examples from their own Christian experience and knowing how to make connections with student contexts can build up this trust, as well as staff participation in Christian practices that frame the learning experience (e.g., Chapel services). Latterly we have instituted small group Bible studies, a very recognisable practice for EPC students, in order to model and encourage critical academic skills with students.[65] Such 'critical piety' flourishes through interactions within a like-minded student body,[66] especially if the forum is perceived 'safe' to speak one's mind. Scripture's own critical reappraisal of itself serves as a particularly powerful tool for modelling questioning of tradition, as an emphasis on Christological readings of the Old Testament has made clear, particularly on topics such as tithing that are deeply embedded within students' traditions. This is one instance of drawing out criticality from within the students' own traditions.

Beyond criticality, other issues with theological reflection specific to our students have been the lack of case studies and examples in the practical theology literature that reflect EPC contexts. There are few 'people like us', especially in entry level works, so staff have written their own case studies to help students see what theological reflection looks like in contexts they recognise. I recall in one class asking students to name practices performed by a congregation and when 'testimony' was offered, realised it was not one I had anticipated or could easily point to in the textbooks.[67] I also wonder how well practical theology addresses the questions that EPC students are asking, which often revolve around how do I encounter God/hear from God in this situation? On this point, there has been a lacuna in practical theology regarding the role of the Holy

110  *Andrew Rogers*

Spirit in theological reflection. While this is changing,[68] it seems that representations of practical theology would benefit from greater awareness of the breadth of theological traditions engaging with the discipline.

I have outlined issues that arise for our Pentecostal students learning practical theology to do with a) the difficulty of theological reflection shared across the traditions b) the encounter with criticality and c) the lack of fit to aspects of Pentecostal theology, spirituality, and practice. There are also many benefits which put these issues in perspective (to return to my first observation). I have found that the simple model of theological reflection that students start with forms them in theologically helpful ways, despite the issues raised. They develop the discipline of taking theology and practice seriously, of recognising how the two inform and are intertwined with each other. This discipline involves paying attention to contexts and not taking them at face value, so learning that being critical of practices and oneself can be a legitimate part of their discipleship. These contexts are not confined to the church, as students discover that they can reflect theologically on pretty much anything. The model also develops students' 'So what?' reflex—a key goad at the heart of practical theology—so they learn to expect that theologising leads to action. Students speak to staff frequently and effusively about the changes in their practice and thinking they experience during the programme, of which theological reflection is a core part. Further empirical research may be needed to capture this dynamic more fully.

This experiential account makes the case that practical theology and its models of theological reflection has a lot to offer our Pentecostal students. Indeed, I would go so far as to say that theological reflection is a gift to EPCs, perhaps a flawed gift, but a gift nonetheless, given the resonances it has with EPC priorities (e.g., experiential, action-orientated, contextual, grassroots focussed).[69] The attraction, as Andrew Root recognises, is because 'too often the move from experience to new practice and action has skipped reflection.'[70] We are working with the 'flaws', through recognising that some models may be best for the early stages of learning skills and disciplines appropriate to theological reflection.[71] This then leads into offering critiques of theological reflection models with students as they progress, as well as evaluating emerging models from EPC scholars.[72] On an ecumenical open access programme, balancing accessibility with theological match is a pedagogical judgement.

## Closing reflections

This story has been about evangelicals learning practical theology—myself and my students. As an autobiographical account, the primary emphasis has been on my experience of this learning while reflecting along the way. I close with five brief reflections on evangelicals learning practical theology emerging from this story.

First, it should be fairly obvious that these learning experiences are rooted in particular stories and contexts, but I hope aspects of them will either resonate with readers or offer interesting contrasts to their own formation.

Second, practical theology is not inimical to EPCs; indeed, far from it. Many of the emphases and disciplines required within practical theology are also valued by EPCs. Questions about where we start in theological reflection can misconstrue what it means to 'start'. In practical theology parlance, Christian tradition is interpreted via our experience; our experience is interpreted through the Christian tradition. There is no innocent starting point. EPCs may well want to start with Scripture in their theological reflection, although to my mind starting points need to be discerned in context. Nevertheless, 'starting' with Scripture or doctrine or the ministry of Christ, and ascribing normativity in some way to these, is a legitimate and valuable approach to theological reflection within practical theology, as has been argued over the last decade.[73]

Third, this story had the potential to illuminate differences between evangelicals and Pentecostals learning practical theology. I did note similarities between my own formation and that of my students, albeit occurring in different times and places. It is difficult to determine, however, if some distinctives were particular to our student constituency (e.g., concerns about critiquing practice), or true more broadly of Pentecostal students. Nevertheless, our students did appear to experience many of the same issues faced by most practical theology students, as well as specific issues encountered by other EPC students. To be more precise than that will require further investigations.

Fourth, EPCs have a great deal to offer practical theology, as well as much to benefit from the discipline and its institutions. I do hope that the 'authentic liberal inclusivity', noted by Rooms and Bennett of BIAPT and its Practical Theology journal, goes from strength to strength in including the EPC constituency.[74] With the growth of Pentecostalism in the UK in particular, it seems that better representation of such traditions is needed in learning resources for practical theology (e.g., pneumatology), alongside greater visibility in its institutions.

Fifth, and finally, EPCs learning practical theology impact church and world. While I can testify to this from my own experience, my selective story also tells of how students develop the habit of theological reflection, leading to transformed understanding and practices with impacts on their churches and wider communities.

## Notes

1 While I am not aware of any statistics to prove this point, key indicators would be the embedding of practical theology within ministry formation programmes across the theological spectrum, the growth of professional doctorate programmes, the intentional diversification of BIAPT (e.g., "Five year strategy for BIAPT 2017–2022"), and renewed attention to the role of the Bible in practical theology. See David Lyall and Paul Ballard, "Soil, Roots and Shoots: The Emergence of BIAPT," *Practical Theology* 13, no. 1–2 (2020): 17; Nigel Rooms and Zoë Bennett, eds., *Practical Theology in Progress: Showcasing an Emerging Discipline* (London: Routledge, 2019), 27; Roger Walton, "Using the Bible and Christian Tradition in Theological Reflection," *British Journal of Theological Education* 13, no. 2 (2003): 133–151.

2 David W. Bebbington, *Evangelicalism in Modern Britain: A History from the 1730s to the 1980s* (London: Unwin Hyman, 1989); Rob Warner, *Reinventing English Evangelicalism, 1966–2001: A Theological and Sociological Study* (Milton Keynes: Paternoster, 2007). The quadrilateral identifies four qualities that have been marks of evangelicalism historically, namely conversionism, activism, biblicism, and crucicentrism. Warner develops this in the English context in terms of two rival axes—conversionist-activist and biblicist-crucicentric. I discuss this further in Andrew P. Rogers, *Congregational Hermeneutics: How Do We Read?* (London: Routledge, 2016), 68f.
3 E.g., Brian Stanley, *The Global Diffusion of Evangelicalism: The Age of Billy Graham and John Stott* (Downers Grove: IVP, 2013).
4 See Andrew P. Rogers, *Being Built Together: Final Report* (London: University of Roehampton, 2013), www.roehampton.ac.uk/BeingBuiltTogether/, §5.3, 102; Andrew Root, "Evangelical Practical Theology," in *Opening the Field of Practical Theology: An Introduction*, eds. Kathleen A. Cahalan and Gordon S. Mikoski (Plymouth: Rowman and Littlefield, 2014), 81. Tania Harris makes a case for where evangelicalism and Pentecostalism diverge in "Where Pentecostalism and Evangelicalism Part Ways: Towards a Theology of Pentecostal Revelatory Experience Part I & 2," *Asian Journal of Pentecostal Studies* 23, no. 1 (2020): 31–56.
5 This terminology appears to originate with Alan Jamieson, *A Churchless Faith: Faith Journeys Beyond the Churches* (London: SPCK, 2002), 11.
6 Andrea Hatcher, *Political and Religious Identities of British Evangelicals* (London: Palgrave Macmillan, 2017).
7 Stephen R. Holmes, "Evangelical Doctrines of Scripture in Transatlantic Perspective: The 2008 Laing Lecture," *Evangelical Quarterly* 81 (2009): 38–63.
8 Heather Walton has written extensively in this area. The form of this chapter most closely resembles what she describes as 'life writing' in *Writing Methods in Theological Reflection* (London: SCM, 2014), Ch. 9.
9 See Rogers, *Congregational*, 14f, 70f.
10 All of life as it was experienced. Not all possible areas of life, e.g., politics was not on the agenda.
11 I have been part of an Anglican evangelical church now for 18 years.
12 E.g., James D. G. Dunn, "The Bible and Scholarship: On Bridging the Gap between the Academy and the Church," *Anvil* 19, no. 2 (2002): 109–118.
13 E.g., the Keswick convention and Spring Harvest.
14 Bonnie Miller-McLemore refers to four distinct yet connected uses of practical theology, where the first is 'an activity of believers seeking to sustain a life of reflective faith in the everyday,' in "Introduction: The Contributions of Practical Theology," in *The Wiley-Blackwell Companion to Practical Theology*, ed. Bonnie J. Miller-McLemore (Chichester: Wiley-Blackwell, 2012), 32. Pete Ward spells out in more detail how practical theology is the 'ordinary life of the church' in *Introducing Practical Theology: Mission, Ministry, and the Life of the Church* (Grand Rapids: Baker Academic, 2017), Ch. 1.
15 Cf. Rogers, *Congregational*, 26f.
16 Cf. Ward, *Introducing*, 14.
17 Named London Bible College at the time.
18 Ward, *Introducing*, 3–4, 76–77.
19 E.g., Kwame Bediako, *Theology and Identity: The Impact of Culture upon Christian Thought in the Second Century and Modern Africa* (Oxford: Regnum, 1992); Justin S. Ukpong, "Rereading the Bible with African Eyes: Inculturation and Hermeneutics," *Journal of Theology for Southern Africa* 91 (1995): 3–14.
20 E.g., Ched Myers, *Binding the Strong Man: A Political Reading of Mark's Story of Jesus* (Maryknoll: Orbis Books, 1988); John Howard Yoder, *The Politics of Jesus:*

*Vicit Agnus Noster* (Grand Rapids: Eerdmans, 1994); Walter Wink, *The Powers that Be: Theology for a New Millennium* (New York: Doubleday, 1998).
21 If not self-explanatory, then it is the experience of encountering a theological idea or practice that profoundly challenges one's existing theological tradition.
22 Dave Tomlinson, *The Post-Evangelical* (London: Triangle, 1995).
23 E.g., J. Richard Middleton and Brian J. Walsh, *Truth Is Stranger Than It Used To Be: Biblical Faith in a Postmodern Age*, Gospel and Culture (London: SPCK, 1995).
24 Some of the weaknesses of Tomlinson's position were spelled out in Graham Cray, *The Post-Evangelical Debate* (London: Triangle, 1997). My own engagement later on was particularly through the 'Deep Church' series, so Andrew P. Rogers, "Reading Scripture in Congregations: Towards an Ordinary Hermeneutics," in *Remembering our Future: Explorations in Deep Church*, eds. Luke Bretherton and Andrew Walker (Milton Keynes: Paternoster, 2007).
25 Fulcrum offers an Anglican sense of this term (www.fulcrum-anglican.org.uk/).
26 Particularly Margaret S. Archer, Andrew Collier, and Douglas V. Porpora, eds., *Transcendence, Critical Realism and God* (London: Routledge, 2004). Andy Wright was our critical realism mentor, see Andrew Wright, *Christianity and Critical Realism: Ambiguity, Truth and Theological Literacy* (London: Routledge, 2014).
27 John Swinton and Harriet Mowat, *Practical Theology and Qualitative Research* (London: SCM Press, 2006), Ch. 3.
28 In my case, combined with a more explicit critical realism.
29 Christian Scharen, ed. *Explorations in Ecclesiology and Ethnography* (Grand Rapids: Eerdmans, 2012); Pete Ward, ed. *Perspectives on Ecclesiology and Ethnography* (Grand Rapids: Eerdmans, 2012). See also Andrew P. Rogers, "Ordinary Biblical Hermeneutics and the Transformation of Congregational Horizons within English Evangelicalism: A Theological Ethnographic Study" (PhD Diss., King's College, London, 2009), §3.2; *Congregational*, 27f.
30 Helen Cameron, "Reflections on the Challenges of Using the Pastoral Cycle in a Faith-Based Organisation," *British and Irish Association of Practical Theology Conference*, 11th July (2012).
31 Cherryl Hunt, "Promoting Biblical Engagement Among Ordinary Christians in English Churches: Reflections on the Pathfinder Project," (PhD Diss., University of Exeter, 2016), https://ore.exeter.ac.uk/repository/handle/10871/23365.
32 Five-year strategy for BIAPT (2017–2022).
33 See www.biapt.org/events/theological-reflection-2006/
34 Elaine Graham, Heather Walton, and Frances Ward, *Theological Reflection: Methods* (London: SCM, 2005).
35 Graham, Walton, and Ward, *Methods*, Ch. 3.
36 Cf. Helen Collins, *Reordering Theological Reflection: Starting with Scripture* (London: SCM, 2020), 23f.
37 Graham, Walton, and Ward, *Methods*, 7.
38 Richard R. Osmer has similarly argued for greater theological diversity in practical theology in the US, in "Toward a New Story of Practical Theology," *International Journal of Practical Theology* 16, no. 1 (2012): 68; cf. Andrew Root, *Christopraxis: A Practical Theology of the Cross* (Minneapolis: Fortress Press, 2014), 10–11. James Packer argued that evangelicals should maintain constant dialogue with non-evangelical theology, cited in Graham McFarlane, *A Model for Evangelical Theology: Integrating Scripture, Tradition, Reason, Experience, and Community* (Grand Rapids: Baker Books, 2020), 65.
39 From an EPC perspective, at least. For example, a committee member has been appointed to encourage Pentecostals to participate in BIAPT. Lyall and Ballard identify a vision for BIAPT from its origins as corporate, adventurous, variegated, and diffuse in "Soil," 15.

40 Co-convened with Zoë Bennett and then Kevin Ellis and Helen Cameron. Conversation partners in this group have been the group itself, but some have helped as catalysts for reflection. Work informed by this group includes Zoë Bennett, *Using the Bible in Practical Theology: Historical and Contemporary Perspectives*, (Farnham: Ashgate, 2013); Richard S. Briggs, "Biblical Hermeneutics and Practical Theology: Method and Truth in Context," *Anglican Theological Review* 97, no. 2 (2015): 201–217; Richard S. Briggs and Zoë Bennett, "Review Article—Using the Bible in Practical Theology: Historical and Contemporary Perspectives," *Theology and Ministry* 3, no. 1–9 (2014), www.dur.ac.uk/resources/theologyandministry/TheologyandMinistry3_7.pdf; Rogers, *Congregational*; Margaret Whipp, "Lucky Lections: On Using the Bible in Practical Theology," *Practical Theology* 5, no. 3 (2012): 341–344.
41 On this point, see also Rooms and Bennett, *Progress*, 154.
42 Roehampton University, "Foundation Degree of Arts Ministerial Theology," (2020), https://ursecure.roehampton.ac.uk/programmedetails/ug20202021/335/
43 N=406, over 2007–2016.
44 N=407, over 2007–2016.
45 N=407, over 2007–2016. The remainder travelled from across Greater London. 'Beyond' in this case includes Coventry, Oxford, Bristol, Nottingham, Swindon, Gloucester, and Peterborough (given in decreasing frequency order).
46 R. David Muir, "Theological Education and Training Among British Pentecostals and Charismatics," in *Pentecostals and Charismatics in Britain: An Anthology*, ed. Joe Aldred (London: SCM Press, 2019), 169.
47 Andrew P. Rogers, "How are Black Majority Churches Growing in the UK? A London Borough Case Study," *Religion and Global Society Blog* (2016), https://blogs.lse.ac.uk/religionglobalsociety/2016/12/how-are-black-majority-churches-growing-in-the-uk-a-london-borough-case-study/#; "Walking Down the Old Kent Road: New Black Majority Churches in the London Borough of Southwark," in *The Desecularisation of the City: London's Churches, 1980 to the Present*, eds. David Goodhew and Anthony-Paul Cooper (London: Routledge, 2018).
48 Richard Burgess, "Education for Conceptual Change: BME Students' Experiences of Learning Theological Reflection," *Developments in Academic Practice (DiAP online)* University of Roehampton (2014): 1–18; Mark Garner, Richard Burgess, and Daniel Eshun, "Submitting convictions to critical enquiry: a challenge for higher education," *Occasional Papers on Faith in Higher Education* 1 (2015), https://cuac.anglicancommunion.org/; John R. L. Moxon, "Biblical Studies—Troublesome or Catastrophic? Strategies in Ministerial Formation," *Practical Theology* 13, no. 4 (2020): 355–371.
49 cf. Moxon, "Biblical," 9f.
50 Laurie Green, *Let's Do Theology* (London: Continuum, 2001); Judith Thompson, Stephen Pattison, and Ross Thompson, *Theological Reflection (SCM Studyguide)* (London: SCM, 2008).
51 61% of students from 2009–2016 were over the age of 40, N=407.
52 Stephen Pattison, "Some Straw for the Bricks: A Basic Introduction to Theological Reflection," *Contact* 99, no. 1 (1989): 2–9. See www.biapt.org/events/the-practical-theologian-as-reflective-practitioner-2018/. See also the commentary on the development of this theme in Gary O'Neill and Liz Shercliff, eds., *Straw for the Bricks: Theological Reflection in Practice* (London: SCM Press, 2018), 18f.
53 Garner, Burgess, and Eshun, "Submitting."
54 Walton, "Bible."
55 A phrase from my colleague, Clare Watkins.
56 E.g., Swinton and Mowat, *Practical Theology*, 6; 25.
57 Burgess, "Education," 8. Quote used by kind permission.
58 Burgess, "Education," 10.
59 Burgess, "Education," 9.

60 Hermeneutical practices that are familiar from my research with evangelical congregations in Rogers, *Congregational*, Ch. 4.
61 Moxon, "Biblical."
62 As many have noted, this standard division of the theological curriculum is not ideal, and so another hope of mine is to develop a more integrated approach. See Graham, Walton, and Ward, *Methods*, 7–8.
63 This raises the question of how far critical skills learned in biblical studies modules extend into theological reflection modules. Put another way, what is an appropriate way of engaging Scripture in practical theology?
64 Garner, Burgess, and Eshun, "Submitting," 69f.
65 An initiative by my colleague, Ash Cocksworth.
66 The phrase 'critical piety' was inspired by my colleague's reflections on the same students, so Moxon, "Biblical."
67 Cartledge has a useful discussion on the significance of testimony as a mode of theology in *Testimony in the Spirit: Rescripting Ordinary Pentecostal Theology* (Aldershot: Ashgate, 2010), 16f.
68 E.g., Mark J. Cartledge, *The Mediation of the Spirit: Interventions in Practical Theology* (Grand Rapids: Eerdmans, 2015); Collins, *Reordering*; Joshua Jones, "Practical Theology and the Holy Spirit," *Theology and Ministry* 6 (2020): 36–61.
69 McFarlane, albeit in his own terms, argues that 'the focus of an evangelical theology is on practical theology,' in *Model*, 61.
70 Root, "Evangelical," 93; cf. McFarlane, *Model*, xi.
71 As in other disciplines. E.g., Pascal programming language in Computer Science.
72 E.g., Collins, *Reordering*.
73 E.g., Collins, *Reordering*; Root, *Christopraxis*; Ward, *Introducing*.
74 Rooms and Bennett, *Progress*, 27.

# 7 Developing reflective practitioners
## Engaging evangelical ordinands in theological reflection

*Liz Hoare*

### Introduction: setting the scene

In one sense evangelical ordinands[1] are no different from anyone else when it comes to encountering theological reflection for the first time. Like all theological students, some are naturally reflective and need little help to do it well, while others resist with varying degrees of statements like 'I'm not reflective' or 'why don't we just do theology?' For evangelicals, however, there is a further set of issues that hinders taking theological reflection seriously and it is these that I wish to focus on here, in the light of twelve years of experience of teaching in an Anglican theological college.

It might be expected that the faith journey of evangelical ordinands immerses them in the practices of theological reflection. Evangelicals believe in working out the relevance of what they believe in their heads with life in the world. They are urged to read, mark, and learn their Bible: to study it in order to live transformed lives. The counter-cultural stance they are expected to inhabit requires adopting a new and different worldview, where God is at the centre and the Christian framework by which the world is understood provides the lens through which it is viewed. Evangelicals are discouraged from learning for learning's sake. They come to college expecting that doctrine will have pastoral implications for example.[2] That 'so what?' question is always hovering at the boundaries of study. They are accustomed to sermons that are applied. A typical sermon is full of illustrations that are meant to earth the Bible passage in real life. Key figures like the late John Stott encouraged evangelicals to 'think Christianly' about the issues that were being discussed and his book *Issues Facing Christians Today* remains mandatory reading for anyone who identifies as an evangelical training for leadership.[3]

The high regard for the Bible as supreme authority in all things pertaining to salvation is combined with high view of the local church and practical Christian ministry. There is a paradox here because, while, as we have just seen, the emphasis in preaching in such churches is on the practical outworking of being a Christian on a daily basis, homiletics, pastoral care, and Christian discipleship are primarily guided by reflection on the word of God, rather than by a systematic study of these practices in themselves.

DOI: 10.4324/9781003094975-10

## Particular issues for evangelicals

Given this background one might assume theological reflection would come naturally and there would be enthusiasm for its inclusion in the curriculum at theological college. This has not been the case in my experience, though the landscape today looks much more encouraging than when I first began teaching in this field twelve years ago. As an instinctive reflector myself, I naïvely assumed others would 'get it' when I explained the mechanics of the reflective process. The reality was very different and it was an uphill struggle for a number of years. In particular, I struggled to find textbooks that I could confidently recommend to students committed to the standpoint that the Scriptures contain all things necessary for salvation and constitutes the supreme authority for anyone seeking to understand God, human nature, and the world. It is a considerable jump for such students to move from what the Bible says, to reading textbooks on theological reflection that are Bible-lite to say the least. The textbooks I used early on were not strong on offering biblical foundations on which to build the structures for learning to become reflective practitioners. It was no surprise to discover Paul Ballard's article 'The Bible in Theological Reflection: Indications from the History of Scripture', and to read that little attention had been given to the place and function of the Bible in the process of theological reflection.[4]

Suspicion arises further still among evangelicals when we turn to the origins of theological reflection. In the early days, there was a more widespread suspicion around many aspects of pastoral care and, for some, the Bible was all that was needed.[5] The linear model was the default model for applying the Bible to every pastoral situation. Resistance was frequently expressed when secular models of counselling and what it means to be human were appealed to as authoritative. With Marxism and Liberation Theology both influencing the origins and development of methods of theological reflection, suspicions are aroused because neither of these is perceived as giving Scripture the kind of final authority that evangelicals regard as a *sine qua non*. A good deal of explanation and reassurance was required in order to gain traction for drawing on secular resources.

This particular area of resistance was nothing, however, compared with the perceived problem of beginning with experience. Almost all the textbooks do this often without comment and it arouses hostility among conservative evangelicals especially. While ordinands from this section of the church accept that the Church of England does her theology by means of Scripture, reason and tradition, Scripture unquestionably has first place. The methodology is a pyramid, not a three-legged stool. As for experience itself, it is regarded as a poor measure of where truth lies. As someone who was taught in Sunday School that life was a bit like a goods train with God in the driving seat and feelings tagging along in the guard's van at the back, I have some sympathy with the struggle involved in getting over this.[6]

The fourth big obstacle encountered was the assumption among students that theological reflection was designed to change students' minds about something they held as important and were deeply and personally invested in. This 'something' was usually something with doctrinal implications and rooted in the Bible. Introducing the pastoral cycle, the most basic theological tool, was therefore beset with bear-traps. Not only does it begin with 'experience' it goes on to analyse, reflect, and finally lead to new action, that probably involves change. Why would a Bible-believing Christian change? This was a serious position that prevented students hearing what theological reflection was inviting them to do.

It seemed that much of the hostility boiled down to the perception that an evangelical perspective was not taken seriously in the practice of theological reflection. Over the years, in spite of the obstacles noted, however, I have detected a significant decrease in resistance to the principles behind theological reflection, so last academic year I decided to put this to the test.

## Research project

Having set up the project according to the university protocols, I explained at the beginning of the module that I wanted to do a small piece of qualitative research to provide some material with which to reflect on my experience of teaching theological reflection. I asked for volunteers to take part in completing an anonymous questionnaire. I explained that we would have four lectures on theological reflection examining what it is, how it is done, the practice of keeping a journal as a reflective aid, and how to put together a ministry portfolio. I asked students to write down their own definition of theological reflection at the beginning of the four lectures and at the end gave them the questionnaire to fill in.

## The questionnaire

1   Please offer your own definition of theological reflection.
2   What is the most important thing you have learned from the course?
3   In what ways do you see yourself using this tool in your future ministry?
4   What questions, if any, do you still have about the practice of theological reflection?
5   What do you consider to be the most important component of theological reflection?
6   Do you consider yourself to be a naturally reflective person?
7   What is your course of study at Wycliffe Hall?

## Analysis of questionnaires

There were 12 respondents: 7 ordinands and 5 independent students out of a class of 35. All participants were in their first year of study. Some of the ordinands in the class were beginning theology degrees through Oxford University, others embarking on either a diploma or degree through Durham University.[7]

The questionnaire was anonymous although students were asked to identify as ordinand or independent student.

Analysing the responses to the questionnaire brought some unexpected results which have led to the content of much of the rest of this chapter. All respondents appear to have understood the purpose of theological reflection and grasped something of its value for them personally and for the church as a whole. Two common phrases about the definition of theological reflection were 'seeing the world through God's eyes', and 'bringing Scripture to bear on a situation'. Another repeated phrase throughout was 'hearing what God says'. Is this because I said that a lot, or because there was a strong charismatic element in the make-up of the class that year? Many responses referred to a 'lens' which was a way of referring to the process I had employed in class. Responses were clearly understanding that an integrated approach was required. Some focused more on theological reflection as a tool or framework, while others stressed prayer and Scripture, but none confined their answers to only one or the other.

In responding to Question 2, the importance of giving the process time was stressed. Given that this is often the main reason why ministers do not practise theological reflection, this was encouraging. If theological reflection is to become a habit along with Bible study and prayer, it all takes time. As a notoriously activist tradition, evangelicalism has tended to emphasise the urgency of the mission, rather than patient waiting on God to reveal his secret purposes.[8]

Turning to Question 3, many said they would be keeping a journal as a valuable means of reflecting regularly. Some focused more on its use in times of crisis to help think through difficulties. Many ordinands begin to keep a journal during the discernment process and there is plenty of material in the evangelical tradition to encourage this as a spiritual discipline. Linking the practice of writing and personal spiritual growth is not difficult in the evangelical world and provides a simple but effective link between the two. This leads naturally to Question 4. The main issue seemed to be how to make theological reflection a habit. This set me thinking about ways to help to foster spiritual disciplines while at college that may enable character formation to take place. Helping students make the link between theological reflection and formation is something that could be emphasised more clearly. This leads to the thinking behind Question 5 and responses to it. One respondent saw the most important part of theological reflection as being the 'opportunity' to change. This is remarkable given the suspicion previously experienced when teaching the pastoral cycle. The most challenging phase of the cycle is 'Action', where it is commonly assumed that the whole aim of theological reflection is to make committed evangelicals give up their principles. Helping students see that change is integral to growth is thus essential if they are to let go of positions held on to for security and identity. Change does not necessarily mean abandoning cherished beliefs or habits of prayer and devotion that have sustained a person over time. Remembering that God is always bigger than our experience of him is one of the most exciting aspects of making theological reflection a life-long habit that should be obvious to the evangelical mind. The key, I think, is to focus on this in such a way as to open up new possibilities that may emerge as a result of bringing all the tools of theological reflection to bear on a situation. The Bible featured most often as the foremost component, which is to be expected in this environment, but all stages of the pastoral cycle were highlighted by one or other respondent. One, for example, saw taking time to engage with their own feelings as the most important aspect of theological reflection.

Question 6 delivered some surprises, though of course it invites a subjective answer which others may not agree with. Of the twelve, eight regard themselves as naturally reflective (one overly so). Two saw themselves as not, one 'moderately' so and one answered, 'when I want to be.' The two Nos were both ordinands. The moderately reflective person said they were challenged most with the idea of keeping a journal. The two Nos still thought they would use theological reflection in their future ministries. Finally, the 'when I want to be' respondent saw theological reflection as 'super-helpful' in their personal spiritual journey.

Overall, the responses to the questionnaire supported my hunch that theological reflection was no longer the suspect phenomenon it was once perceived to be. Clearly something has changed over time and for the sake of good pedagogy it seems important to tease out some of the possible reasons. One very obvious observation could be that I have got better at teaching this topic! I am in no doubt that I have been able to build on experience and a certain determination to find a way through the impasse of old. What follows is my attempt to document this progress.

## My journey

I received no training in how to do theological reflection at theological college in the late 1980s. Indeed, the phrase was never mentioned. I owe a lot to one particular tutor, whose job was split between teaching and a parish ministry, who helped us to make the connections between academic theology and pastoral care. So how did I learn to understand and practise theological reflection? I suppose I learned it backwards. I have journaled since I was 12 and thus developed reflexivity without realising it. I grew up in an evangelical free church that taught the Bible with no bits un-explored or left out. I read and studied the Bible for myself and used guides that helped me to apply it to daily life. Later on, I had a friend who was always asking 'So what?' when presented with any profound theological concept. The real key for me, however, was spiritual direction, which I have been receiving since my early twenties and giving for almost as long. When I began to read textbooks on theological reflection my first response was how like spiritual direction it seemed. Tutors are often taken on to teach a specific subject at theological college and soon find themselves with responsibility for a number of other courses they didn't originally sign up for. Thus, I found myself with some classes on theological reflection.

## Changes in the student body

Over the course of that time I have noticed a number of trends including the following:

First, in order to do theological reflection well, students need to know their way around the Bible. Ironically, it is often those ordinands who have been thoroughly grounded in the Bible who find most difficulty with theological reflection. It is sometimes claimed that there is less emphasis on Bible teaching in evangelical churches today than previously, so one would expect students to arrive at theological college with a weaker knowledge of the Bible than before. Many of our ordinands have come to faith as young adults from little or no Christian background, but this is not something new.[9] The much-reduced level of biblical literacy in the wider culture, however, is new. A recent convert to Christian faith would therefore be starting further back than one from a previous generation. My hunch from listening to students, is that they are eager to catch up with knowledge and use of the Bible and to learn from peers who are more familiar with handling it. Programmes for reading the Bible in a year, for example, are popular among ordinands, and exposure to the daily lectionary in college chapel, along with homiletics teaching encourages rigorous engagement. It would be very interesting to do some further research into the way that familiarity with Scripture, for example, its imagery, over-arching themes, the way the Old Testament is treated by the New, impacts the practice of theological reflection.[10]

Second, when I began to teach theological reflection some of the classes were composed almost entirely of young white men. While there were students with a strongly developed reflexivity present, they were not often willing to reveal this in such a dominant British white male culture whose evangelicalism was of a more conservative flavour. The growing number of women in classes has been one of the most important factors in opening up conversation around faith and life in small groups and during Q&A slots in class. While I do not wish to collude with the stereotyping of women as being more naturally reflective than men, it has been the case in my experience that female students are quick to draw on their personal life stories to share with their peers in ways that provide opportunities to demonstrate how theological reflection works. Increased numbers of students from the charismatic tradition background has also helped to foreground experience alongside Scripture and the impact of this has been deeply significant. Classes have also grown more mixed in age and background. The most recent class I taught, for example, included a number of older students who were rooted in the workplace and could bring that experience to theological reflection. The growing number of students from overseas in the classroom has also led to the sharing of a greater range of life experience.

Third, when I first started teaching theological reflection, classes were offered as a stand-alone topic in an overcrowded timetable. A more integrated approach to learning such as linking placements to forms of assessment, emphasising the relationship between subjects taught across the curriculum, including more practical subjects like preaching along with doctrine with all having a place at the table is a given. Theological reflection is taught as part of a module undertaken by all students which has a number of components, theological reflection being just one. While everyone in the class is in their first year, we ask all our ordinands to attend whatever pathway they are on. One of the positive outcomes of this module has been the shaping of a kind of 'Theology 101' for all students.

It is acknowledged that different pathways involve different approaches to learning. While Common Awards[11] assumes the integration of theology and practice from the start, for example, a first-year student studying for the Oxford degree in Theology and Religious Studies will be writing three academic theology essays every fortnight with little or no attention being drawn to their ministerial relevance at this stage. They may, therefore, need to make more effort to engage with the layers of how theological reflection works and need more encouragement to draw out personal and pastoral implications. My experience of teaching theological method to postgraduates often with ministerial experience bears this out.[12]

## Changing perceptions

A key development in the approach to teaching theological reflection in my context came in the wake of an article co-written by myself and a colleague entitled 'Evangelicals and Contextual Theology: Lessons from Missiology for Theological Reflection'.[13] We had both noticed the lack of regard for pastoral and practical theology among some evangelicals, especially from the more conservative end of the spectrum. These were seen as carrying less weight academically and could possibly be a threat to the stress on personal salvation as opposed to salvation by works. We also drew attention to the paradox that the same evangelicals who have been in the forefront of mission and evangelism overseas have often taken the lead in reflecting on the need for, and the nature of, contextualisation in this field. Could it be the case that evangelical missiological reflection on contextual theology might help develop models and methods for theological reflection that would be faithful to the biblical witness and attractive to evangelical students in the UK? We hoped that a positive conclusion would enable students to engage with questions of theological reflection closer to home.

We took five of Stephen B. Bevans six models of contextual theology as our starting point.[14] The aim was to show that the main models currently used in the UK reflect Bevans' anthropological, praxis, and synthetic models and to highlight some of their shortcomings in light of an evangelical understanding of the principle tenets of historic orthodox Christian faith.[15] Given that evangelical missiologists have been at the forefront of developing and applying these models, we went on to ask what contextual theology and theological reflection would look like in line with Bevans' translation and countercultural models. Acknowledging that contemporary practitioners need a range of models for contextualisation and theological reflection for the full range of tasks that Christian presence, witness, and discipleship require in our multicultural world, we concluded that this is possible without compromising evangelical respect for the supreme authority of the Christian Scriptures as the revelation of the gospel of salvation in Christ. Using case studies, we mapped contextual and theological reflection onto Bevans' models to test this out.

The article pointed out that all five models of contextual theology examined can contribute to culturally incarnating the gospel in ways that are both faithful and relevant. The translation model is crucial in initial cross-cultural evangelism; the counter-cultural model for the nurturing of disciples; the praxis model for working out the social implications and impact of the gospel in a certain context; the anthropological model will help us attend to how God has been present and at work in a given context before missionaries and evangelists arrived and how God is working in concrete Christian communities; the synthetic model will help set up a critical and creative dialogue between Christ and context.

## Fresh approaches

With the benefit of experience and time for reflection I learned to challenge misconceptions around theological reflection in ways that sought to engage and make sense. The following were the main actions taken to counteract misconceptions and assumptions.

First, textbooks. This is an industry in itself. Students need help to navigate the plethora of names in the field, competing methodologies, and critical studies. For evangelical students most textbooks carry a health warning which needs unpacking. Being able to refer students to the article written with my colleague as described above, has been helpful in this respect helping to build confidence among students in order to navigate the literature in the field. For the most part, I have created my own exercises, worked examples, and illustrations to help students find their way in. The type of straw needed to make bricks in the evangelical world must be biblical in shape and ethos if it is to be productive and there is no reason why this should not be the case. Examples from contexts that are familiar to students and arising out of their personal experience encourages the process of learning to see their story as part of God's overarching story set out in the Bible.[16]

The next challenge was to find metaphors for theological reflection that resonated. I explain theological reflection as a skill, a process, a perspective, and a conversation. For years I referred to the advanced driving test.[17] When someone signs up for this, everything they have ever learned has to be dismantled, described, and analysed in the presence of the instructor. In all the years I used this illustration, there have been three students who had experienced the test. (I have never taken it myself either!) I now use an illustration much dearer to my heart: that of baking a cake with a seven-year-old, which I have done. I learned to bake as a child from my mother with a cake-mix, graduating to sophisticated creations that would have qualified me to apply for The Great British Bake-off. I enjoyed going right back to basics to encourage my seven-year-old friend to learn how to bake for herself, to understand her ingredients, and what to do with them to produce a great cake. Using this illustration involves the whole of me with a strong dose of real experience and enthusiasm. I can see the value of it from my own perspective. I am certain that students pick up on this and start to make their own connections.

I tackled the issue of changing minds in three ways. First, beginning with the Bible. For some students this is the only way to gain a hearing. I once taught a class in Christian spirituality on the theme of forgiveness and half-way through one student said she had lost me because I started with a set of scenarios rather than with the Bible. I therefore introduced the relationship between experience and the Bible by inviting students to think about the Apostle Paul and what he wrote in his letters. So much of his experience of Christ lies behind his great statements of faith. How, for example, could he say, 'for I know the one in whom I have put my trust, and I am sure that he is able to guard until that day what I have entrusted to him' (2 Tim 1:12), unless he had first experienced it in his own life? Looking at what might occur as a result of reflecting theologically also helped to avoid the zero-sum game of whether or not to start with the Bible or experience. The two are inextricably inter-linked.

Second, I sought out concrete examples that the ordinands in front of me could relate to as moments when they might have engaged in what could be regarded as theological reflection that led to some kind of change in outlook or behaviour. That Bible study with undergraduate students, for example. Why did it go so badly? What led to a different approach the next time? Or take the Christian holiday you attended as part of a team of leaders. When you met together afterwards for the debrief, what did you learn about the way it went, how others perceived it, what you achieved and what changes you intend to make for next year so it goes just as well if not better that this?

Third, I offered the reassurance that 'change' is a simplistic way of understanding the outcome of theological reflection. Sometimes no change occurs because we have been affirmed in our beliefs and/or practice. But something has happened nonetheless, because through theological reflection we have recognised a gospel truth and seen its expression in our lives. This may be especially helpful when faced with criticism in the future over a particular course of action or when periods of self-doubt set in. 'Growth' may therefore be a better way of understanding how theological reflection contributes to faith and practice. This resonates with the emphasis on discipleship and developing a Christ-like character that is so central to evangelical spirituality.

The concept and practice of reflection has gained more traction in the institution as a whole over the years. 'Reflective worship' has a place in the life of the college community. 'Being reflective' is no longer seen as something fluffy that belongs to a sort of feminised spirituality best left to Christians of a liberal persuasion. There is greater acknowledgement of the importance of deepening self-awareness and that it is not narcissistic to do so. Rather, it is regarded as essential to avoiding doing a great deal of damage in pastoral ministry. Students are exhorted to work at ways to bridge the gap between intentions, actions, and impact. The responses to a number of the questions put to students in the questionnaire suggest that this whole approach has become embedded in the culture of the college.

There is no doubt that integrating the curriculum much more has gone a long way to raising expectations. I have learned to keep on reminding students of other parts of the curriculum that will help them with material for analysis and reflection. It might be a prayer practice from the spirituality course, a doctrine they have been unpacking, something they have been wrestling with in an Old Testament essay or issues in Christian ethics. Approaches to homiletics is especially useful for helping evangelicals to think about the relationship of the Bible to life. Joined up thinking ensures a multidimensional approach to the pastoral cycle and indeed all reflective processes.

Challenging students to notice their positions on a range of topics is enlightening for many. Attitudes and beliefs that go with the territory of evangelicals are as open to prejudice and bad hermeneutics as elsewhere within the church and need challenging. This is another area where students may feel threatened, especially if they have never been asked to question their positions on emotive issues such as the beginning and end of life, race, gender, or money. Our positions are usually deep-rooted and instinctive, and it takes courage to confront them and be open to change.[18] Over and over again we are reminded that making theological reflection a habit requires practice. I have altered the balance between me talking and students listening during class time. There is now more time allotted to partnered conversation and group exercises, often using case studies that students can relate to that offer ways in to beginning the habit. Using testimony, a strong tradition among evangelicals, has contributed to helping students listen to each other as well as to the lecturer and is a reminder that God is in the process.

Getting away from teaching theological reflection as a 'thing' and emphasising it as a tool or a skill that involves my perspective, along with those of other conversation partners, helps students to value it as a way to foster discipleship in the world. It encourages us to pay attention to context as the arena in which we live out our faith and also how we live it out in terms of practices and attitudes. Furthermore, it constantly reminds us of God who is the focus and goal of all our living and drives us back to the Bible to ponder it again with fresh perspective.[19] Making the link between theological reflection and discipleship has been one of the most important keys to helping evangelical ordinands see its value. Discipleship is a given. We may emphasise conversion in an evangelical context[20] but most evangelical church leaders in the UK avoid the travesty of leading people to faith and then failing to help them to keep going. The Christian life is understood as dynamic; it is faith that is going somewhere and thus change is not only to be expected but welcomed. To grow is to change. As one respondent commented 'This will be super-helpful in my personal spiritual journey as I engage with ministry.'

Rather than detailed instructions on prayer or Bible study or lifestyle, Roger Walton talks about rhythms of life which inculcate attitudes or orientations. He lists these as courageous openness, careful accountability, conscientious immersion in the Tradition, constant prayerfulness, and faithful reflection.[21] Bringing values into the discussions around theological reflection helps students to take the long view and see where the process could make a real contribution to the development of a more reflective church. There is no doubt that the question of how to engage others was an important one to those responding to the questionnaire.

### Insights from spiritual direction

Elsewhere in the curriculum, students are introduced to some of the main traditions of prayer available to Christians including Celtic, Benedictine, Franciscan, and Ignatian. Greater openness among evangelicals to a wider variety of ways of reading the Scriptures has led to more reflective and less cerebral approaches to God's word. Discovering the riches of the church's treasury of prayer has opened up new vistas of faith and life for many. Ignatian spirituality, in particular, encourages habits of reflection in times of prayer and because it is Bible-based, evangelicals are usually more open to exploring it.[22] It requires a reflective approach and inculcates the habit of noticing what is happening in prayer as well as connecting experience with Bible text and tradition. Students are introduced to the *examen* which takes the happenings of the day, both ordinary and extraordinary, to ask 'Where was God?' This also helps develop habits of reflecting on God's action in our daily lives. Linking the *examen* with journaling fosters paying attention to life in the light of God and God's word. Such practices encourage deep immersion in Scripture that impacts our emotions, feelings, assumptions, and attitudes, discouraging engagement with God's word purely on a cerebral level. They deepen the understanding of how the Holy Spirit works with the word to deepen, enliven, and challenge us to grow.

Spiritual direction teaches us to pay attention and to make connections. The models described in the theological reflection textbooks that resonated most with me were 'theology by heart' and the habitus models.[23] Theology by heart draws deeply on human experience that is felt as well as understood and this reminds me of the process in spiritual direction. Ordinands are encouraged to have a spiritual director while they are at college. Some begin the practice during the discernment process while others want to start direction for the first time. The number of students requesting a spiritual director has grown exponentially in the last decade. There is no doubt in my mind that students who see a spiritual director regularly are helped to grow in reflexivity. Since many arrive at college from busy, programme-heavy churches, it seems ever more important that we help these future leaders learn to press pause and pull back from the action-reaction dynamic that besets so much of contemporary church life. Realising that reflection draws on the very things they know to sustain them: prayer, Scripture, thoughtful analysis, and practice, and that doing so will lead to wiser and more-informed action in the future is vital for long term health in ministry and also the spiritual health of the churches they will lead.

Roger Walton has two helpful insights in his final section on practice in *The Reflective Disciple*, both from Scripture. He advocates that reflective disciples practise attentiveness pointing to Luke 2:19 where it is stated that Mary 'kept all these things and pondered them in her heart.' Luke uses the word *suneterei* which can mean held, protected, or treasured. Walton also urges reflective disciples to practise making connections. In Luke 2:19 the word translated 'pondered' is made up of two words: *sum-ballo*, one meaning 'together' and the other 'to put or place or throw'.[24] It seems that Mary actively explored the way things came together, how events related to each other. Relating the Bible to life does this as all evangelicals know from the beginning of their Christian lives. This process works both ways. In response to Question 2 'What is the most important thing you have learned from the course?', almost all highlighted the reflective process in relation to slowing down and 'seeing what God is doing'. This was described by one as 'prayer being central to the process' while another wrote, 'It is best to give God time to speak to my heart.' One commented that without reflection 'one misses hearing God's voice and recognising his hand at work'. Slowing down was mentioned more than once, taking time by another and a third wrote, 'Asking the question 'Where was God?' is the vital key. The same question is posed time after time by spiritual directors when the person before them has told their story.

**Summary**

It seems to me that ministry demands ongoing reflexivity. The part that the self plays in theological reflection is crucial to recognise in order to break free from cultural stereotypes, expectations of others and ourselves and all the other image-making processes we practise every day in our subconscious lives. The personal journey of the teacher is therefore a key priority in thinking pedagogically about theological reflection. This has occurred alongside other pedagogical considerations discussed here: textbooks; metaphors; biblical examples; examples from students' experience; growth over change; exercises, testimonies, and discussion; and making connections with discipleship and spirituality.

A further key consideration is the context both immediate—'who is in the classroom?'—and more widely in the institution. Responding to the changing evangelical context over the last twelve years has been important personally and pedagogically. It includes a more diverse student body which makes it easier for students to inform each other's learning. There has also been greater institutional commitment to reflection that has reinforced classroom practice. This includes a commitment to understanding contemporary missiology which has led to a clearer focus on context which in turn paves the way for theological reflection. Finally, the widespread adoption of spiritual direction by evangelical ordinands has increased their reflective capacity and their ability to see the point of theological reflection.

Overall, I have learned that to teach theological reflection in a way that enables evangelical students to be receptive involves taking seriously where they are coming from. It means making the effort to use language and concepts they can relate to. We often talk of 'wrestling' with Scripture and do so in the context of holding it in high regard. This should not be incompatible with taking the contributions of recent scholarly efforts to embrace a variety of approaches to theological reflection, so long as the expectation that God will speak remains, our task being to listen and respond.

Evangelicals have a vital contribution to bring to the theological reflection table. Their commitment to see lives changed as a result of encounter with God through word and Spirit will ensure that theological reflection remains grounded in God rather than human comment. Instead of being made to feel defensive, encouraging an approach that takes the Bible seriously along with personal insight and spiritual growth has the potential to deepen the church's engagement with this crucial practice. As Ballard and Pritchard put it: 'Theological Reflection is simply the art of making theology connect with life and ministry so that the Gospel truth comes alive.'[25] I think that those who completed the questionnaire would agree.

## Notes

1 Women and men who are training for ordained ministry in the Anglican Church.
2 Ellen Charry, *By the Renewing of Your Mind. The Pastoral Function of Christian Doctrine* (Oxford: Oxford University Press, 1997). One of Charry's aretegenic texts is Calvin's *Institutes*, a key theologian for conservative evangelicals.
3 John Stott, *Issues Facing Christians Today*, rev. ed. (London: Marshall Pickering, 1999).
4 Paul Ballard, "The Bible in Theological Reflection: Indications from the History of Scripture," *Practical Theology* 4, no. 1 (2011): 35–47.
5 Roger Hurding, *Five Pathways to Wholeness* (London: SPCK, 2013), 9.
6 I had a take-home drawing to remember the correct ordering of things and failed to see the irony of needing a guard's van to police one's feelings.
7 Durham University is the validating body for the Church of England's theological training.
8 David W. Bebbington, *Evangelicalism in Modern Britain: A History from the 1730s to the 1980s* (London: Unwin Hyman, 1989) refers to activism as one of the four key components of evangelical spirituality, the others being crucicentrism, biblicism, and conversionism.
9 The Billy Graham missions of the 1950s created a huge influx of ordinands.
10 Helen Collins, *Reordering Theological Reflection: Starting with Scripture* (London: SCM, 2020) came out as this chapter was completed.
11 The name of the Church of England's training scheme validated by Durham University.
12 For a Master of Arts in Applied Theology.
13 B. van den Toren and E. Hoare, "Evangelicals and Contextual Theology: Lessons from Missiology for Theological Reflection," *Practical Theology* 8, no. 2 (2015): 77–98.
14 Stephen B. Bevans, *Models of Contextual Theology*, rev. ed. (Maryknoll: Orbis, 2014).
15 Stephen Pattison, "Some Straw for the Bricks: A Basic Introduction to Theological Reflection," in *The Blackwell Reader in Pastoral and Practical Theology*, eds. James Woodward and Stephen Pattison (Oxford: Blackwell, 2000). Key textbooks used in

theological colleges at this point included Laurie Green, *Let's Do Theology: A Pastoral Cycles Resource Book* (London: Continuum, 1990); James Woodward and Stephen Pattison, eds., *The Blackwell Reader in Pastoral and Practical Theology* (Oxford: Blackwell, 2000); Paul Ballard and John Pritchard, *Practical Theology in Action: Christian Thinking in Service of Church and Society* (London: SPCK, 1996); Judith Thompson, *The SCM Study Guide to Theological Reflection* (London: SCM, 2000); Elaine Graham, Heather Walton, and Frances Ward, *Theological Reflection: Methods* (London: SCM, 2005).
16 Cf. N. T. Wright, *Scripture and the Authority of God* (London: SPCK, 2005).
17 A metaphor I owe to my friend and former colleague the Revd Judy Hirst.
18 Robert L. Kinast, *Let Ministry Teach. A Guide to Theological Reflection* (Collegeville: The Liturgical Press, 1996).
19 Cf. Walton, Roger, *The Reflective Disciple* (London: Epworth, 2009).
20 Bebbington, *Evangelicalism*, 5–10.
21 Walton, *The Reflective Disciple*, chs. 4 and 5.
22 Cf. Anne Netherwood, *The Voice of this Calling: An Evangelical Encounters the Ignatian Exercises* (London: SPCK, 1990).
23 Described respectively in Graham, Walton, and Ward, *Theological Reflection*; and Ballard and Pritchard, *Practical Theology*.
24 Walton, *The Reflective Disciple*, 137–138.
25 Ballard and Pritchard, *Practical Theology*, 118.

# Part III
# Engaging with practice

# 8 Educating for the common good
## Engaging relational truth in a world of ideas

*Olwyn Mark*

## Introduction

The practical outworking of the Christian gospel in pluralistic, democratic societies in the West continues to present opportunities for constructive political engagement. This active pursuit of the public good is in line with the ongoing commitment of evangelicals to both evangelism and social action. This chapter appeals, in particular, to a Transformationist tradition of cultural engagement within the church, a tradition that is committed to 'culture-making' and the reordering of society in line with the norms of creational flourishing and in response to the call to love our neighbour. Christians pursue reform in social and political life in pursuit of the *shalom* of the kingdom of God for the common good.[1] Law and policy are regarded as modes of common grace, and the operation of the Spirit in wider culture enables Christians to work collaboratively and find common cause with non-Christians in the pursuit of social justice and human flourishing. This theological engagement recognises the 'general revelation' of God in creation alongside affirming the universal truth that is clarified and confirmed in Scripture and the life and teachings of Jesus Christ.

As an exercise in public theological engagement with the wider world, this chapter gives particular attention to a recent change in policy and curriculum content within schools in England, and begins to articulate a case for a distinctly Christian approach to Relationships and Sex Education (RSE). In September 2020, it became compulsory for all secondary schools in England to teach RSE and for all primary schools to teach Relationships Education. In light of this policy context and the statutory nature of these subjects, questions arise as to how the Christian community can help to create and facilitate a constructive context for the teaching of Relationships Education and RSE, as well as be able to offer a distinctly Christian contribution to the content of what is taught.

In exploring these questions, it should be acknowledged that, even for Christians committed to forging a common life with their neighbours, it can be an attractive and tempting prospect simply to withdraw from the policy discussions or the teaching and learning that accompanies culturally sensitive and

DOI: 10.4324/9781003094975-12

contentious subjects like RSE. To do so can often be viewed as a means of protesting against the exposure of children and young people to corrupting ideas and emerging cultural norms. However, notwithstanding the importance of asserting the role and responsibility of parents as primary educators, and the need to promote and protect the welfare of all children, the danger of automatically adopting this posture within the common life of the school is that Christians move towards what Miroslav Volf calls a 'separatist programme' of being present in culture but remaining completely external to it. Except in exceptional circumstances, where a culture has gone 'seriously awry', he contends that 'Christian "difference" should always remain *internal* to a given cultural world.'[2] This is to recognise and adopt a theological understanding of the transforming role and responsibility of Christian public witness and engagement in the midst of cultural plurality. He warns that if 'Christian communities withdraw from the world and turn inward, the result will be the idleness of the Christian faith as a prophetic religion.'[3]

On account of these curriculum changes in England, the influence of the school in this subject is only increasing, and young people point to it as their preferred source of information on sex and relationships.[4] The consequence of Christian 'idleness' on this subject would thus be to neglect the opportunity to impact millions of children and young people's lives. My own interest and engagement on this issue began 15 years ago when I started working for a Christian RSE project in N. Ireland. At that time, *Love for Life* was developing RSE programmes for children and young people in primary and post-primary schools, as well as pursuing strategic influence. Over the years, the organisation has grown and expanded its work in communities across N. Ireland, and we remain committed to supporting schools across N. Ireland in their delivery of RSE. With a background in politics and public policy, my early involvement led to an academic interest in the ethical debates and policy responses to the issues surrounding RSE, and subsequent doctoral studies led to the articulation of a theological response.[5]

In light of this, and from a theological stance that pursues transformative engagement, I will make the case in this chapter for why the Christian community should seek to posture their presence and practice towards seeking the common good of all children and young people. In continuing to contend for freedom of thought and expression in education, there is an opportunity for Christians to engage in constructive apologetics in schools and communities in England. In commending this apologetic approach, Elaine Graham highlights the many areas of public life that public theology is engaged with, including those to which my subject will give particular attention—government, public health and education.[6] She notes the commitment of public theology to engage with non-theological sources, demonstrating its apologetic credentials.[7] Critical engagement with insights from philosophy and the social sciences opens up opportunities for a public dialogue that affirms the moral law and common grace evident in the creational order and allows for points of contact to be found where the truth claims of Christianity can be commended.

In mapping a way forward in this discussion, I will in the first instance give attention to the implicit and explicit moral questions that shape the moral framework of teaching and learning in RSE. I will go on to explore the possibility of confessional diversity in how the content and delivery of this subject is understood. Finally, I will argue that a Christian contribution to Relationships Education and RSE will give particular attention to the formation of relational and sexual values, attitudes, habits, and practices. This contribution begins by articulating and presenting a distinctly Christian vision of what it is to be human and what the true, flourishing life is and how to live it well. Miroslav Volf and Matthew Croasmun suggest that this is the forgotten purpose of Christian theology: 'to critically discern, articulate, and commend visions of the true life in light of the person, life and teachings of Jesus Christ.'[8] Indeed, when it comes to a contribution within the public square, Volf affirms that 'a vision of human flourishing—and the resources to realize it—is the most important contribution of the Christian faith to the common good.'[9] Questions over human identity, worth, and purpose, alongside ideas of relational and societal flourishing, will continue to lie at the heart of debates around RSE going forward. As long as there is the freedom and opportunity to do so, I contend that Christians should seek to offer their distinctive contribution both at a political level and in the classroom.

## Mutual engagement and moral judgements

During the consultation process around the new guidance for schools, Nigel Genders, the Church of England's Chief Education Officer, expressed concern about the risk of 'ghettoising faith perspectives on relationships' by only teaching faith perspectives within RSE in schools of a faith character. The implication of this would be that other schools would only cover faith perspectives in Religious Education.[10] He warned that this only 'serves to problematise religion, rather than giving children and young people the skills and knowledge they need for life in pluralistic communities with diverse belief, faith, religion and culture.'[11]

Humanists UK, on the other hand, believe that the 'religious character of a school should not deprive children of their entitlement to comprehensive, evidence-based, and age-appropriate teaching in this area.'[12] The inference in their statement is that religious-based education sells young people short and cannot provide adequate or objective education on this subject. This judgement is in line with their pursuit of a secular Britain—the creation of a neutral public space where citizens are neither privileged nor disadvantaged on grounds of their beliefs; the creation of this perceived level playing field is civilised through democracy and the rule of law, and is undergirded with a commitment to equality and human rights.[13]

This debate draws into particular focus the challenge that pluralism presents for the formation and sustaining of a common life within public schools. As James K. A. Smith suggests, the challenge of pluralism is 'how to forge common life' in the midst of what he calls '"confessional" diversity.'[14] He states:

> The challenge of pluralism is the challenge of forging a life in common in neighbourhoods, communities, territories, and states that are populated by citizens with divergent worldviews, different ultimate beliefs about the good, and different practices and rituals that they understand to constitute a life well lived.[15]

This challenge is of course intensified by the nature of the school subject in question, for there is embedded in the teaching and learning in RSE foundational truth claims about what it is to be human and the meaning and purpose of our relational lives and sexual identity. Forging a common life in the midst of diverging beliefs around human sexuality will certainly test a collective understanding of tolerance in this cultural moment.

Nevertheless, the finalised statutory guidance for schools seeks to accommodate confessional diversity, giving particular allowance to schools with a religious character to teach a distinctive faith perspective on relationships, as well as giving opportunity for all schools to teach about faith perspectives in RSE. This is alongside recognising that 'a good understanding of pupils' faith backgrounds and positive relationships between the school and local faith communities help to create a constructive context for the teaching of these subjects.'[16]

The debate around the teaching of faith perspectives within RSE is set within a wider debate around the role and place of faith schools within a 'secular' state—a political arrangement that is perceived to create a more democratic, equal and neutral public square. In his book, *Christ and the Common Life*, Luke Bretherton helpfully makes the distinction between secularism as a regime of governance which seeks to manage and regulate religious life in the pursuit of a neutral public space and secularity (or plurality) as a theological commitment and a political good that can configure a common life that is religiously plural and morally diverse. In setting out a constructive political theology, he advocates for the role of democratic politics in developing and sustaining a common life, and this, he suggests, 'entails a commitment to *mutual* rather than *neutral* ground.'[17]

In preparing the ground for mutual and constructive policy engagement in education, it is important, therefore, to challenge the assumption that secular humanism secures a neutral public space in schools. Where 'Doing God' in education is seen by secular humanists as irrational and unfair, Trevor Cooling points out that the humanist belief in the objective nature of human knowledge as the basis for public education does no more to create a so-called level playing field or neutral public space than using Christian beliefs.[18] The philosophical logic behind an aspiration to neutrality in education is rightly challenged by political and educational philosophers and theologians alike. To negate or actively seek to remove the philosophical moorings that give content and meaning to moral knowledge is to judge one position as morally tenable as the next, which itself is a philosophical position; it also dismisses the necessity of having a reason or defence for your position in the first place.[19]

In RSE, the learning deemed necessary for pupils at different ages and stages will inevitably be filtered through a 'values' or worldview lens as the following questions are explicitly or implicitly explored: What are the principles and fundamental convictions about relationships and sex that should guide a young person or an adult's behaviour? Indeed, is there a difference in how a young person or an adult's decisions around sexual behaviour are viewed and judged? What are the ideals in relationships towards which a young person should strive? What sexual choices are good, right, desirable, or worthy of respect? In public education, who decides what sexual information or sexual choices are deemed good and worthwhile? Further, what habits and practices constitute the vision of a sexually and relationally educated young person or adult?[20]

In exploring these questions, the moral judgements and the moral vision for teaching and learning will come to the fore. This would be the case if these questions were applied to Humanists UK's belief statement on RSE[21] as it would be to any other belief statement. The end or the purpose of an RSE lesson unavoidably involves reaching conclusions on the individual and social good of the curriculum subject, including what it means to live a healthy and flourishing life and how and why we should relate well, one to the other. This is inevitably determined by a particular vision of human identity, the rights and responsibilities of the moral self, and a vision of human flourishing. Consequently, in configuring and creating RSE policy direction through democratic discourse, secular humanism can no more provide a neutral or unbiased account of education than a Christian account can. In putting the subjects of Relationships Education and RSE on a statutory footing, values inevitably move beyond a matter of private belief or opinion to become animated in the public domain.

In engaging on this mutual ground, Smith cautions, however, against reducing the political simply to the space in which we exchange beliefs and ideas rather than perceiving the formative influence of public policy and political arrangements. Freedom of thought and expression, he suggests, takes place within a cultural script in which loves and desires are being shaped and formed: 'Every society *makes* a "people"; every *polis* breeds character. Laws function as "nudges" that are habit-forming.'[22] In light of this, he argues that

> we shouldn't shrink from hoping to bend our policy and public rituals in the direction of rightly ordered love, not so we can "win" or "be in control," but for the sake of our neighbours, for the flourishing of the poor and vulnerable, for the common good.[23]

This is arguably all the more important when it comes to policies that shape a social vision for education, like the guidance for Relationships Education and RSE, as within it is articulated a particular vision of a full and flourishing life that can capture hearts and imaginations, and shape habits and practices. As Smith affirms: 'If we are convinced (convicted) that in Christ and his Word we know something about *how to be human*, then shouldn't we seek to bend social practices and policy in that direction *for the good of our neighbours?*'[24]

## Teaching faith perspectives

Government guidance accommodates confessional diversity in the teaching of Relationships Education and RSE, both in regard to an awareness of the faith background of pupils but also in offering an opportunity for distinctive faith perspectives to be taught. The teaching of faith perspectives is framed within the guidance by the rule of law, in particular, the Equality Act 2010.[25] In the teaching of RSE, it is advised that

> pupils should be well informed about the full range of perspectives and, within the law, should be well equipped to make decisions for themselves about how to live their own lives, whilst respecting the right of others to make their own decisions and hold their own beliefs.[26]

In light of this, it is important to note that the outworking of the Equality Act 2010 does not have implications for the content of what is taught but for the way that it is taught.

Government advice for schools points out that by excluding the content of the curriculum from discrimination law it

> ensures that schools are free to include a full range of issues, ideas and materials in their syllabus, and to expose pupils to thoughts and ideas of all kinds, however challenging or controversial, without fear of legal challenge based on a protected characteristic.[27]

Schools at the same time 'will need to ensure that the way in which issues are taught does not subject individual pupils to discrimination.'[28] In other words, in the outworking of the Equality Act, the content is explicitly excluded but the delivery is explicitly included.

If a school, for example, does a project to mark Gay Pride Week and a Christian or Muslim pupil objects to it on religious grounds, this will not give rise to a valid complaint under the Equality Act. Valid complaints may still arise in terms of how it is delivered, but the content is not viewed as discriminatory.[29] The same logic could, therefore, be applied if a school does a project exploring a biblical understanding of human sexuality and marriage. As such, in a multi-cultural and pluralistic context, so-called 'faith sensitive and inclusive'[30] RSE will only be truly sensitive and meaningfully delivered if it can accommodate different understandings of human sexuality. This will include engaging with comprehensive and coherent faith perspectives.

Beyond the teaching of particular faith perspectives on human sexuality, I want to suggest that there are also significant opportunities within the guidance for faith perspectives to frame and bring meaning and life to the language around healthy and flourishing relationships as a means of enriching the common life and serving the common good. As the guidance states:

> The aim of RSE is to give young people the information they need to help them develop healthy, nurturing relationships of all kinds, not just intimate relationships. It should enable them to know what a healthy relationship looks like and what makes a good friend, a good colleague and a successful marriage or other type of committed relationship.[31]

To educate in relationships will require the educator to engage with moral language that defines what a 'healthy and nurturing relationship' consists of. It will also involve building knowledge and life-skills, centred on personal and relational development, which encourage the exercise of thinking skills and personal capabilities such as working with others, self-management, problem-solving, and decision making that contribute towards the goal of healthy relationships of all kinds. The language and direction of the guidance affords the Christian community a significant opportunity to play a strategic role in challenging what Dale Kuehne coined the 'iWorld'—a world shaped by the insecurity of individualism. Transformative engagement in the classroom and beyond enables Christians to present a 'new relational scaffolding' that helps to construct instead what he calls the 'rWorld,' where healthy and flourishing relationships enrich and restore a common life.[32] The Bible, Kuehne contends, is 'effectively an rWorld textbook.'[33]

A distinctly Christian contribution to RSE will, accordingly, point to a Christian vision of human flourishing that gives particular attention to our relational nature, with an appreciation of the framework of relational associations that we inhabit, including family relationships and friendships. Teaching and learning in Relationships Education and RSE will provide children and young people with this conceptual framework—along with the necessary moral resources—to understand and live out their relational lives. The vision will be both normative and transformative, giving dignity and worth to the individual while equally affirming their interconnectedness to their neighbour, their created capacity for relational intimacy and the moral responsibilities that lie therein. As an antidote to radical individualism, a constructive Christian contribution offers the opportunity to tell a better story about human relationships and to do so in pursuit of the common good and the flourishing of a common life.

## Attributes of healthy and flourishing relationships

To engage with the attributes of a healthy and flourishing relationship accords with the attention given in the guidance for Relationships Education to the cultivation of positive personal attributes and character traits as a means for children to form strong, positive, caring and respectful relationships:

> A growing ability to form strong and positive relationships with others depends on the deliberate cultivation of character traits and positive personal attributes, (sometimes referred to as "virtues") in the individual ... Alongside understanding the importance of self-respect and self-worth, pupils should develop personal attributes including honesty, integrity, courage, humility, kindness, generosity, trustworthiness and a sense of justice.[34]

The guidance for RSE further points to the need to teach young people the fundamental building blocks and character traits of healthy, nurturing, and positive relationships:

> As in primary, secondary Relationships Education can be underpinned by a wider, deliberate cultivation and practice of resilience and character in the individual. These should include character traits such as belief in achieving goals and persevering with tasks, as well as personal attributes such as honesty, integrity, courage, humility, kindness, generosity, trustworthiness and a sense of justice, underpinned by an understanding of the importance of self-respect and self-worth.[35]

When it comes to intimate and sexual relationships, the guidance suggests that pupils should know by the end of secondary school 'how to recognise the characteristics and positive aspects of healthy one-to-one intimate relationships, which include mutual respect, consent, loyalty, trust, shared interests and outlook, sex and friendship.'[36] The guidance gives explicit attention to moral attributes that are often absent from a risk-reduction approach to sex education and sexual health—an approach that is primarily concerned with reducing unintended pregnancies and cases of STIs through widespread access to, and education around, contraception. The inclusion of moral attributes is more akin to what Sharon Lamb calls for in an ethics-based sex education.[37]

The attention given to personal attributes or virtues reflects a renewed interest in a virtue ethical approach to education more broadly.[38] Agreement can be found within public education on essential values and virtues, even if there is disagreement over their source.[39] The role of character in the moral life also has deep roots in the Christian tradition, and the 'What if Learning' approach to teaching offers an example of how Christian distinctiveness can be understood in the nurturing of character in teaching and learning.[40] Joshua Heyes notes that a virtue ethical approach to RSE can move the discussion beyond the legal facts around rights and consent and centralise the discussion instead on 'how *best* to act' in the realm of sexuality.[41] In his exploration of this approach, he concludes: 'We must teach young people the law, and we must teach them their rights. But if we are to form a generation of young people towards sexual and romantic flourishing, we must not settle for the ethical "lowest common denominator".[42]

Despite the attention given to numerous personal attributes and character traits in the new guidance, it is of note that the concept of love is only explicitly mentioned within the context of family relationships. It does not feature in the list of personal attributes, though as the principal relational norm and ideal, it arguably underpins them all. It is also worth noting that there were two virtues which were removed from the list in the guidance following the consultation process—self-control and self-sacrifice.[43] Concern was expressed that the message it would give pupils is that 'relationships are about self-sacrifice, rather than about equality and enjoyment for example.'[44] What their removal at least highlights is the need to provide a coherent moral narrative and conceptual framework for thinking about healthy and flourishing relationships, including sexual relationships. Such a narrative provides a moral language that gives the identified values and virtues content and meaning, including those of self-control and self-sacrifice. In an 'Age of Authenticity', it is perhaps unsurprising that these personal attributes are particularly unpalatable. As Charles Taylor notes: 'The pursuit of happiness has come to seem not only not to need a restrictive sexual ethic and the disciplines of deferred gratification, but actually to demand their transgression in the name of self-fulfilment.'[45] Their dismissal, however, overlooks not only the necessity of self-control and self-sacrifice in the pursuit of sexual and relational flourishing, but their importance in the flourishing of a common life.[46]

A transformative Christian contribution to RSE can provide children and young people with a narrative that transcends self and makes sense of their relational selves—one that can inspire their choices and practices. A Christian account of love, for example, is not one that is predicated on the realisation of self-authenticated pleasure and fulfilment, but one that witnesses to the fullness of love that is found in the gospel. In view of this revelation, it is within the Christian account that we are instructed to love not just those who love us, but those we regard as our enemies; and love is demonstrated most profoundly in the laying down of one's life for one's friends. Love by its nature is not self-serving, but is costly and sacrificial—for it is in losing one's life that you find it.

## Delaying sexual activity: a reason to say 'no'

Along with a conceptual framework to understand relational norms and commitments, what is increasingly absent in the Western cultural narrative around relationships and sex is a reason for young people to delay sexual activity, as well as a normative link between sex and love, or indeed, any relational context or commitment. Stripped of any inherent meaning or purpose, sex becomes merely a subjective pursuit of sexual experience and pleasure. In his observations of relational and sexual behaviour within American culture, sociologist Mark Regnerus notes: 'Great (infertile) sex is now a priority, a hallmark of the good life, signalling that our genital and psychosexual life—sexual expression and how we experience it—is close to the heart of being human.'[47] In light of the normative cultural narrative that we inhabit in the West, what good reason do young people have to say 'no' or to delay first sex? One outcome of this cultural script is that young people, on their own admission, are having sex too early.

Research highlights that 'the most commonly reported negative feature of first sex was that it was not felt to have occurred at the "right time" (39.7% of women and 26.5% of men).'[48] According to data from the third National Survey of Sexual Attitudes and Lifestyles (Natsal-3) in Britain, participants aged 17–24 years old were categorised as 'sexually competent' if the following self-reported criteria applied to the event of first heterosexual intercourse: 'contraceptive use, autonomy of decision, both partners "equally willing", and occurrence at the perceived "right time".'[49] Sexual competence was noted to be significantly lower amongst those who were younger at first intercourse; 77% of women and 64.7% of men who reported first intercourse at age 13–14 years were categorised as not sexually competent.[50]

The concept of sexual competence in sex education discourse is associated with a broader, more holistic understanding of sexual health, one that encompasses both physical health and psycho-social well-being. Julia Hirst suggests that sexual competence refers to 'the ability to be involved in sexual practices with successful *processes* and *outcomes*.'[51] She points out that successful outcomes would include a positive sexual experience that promotes physical, emotional, mental, and social well-being. A successful process would involve participating in a sexual practice that is 'chosen, satisfying, and involved emotional connection and negotiation.'[52] Determining successful processes gives attention to the interactions and the rights of the individuals involved in achieving the desired outcomes.

Hirst readily points out that identifying outcomes and processes associated with sexual competence and articulating the concept itself should not 'minimise the difficulties inherent in achieving it.'[53] It is argued that sex education itself 'contributes to sexual competence.'[54] Hirst accepts, however, that 'while sex educators can do little to influence the contexts for sex, they can acknowledge that sex is often furtive, clandestine and rushed, and, together with alcohol, this can influence sexual negotiation, autonomous decision-making and young people's sense of self.'[55] Arriving at a sense of what educating for sexual competence might entail, she concludes that both students and educators would most likely agree that 'competencies of autonomy and safer sex are skills worth developing.'[56] She concedes that sexual competence may not always be achieved, but confirms that 'the quest is to work towards feeling competent *more of the time.*'[57]

Despite her dismissal of the educator's influence over the contexts for sex, it is worth pointing out that a further finding from Natsal-3 was that the stability of the partnership was associated with a more positive first sexual experience and that the status of the relationship with the partner had a strong association with sexual competence.[58] It would seem, therefore, that giving more attention to the relational context and circumstances of first sexual intercourse would accord with a commitment to evidence-based practice and would be necessary in order to promote sexual health and well-being. Educating for sexual competence, as a result, would involve going beyond Hirst's focus on skills for autonomous decision making and safer sexual practices. This arguably offers a limited understanding of what is required to secure psycho-social well-being. Instead, educating young people to identify, cultivate and inhabit positive relational attributes and practices would enrich their sense of self in relation to the other. Giving greater attention, therefore, to *relational* competence could arguably achieve higher levels of sexual competence.

With importance placed on autonomous decision making, it is worth pointing out that promoting freedom of choice in relational and sexual decision making does not sit in antithesis to Christian belief or doctrine. Smith asserts that 'despite all the ways that freedom has morphed into autonomy in late modernity, we shouldn't demonize freedom or liberty as such.'[59] As Hirst's judgement on sexual competency demonstrates, attention is placed on encouraging young people to make informed, autonomous choices in line with the ideals of a liberal education. Thus, it is argued, 'We should be as free in our sexual lives as it is alleged we should be in every other part of our life. And we should teach sex in a way that is consistent with that ideal.'[60]

In pursuit of this liberal ideal in education, we should not overlook the fact that this is an ideal that 'finds its antecedents in the Christian doctrine of freewill.'[61] Freedom to choose is in and of itself a God-given moral right and responsibility, and it should be commended and actively affirmed within a Christian approach to education. It is coercion and the denial of freedom that goes against the universal truth presented in the Christian gospel. As Lesslie Newbigin contends:

> We must affirm the gospel as truth, universal truth, truth for all peoples and for all times, the truth which creates the possibility of freedom; but we negate the gospel if we deny the freedom in which alone it can be truly believed.[62]

Freedom of choice is also dependent on, and guaranteed by, freedom of thought and expression. The philosopher, Stephen Law, argues for a liberal education that encourages children to think carefully and critically for themselves about moral issues, regardless of where moral beliefs come from: 'Reason alone may be incapable of determining right and wrong, but that is not to say that establishing what is right and wrong has nothing to do with reason.'[63] Christian educators should welcome calls for more robust philosophical engagement in the classroom. Through careful and considered investigation, we should be confident that Christian beliefs and values can stand up to critical scrutiny, including Christian truth claims concerning human relationships and sexuality.

Alongside a robust engagement of ideas, the educator must also recognise that the learner is embodied in 'cultural liturgies' that are shaping motivations and desires towards a particular end: 'A vision of the good life captures our hearts and imaginations not by providing a set of rules or ideas, but by painting a picture of what it looks like for us to flourish and live well.'[64] Thus, in drawing their attention to the reality of themselves as embodied participants in a cultural script, young people should have the opportunity to give critical attention to the content of that script and the picture of human flourishing that it paints. In engaging in a constructive apologetic, we seek to make Christian truth claims and practices accessible to a generation of young people, as we both serve and cultivate a common life and witness to and demonstrate gospel hope.

When it comes to exploring the initiation of sexual activity, the opportunity and need for this apologetic approach is particularly apparent. On the matter of first sex, the guidance states the following: 'Effective RSE does not encourage early sexual experimentation. It should teach young people to understand human sexuality and to respect themselves and others. It enables young people to mature, build their confidence and self-esteem and understand the reasons for delaying sexual activity.'[65] It continues: 'Effective RSE also supports people, throughout life, to develop safe, fulfilling and healthy sexual relationships, at the appropriate time.'[66] Here we see articulated a normative vision for the initiation and management of sexual behaviour; delaying first sex is encouraged, but what is increasingly absent is a coherent community narrative and the corresponding moral content that is needed to make such an aspiration achievable or, indeed, desirable. As noted earlier, in our collective pursuit of happiness it is not clear why someone would choose to defer what is deemed to be pleasurable and consensual sexual activity, resulting in moral ambiguity around the initiation of sex.

The NHS, for example, gives tenuous relationship 'advice' on sexual decision making. In answering the question 'Are you ready for sex?', it states on the one hand that, 'There are no rules about how long you have to be going out with someone before you have sex;' on the other hand, it suggests two questions an individual might ask themselves before having sex: 'Do I love my partner? Does he/she love me just as much?'[67] This highlights the vague and volatile nature of love and sexual encounter in the current cultural script. Casual relationships such as hookups and one-night stands are morally legitimised on the basis that the boundaries of the relationships are clarified in advance.[68] However, the evidence would indicate that casual sexual relationships and experiences cannot be so easily disentangled from unintended psychological and emotional outcomes.[69]

Scientific findings also point to the particular importance of companionate love—'feelings of intimacy, commitment and deep attachment towards others, romantic or otherwise.'[70] Over and above passionate love, companionate love is deemed to be necessary for the long term stability of a romantic relationship: 'developing a strong friendship with a romantic partner may ultimately be more important for the long-term success of the relationship.'[71] Of course, scientific insights do not correspond with moral imperative in relational decision making, but in pursuit of an evidence-based approach to policy-making this is a significant observation in terms of what contributes to relational flourishing and one that accords more closely with the steadfast nature of Christian love.

In engaging pupils' imaginations towards the pursuit of moral clarity and coherent action, a Christian contribution will encourage reflection on the safest and most secure context for sexual activity, nurturing the relational values and personal attributes that will allow that context to flourish. A Christian vision of human flourishing will also expose and disentangle the cultural myth that sexual expression corresponds with human purpose and fulfilment. C. S. Lewis warned of the 'god-like' nature of *eros* in his classic account of 'The Four Loves'. For him, the real danger of *eros* was 'not that the lovers will idolise each other but that they will idolise Eros himself'.[72] A Christian account of love is instead determined by an account of personhood that recognises and makes sense of the inter-related nature of our existence—to God, to others and to creation. The normative context of a sexual relationship is such that *eros* is tempered by *agape*—an other-regarding love that is directed towards sexual faithfulness and commitment.

A distinctly Christian contribution will thus present an enriched moral narrative that can inform young people's sexual choices and practices—a narrative that focuses on relational competence and context and not just on sexual competence or consent. In echoing Dennis Hollinger's observation: 'It's in the meaning of sex that we find a framework by which we make sense of our sexuality as human beings.'[73] In exploring this meaning and the corresponding framework, a Christian account of human flourishing will give a reason why someone would choose to wait until marriage to engage in a sexual relationship, and indeed give an account for why someone would choose to never have sex at all.

## Conclusion

Evangelicals affirm that social responsibility is an outworking of faith, and the desire and duty to pursue social justice and transformation is coupled with evangelism. The constructive and transformative approach to public engagement presented in this chapter is one that is enabled by the wider societal commitment to nurture the mutual ground on which a common life is built. This will include an ongoing commitment to freedom of thought and expression within public education, and will also involve an ongoing commitment from the church towards nurturing hospitable public engagement.

Importantly, the endeavour to find commonness, to respect plurality and to seek to shape public outcomes should not be done at the expense of the Christian community witnessing to, and actively pursuing the life in Christ that marks it out as distinctive. In a world that is relationally fractured and sexually confused, the current changes in RSE in English schools presents an opportunity for Christians to live out and tell—with imagination, conviction, compassion, and courage—a hopeful and grace-filled account of sexual and relational flourishing.

## Notes

1 James K. A. Smith, "The Reformed (Transformationist) View," in *Five Views on the Church and Politics*, ed. Amy E. Black (Grand Rapids: Zondervan, 2015), 139–162.
2 Miroslav Volf, *A Public Faith: How Followers of Christ Should Serve the Common Good* (Grand Rapids: Brazos Press, 2011), 89.
3 Volf, *Public Faith*, 88.
4 From 1990–2012, the proportion of 16- to 24-year-olds who cited school lessons as their main source of information about sex increased from 28% to 40% (Pandora Pound, Sarah Denford, Janet Shucksmith, Clare Tanton, Anne M. Johnson, Jenny Owen, Rebecca Hutten et al., "What is Best Practice in Sex and Relationship Education? A Synthesis of Evidence, including Stakeholders' Views," *BMJ Open* [2017]: 4).
5 My doctoral studies focused on the ethical debates and policy responses in England. Due to the differences in political and education systems, even within the UK, different possibilities for transformative engagement will emerge. In N. Ireland, RSE has been a statutory component of the Curriculum since 2001, and is currently shaped within the Personal Development strand of the Curriculum which gives particular attention to the key elements of personal understanding, mutual understanding, personal health, moral character, and spiritual awareness. Love for Life's programmes complement this holistic approach. Best practice in RSE includes making clear linkages and explicit connections with the aims, values, ethos, moral and ethical framework of the school. Therefore, all schools in N. Ireland, including those with a Christian ethos, can shape RSE in line with their beliefs and values.
6 Elaine Graham, "Between a Rock and a Hard Place," *Practical Theology* 7, no. 4 (2014): 242.
7 Graham, "Between," 242.
8 Matthew Croasmun and Miroslav Volf, *For the Life of the World: Theology That Makes a Difference* (Grand Rapids: Brazos Press, 2019), 45.
9 Volf, *Public Faith*, 63.
10 "Risk of 'Ghettoising' Faith in Schools," Church of England, accessed March 12, 2019, www.churchofengland.org/more/media-centre/stories-and-features/risk-ghettoising-faith-schools.
11 "Risk of 'Ghettoising'."
12 "PSHE and Sex and Relationships Education," Humanists UK, accessed April 6, 2020, https://humanism.org.uk/campaigns/schools-and-education/school-curriculum/pshe-and-sex-and-relationships-education/.
13 "Secularism," Humanists UK, accessed April 6, 2020, https://humanism.org.uk/campaigns/secularism/.
14 James K. A. Smith, *Awaiting the King: Reforming Public Theology* (Grand Rapids: Baker Academic, 2017), 132.
15 Smith, *Awaiting*, 132.
16 Department for Education, *Relationships Education, Relationships and Sex Education (RSE) and Health Education: Statutory Guidance for Governing Bodies, Proprietors, Head Teachers, Principals, Senior Leadership Teams, Teachers* (London: Department for Education, 2019), 12 (para. 19).
17 Luke Bretherton, *Christ and the Common Life: Political Theology and the Case for Democracy* (Grand Rapids: Eerdmans, 2019), 254.
18 Trevor Cooling, *Doing God in Education* (London: Theos, 2010), 22.
19 See Olwyn E. Mark, *Educating for Sexual Virtue: A Moral Vision for Relationships and Sex Education* (Oxford: Peter Lang, 2018), 16–19.
20 These questions reflect Mark Halstead and Michael Reiss's definition of values: 'Values are *principles and fundamental convictions which act as general guides to behaviour; enduring beliefs about what is worthwhile; ideals for which one strives;*

*broad standards by which particular beliefs and actions are judged to be good, right desirable or worthy of respect*' (Mark Halstead and Michael Reiss, *Values in Education: From Principles to Practice* [London: RoutledgeFalmer, 2003], 5).
21 'We believe that all children are entitled to comprehensive RSE, including education about forming and maintaining rewarding relationships and unbiased information on contraception, STIs, abortion, sexual orientation, as well as the many different forms of family relationship conducive to individual fulfilment and the stability of society' ("PSHE and Sex and Relationships Education").
22 Smith, *Awaiting*, 34.
23 Smith, *Awaiting*, 34.
24 Smith, *Awaiting*, 142.
25 Department for Education, *Relationships*, 12 (para. 20).
26 Department for Education, *Relationships*, 26 (para. 78). Further, the guidance states that 'key aspects of the law relating to sex which should be taught include the age of consent, what consent is and is not, the definitions and recognition of rape, sexual assault and harassment, and choices permitted by the law around pregnancy.'
27 Department for Education, *The Equality Act 2010 and Schools: Departmental Advice for School Leaders, School Staff, Governing Bodies and Local Authorities* (London: Department for Education, 2014), 14.
28 Department for Education, *Equality*, 14.
29 Department for Education, *Equality*, 14.
30 See, for example, how the Church of England Education Office understands 'faith sensitive and inclusive' Relationships Education and RSE. ("Relationships Education, Relationships and Sex Education (RSE) and Health Education in Church of England Schools," Church of England, accessed April 14, 2020, www.churchofengland.org/sites/default/files/2019-11/RSHE%20Principles%20and%20Charter_0.pdf).
31 Department for Education, *Relationships*, 25 (para. 69).
32 Dale S. Kuehne, *Sex and the iWorld: Rethinking Relationships beyond an Age of Individualism* (Grand Rapids: Baker Academic, 2009), 178.
33 Kuehne, *Sex and the iWorld*, 112.
34 Department for Education, *Relationships*, 20 (para. 60).
35 Department for Education, *Relationships*, 25 (para. 74), 26.
36 Department for Education, *Relationships*, 29.
37 Such an approach, she suggests, addresses the perceived separation between sex education and moral education. A 'sex-in-relationship' focus moves beyond a discourse of health and healthy choices, and takes account of the treatment and care of other people; mutuality is the 'moral center' of the ethics-based approach that she advocates—an approach that includes the exploration of religious and multicultural values. (Sharon Lamb, "Just the Facts? The Separation of Sex Education from Moral Education," *Educational Theory* 63, no. 5 [2013]: 460).
38 See "Cultivating Virtue in Moral Education: An Enriched Vision for RSE," in Mark, *Educating*, 143–67.
39 Mark A. Pike, "Christianity and Character Education: Faith in Core Values?" *Journal of Beliefs and Values* 31, no. 3 (2010): 311–321.
40 "The Prize is Virtue: Subject Teaching and Character Development," What If Learning, accessed April 14, 2020, www.whatiflearning.com/big-picture/virtues/. See also "*What If Learning* and Church School Education," in *Christian Faith in English Church Schools: Research Conversations with Classroom Teachers*, eds. Trevor Cooling, Beth Green, Andrew Morris, and Lynn Revell (Oxford: Peter Lang, 2016), 17–35.
41 Joshua M. Heyes, "Towards a Virtue Ethical Approach to Relationships and Sex Education," *Journal of Moral Education* 48, no. 2 (2019): 177.
42 Heyes, "Towards," 177.

43 "The New RSE Guidance—Your Questions Answered," Sex Education Forum, accessed June 10, 2019, www.sexeducationforum.org.uk/news/news/new-rse-guidance-your-questions-answered.
44 Lucy Emerson, "New Relationships and Sex Education Guidance is Here—But Does it Do the Job?" accessed June 10, 2019, https://schoolsweek.co.uk/new-relationships-and-sex-education-guidance-is-here-but-does-it-do-the-job/.
45 Charles Taylor, *A Secular Age* (Cambridge, MA: Harvard University Press, 2007), 493.
46 This is keenly evident in the current global pandemic of Covid-19 in which we are all being asked to sacrifice our liberty and to control our desires for the sake of the public good.
47 Mark Regnerus, *Cheap Sex: The Transformation of Men, Marriage, and Monogamy* (Oxford: Oxford University Press, 2017), 196.
48 Melissa J. Palmer, Linda Clarke, George B. Ploubidis, and Kaye Wellings, "Prevalence and Correlates of 'Sexual Competence' at First Heterosexual Intercourse Among Young People in Britain," *BMJ Sex Reprod Health* 45 (2019): 129.
49 Palmer et al., "Prevalence," 127.
50 Palmer et al., "Prevalence," 130.
51 Julia Hirst, "Developing Sexual Competence? Exploring Strategies for the Provision of Effective Sexualities and Relationships Education," *Sex Education* 8, no. 4 (2008): 402.
52 Hirst, "Developing," 402.
53 Hirst, "Developing," 403.
54 Simon Blake in conversation with Peter Aggleton, "Young People, Sexuality and Diversity. What Does a Needs-led and Rights-based Approach Look Like?" *Sex Education* 17, no. 3 (2017): 363–369.
55 Hirst, "Developing," 411.
56 Hirst, "Developing," 410, 411.
57 Hirst, "Developing," 411.
58 Palmer et al., "Prevalence," 130.
59 Smith, *Awaiting*, 103.
60 David Archard, "How Should We Teach Sex?" *Journal of Philosophy of Education* 32, no. 3 (1998): 448.
61 Mark A. Pike, "British Values and Virtues: Schooling in Christianity and Character?" *British Journal of Religious Education* 41, no. 3 (2019): 355.
62 Lesslie Newbigin, *The Gospel in a Pluralist Society* (London: SPCK, 1989), 10.
63 Stephen Law, *The War for Children's Minds* (Abingdon: Routledge, 2006), 116.
64 James K. A. Smith, *Desiring the Kingdom: Worship, Worldview, and Cultural Formation* (Grand Rapids: Baker Academic, 2009), 53.
65 Department for Education, *Relationships*, 25 (para. 70).
66 Department for Education, *Relationships*, 25 (para. 70).
67 "Are you Ready for Sex?" NHS, accessed April 14, 2020, www.nhs.uk/live-well/sexual-health/are-you-ready-for-sex/.
68 See, for example, the 'Click' relationships on-line resource which suggests: 'It might help to think of it as a consent issue. In the same way you should always respect sexual boundaries, you shouldn't enter into any kind of sexual relationships without being clear about the boundaries around it. When everything's laid out on the table, there's no reason a casual relationship shouldn't work.' (Click. "Understanding Casual Relationships," Click, accessed April 14, 2020, https://click.clickrelationships.org/content/all-issues/casual-relationships/).
69 Sophie Dubé, Francine Lavoie, Martin Blais, and Martine Hébert, "Consequences of Casual Sex Relationships and Experiences on Adolescents' Psychological Well-Being: A Prospective Study," *The Journal of Sex Research* 54, no. 8 (2017): 1006–1017; Carl Rodrigue and Mylène Fernet, "A Metasynthesis of Qualitative Studies on Casual

Sexual Relationships and Experiences," *The Canadian Journal of Human Sexuality* 25, no. 3 (2016): 225–242; Sara E. Sandberg-Thoma and Claire M. Kamp Dush, "Casual Sexual Relationships and Mental Health in Adolescence and Emerging Adulthood," *Journal of Sex Research* 51, no. 2 (2014): 121–130.
70 Garth Fletcher, Jeffry A. Simpson, Lorne Campbell and Nickola C. Overall, *The Science of Intimate Relationships* (Chichester: Wiley-Blackwell, 2013), 172.
71 Fletcher et al., *Science*, 175.
72 C. S. Lewis, *The Four Loves* (London: HarperCollins, 2002), 135.
73 Dennis Hollinger, *The Meaning of Sex: Christian Ethics and the Moral Life* (Grand Rapids: Baker Academic, 2009), 13.

# 9 Salvation's song

*Matt Spencer*

Growing up as a child of mixed Jamaican and British heritage, I was aware of racial prejudice and injustice, even within the church. As the sibling of a disabled brother, I further understood from an early age that faith must be 'worked out' and salvation understood within the context of significant challenges to overly simplistic interpretations of God's nature and will. I learnt to complexify issues of faith as I reflected upon them within the contexts of disability and racial (in)justice. This complexification led me to conclude, early in life, that any understanding of the church's role in the world which focussed solely upon narrow, personal, 'spiritual' salvation to the exclusion of the wider issues impacting people's lives, was inherently flawed. As a Salvationist, I was aware that the movement to which I belonged was motivated by love for God, to serve the world, and yet even within that context, I was mindful of theological tensions within the denomination concerning the nature of the salvation central to its very name and identity. Indeed, The Salvation Army's Handbook of Doctrine[1] states that, 'Salvation begins with conversion to Christ, but it does not end there.' Whilst this statement hints at a broader understanding of salvation than mere conversion, it still places conversion (understood as a personal acceptance of Christ as Saviour) as the gateway to salvation, through which one must pass in order to experience other aspects of salvation's expansive scope. Growing up alongside a brother who almost certainly cannot grasp the abstract concept of 'conversion to Christ', let alone give personal assent to it, I am convinced that the salvation at the heart of God's mission far exceeds an individual's relationship to certain theological precepts.

This conviction fuelled my research into the 'greater than' aspects of salvation, which I considered through the lens of singing.[2] As a singer, songwriter, worship leader, choir master, and leader of a local church, singing features heavily in my life and the lives of those around me. My doctoral research asked two key questions: *What is the lived experience of singing for members of the church/choir I lead?* and *What are the implications for Salvationist missiology and practice arising from analysis of those experiences?*

Along with my wife Emma, I have been privileged to lead The Salvation Army corps (church) in New Addington (known locally as NASA) since 2008. NASA is a relaxed, community-minded expression of Salvationism, running the

DOI: 10.4324/9781003094975-13

local food bank and partnering in multi-agency initiatives to serve one of London's most deprived communities. One of NASA's outreach ministries is SingCR0nise Community Choir, which I lead (the CR0 refers to the local postcode). SingCR0nise has members from different musical, cultural, educational, religious, and socio-economic backgrounds, making it the ideal context within which to consider singing's impact on people with a variety of lived experiences. My research invited creative responses to the phrase 'Songs, Singing, NASA and Me'[3] and the resulting paintings, collages, 'Wordles' and so on formed the basis of one-to-one conversations between myself and the participants[4] and then, later in the process, they stimulated discussion amongst all the participants as they considered one another's creative pieces and the issues arising from them.[5]

The answer to the first question concerning singers' lived experiences of singing is summarised thus: singing engenders belonging, elicits emotions, enriches spirituality, and enables transformation. These findings resonate with other ethnomusicological studies evidencing singing's contributions to the human experience. I then considered these influences upon wellbeing within the context of a broad and expansive understanding of God's mission, describing the church's role in terms of five Ways of Being: the facilitation and nurture of community; the empowerment for and engagement in ministry; the integration of internal structures with external action; the authentic communication of the truth; and the embodiment and enactment of Christian hope. Each is considered in turn below, and whilst the lens of singing is utilised here, it may be true that other activities could also engage with and impact upon these Ways of Being.

## Singing and the facilitation and nurture of community

The notion of community lies at the heart of the Trinity. The outworking of God's communal nature is further evidenced in the incarnational 'dwelling among' of Jesus with humanity[6] and permeates the *missio Dei*, which seeks the restoration of relationship, both divine and human, which is God's will for creation. The church engaged in the *missio Dei* will therefore embody ways of being which facilitate and nurture such communion.

My data demonstrated that SingCR0nise provides a physical and experiential space for the nurture and facilitation of relationships, engendering a sense of belonging among members which is integral to healthy, functioning communities. As people gather to sing, they enter an environment wherein there is shared purpose, learning, anxieties, and vulnerabilities. Sharing such experiences effectively 'fast-tracks' relationships as people not only sing, but laugh and sometimes cry together. The bringing together of diverse individuals, with different reasons for participation and different ways of understanding the world, provides opportunities for what Cathy Ross calls 'seeing otherwise' to occur.[7] In 'seeing otherwise' individuals are introduced to new ways of viewing and understanding the world via experiencing and seeking to understand another's perspective. The nurture of community relies upon the existence of spaces in which people who 'see otherwise' might interact, enlightening one another with their differing viewpoints. The community choir provides such a space. In this regard, the choir represents what Paul Weston refers to as a 'third-space'[8] wherein disparate parties pursue a common aim, with the potential outcome of discovering something new together, not only musically, but, through the convergence of diverse worldviews, backgrounds, and experiences, about life itself.

The community choir is not preoccupied with internal ecclesial concerns, nor is it a space to which unbelievers are invited to hear the gospel. Rather, it is a community of hospitality and welcome, in which Christ is present by his Spirit, wherein everyone, from the leader to the newcomer, can experience something of the community of belonging which lies at the heart of the *missio Dei*. John Sloboda notes that whilst 'music cannot, in and of itself, create community,'[9] it can provide a purpose—such as a choir for instance—around which a community gathers and therefore to which others might belong. Participation in a group such as a choir, in which melody, countermelody, harmony, and rhythmic synchronicity play an important part, can draw people together not only in terms of their physical presence in the same space, but in terms of their shared encounter with the music and lyrics, their shared identification with the group, and the ensuing affirmation of a common humanity. Group singing not only combats isolation, it provides a context in which disparate human beings find their place within a purposeful whole, which becomes something of beauty and unity, the uniqueness of which is entirely due to each individual's participation. Such unity-in-diversity both reflects the Trinitarian nature of God-in-community and exemplifies the church's call to nurture and facilitate community as it participates in the *missio Dei*.

The church must both facilitate and nurture loving fellowship among its members, and be proactively hospitable in reaching beyond itself to enable others to experience the benefits of belonging. The faithful witness of the community as it lives in and lives out Christ is both attractive and authentic. There is no need for a covert agenda behind actions which challenge loneliness, isolation and so on, as they bear witness to Christ whose victory over such evils is already assured. Holistic, or one might say 'practical' soteriology embraces that which might be considered as 'small victories', within the breadth of Christ's saving work. The lonely person finding friendship in a choir, and connection with other people via the intimate actions of listening to others' voices, breathing and moving in unison with them, and engaging in collective expressions of deep emotions, can experience the transformative defeat of the evils of loneliness and isolation, which, to borrow Lesslie Newbigin's phrase, is 'an authentic part of the victory of the Lamb.'[10]

Whilst musical groups undoubtedly contain the potential for community, they do so only to the extent that they are hospitable entities, which implies risk. An open door not only permits, but actively encourages the entry of the tuning-deficient and rhythmically-challenged! The significance of such risks dissipates however, when participation is prioritised over professionalism. The risk level correlates with the desired standard of performance. The lower the musical expectation placed upon a group, the lower the risk of a newcomer negatively impacting it. It seems appropriate then, in the context of mission, for the bar of entry into a musical group such as a community choir to be as low as possible to facilitate participation by as many as so desire. Once welcomed into the fold, lyrical and musical accessibility and inclusivity become key in the maintenance of a hospitable environment. Recognising that many people are not musically literate and some struggle even to read words, in my own choir, sheet music is never used, and written lyrics are rarely given out (except to those who specifically ask for them, or to newcomers whose inclusion might be expedited by having written words to follow). Participation in the choir is free of charge, so no one is excluded on financial grounds. There is no audition or expectation of musical knowledge or ability. Sporadic attendance and 'loose' commitment is met with understanding rather than judgement, with individuals participating according to their own priorities and pressures, rather than a demand for a particular level of commitment.

Some may say this lacks the discipline necessary for the choir to function effectively, but by what measure of effectiveness? My participants confirmed that the choir facilitates for them aspects of the reconciliatory purpose for which Christ came, which is the type of effectiveness SingCR0nise pursues. Some spoke of a deep connection with God, some of the development of relationships with others and some of the restoration of their own sense of self-worth and confidence. Through group singing, disparate individuals are connected via mutual participation, many experience a range of emotions which help to reintegrate their inner selves, and for some, this ultimately results in a connection with the Divine. The choir is more than a space in which non-Christians might encounter God, or even a space in which Christians might come to know more of God, although it is clear from my research that both take place. When the facilitation and nurture of community are understood as legitimate missional aims, the 'third-space' community of the choir participates in the *missio Dei* as it combats isolation and loneliness, promotes physical and mental wellbeing, and facilitates harmonious relationships. There is, inherent in this 'third-space', a blurring of the boundaries of participation in mission, and indeed ministry, as we will consider next, as God works his purposes through the choir, whose members do not all identify as Christians.

## Singing and empowerment for and engagement in ministry

Effective engagement in ministry relies upon empowerment and opportunity. Whilst the Christian's primary source of power is the Holy Spirit, through whom all forms of ministry are undertaken, empowerment understood more broadly encompasses the motivation to engage in ministry, and the physical, emotional, and intellectual strengthening of individuals in order that they possess the resilience and resources required to effectively participate in it.

Regarding motivation for ministry, the choir has provided at least one participant with such.

> When I'm singing, and you get certain words and certain phrases and certain songs, and you can relate to them and think 'how lucky am I to be able to be doing all this, when there's people out there that are not as lucky as I am, that actually live in abject poverty' … I see so many sad, beaten faces. Grey. Downtrodden … that's unacceptable to me … as human beings, that's completely unacceptable to me.

Singing with the choir elicits strong emotions in this individual, particularly concerning the political and spiritual imperatives which motivate their engagement in ministry. The experience described above encompasses both the songs themselves and the contexts in which they are sung. Participation in the choir increases prosocial thoughts, deepens empathy, and fuels a desire for transformative action, both through the singing of songs which evoke gratitude in the singer regarding their own circumstances relative to others, and through the provision of opportunities for ministry with the choir in locations and contexts which arouse feelings of injustice. One such experience involved the choir giving an outdoor performance yards away from a site where, just weeks earlier, a teenage asylum-seeker had been subjected to a violent, unprovoked attack by a group of six men. More than one choir member alluded to SingCR0nise's performance having a redemptive quality in that context, as it brought joy to a place which had experienced an act of such depravity, singing words of love and hope over a community in shock and fear.

Such engagement in ministry requires appropriate physical, emotional, and spiritual empowerment. The principle of worshipful living found in Romans 12:1b–2a offers a helpful lens through which to consider singing's role in such empowerment.

> … present your bodies as a living sacrifice, holy and acceptable to God, which is your spiritual worship. Do not be conformed to this world, but be transformed by the renewing of your minds …

Here, the importance of an integrated and holistic understanding of Christian living is emphasised. Body, mind, and spirit are implicated in the Christian's offering to God, and body, mind, and spirit are involved in mission and ministry. Whilst hesitating to press the internal imagery beyond appropriate boundaries of the intended language of this passage, I would suggest that a tacit inference is that an activity such as singing, which positively impacts upon bodily wellbeing and plays a part in the literal renewal and transformation of the mind via a variety of brain processes, is consequently implicated in preparing and empowering individuals for ministry. Several participants in my research referred to feeling empowered and emboldened through singing, either with the choir or during the worship service.

I've never, ever been able to sing a note, and you all put up with me, and you're all singing something and I'm singing something else, but it doesn't matter! (laughs) But it's this thing where "you can do it! You will do it! You're not going to be put down!" That's, that's the empowerment.

The music, it just fills me up with so much more that it just lifts me and emboldens me to just go "Yeah! You can pray! You can sing out loudly" and no one is gonna go "why are you singing so loudly?" You contribute to the atmosphere.

Singing is a powerful activity. Yes! It's extremely powerful. It really strengthens the heart, it strengthens the conviction, it just uplifts a person. ... it's just liberated me to be able to sing in public.

The empowerment for ministry described above begins with the sense of security felt as a result of belonging to the group; a knowledge that no one is going to 'put you down'. This security relies upon the aforementioned philosophy of 'participation over professionalism', wherein belonging is not contingent upon ability, and the corresponding empowerment enables uninhibited participation. This liberated participation then has the impact of emboldening and encouraging singers to engage in other activities and embrace their potential contribution to other forms of ministry. This empowerment for ministry is a form of transformation, with singers identifying a distinction between their confidence and willingness to move outside of their 'comfort zones' before and after their engagement in group singing, particularly in the context of the community choir. These transformations, however insignificant they might seem, are evidence that those who participate in ministry can become beneficiaries of the very ministry in which they are engaged. The building up of confidence, enhancement of wellbeing and experience of being blessed through blessing others, has far-reaching implications for singers' lives beyond the context of the choir, as they are emboldened to participate in other opportunities for ministry.

One choir member began singing with the choir as a self-professed 'Angry Atheist'. The hospitality and inclusion they experienced led to them joining the cast of the church's annual community pantomime, and then attending Sunday worship and soon afterwards (still professing atheism) playing in the worship band, and gradually an atheistic worldview was replaced with a Christian one. Throughout their journey, this individual participated in the ministry of the church, even as an atheist, whether or not they understood their involvement in those terms. Since becoming a Christian, they even speak of their day-to-day working life using the language of ministry, evidencing a rich understanding of ministry's expansive scope.

The choir facilitates a blurring of the boundaries of participation in ministry, akin to that which has already been considered concerning the facilitation and nurture of community. The involvement of non-Christians in the ministry of the choir (and the pantomime and even the worship band) invites reflection on the notion of 'The Priesthood of All Believers'. As individuals who do not

156  *Matt Spencer*

profess a Christian faith add their voices and presence to the choir, they not only demonstrate solidarity with the choir's ministry, but they also participate in it. In this regard one might suggest a comparison with the Gentiles whom Paul describes as doing 'by nature things required by the law ... even though they do not have the law' (Rom 2:14). Those who do not possess the Spirit of Christ by faith may still act in ways which contribute to the advancement of the Kingdom of God, which is the essence of ministry. If ministry is only understood as service motivated by Christian faith, then the actions of those not possessing such a faith are clearly unable to be considered within its scope. However, the undeniable contribution of non-Christians to groups such as SingCR0nise, calls for a broadening of the boundaries of ministry beyond 'The Priesthood of Believers', to include those who are entirely unaware that their actions and energies are contributing to the ministry of the church in the world and thus, the advancement of God's Kingdom.

## Singing and the integration of internal structures with external action

The integration of internal structures with external action as a missional way of being requires that such internal benefits as singing provides find outward means of expression, and community choir singing can be an exemplar in this respect. Singing in The Salvation Army has historically served the primary purposes of performance, proclamation, proselytisation, pedagogy, praise, and pastoral ministry. In this context, singing fulfils what Paul Weston refers to as 'First-space' and 'Second-space' purposes.[11] In the 'First-space' people are invited to 'come and hear' songs about God's goodness, love, and salvation. In the 'Second-space' singers 'go and tell' the message outside the context of the church, for instance in an 'Open Air Service'. Whatever the merits of these two approaches, I contend that true integration of internal structures with external actions requires 'Third-space' approaches, such as a community choir provides. In the context of the community choir, there is no 'them and us', only 'we', and participation, inclusivity, and accessibility are key. The choir is a truly integrated space, which both strengthens the internal life of the church, improves the emotional, physical and spiritual wellbeing of choir members, and engages in external actions of benefit to communities beyond the choir.

The biochemical and physiological evidence of singing's capacity to positively impact mental and physical health and wellbeing is well-documented.[12] Such benefits are, in the most literal sense, internal, and yet they are generated and experienced through the external action of singing. There is an inherent integration between the internal physiological responses to singing and the outward physical and social manifestation of it. The old Spiritual which says, 'I sing because I'm happy' could equally, according to the scientific and experiential evidence, say 'I'm happy because I sing' and the positive feelings which singing engenders can in turn lead to positive actions. The human response to the internal release of chemicals which singing generates is often to feel differently inwardly and to act differently outwardly. This is in a sense analogous to the

Christian's and indeed the church's response to the internal activity of God which both inspires the individual or community and requires an outward response.

In describing their own experience of this phenomenon, one choir member referred to the choir's concerts for a local Mencap group.

> ... once a year we would [sing] for the disabled people ... and those people would join in with such bliss and fun and it would make everyone smile and it would make us all happy about what we're seeing, and there it is in front of our eyes, and it's uplifting, and it brings you back to reality about what life is about ...

What is described here is the outward manifestation of the choir's internal practice of inclusion. This event was challenging for some members of the choir who found certain audience members' behaviour disturbing. However, as is noted above, the concert brought joy to the audience, engendered gratitude amongst choir members, and ultimately lifted everyone's spirits. Jeremy Begbie contends that music can illuminate doctrinal truths and play a part in the 'life, worship and witness of Christians'[13] as it creates tension, suggests incompleteness, and moves towards resolution. Whilst Begbie is speaking of music itself, I would expand his contention to include the performance of music, such as took place at the Mencap concerts. It was singing which led the choir into an environment in which they experienced tension and disquiet, as some members felt dis-ease not only with the unfamiliar behaviours they encountered, but perhaps also with their own responses to them. Singing brought choir members face to face with difference and challenged their perceptions of wholeness, as the happiness with which many of the Mencap members received the choir was juxtaposed with some choir members' discomfort. For some singers, this experience elicited powerful emotions which proved to be transformative, as an activity as seemingly innocuous as giving a concert with a community choir opened their eyes to a world which they had never seen, and shone a light on their own responses to it. This experience illustrates that integrating internal structures and philosophies (such as inclusion) with external actions which reflect and enact them, can generate tension and challenge. The choir's activity of singing for the Mencap group is both reflective of its internal commitment to inclusivity and challenging to it, thus strengthening such internal values as are tested in practice. Singing in potentially challenging contexts such as this serves to integrate the internal life of the choir with an outward-focussed activism which recognises that it exists for a purpose which goes beyond its own satisfaction. This exemplifies the potential role which a community choir can play in the process of transformation to which the Church is called. One member expressed the sentiment thus;

> ... I think more people should sing ... it would help a lot of people in different situations, to have that feeling of being part of the group ... music

and singing would really make a difference. I always say to people 'give it a go' ... it can change your life ... if it can change it in a little, small way, then that sort of knocks on to lots of other parts ...

These words echo David Bosch's expansive assertion that 'salvation is as coherent, broad, and deep as the needs and exigencies of human existence.'[14] Perhaps considering some of these various needs and exigencies (loneliness, isolation, mental dis-ease and so on) the singer quoted above notes that singing and belonging to a group such as the choir helps 'a lot of people in different situations' in small but potentially life-changing ways. The physiological and psychosocial benefits of group singing are integral to its role in the church's participation in God's mission. Whilst increased endocannabinoid levels in the bloodstream,[15] for instance, might seem to be outside the concerns of mission, the opposite is true if physical and emotional well-being, mental health, cognition, and memory are encompassed within mission's scope. It must then be incumbent upon the church, which has at its disposal the capacity and skill to offer opportunities for people to experience such physical and mental health benefits as singing provides, to make such available to the communities it serves. To do otherwise is to fail to integrate internal structures, in which singing plays a significant part, with external action. The Salvation Army's Older People's Services department has embraced this missional imperative in its 'Singing by Heart' programme, which provides singing groups for people with dementia, in which they can 'connect with others and bring back memories.'[16] In recognising singing's capacity to enhance the lived experiences of people with dementia and their carers, this programme evidences an embrace of the missional significance of such benefits.

Singing, particularly in the 'Third-space' context of a community choir, provides a model of the integration of internal structures with external action through the generation of physiological, psychological, social, and spiritual benefits, which challenge, equip, and motivate the singer for further outward actions, either through singing with the choir in concerts and public events, or other means of engagement in the world. These outward actions, particularly those involving singing, then contribute further to the physiological, psychological, social, and spiritual benefits derived by the singers themselves, as they not only experience the direct benefits of singing, but also derive an increased sense of self-worth as they participate in activities which are of benefit to others.

### Singing and the authentic communication of the truth

The first of The Salvation Army's Eleven Articles of Faith states,

> We believe that the Scriptures of the Old and New Testaments were given by inspiration of God, and that they only constitute the Divine rule of Christian faith and practice.

This statement asserts that the Bible is the Salvationist's primary (if not only) source of truth concerning Christian living, and thus I begin this consideration of singing's relationship with the communication of the truth with reference to singing and the Bible. Around one third of those who participated in my research credit singing with enabling them to better understand and engage with the Bible and relate the truths they perceive within it to their everyday lives.

The singing of songs with scripturally-based lyrics clearly assists in the communication of biblical truth to the singer, but singing also possesses a wider reach in terms of truth communication, beyond straightforward engagement with the text of the Bible. When SingCROnise sang opposite the location of the horrific attack on the young asylum-seeker, witness was borne to the truth that love conquers evil. Performing songs with such titles as 'One Love', 'Lord You Are Good', 'Lean on Me', 'Better', and 'Brighter Day', the choir literally sang words of love and truth over the ground. On that occasion SingCROnise embodied the 'glad and spirited and peaceful' expression of the gospel for which Karl Barth once praised The Salvation Army.[17] Barth's entreaty to the church to proclaim freedom, not law; the promise of life, not the threat of hell; and 'the artless indication of the truth' rather than 'clever or attractive apologetic' was evident in SingCROnise's activity that day. If Scripture's central claim about God is that God is love (1 John 4:8) then singing of love in a place where an act of hatred has taken place is an authentic witness to the truth of who God is.

For the church to fully participate in God's mission, it must bear witness to the whole truth of the whole gospel—salvation in its fullest sense: spiritual, physical, emotional, psychological, relational, structural, economic, and political. Singing can engage with each of these elements in multiple ways. The example above in one sense describes an act of political engagement—a demonstration of defiant love challenging the hate-filled ideology which fuelled the attack on an innocent Kurdish-Iranian teenager. In communicating the truth of God's love on and over that ground, the choir also brought emotional and relational healing to those who gathered to listen, and contributed to a wider work of restoring trust and social cohesion in a community in pain. Whilst the lyrics sung on the occasion described above were undoubtedly at odds with the hatred which had motivated the attack, the choir's very presence also represented an embodied, authentic witness to the truth of God's love. The choir's own ethnic, socioeconomic, cultural, generational, and religious diversity testified to an inclusivity which stood in direct opposition to the worldview of those who had unleashed their violent aggression just days earlier in the same space. According to Barth, 'Christians are either the messengers of God (with or without words) … or else they are not Christians at all.'[18] Whilst not all members of SingCROnise are Christians, the choir is a ministry of the church and as such, seeks to be a messenger of God which authentically communicates gospel truth. Barth asserts that this communication may be undertaken by means other than words. Where actions are commonly contrasted with words, I would suggest that in the context of the community choir 'essence' is a more appropriate concept, for by its very essence, the choir authentically communicated the truth of the gospel on the occasion described above.

The inclusive hospitality, focus upon participation, and building up of singers' confidence and self-worth, which characterise the choir's ethos, are reflective of the 'free act of the free grace of the free God' which Barth calls 'good news'[19] and of which Newbigin calls the church to be a living hermeneutic.[20] Singing next to the attack site, the choir did not need to speak of what had taken place—its presence was a prophetic witness against it. Barth describes the goal of mission not as conversion to personal salvation (which is the work of God alone) but as attesting to the work and Word of God. He further notes that the work of mission must 'lead the heathen themselves to become witnesses.'[21] Barth's words can be understood as finding fulfilment outside the context of conversion, as non-Christian members of the choir—'the heathen' as Barth might call them—did indeed become witnesses to the truth. The entire choir, Christians and non-Christians alike, became a credible and attractive manifestation and embodiment of the gospel, which is the means by which the authentic communication of the truth takes place. Through love-filled lyrics and the living testimony of its own diversity and inclusivity, SingCR0nise undertook the prophetic act of restoring dignity and justice to a place which had experienced anger and aggression, and in so doing, blurred the boundaries of participation in the communication of eternal truth.

In providing a purpose around which people gather, community choir singing not only communicates the truth of the good news that the gospel of Christ involves the salvation of the whole person and the restoration of the whole creation, but it also enables people to experience elements of that salvation for themselves. Some choir members sing Christian lyrics, often taken directly from Scripture, seemingly without them impacting upon their belief system, and yet if in gathering to sing, those individuals feel less isolated, lonely, anxious, or depressed and become more connected to other human beings, then an aspect of the truth of the gospel is being communicated to them and they in turn are part of communicating it to others.

There is another sense in which singing contributes to the authentic communication of the truth, which is alluded to by several participants in my research. It's encapsulated in the following quote from one choir member:

> When I sing, when I hear music, it sort of makes me come out of me.

This individual suggests that in singing, they become a more authentic version of themselves. Through its capacity to elicit emotions, singing has a disinhibiting effect, enabling singers to 'let down their guard' and express feelings and engage with aspects of themselves which are otherwise hidden. The truth communicated in this instance is the authentic expression of who the singer really is. Of course, not all singers experience this phenomenon of tapping into deep-seated aspects of their psyche in a positive way. A significant minority referred to their perceived vocal inadequacies, which for some, stemmed from negative childhood experiences.

> I know I'm tone deaf; I've been told that since I was that high.
> ... when I was at Junior School I was gonna sing one of the solos in 'We Three Kings of Orient Are' and when it come to the crunch, I just lost my voice ... it was very, very embarrassing for me.
> I'm sure I could psychoanalyse it and find reasons and probably say "well I was in the choir at school but I didn't get in first time, it took the second bash", you know, things like that.

Each of these singers tells their own story of experiences in their past which impact upon their relationship with singing in the present. One experienced repeated negative messaging concerning their singing throughout their childhood, which reinforced their belief in their inability to sing in tune. For another, a specific embarrassing childhood experience undermined their confidence in singing even into late adulthood. For another, despite being accepted into the school choir on the second round, the initial sense of rejection was overwhelming, negatively impacting their relationship with singing for decades. Having heard all three of these people singing in the choir, I am convinced that their vocal disenfranchisement[22] owes more to their negative childhood experiences than to any genuine vocal deficiency. According to John Bell, such vocal disenfranchisement can be combatted by exposing individuals to a different 'truth' concerning their singing ability in order to nullify the negative messaging which undermines their confidence. Bell refers to the speaking of this different truth as 'renaming.' He notes that 'God is in the renaming business' (Abram-Abraham; Sarai-Sarah; Simon-Peter) and as such, God 'delights to get rid of the rumours, nicknames and debilitating labels of the past.'[23] Whilst in the context of SingCR0nise the process of renaming is not quite so explicit, the choir members quoted above have, through gradual encouragement and participation in the collective experience of singing with the choir (and even through participation in the research process itself), begun to understand their singing ability in more positive terms, perhaps renaming themselves as 'Choir Members' as opposed to 'Non-Singers'. This process has facilitated the replacement of the negative voices of their childhood with a more accurate understanding of the truth concerning their vocal abilities, which liberates them to sing with greater confidence and rediscover the joy of singing, which for some, was lost many years ago. The transformative impact of this experience for the individuals concerned must not be underestimated, as it extends beyond their relationship with singing to encompass their entire sense of self-worth, redeeming a part of their past which has had a powerful hold over their lives for many years.

This section has demonstrated singing's role in the authentic communication of the truth. First, songs themselves are recognised as effective tools for communication, making challenging concepts accessible in ways which words alone may not. As these concepts are accessed and understood by singers who might not otherwise have encountered them, the impact can be spiritually transformative. Second, the act of singing in itself, particularly by a diverse group of people, can be a prophetic witness to an alternative truth, countering hatred and anger. Third, singing can communicate transformative truths over previously held beliefs which impact upon confidence and self-worth, via a process of renaming, which restores and transforms individuals' understanding of their true selves. Singing, particularly in the context of the choir, blurs the boundaries of participation in truth communication, embracing non-Christians within the embodied witness, as they both communicate and encounter the truth of the gospel.

## Singing and the embodiment and enactment of Christian hope

Christians frequently sing about hope. However, the embodiment and enactment of Christian hope goes beyond merely singing about it. Embodied and enacted hope is hope lived out—hope evidenced and glimpsed. Hope, by its very nature is not fulfilled and yet there are actions into which God invites the church to participate, which offer insights into the ultimate hope described above. Many of the participants in my research process spoke of experiences of transformation through singing in the choir, indeed the enabling of transformation is one of four key findings of my research into singing's role in mission, alongside the engendering of belonging, the eliciting of emotions, and the enriching of spirituality. Participants testified to overcoming shyness and anxiety, addressing long-held insecurities around their capabilities, and becoming emotionally stronger and more confident. Such experiences of personal transformation bear witness to the transformation of all creation for which Christians hope, providing glimpses of God's transformative activity in the present which is a precursor to the promised hope for the future.

For some choir members, the choir represents hope in a very simple, yet profound way, as evidenced in these interview extracts:

> ... things that's happened in my life I, I sort of, a lot of things that I keep, keep in, so, in a way, singing is another thing for letting it all out really, and still being private ...
> ... you can forget your problems for a little while ...
> ... I think I'm dyslexic ... it's quite embarrassing really, I feel as though I can perhaps forget that bit, and just do what I can.

Whilst this individual still lives with many challenges, the emotions which singing elicits and the sense of belonging experienced through the choir enable them to temporarily forget some of the issues they face. This experience mirrors the now and not yet of Christian hope. In belonging to the choir, they glimpse something of the future liberation from earthly suffering for which Christians hope, when 'there will be no more death or mourning or crying or pain' (Rev 21:4). In singing with the choir, they are temporarily distanced from the problems of their life. They experience momentarily a hint of that for which Christians hope eternally.

One of the many challenges of the Covid-19 pandemic has been its impact upon people's ability to engage in the hope-filled act of corporate singing. During a time of immense disorientation, a coping strategy to which many might have turned has been unavailable. Our church and choir, like many others around the world, turned to virtual means of producing music, featuring singers and instrumentalists from our various musical contexts, but, however helpful these may be, they are but shadows of the truly hope-inspiring experiences of collective musicking which have been curtailed.

This section has considered the role of singing in the embodiment and enactment of hope. It has described the means by which the hoped-for transformation of human experience can be glimpsed through the act of singing, as the singer is transported, albeit temporarily, into an experiential space in which singing overwhelms such things as stifle hope.

This chapter has brought the experiences of singers into dialogue with five key missional Ways of Being, exploring singing's relationship and contribution to them. The specific conclusions drawn can be summarised thus:

- Singing engenders belonging and contributes to the facilitation and nurture of community through a commitment to inclusivity and accessibility, characterised by the facilitation of a hospitable 'Third-space', benefitting both the community of the choir and the wider community beyond it.
- Singing facilitates empowerment for and engagement in ministry through its transformative impact upon singers' confidence and wellbeing, and the provision of ministry opportunities to both Christians and non-Christians who contribute to the choir's ministry.
- Singing exemplifies the integration of internal structures with external action through a virtuous circle of physical, social, emotional, and spiritual benefits, which motivate, equip, and enable singers for outward actions, benefitting the wider community and contributing to the singers' sense of fulfilment, confidence, and self-worth.
- Singing facilitates the authentic communication of the truth through songs' capacity to make biblical concepts more accessible. Singing prophetically communicates transformative truths over individuals and situations, embracing non-Christians within the embodied witness, as they both encounter and communicate the transformative truth of the gospel.
- Singing contributes to the embodiment and enactment of hope through the creation of experiential spaces in which the act of singing produces physical, psychological, social, and spiritual benefits which overwhelm such things as stifle hope.

Together, these conceptual conclusions, underscored by holistic understandings of soteriology and missiology, lead to the central conclusion that the more expansive one's view of God's mission and the scope of salvation, the greater the blurring of boundaries between the church and the world and the more activities such as community choirs can be understood to contribute to the *missio Dei*.

Whilst choral singing has provided a lens through which this chapter has looked, the principles considered have far wider-reaching implications for the church engaged in mission, not least the church which I am privileged to lead. Just as singing has functioned in this chapter, each attitude and activity of the church might equally be considered according to its relationship to the values which underpin the five Ways of Being in God's mission. As one with responsibility for leading a church fellowship, my research journey now speaks beyond singing into my wider ministry, leading me to ask of the activities in which we as a church engage and the attitudes and postures we adopt, and even the physical spaces we inhabit: 'Is it hospitable and inclusive?'; 'Does it facilitate and nurture community?'; 'Does it provide empowerment and opportunity for people to engage in ministry?'; 'Does it look beyond internal concerns to Kingdom growth?'; 'Does it facilitate the communication of essential truths?'; and 'Does it nurture hope and combat despair?' Such interrogation invites reflection on the church's essence and being, which in turn assists the church in finding its unique role in serving the world and participating in God's mission.

## Notes

1. The General of The Salvation Army, *The Salvation Army Handbook of Doctrine* (London: Salvation Books, 2010).
2. Matthew Spencer, "Salvation's Song: Insights into Salvationist Missiology from Practices of Communal Singing at New Addington Salvation Army Community Church" (DProf diss., Anglia Ruskin University, 2019). Full thesis can be found at https://arro.anglia.ac.uk/id/eprint/705887.
3. The 'Solo Phase'.
4. The 'Duet Phase'.
5. The 'Chorus Phase'.
6. John 1:14.
7. Cathy Ross, "Hospitality: The Church as 'A Mother with an Open Heart'," in *Mission on the Road to Emmaus: Constants, Context and Prophetic Dialogue*, eds. Cathy Ross and Stephen B. Bevans (London: SCM Press, 2015) 67–84.
8. David Male and Paul Weston, *The Word's Out: Principles and Strategies for Effective Evangelism Today*, rev. ed. (Abingdon: The Bible Reading Fellowship, 2019), 103.
9. John Sloboda, "Music and Worship: A Psychologist's Perspective," in *Creative Chords: Studies in Music, Theology and Christian Formation*, eds. Jeff Astley, Timothy Hone, and Mark Savage (Leominster: Gracewing, 2000) 110–125, 124.
10. Lesslie Newbigin, *The Open Secret*, rev. ed. (Grand Rapids: Eerdmans, 1995), 108.
11. Male and Weston, *The Word's Out*, 91ff.
12. Raymond MacDonald, Gunter Kreutz, and Laura Mitchell, *Music, Health, And Wellbeing* (Oxford: Oxford University Press, 2013).
13. Jeremy S. Begbie, *Theology, Music and Time* (Cambridge: CUP, 2000), 127.
14. David J. Bosch, *Transforming Mission: Paradigm Shifts in Theology of Mission – Twentieth Anniversary Edition* (New York, NY: Orbis Books, 2011), 410.

15 Nicole L. Stone et al., "An Analysis of Endocannabinoid Concentrations and Mood Following Singing and Exercise in Healthy Volunteers," *Frontiers in Behavioural Neuroscience* 12:269 (2018), https://doi.org/10.3389/fnbeh.2018.00269.
16 "Salvation Army launches group singing programme for people living with dementia," The Salvation Army, published 30 January 2018, salvationarmy.org.uk/salvation-army-launches-group-singing-programme-people-living-dementia.
17 Karl Barth, *Church Dogmatics IV:3: The Doctrine of Reconciliation* (Edinburgh: T&T Clark, 1962), IV:3:874.
18 Karl Barth, *Church Dogmatics III:3: The Doctrine of Creation* (Edinburgh: T&T Clark, 1960), III:3:64.
19 Barth, *Church Dogmatics IV:3*, IV:3:462.
20 Lesslie Newbigin, *The Gospel in a Pluralist Society* (London: SPCK, 1989), 227.
21 Barth, *Church Dogmatics IV:3*, IV:3:876.
22 John L. Bell, *The Singing Thing: A Case for Congregational Song* (Glasgow: Wild Goose Publications, 2000), 95ff.
23 Bell, *The Singing Thing*, 103.

# Part IV
# Engagement by students

# 10  Developing critical thinking within the context of a small group Bible study

*Isaac McNish*

## Introduction

'Critical thinking must be a distinguishing mark of the mature follower of Jesus.'[1] If Donald Sanders is correct, how is critical thinking developed in practice? In my own experience, a small group Bible study can readily become an exercise in which the participants are guided to adopt the views of the group leader rather than critically forming their own view. Using Alistair McKitterick's Theological Imperative Model for Practical Theology,[2] I shall critically reflect upon my experience of leading a Bible study group to understand how I may better facilitate learning.

## Personal encounter

McKitterick writes, 'we encounter people and engage with their stories and face their tensions with them.'[3] I lead a Bible study group of six Christian adults. At a particular meeting, the group engaged with the biblical concept of heaven. I spoke about heaven and earth coming together in contrast to heaven being a place we escape earth to reach. One member of the group, Mary,[4] found this challenging and said: 'now don't take heaven away from me as well, I'm looking forward to that!' She explained she had always understood heaven differently. Daniel commented that it is not a central issue to our salvation and therefore we can each have differing views. In a self-deprecatory manner, Mary said, 'I'm no good at theology, I am not a theologian.' During this exchange, I was uncomfortable and defensive; I felt the urge to respond by minimising the differences between viewpoints. Mary said, 'it's scary when you've gone down one way all your life, it's hard to change.' We prayed together about this at the end of the meeting. The Theological Imperative model prompts the practical theologian to ask: 'who am I in relation to the person encountered?'[5] My relationship with the members of this group is multivalent. We are friends and co-workers in church-based youthwork. I am also a member of the church leadership team and I am student studying theology. The latter two relations in particular can create a dynamic in which it is expected that I hold 'the right answers' on any explicitly theological matter.

DOI: 10.4324/9781003094975-15

## Critical description

The Critical Description is a 'theory-laden articulation' of the Personal Encounter. John Swinton and Harriet Mowat write of 'complexifying'[6] our understanding by paying attention to the multifaceted nature of human interaction. The following description, presented as a trialogue in the indicative mood, analyses the issues raised in the Personal Encounter by drawing on sociological, psychological, and theological resources. On the relationship between science and theology, J. P. Moreland remarks that a warfare metaphor (the two disciplines as antagonistic and irreconcilable) 'paints a simplistic, false picture.'[7] Evangelical practitioners may glean a wealth of valuable insights by humbly engaging with perspectives from other disciplines. However, as the social sciences typically operate with a secular methodology, a model of integration is required that is cognisant of these implicit philosophical presuppositions.[8] In recognising that 'science is of necessity a descriptive discipline,'[9] the Theological Imperative model restricts any normative statement during the Critical Description, thus avoiding uncritically importing a secular imperative. Therefore, during this stage I shall describe what is, rather than what ought to be, happening within the Personal Encounter, purposefully refraining from 'expressing a moral perspective'[10] on the issues raised.

### *Social psychology: language and groups*

The topic of discussion in the Personal Encounter was the biblical concept of heaven. Carmer Granito, Claudia Scorolli and Anna Maria Borghi have demonstrated that 'abstract concepts and words are hard to learn' and that 'language plays a major role'[11] in their representation. Jochim Hansen and Michaela Wänke have conducted research into the perceived truthfulness of concrete and abstract language. They have found that 'linguistic concreteness' and 'increased imaginability'[12] result in the greater likelihood of a statement being believed. They suggest that 'language as a means of social communication also affects social reality. How something is said is sometimes at least as important as what is said.'[13] The 'social reality' in the Personal Encounter is a 'small group', which Martin Ringer describes as a 'small complex dynamic social system where the leader is an integral part of that system.'[14] Therefore, as the group leader, my use of abstract language ('heaven and earth coming together') may have unconsciously been received as unlikely or untrustworthy.

Alternatively, the group may exhibit the phenomenon of 'groupthink', a term coined by Irving Janis.[15] Donald Pennington describes this as when a group pursues 'concurrence, consensus and unanimity among themselves rather than critically looking at all options.'[16] In groups which display a high level of cohesiveness, such as within church contexts, 'the desire to encourage unity … can encourage a groupthink dynamic.'[17] By seeking to resolve the tension within the group, Daniel may have acted as a so-called 'mindguard', creating an atmosphere in which further contributions must 'fit in or add confirmation'[18] to previously held beliefs. Richard Gross suggests that a dissenting voice, such as my comment, may demonstrate that disagreement is a possibility.[19]

*Psychology: learning*

As the group meets to learn together, it seems pertinent to ask, what is learning? Jennifer Moon describes learning as 'transforming conceptions'; learning is a dynamic process in which one 'continuously constructs and reconstructs a view of the world'[20] in light of new information. John Hull understands learning as an evolution of the self. He describes the sense of grief involved, as one emerges 'from the embedded self into something which [is] not yet recognisable as being me.'[21] Frances Ward observes that learning is not easy, it can 'stir defences, anxieties, fear of failure and resistance to change.'[22] Thus, learning is characterised as an active and challenging process in which we construct meaning.

This description of learning has resonances with Jean Piaget's theory of constructivism. Piaget theorised that thoughts are organised into 'schema'. New information is 'assimilated' into our current schema. However, when we encounter information that cannot be organised into our existing schema we may distort the idea to 'force it to fit in'[23] and so misunderstand. Alternatively, we may 'accommodate' the new information by realising we require a whole new schema. Barrett McRay argues that this internal dialogue between assimilation and accommodation is the place 'in which learning occurs.'[24] Cognitive development is driven by a state of disequilibrium, which Piaget contends is necessary to go beyond one's 'present state and to seek new equilibriums.'[25] Denis Haack describes disequilibrium as 'the state of discomfort or unease, sometimes severe, that occurs when a person experiences or learns something that does not fit his or her preconceived view of life or reality.'[26] Thus, Mary's stated unease may be indicative of a state of disequilibrium and therefore active engagement in the learning process.

Focusing on the social context of learning, Vygotsky proposed a distinction between a learner's 'actual developmental level,' what they can achieve independently, and their 'zone of proximal development' (ZPD), that which is possible 'in collaboration with more capable peers.'[27] For example, I can thread a sowing machine independently, but would only be able to sow a shirt together with the guidance of an experienced sower (this is my ZPD). Thus, learning is optimal when the learner is appropriately supported in 'activities that appear to be beyond their current level of development.'[28] Analogously, Mary's statement 'I am not a theologian,' may indicate her perception of the discussion as either within her ZPD (but lacking the peer support to actualise the learning) or beyond it (and therefore not yet accessible). Importantly, the greater the distance in ability between two people, the less likely the 'teacher' will accurately gauge the ZPD of the 'student'.[29] As such, Daniel's comment, rather than engendering a groupthink dynamic, may instead reflect a greater sensitivity than mine to the contours of Mary's ZPD.

## Theology: journey

The psychological description of learning as a process of change evokes the language of journey. Robert Mulholland remarks that journey is 'a core reality of historic Christian experience,' citing Abraham's journey 'from known, comfortable Haran to an unknown land that God would show him.'[30] This journey is prompted by God's command to 'go from your country and your kindred and your father's house to the land that I will show you' (Genesis 12:1). The 'deep pathos'[31] of Abraham's journey is indicated by the triple object of the imperative 'go': country, kindred, and father's house, in order of ascending intimacy.[32] This imagery of departing resembles Piaget's notion of disequilibrium; relationship with the familiar is transformed as one undertakes the challenging journey to the 'land I will show you'. Commenting on Genesis 12:1, Miroslav Volf states that journey begins with departure which is a 'temporary state, not an end in itself.'[33] This may be correlated with the psychological description of learning by positing that Mary's response was provoked by a sense of grief over a (learning) journey begun (the interrogation of the old schema) but not yet concluded (formation of a new schema). The theological language of journey emphasises the deep pathos of Mary's disequilibrium experience and the empathic dimension of Daniel's comment.

The metaphor of journey is described by Sheldrake as 'a movement of ongoing transformation' which portrays the 'radically dynamic rather than static nature of Christian experience and practice.'[34] The destination of Abraham's journey 'is described in the vaguest possible terms.'[35] In the Personal Encounter, the end of the journey (the, as yet, abstract and unknown 'land I will show you') is new understanding of the concept of heaven. The journey metaphor adds a time-dimension to Hansen and Wänke's conclusion; learning entails increasing the 'imaginability'[36] of an abstract concept over time. Jonathan Sacks states that as the 'biblical drama is set in the arena of time' and that profound change of its characters is wrought through time, 'the ability to live with delay'[37] is thus a characteristic of faith. Likewise, Volf states that Abraham's call emphasises that departing from 'enmeshment in the network of inherited cultural relations is a correlate of faith.'[38] Mary's concluding description of 'going one way her whole life' reflects something of this enmeshment. This theological description underscores that learning is not only a process of wrestling with new ideas but may also be understood as an act of faith.

## *Kairos* moment

The shift from the indicative to imperative mood is marked by the *Kairos* moment, which is envisioned as 'a revelatory moment of discernment guided by the Holy Spirit.'[39] Swinton and Mowat argue that the practical theologian is 'the primary tool that is used to access the meanings of the situation being explored;'[40] an aspect of the Theological Imperative model's reflexivity is seen in the invitation for the practical theologian to bring their faith in God to the reflective process in prayer. The presentation of the *Kairos* moment in revelatory terms does not however preclude the Theological Imperative, the fruit of critical reflection, from being 'itself subject to critical reflection.'[41] Throughout the Critical Description, I have refrained from describing Mary's experience of tension or disequilibrium in negative terms (which would risk smuggling in an imperative too early, namely, 'this situation ought to be avoided'). Emerging from the critical correlation of the call of Abraham with the psychological description of learning is the notion that the discomfort of disequilibrium may be regarded as a positive, even necessary, feature of the learning process. The insights within the Critical Description are held together by this new idea or perspective on the Personal Encounter which 'initiates the momentum, and sets the direction, for Christian Praxis.'[42]

## Theological imperative: be transformed

Bonnie Miller-McLemore writes 'many would argue practical theology is, in fact, not complete without a move from description to normative construction and action.'[43] The normative dimension here, the Theological Imperative, is described as the 'hope for change and renewal … framed in the language of moral obligation and theological concepts.'[44] This purposeful turn to the Christian tradition, 'most especially Scripture,'[45] provides the methodological grounding for the authoritative role of Scripture in shaping the Christian praxis. In Romans 12:2, Paul writes: 'be transformed by the renewal of your mind.' Sanders delineates the teleological component of Paul's command: 'the purpose of critical thinking for the Christian is to pursue the will of God and the goal is to live in accordance with that revealed will.'[46] Echoing the description of Abraham's departure, Ben Witherington describes this imperative as a 'process of de-enculturation and reorientation.'[47] Capturing the notion of learning as an active process, Anthony Thiselton explains that 'be transformed' is in the present continuous tense, rendering the meaning as 'go on being transformed.'[48] Transformation is inextricably linked with what Paul Ballard and John Pritchard describe as a 'corporate spirituality,'[49] it requires mutual commitment to one another's learning and growth (cf. Vygotsky). Paul's paraenesis in Romans 12:1–5 employs the Greco-Roman analogy of the 'body politic'[50] to express the unity of the Christian community as a concrete example of renewal of the mind. According to Witherington, Paul does not seek outward conformity (such as groupthink) but 'inwards transformation which is outwardly expressed.'[51] Therefore, to 'be transformed' is not merely mental assent to new ideas but is chiefly manifested in transformed living. This is further evident in Frank Matera's comment that the believer's body refers to 'the embodied self'[52] or as James Dunn states 'the concrete relationships that constitute our everyday living.'[53] Dunn argues that Paul 'saw offering of the body as a piece with renewal of the mind … the integration of rationality with the total transformation of the person.'[54] This process of transformation is not limited to the efforts of the individual self, but as Pete Ward remarks, 'knowing

God is a work of the Holy Spirit in the believer.'[55] It is apposite that Paul's phrase 'do not conform' (*syschēmatizesthe*, cf. 'schema') offers a tangible link with the language of constructivism. If then, as Haack argues, disequilibrium should be regarded as a 'biblically normative expectation in the Christian's growth in maturity,'[56] then learning as a journey of faith in response to God's calling should be pursued as a corporate activity with the empowerment of the Holy Spirit.

## Christian praxis

The vision of the Theological Imperative is implemented in returning from the reflective to the active mode. Whilst Mary's discomfort was initially approached as an experience to avoid, a central outcome of this process is that it gives me courage to act differently, hopefully with a 'new, creative and informed'[57] response to the Personal Encounter:

- As the imperative 'be transformed' is corporate in nature, I shall present the 'shared journey of faith' to the group as the guiding metaphor for understanding the purpose of our meetings. Thus, disequilibrium shall be addressed as an explicit and intended aspect of the Bible study. Learning as a shared journey of faith involves: (1) departing, to be willing to leave the 'comfortable' of what may be a long held understanding; (2) together, to acknowledge that this is a shared journey and thus to be mindful that the pace of learning does not overtake any individual's ability to form their own view; (3) faith, to recognise that this journey is an act of faith, believing that God's Spirit is active within the discussion and a new, more critically held understanding, will form.
- When the course of the conversation takes individuals to an uncomfortable place where their understanding is being challenged, in contrast to my initial urge to minimise the differences between viewpoints, I shall be willing to present a dissenting voice.
- I will invite the group to purposefully use the content of our discussions, and any ongoing disequilibrium or tension, as a resource to use in our corporate prayer following each meeting.

## Conclusion

How is critical thinking developed in practice? Using McKitterick's Theological Imperative Model, I have proposed a Christian praxis drawing on the description of learning as a shared journey of faith. The act of departing is characterised by discomfort and uncertainty. It is the transformative action of God's Spirit within the Christian community that enables the goal of new understanding to be realised, so that together we may discern and live according to

*Developing critical thinking* 175

the will of God. My hope, then, is that in developing our critical thinking we shall become more mature followers of Jesus.

## Notes

1 Donald Sanders, "From Critical Thinking to Spiritual Maturity: Connecting the Apostle Paul and John Dewey," *Christian Education Journal* 15, no. 1 (2018): 103.
2 Alistair J. McKitterick, "The Theological Imperative Model for Practical Theology," *Journal of European Baptist Studies* 16, no. 4 (2012): 5–20.
3 McKitterick, "Theological Imperative," 8.
4 The names of all individuals involved have been changed.
5 McKitterick, "Theological Imperative," 9.
6 John Swinton and Harriet Mowat, *Practical Theology and Qualitative Research*, 2nd ed. (London: SCM, 2016), 13.
7 J. P. Moreland, "Science and Theology," in *Evangelical Dictionary of Theology*, eds. Daniel J. Treier and Walter A. Elwell, 3rd ed. (Grand Rapids: Baker Academic, 2017), 1427.
8 Jeffrey S. Reber, "Secular Psychology: What's the Problem?" *Journal of Psychology and Theology* 34, no. 3 (2006): 202.
9 McKitterick, "Theological Imperative," 7.
10 McKitterick, "Theological Imperative," 10.
11 Carmer Granito, Claudia Scorolli, and Anna Maria Borghi, "Naming a Lego World: The Role of Language in the Acquisition of Abstract Concepts," *PLoS ONE* 10, no. 1 (2015): 18.
12 Jochim Hansen and Michaela Wänke, "Truth from Language and Truth from Fit: The Impact of Linguistic Concreteness and Level of Construal on Subjective Truth," *Personality and Social Psychology Bulletin* 36, no. 11 (2010): 1585.
13 Hansen and Wänke, "Truth from Language," 1586.
14 T. Martin Ringer, *Group Action: The Dynamics of Groups in Therapeutic, Educational and Corporate Settings* (London: Jessica Kingsley, 2002), 18.
15 Irving L. Janis, *Victims of Groupthink* (Boston: Houghton Mifflin, 1972).
16 Donald C. Pennington, *The Social Psychology of Behaviour in Small Groups* (London: Routledge, 2014), 179.
17 Sally Nash, Jo Pimlott, and Paul Nash, *Skills for Collaborative Ministry*, 2nd ed. (London: SPCK, 2011), 29.
18 Pennington, *Small Groups*, 14.
19 Richard Gross, *Psychology*, 6th ed. (London: Hodder Education, 2010), 407.
20 Jennifer A. Moon, *A Handbook of Reflective and Experiential Learning: Theory and Practice* (Abingdon: RoutledgeFalmer, 2004), 17–18.
21 John M. Hull, *What Prevents Christian Adults from Learning* (London: SCM, 1985), 178.
22 Frances Ward, *Lifelong Learning* (London: SCM, 2005), 153.
23 Fraser Watts, Rebecca Nye, and Sara Savage, *Psychology for Christian Ministry* (London: Routledge, 2002), 125.
24 Barrett McRay, "How People Develop in Their Thinking," in *Teaching the Next Generations: A Comprehensive Guide for Teaching Christian Formation*, ed. Terence D. Linhart (Grand Rapids: Baker Academic, 2016), 62.
25 Jean Piaget, "Genetic Epistemology," in Richard L'Evans, *Jean Piaget: The Man and His Ideas*, trans. Eleanor Duckworth (New York: E. P. Dutton & Company, 1973), xliv.
26 Denis Haack, "When Spiritual Growth Involves Disequilibrium," *Presbyterian: Covenant Seminary Review* 41, no. 1 (2015): 31.

27 Lev S. Vygotsky, *Mind in Society: The Development of Higher Psychological Processes*, ed. Michael Cole et al. (London: Harvard University Press, 1978), 86.
28 Dennis M. McInerney and David W. Putwain, *Developmental and Educational Psychology for Teachers: An Applied Approach* (London: Routledge, 2016), 112.
29 Watts, Nye, and Savage, *Psychology*, 131.
30 M. Robert Mulholland Jr., "Spiritual Journey," in *Dictionary of Christian Spirituality*, ed. Glen G. Scorgie (Grand Rapids: Zondervan, 2011), 551.
31 James McKeown, *Genesis*, Two Horizons New Testament Commentary (Grand Rapids: Eerdmans, 2008), 285.
32 Victor P. Hamilton, *The Book of Genesis* Chapter 1–17, New International Commentary on the New Testament (Grand Rapids: Eerdmans, 1990), 371.
33 Miroslav Volf, *Exclusion and Embrace: A Theological Exploration of Identity, Otherness, and Reconciliation*, 2nd ed. (Nashville: Abingdon, 2019), 31.
34 Philip Sheldrake, "Spiritual Journey," in *The New SCM Dictionary of Christian Spirituality*, ed. Philip Sheldrake (London: SCM, 2005), 388.
35 McKeown, *Genesis*, 75.
36 Hansen and Wänke, "Truth," 1585.
37 Jonathan Sacks, *Genesis: The Book of Beginnings, Covenant and Conversation* (Jerusalem: Maggid Books, 2009), 92–93.
38 Volf, *Exclusion*, 29.
39 McKitterick, "Theological Imperative," 15.
40 Swinton and Mowat, *Practical Theology*, 57.
41 McKitterick, "Theological Imperative," 16.
42 McKitterick, "Theological Imperative," 14.
43 Bonnie J. Miller-McLemore, "Introduction: The Contributions of Practical Theology," in *The Wiley-Blackwell Companion to Practical Theology*, ed. Bonnie J. Miller-McLemore (Chichester: Blackwell, 2012), 17.
44 McKitterick, "Theological Imperative," 15.
45 McKitterick, "Theological Imperative," 15.
46 Sanders, "Critical Thinking," 98.
47 Ben Witherington III, *Romans: A Socio-Cultural Commentary*, in collaboration with Darlene Hyatt (Grand Rapids: Eerdmans, 2004), 286.
48 Anthony Thiselton, *Discovering Romans*, Discovering Biblical Texts (London: SPCK, 2016), 221.
49 Paul Ballard and John Pritchard, *Practical Theology in Action*, 2nd ed. (London: SPCK, 2006), 187–188.
50 Thomas H. Tobin, *Paul's Rhetoric in Context: The Argument of Romans* (Peabody: Hendrickson, 2004), 391.
51 Witherington III, *Romans*, 286.
52 Frank J. Matera, *Romans*, Paideia Commentaries on the New Testament (Grand Rapids: Baker Academic, 2010), 287.
53 James D. G. Dunn, *The Theology of Paul the Apostle*, 2nd ed. (London: T&T Clark, 2003), 58.
54 Dunn, *Theology of Paul*, 74.
55 Pete Ward, *Introducing Practical Theology* (Grand Rapids: Baker Academic, 2017), 29.
56 Haack, "Disequilibrium," 44.
57 McKitterick, "Theological Imperative," 19.

# 11 Theodrama

## A contemporary application

*Samuel Norman*

### Introduction

Life feeds us a narrative. It tells us how the world is, how it functions, and how we should respond to it. It is as if someone has dropped you into the middle of a play. Take for example Julius Caesar. Who are you going to be? Are you going to be Julius, triumphing at all that he does living out his famous motto, 'I came, I saw, I conquered,' or are you going to join those who end up stabbing him in the back? Narrative and identity formation come hand in hand. However, within my experience as a university student prior to studying at Moorlands College, and through my encounters with relativistic philosophy, life was presented as being thrust into a multitude of Shakespearian plays all at once. In a plurality of narratives, choosing and establishing one's character becomes ever more confusing. The inability to navigate such a scenario can lead individuals to a place of passivity about objective truth, resulting in a relativistic position of some kind.

Cahalan states that practical theology 'can be strengthened by further attention to the philosophical assumptions that inform each perspective.'[1] Therefore, I will first engage with the philosophical position of relativism in its explicit form, demonstrating how an effective application of a theodramatic approach can provide a bridge to communicate the good news of Jesus and ultimately establish real identity for those that embrace such a philosophy.

The second area that I will address is theological education. Reflecting on his own undergraduate training in theology, Pete Ward observes that, although he grew substantially in his knowledge of and appreciation for the Christian tradition, he struggled to relate what he was learning about the Bible, church history and doctrine to his role as a youth worker.[2] Others claim more strongly that theological education is too theoretical with an inadequate amount of focus on lived out faith and therefore is 'irrelevant for training people for church ministry.'[3] Although I can personally attest that not all centres of theological training are like this (having studied at one that emphasises practice), this general reputation is of concern. Therefore, I will explore the implicit relativism that undergirds such a divorce between theory and practice. After identifying the issue at hand, I will propose a theodramatic approach as an effective way to uncover relativistic ideas and re-establish the link between orthodoxy and orthopraxy.

DOI: 10.4324/9781003094975-16

## Relativism

Relativism, Boa and Bowman state, is the 'belief that statements of fact or value are true from some perspectives but not from others.'[4] Many evangelical scholars have been vocal about the danger that relativism poses to society and Christianity. D. A. Carson states that 'relativism is treason against God and his word.'[5] The rejection of absolute truth is a rejection of God's truth and its subsequent outworking in the world. Others, such as Carl Trueman, remark that some within evangelicalism accept relativism without taking it to its logical conclusion. If they had sat in 'university environments where postfoundational relativism is used to justify everything from female circumcision to infanticide,' he says, 'they might have a different take on the dark world into which their superficial grasp of complex secular philosophy is merrily leading us.'[6]

However, others such as James K. A. Smith have pointed out that those opposed to relativism are often imprecise in their definition of it. Smith comments that '[w]e confuse something's being "relative" with being arbitrary or subjective or governed only by fleeting whims.'[7] Smith defines relativism as 'claims or accounts that are ... relative—related to something or Someone.'[8] Rather than relativism meaning nothing matters, he states that it means 'everything depends.'[9] Additionally, William Knorpp states that truth is relative to the 'culture, or belief, or whatever it is *supposed* to be relative to' (emphasis added).[10] Therefore, relativism in and of itself is not controversial; what one may decide truth is *supposed* to be relative to, is.

It is possible by Smith's standards to be both a relativist and a Christian so long as one says that truth is relative to Jesus who is 'the truth' (John 14:6). However, although Smith maintains that relativism is wrongly used as a synonym for subjectivism, in most cases relativism is seen to be anchored to something that fluctuates rather than something fixed. For example, an American study carried out by Pölzler and Wright found that participants 'seemed to have the intuition that either moral truth is mainly determined by their own or by culturally dominant moral beliefs, or that there is no moral truth at all.'[11] In all three of these intuitions, truth is relative either to the individual, society, or nothing. Therefore, relativism by Smith's own definition can and does encompass situations where differing truth claims co-exist, and does so in the majority of cases. This is most likely why leading dictionaries define relativism as having no absolute right or wrong since truth claims are almost always relative to something that can change.[12] Therefore, I shall define relativism as the belief that truth is relative to a variable and is not absolute.

## Explicit and implicit relativism

Throughout my time at university, I encountered two types of relativistic philosophy: explicit relativism and implicit relativism. The first type I experienced through debates and conversations with individuals holding differing beliefs and opinions on various issues. In order to avoid conflict or confront their own perception of reality some would result to a form of relativistic reasoning to justify their own (or someone else's) narrative whilst living beside others who hold contradictory ones. Such a position is typified by phrases such as 'that's just your opinion' or 'that's just your truth.'[13] Unsurprisingly, this phenomenon is not uncommon in the education system (particularly in universities), so much so that Stephen Satris coined the term 'student relativism' to describe it.[14] Although I have personally met and conversed with Christians who hold such a philosophy, it is more common outside the church. My experience of 'explicit' relativism—that is relativism that is openly admitted in order to justify the existence of contradictory truths—has provoked me to explore how I can reach those who identify with this philosophy with the good news of Jesus who is the absolute truth.

The second type, implicit relativism, is something that I encountered at university and continue to observe within Christian teaching contexts. Implicit relativism is characterised by an outward theoretical rejection of relativistic philosophy alongside a simultaneous acceptance of it through actions that are not in line with the more objective truths that are espoused. Stevens observes that theology is often considered to be abstract in nature, reduced to propositions and categorised into sections.[15] In line with this observation, Swinton and Mowat note that '[o]ne of the most persistent criticisms of academic theology is that, rather than encouraging the activity of faith, it can create significant distancing from the life of faith.'[16] As such, calls for theology to recover its position as a practical discipline have been steadily increasing since the 1980s, with those such as Helmut Gollwitzer proposing that theology establishes itself as a 'second-order activity whose primary task is to mediate between present and future praxis.'[17]

Although there has been significant work done in the past forty years to bridge the gap between theory and practice, particularly with the rise of practical theology, one observation I had whilst studying theology was that there is no clear self-reflective structure for students (and perhaps teachers) to link orthodoxy and orthopraxy within the classroom. A disconnection in the classroom between beliefs and practice fails to challenge individuals who may say that they believe one thing, but do not act out the implications of that truth. Swinton and Mowat maintain that 'faith exists in situations within which the gospel is embodied, interpreted, shaped and performed.'[18] Whilst the author of Hebrews defines faith as the 'confidence in what we hope for and assurance about what we do not see' (Heb 11:1), Scripture also affirms that faith without action is not really faith at all (Jas 2:17). If one is to faithfully believe in God's word, such faith should produce consistent action. Anything else unwittingly conveys a relativistic claim that truth is not absolute, even if this is done implicitly through action rather than explicitly through words. Therefore, Christians need to be able to engage with the relativistic philosophy and its influence both in the church and the world in order to effectively join the mission of God in making disciples and reaching the lost. Theodrama contributes to this goal.

## Theodrama: an introduction

The term theodrama was first coined by Hans Urs von Balthasar in the late 20th century with the printing of his four-volume work *Theodramatik*.[19] Although the core of his work was to explore how it is that God can allow human beings to have 'relative liberty' yet still have 'absolute liberty,'[20] the principle of using theatrical language in theological discussion is widespread. Elements of theodrama are seen in the works of N. T. Wright, first in his book *The New Testament and the People of God*. Wright uses the metaphor of a Shakespearian play in which the last act is missing and the actors have to use what has gone before to act out the rest of the drama.[21] Similarly, he suggests that Christians are to faithfully improvise as if they are characters in the biblical narrative without most of the fifth act, carefully 'puzzling over what has gone before.'[22] He has built upon this concept in his more recent publication *Scripture and the Authority of God*, in which he reaffirms his proposal of a five-act hermeneutic and stresses the importance of the church acting in 'the appropriate manner for *this* moment in the story.'[23]

Kevin J. Vanhoozer has also contributed significantly to the discussion surrounding theodrama and improvisation, particularly in his work *The Drama of Doctrine*. He suggests a five-act theodrama,[24] 'set in motion by a divine act' as seen in the biblical narrative, identifying the five acts as creation, the election of Israel, Christ, Pentecost and the church, and consummation.[25] Vanhoozer's identification of the five acts differs from that of Wright, who proposes the acts of creation, 'fall', Israel, Jesus, and the church.[26] Wright's highlighting of the fall has its own merits. However, Vanhoozer's model has two distinct advantages. The identification of the fifth act as 'consummation' discourages the adoption of an over-realised eschatology. Additionally, Vanhoozer's fifth act reminds the church that it 'does not have to work out the ending so much as to live in its light.'[27] Whatever one concludes the order should be, however, the core principles of theodrama, particularly improvisation, remain the same. Theodrama can therefore bring new light to important areas, specifically revolving around the question: how should the church improvise within the divine epic?

## Linking doctrine to practice

At this point we return to the problem I identified earlier, namely the lack of a self-reflective structure to link doctrine and practice within teaching contexts. Every drama requires a script. If we see God as the great director and dramatist—or as Lugt puts it, 'the playwright who is free to act in his own play'[28]—it is fitting to see God's word as a script. Viewed in this way, Scripture ceases to be only a collection of interesting stories, poetry, and propositions, but becomes a 'collection of authoritative stage directions for performing the Christian way of life in the truth.'[29] As such, the script 'calls not only for responsive reading but for responsive action and embodiment.'[30] In viewing Scripture as a script, it becomes by its very nature practical. It calls forth action on its own terms. It reconnects biblical teaching with the lived-out life of believers in Christ.

In this way, theodrama 'naturally connects doctrine and discipleship in such a way that orients us in the world as actors, participating in God's drama of redemption.'[31] Theodramatic theology requires a bridge between doctrine and lived out discipleship, a focal interest of practical theology (concerned with 'interactive performance').[32] Vanhoozer notes that doctrine does not just offer a blueprint for behaviour, but equips us to improvise when new situations and new problems arise rather than acting from memorisation.[33] Doctrine is character building so that one can be creative in how they live their lives towards God.

However, improvisation rooted in Scripture is not an excuse to exercise one's prejudice or presupposition of what they want Scripture to say, rather than what it does say. A theodramatic endeavour requires individuals to be ever more vigilant to stay in character, in line with the scriptwriter. Though there is scope to be creative in how one acts, it is within scriptural limitations set out by the author. As Lugt notes, 'just because improvisation is spontaneous ... does not mean it can be accomplished without preparation or discipline.'[34] To imitate Christ faithfully, one must 'understand the drama of redemption,'[35] and then imitate with fidelity to Christ. It is only then that one can act with creativity, 'if one is to continue the *same* pattern in a *different* situation.'[36] Vanhoozer argues that the role of theology is 'to hand on the truth...to disciples in new times and places; to continue the tradition by keeping it vital and vibrant.'[37] If Christians are to teach theology and doctrine effectively, it must be taught as something that can and should be embodied today. Doctrine should equip the church with virtue and wisdom to improvise effectively, in character, and coherently with the playwright (God).

Doctrine also raises another major aspect of theodrama: the characters. Within a drama, characters are not self-defining. They cannot decide to redefine themselves on their own terms. Characters are defined by the script as written by the script writer. Scripture and doctrine not only teach and inform characters of what to do and how to act but also define who they are and whose they are. This is seen explicitly through the theodramatic interpretation of the atonement. Vanhoozer states that 'who we are is ultimately defined in terms of Jesus' person and work.'[38] When we look at the doctrine of the atonement theodramatically, it points us to ponder on our union with Christ and acceptance before God.[39] The danger with any study that stops short of thinking about how it affects one's own self is that it can puff up (1 Cor 8:1) rather than build up (Col 3:16). Hence, the emphasis of doctrine taken theodramatically is how it affects the divine drama, including the characters. As such, the atonement ceases to be a faraway event with little relevance. On the contrary, it becomes central to a Christian's identity, which in turn affects how they act in the divine drama. It is in this way that 'doctrine itself [becomes] a means of character and spiritual formation insofar as it strips up our false masks (our persona) and discloses our true faces: faces that reflect the glory of God; faces that "speak" Christ.'[40]

When doctrine is viewed theodramatically there becomes very little room for orthodoxy without orthopraxy. Implicit relativism cannot manifest itself within believers who reflect and act consistently with their character. Additionally, the theodramatic approach invites students and teachers (whether within the church or academic contexts) to explore the practical implications of doctrine for character development and subsequent practice. Therefore, when implemented holistically, theodrama can become an effective self-reflective structure for learning which naturally leads to action.

## An antidote to relativism

Theodrama certainly has benefits within a theological teaching context (either in the church or theological training centres), but it also has advantages in engaging with those with a relativistic philosophy. The word 'identity' has become something of an ironic buzz word in Western culture. Concepts such as 'identity politics' increasingly drive decisions and culture, whilst discussions surrounding gender and sexual identity have become ever more prominent and controversial.[41] The increase in its prominence points to a lack of fulfilment in humanity's sense of identity and meaning. Relativism and its subsequent outworking may provide a momentary delusion of real identity, but whilst individuals and societies are bound by its ideology any search for identity by a relativistic method will only be grasping for the wind.

For Christians who struggle with an explicit form of relativism, theodrama provides a bridge to reconnect individuals to the absolute truth of Jesus and the narrative that is revealed through Scripture. It provides a way to participate in the divine drama, to find real grounding and identity. Scripture provides the basis for knowing who we are and whose we are, what our character is defined by, and how our creator has made us to function for our good and his glory. For those adhering to an openly relativistic philosophy within the church, the theodramatic model communicates wisdom and knowledge that leads us to improvise in accordance with the director's intentions.

Theodrama also has benefits for those outside the church struggling with the effects of relativism. Just as theodrama reveals to Christians who they are, the divine drama also informs those who do not know Jesus where they are in the story. Theodrama reveals to people their status before God (1 John 3:10) and what awaits such characters if they do not turn to God (Rom 6:23, Rev 20:14–15). The script also provides the way to everlasting life (John 3:16), lasting character change (1 Thess 4:3; Rom 6:22), and the present reality and future hope in Christ (Rev 21:1–8). Both Scripture and doctrine provide a solid foundation for establishing truth, particularly when it comes to character and identity formation. Practically, this involves bringing non-Christians to read Scripture, explaining the grand narrative to them, and explaining where they fit into the divine epic. Even if a person isn't following the script, they are still defined by it. However, for both Christians and non-Christians, we must pray that the wisdom of the word by the enlightenment of the Holy Spirit leads them to action. For relativism ceases to have power over those who look to the director's script to find themselves, and ultimately find themselves in Christ.

## Conclusion

In this chapter I have attempted to address two problems. The first is the lack of a structure to link orthodoxy and orthopraxy within teaching environments, which can exacerbate contradictions between what Christians say and what they do. To address this dilemma, I have suggested the use of theodramatic reflection to effectively link what Christians believe and how they act. The second problem I have addressed is how to reach out to those who hold to an explicit relativistic position by explaining the narrative and truth of Scripture to them, revealing their position in the grand narrative of life, thereby creating a bridge between their relativistic stance and the truth of the gospel.

## Notes

1 Kathleen A. Cahalan, "Three Approaches to Practical Theology, Theological Education, and the Church's Ministry," *International Journal of Practical Theology* 9, no. 1 (2005): 92.
2 Pete Ward, *Participation and Mediation: A Practical Theology for the Liquid Church* (London: SCM, 2008), 25.
3 James K. Mwangi, "An Integrated Competency-Based Training Model for Theological Training," *HTS Teologiese/Theological Studies* 62, vol. 2 (2010): 1.
4 Kenneth Boa and Robert M. Bowman Jr., *Faith Has Its Reasons: Integrative Approaches to Defending the Christian Faith* (Westmont: InterVarsity Press, 2006), 74.
5 D. A. Carson, *The Intolerance of Tolerance* (Grand Rapids: Eerdmans, 2012), 132.
6 Carl Trueman, "Postmodernism, Free Markets and Prophetic Margins," *Themelios* 30, no. 2 (2005). https://themelios.thegospelcoalition.org/article/postmodernism-free-markets-and-prophetic-margins/.
7 James K. A. Smith, *Who's Afraid of Relativism?: Community, Contingency, and Creaturehood* (Grand Rapids: Baker Academic, 2014), 179.
8 Smith, *Who's Afraid of Relativism?* 179.
9 Smith, *Who's Afraid of Relativism?* 180.
10 William Max Knorpp, "What Relativism Isn't," *Philosophy* 73, no. 284 (1998): 277–300.
11 Thomas Pölzler and Jennifer Cole Wright, "Anti-Realist Pluralism: A New Approach to Folk Metaethics," *Review of Philosophy and Psychology* 11 (2020): 71.
12 Cambridge Dictionary, "Meaning of Relativism in English," accessed Friday 14th August 2020. https://dictionary.cambridge.org/dictionary/english/relativism; Lexico, "Meaning of relativism in English," accessed Friday 14th August 2020. www.lexico.com/definition/relativism.
13 Nicholas Rosado, "My Experience with (Cultural) Relativism in the University," *Medium*, March 21, 2020. https://medium.com/@NickRosado/my-experience-with-cultural-relativism-in-the-university-53a1733b49e6.
14 Stephen A. Satris, "Student Relativism," *Teaching Philosophy* 9, no. 3 (1986): 193–205.
15 R. Paul Stevens, "Living Theologically: Toward a Theology of Christian Practice," *Themelios* 20, no. 3 (1995): 4.
16 John Swinton and Harriet Mowat, *Practical Theology and Qualitative Research*, 2nd ed. (London: SCM Press, 2016), 14.

talk and she then told me she was remembering a very moving Oberammergau Passion Play she had seen with her husband. She was surprised it had come to her mind.

I chose this encounter for reflection because, in the silence, Jenny remembered and then shared with me about the Passion Play. Without the silence, there may not have been space for Jenny to make the connection.

Let me explain a bit more about the encounter. We had just started chatting informally about things that mattered to her. Jenny spoke of her family and about her niece and nephew who were, in her opinion, very forthright about their Christian faith. Jenny herself was not a church goer but had been to Sunday school as a child. She shared her worry that her recent falls were a sign of her illness progressing. I might add here that Jenny is an actively minded and, on the whole, able-bodied 94-year-old and she looks after, with a bit of help, her husband who is 93.

Before finishing the service, it seemed right to leave some space. I chose not to move, clear away or even to speak. I could sense something was going on. Eventually Jenny told me about the play she had seen many years before in Germany with her husband. The recollection had clearly taken her by surprise. In the silence, Jenny had been taken back to a time when she was in another place, in a difference space, being confronted in a different way with the same gospel. It seemed to me that God was guiding Jenny back to a place which had meaning back then but also meaning for her now. In the silence of this chapel space, Jenny was being challenged again by the sacrifice Jesus made on the cross.

## Reflection

Reflecting on this encounter and complexifying it, as Swinton and Mowat encourage in their model of practical theology, I recognise there were various things going on.[1] As the service leader, who I am and what has impacted me over the years was influencing my practice on that day. As the participant, Jenny's own experience of church and how she viewed God and Jesus was affecting how she was choosing to engage and share. And how Jenny responded to my informal style of leadership and the opportunity to sit in silence together at the end would, again, have bearing on her participation and perhaps even her willingness to be open to God.

There are various different avenues of analysis and reflection which I could consider here but I have chosen to focus on just one, silence, and whether including periods of stillness and silence during the service is helping achieve my aim of creating space for hospice patients to meet with God.

### Creating space: stillness

> Be still and know that I am God. (Ps 46:10)

This familiar verse in Scripture is often quoted in relation to contemplation. As Goldingay affirms, 'it suggests an atmosphere of meditation and quiet.'[2] His own preference, however, is for the TEV (GNT) translation which replaces 'Be still' with the stronger command to 'Stop fighting'. Although fighting infers war, Kidner points out that the context into which this psalm was written is unidentified.[3] He concludes it is likely to be a crisis in a world 'devastated and forcibly disarmed.'[4] Harman writes that the command was for battle opposition and the Hebrew verb means more 'to abandon' because, as the enemy, they need to submit to God and his authority.[5] To whomever the instruction is directed, it is a command to cease action, to remember who God is and to recognise his power amidst trouble.[6] Frost comments on the same verse, 'In a world of growing pressure and pain, I need to discover a form of Christian spirituality which does not separate me from the world ... but which enables me to find the stillness of God's presence in the thick of the action!'[7]

I wonder if Psalm 46:10 could therefore be interpreted as follows:

Stop, know that I am God in the midst of this crisis,
acknowledge my power to save—trust in me.

Upon reflection, this is a large part of what I am hoping to achieve when I am creating space in chapel to be still. I want to allow opportunity for patients to experience God's presence and for them to discover that they too can trust God 'in the thick of the action', in the midst of their 'devastated and forcibly disarmed' worlds.

Stillness and silence are harder for some people than for others. I recognise that not everyone who attends chapel has come from the same churchmanship as me. My experience and the opportunities I have had to meet with God have been in fairly low church evangelical Anglican churches where, generally, time for quiet reflection is minimal. More recently I have come to value contemplative worship and prayer. A personal study on evangelical spirituality and the writings of Brother Lawrence revealed that I enjoy some practices encouraged by the monk. Although he struggled with meditation and wandering thoughts, Lawrence persevered.[8] He acknowledged 'holy inactivity,' recognising the presence of God in stillness.[9] His call to ceaseless prayer in giving 'attention to keeping your mind in the presence of the Lord' is another practice that I have benefitted from.[10] These practices are consistent with the evangelical spirituality that I am familiar with: yielding one's body, mind, and spirit to God (Mark 12:30). Foster observes that the contemplative tradition 'forces us beyond merely a cerebral religion.'[11] So in as much as I value stimulating sermons, vibrant worship, and corporate intercessory prayer, I also cherish sitting in silence with God. It is these different experiences of church and prayer which significantly influence my practice as service leader in chapel.

Knowing a little of Jenny's church background, as the participant, she was of the era in the 1930s when attending Sunday school was the norm as a child. Services were likely structured and led from the front, without any lengthy times of quiet for personal contemplation. Jenny told me previously that she was sad she had stopped attending church but that she had never lost her faith. She also shared with me that as she had matured in age and become more housebound, she delighted in just being able to sit down and let her thoughts drift away. In effect, she had mastered the art of being able to 'switch off' the world and just be. So perhaps this skill (or could it be called a gift?) that she had developed in her later years enabled Jenny to respond positively to my leading times of quiet and stillness in chapel services each week.

*Creating space: silence*

At the hospice, just as in regular church, patients come from all walks of life. Sickness, and in particular cancer, is one of life's levellers. Gathered together, there are many different personalities present. Ruth Fowke, in her book *Personality and Prayer*, writes that 'intuitive people value silence for much of their prayer.'[12] As I read, I learned that even some extroverts appreciate and have need for silence too.[13] An extrovert myself, I have discovered that I extrovert my intuition. What does that mean? Fowke quotes Bruce Duncan who explains that 'extraverted intuition scans the outer world like a minesweeper, picking up any perceptions that have special meaning.'[14] Duncan continues by saying that 'extraverted prayer is always seeking to find new and ingenious ways of co-operating with God to transform the world into God's Kingdom. The inner vision alone is not enough, unless it can be turned into external reality.'[15] I may love praying and being silent, musing things over with God, but as Fowke says, I will 'want to share my reflections with others ... in order to progress and grow in the spiritual life.'[16]

Returning to Jenny in the chapel, my thought process in the stillness of that moment was immediately to take her memory about the experience of the Passion Play years before and see if it would speak into her experience as she had received Holy Communion and focussed on Jesus. Was this an opportunity for Jenny to progress and grow in her own spiritual life? In the silence, I believed that God was doing something in Jenny that was significant and I wanted to co-operate with God, grasp it by the horns and run with it. I wonder if Jenny had accidentally discovered what Margaret Silf would call a 'sacred space'? A place in her imagination using her memory where she would be able to meet with God.[17]

Wilcock speaks of entering into a place of silence and compares it to 'wandering unexpectedly into a glade in a wood. Silence, suddenly opening out—not just a gap or an interlude, but a real place of its own.'[18] Wilcock shares her wisdom for the spiritual care giver (that person would be me in my role as chaplain) to 'permit the momentousness of its presence, the intimacy of its stillness, the deep, unspoken exchanges that take place there.'[19] In caring well for Jenny, I was to stay silent, rather than satisfy the cravings of the evangelical spiritual activist within me that was desperate to speak. I needed to attend the communicative voice of silence and quietly accompany Jenny, allowing her time to be still in that space she had unexpectedly found herself in.[20] We both needed to tune into 'the cadence of God's time'.[21]

## Creating space: in the midst of chaos

Silence was okay for Jenny. But what about for those patients who find silence uncomfortable. Greig describes the world as 'one loud reverberating echo-chamber' with the fear of silence being evidence of our broken culture.[22] He encourages Christians to make space for silent prayer, as does Comer in his book about '[h]ow to stay emotionally healthy and spiritually alive in the chaos of the modern world.'[23] Comer explores the desert or wilderness place (translated from the Greek word *eremos*) where Jesus went after his baptism. There are various meanings but Comer prefers 'quiet place.'[24] He is challenged by the scene and asks questions about why Jesus had to go there. He concludes that the wilderness, *eremos*, was not a place where Jesus was weakened but strengthened. It was only after he had fasted and prayed for forty days in the *eremos* that Jesus had the 'capacity to take on the devil himself and walk away unscathed'.[25] Jesus gained internal strength from being in a quiet place with God:

> It is not easy to enter into the silence and reach beyond the many boisterous and demanding voices of our world and to discover there the small intimate voice saying "You are my Beloved Child, on you my favour rests."[26]

The patients in chapel are perhaps dealing with more than most when it comes to demanding distractions: physical pain and discomfort, frustration, and sadness at not being able to do what they used to do ever again, tiredness and anxiety about the future, especially as the time of letting loved ones go draws near. I wonder, does having extended periods of silence in chapel give patients too much time to think? And if the answer to that question is yes, but I still believe silence to be a good thing, then surely it is my responsibility to guide people into and out of that silence effectively, to make it less daunting. How I frame that silence is important.

I also ask is not God, who was victorious over chaos when he created the world, not able to speak into and through distractions?[27] I can surely learn again from Nouwen when he notes that being still each day in the presence of God, 'in total confusion and with myriad distractions', radically changed his life.[28] And I wonder, could not inner joy be an end result of silence? Augustine wrote about silence and stillness many centuries ago in the poem 'Entering into Joy'.[29] Each line calls to our imagination: 'Imagine if all the tumult of the body were to quiet down, along with all our busy thoughts about earth, sea, and air; if the very world should stop, and the mind cease thinking about itself, go beyond itself, and be quite still.' At the end we are left to ponder Augustine's question, 'Would this not be what is bidden in Scripture, Enter thou into the joy of thy Lord?'[30]

## Final thoughts

Having theologically reflected on this encounter, I have one further question to ask myself: what do I need to do differently or be more aware of going forward? I can see that it is important to carefully consider the starting point from which people come into chapel. I must not assume that they have given God even a moment's thought that day. And perhaps I need to give more thought to those patients who better connect with God when liturgy is spoken throughout and not during periods of silence. I conclude that it is therefore essential to have prepared myself (and my words) well for each service, but it is just as essential that I pay extra attention to the leading and guiding of the Holy Spirit. If silence, as Wilcock describes, is a language which 'can be read, heard, [and] beheld,' I need to be spiritually alert for moments where God is communicating in a deep and transformative way.[31] As Wilcock concludes, both silence and words are necessary, 'for we arrive at silence through words, and words find their value in silence.'[32]

## Postscript

On that day with Jenny in the hospice, a place where people are faced with their own mortality, I had prepared to share words from Scripture which spoke of God's immortality (1 Tim 6:16). I had also planned for us to sing the hymn, Immortal Invisible, based on that same text. However, I did not realise until later that verse two of the hymn contains many words which describe God, the second of them being 'unhasting.'[33] Fifteen weeks later, when given the opportunity choose a favourite hymn to share with the rest of the chapel folk, Jenny chose 'Be Still for the Presence of the Lord.'[34]

## Notes

1. John Swinton and Harriet Mowat, *Practical Theology and Qualitative Research*, 2nd ed. (London: SCM, 2016), 13–15.
2. John Goldingay, *Songs from A Strange Land: Psalms 42–51*, BST (Leicester: IVP, 1978), 109.
3. Derek Kidner, *Psalms 1–72*, Tyndale OT Commentaries (Leicester: IVP, 1973), 174.
4. Kidner, *Psalms*, 176.
5. Allan Harman, *Psalms Vol 1 (Psalms 1–72): A Mentor Commentary* (Fearn: Christian Focus, 2011), 374.
6. Goldingay, *Songs*, 100–110.
7. Rob Frost, "Foreword," in *Into God's Presence*, ed. Liz Babbs (Grand Rapids: Zondervan, 2005), Foreword.
8. Brother Lawrence, *The Practice of The Presence of God* (USA: Mockingbird Classics Publishing, 2015), 15.
9. Lawrence, *Practice*, 39.
10. Brother Lawrence, *The Practice of the Presence of God*, trans. E. M. Blaiklock (London: Hodder & Stoughton, 1981), pp. 49–50 as cited by Julie Lunn, "Paying Attention: The Task of Attending in Spiritual Direction and Practical Theology," *Practical Theology* 2, no. 2 (2009): 219–229, 220.

11 Richard J. Foster, *Streams of Living Water* (London: Fount, 1999), 51.
12 Ruth Fowke, *Personality and Prayer* (Guildford: Eagle, 1997), 45.
13 Fowke, *Personality*, 45.
14 Bruce Duncan, *Pray Your Way* (London: DLT, 1993), 110, in Fowke, *Personality*, 43.
15 Duncan, *Pray Your Way*, 111, in Fowke, *Personality*, 43.
16 Fowke, *Personality*, 46.
17 Margaret Silf, *Taste and See: Adventuring into Prayer* (London: Darton, Longman & Todd, 1999), 17.
18 Penelope Wilcock, *Spiritual Care: Of Dying and Bereaved People* (Abingdon: BRF, 2013), 61.
19 Wilcock, *Spiritual Care*, 61.
20 Julie Lunn, "Paying Attention: The Task of Attending in Spiritual Direction and Practical Theology," *Practical Theology* 2, no. 2 (2009): 224–225.
21 John Swinton, *Becoming Friends of Time: Disability, Timefullness, and Gentle Discipleship* (London: SCM, 2016), 65.
22 Pete Greig, *How to Pray: A Simple Guide for Normal People* (London: Hodder & Stoughton, 2019), Tool Shed index of Thirty Prayer Tools, Contemplation 17: Silent Prayer.
23 John Mark Comer, *The Ruthless Elimination of Hurry* (London: Hodder & Stoughton, 2019).
24 Comer, *Ruthless Elimination*, 124.
25 Comer, *Ruthless Elimination*, 125.
26 Henri J. M. Nouwen, *Life of The Beloved* (London: Hodder and Stoughton, 1992), 62–63.
27 Goldingay, *Songs*, 101.
28 Henri J. M. Nouwen, "Sitting in the Presence," in *Primacy of the Heart* (Madison: St Benedict Center, 1988), 9 cited by Philip Yancey, *Prayer* (London: Hodder & Stoughton, 2006), 144.
29 St Augustine, "Entering into Joy," Bmcm.Org. Accessed April 20, 2020, www.bmcm.org/inspiration/passages/entering-joy/.
30 St Augustine, "Entering into Joy," in Comer, *Ruthless Elimination*, 131.
31 Wilcock, *Spiritual Care*, 63.
32 Wilcock, *Spiritual Care*, 62–63.
33 Walter Chalmers Smith, "Immortal Invisible," Words: Public Domain.
34 David J. Evans, "Be Still for the Presence of the Lord," © 1986 Thankyou Music (Admin. by Integrity Music).

# 13 An Elim community pneumatologically engaged in corporate theological reflection

*Sheryl Arthur*

Pentecostal pneumatology is 'primarily concerned with the critical experience, reception, or filling of the Spirit as described, especially, by Luke in Acts.'[1] Notably, this 'critical experience' (understood to be available to all believers today[2]) is not simply seen as a momentary event, but marks the start of a lifestyle of being continuously filled with (and empowered by) the Spirit to reach out to others.[3] In practice, therefore, the Spirit-filled life shapes not only how Pentecostals see the world, but also how they participate in it.[4] That is to say, it is central to how Pentecostals 'do' practical theology.

It was in view of the above, that I set out to design and conduct my own congregational study in a manner that reflected the Pentecostal movement I was researching, and to which I belonged.[5] In this chapter I share just a small part of that study which explores how Elim Pentecostal believers interpret their lived experiences of Spirit baptism in relation to those experiences recorded in the book of Acts. Specifically, I attend to how I adopted a pneumatological approach to corporate theological reflection through the design and facilitation of my focus groups.

I begin, therefore, by providing a theological framework for my approach, drawing primarily on Cartledge's, *The Mediation of the Spirit: Interventions in Practical Theology*.[6] Following this, I narrate how I intentionally created space for congregants (and indeed myself) to wait upon, and respond to, the lead of the Spirit in order to make meaningful connections between Scripture and personal Holy Spirit encounter. After reflecting (albeit briefly) on this process, I offer three caveats, concluding that whilst researching collaboratively *with* a congregation requires a theologically tailored approach to research design, such an approach has the potential to generate data that authentically represents congregants' faith and praxis.

## A theological framework for my approach

Early on in the design of my congregational study, I came to the decision that the use of focus groups, as a means to engage the congregation in corporate theological reflection, would be instrumental in implementing my pneumatological approach. Here I use Heather Walton's description of 'corporate theological

DOI: 10.4324/9781003094975-18

reflection', that '[t]he community generates corporate narratives in the course of life together that function to describe the community to itself and articulate its sense of purpose and mission.'[7] Theological reflection, therefore, 'identifies and interprets these shared stories.'[8] My decision to use focus groups in this way was, in part, influenced by how I felt about my insider status to the research project. That is, I did not feel entirely comfortable utilising an approach where I predominantly '*did*' my research *on* the congregation, rather I wanted to embrace a model that enabled me to conduct my research in critical collaboration *with* them.

A further influence came from my wider reading of Pentecostal theology, where the importance of the community emerged as a recurrent theme. One work of significance was Cartledge's *The Mediation of the Spirit*, in which he evidences from within the book of Acts[9] the ways that the Spirit both mediates and is mediated. Cartledge suggests a number of pneumatological 'interventions' for practical theology, asserting that since 'the Holy Spirit not only constituted the early church but continues to constitute the church in present-day reality, one would expect to be able to discern the continual mediation of the Holy Spirit through the concrete ecclesial communities and intermediaries today.'[10] In particular, it was his treatment of Acts 15 (where the Jerusalem Council deliberate over the admittance of newly converted Gentiles into the Christian community) that informed the design of my focus groups. That is, Cartledge's insights into how '[t]he Jerusalem Council's decision making mediates the presence of the Holy Spirit among its members by recalling the signs and wonders, by interpreting Scripture, and through its own communal reasoning processes,'[11] reinforced my decision to engage members of the congregation in corporate theological reflection.

Whilst I am aware that Cartledge is not alone[12] in referencing the importance of Acts 15 as 'a model for describing the relationship between the text of Scripture, the role of the community, and the experience of the Holy Spirit,'[13] I specifically cite his work because of his emphasis on the Spirit's mediation. Other works that consolidated my choice of approach were those that explicitly highlighted the value of the Acts 15 triadic for Elim's faith and praxis. Frestadius, for example, in his philosophical theology of the Elim movement proposes that Elim 'increasingly embrace the model represented in Acts 15, as it provides a biblical precedence for its hermeneutics and also naturally fits with Elim's rationality and historical practice',[14] and Carter, in his empirical study on hermeneutics (in relation to women in ministry), observed that '[w]hen considering a contentious topic, a triadic hermeneutical approach is evident in the practised theology of many Elim Pentecostal lay leaders.'[15]

Mindful, therefore, of the above, I sought within my own study, to enable an Elim community to reflect theologically on their experiences of Spirit baptism in relation to the Bible (as 'the fully inspired and infallible Word of God and the supreme and final authority in all matters of faith and conduct'[16]), expectant that, as a group, *we* would be able to discern the mediation of the Holy Spirit through our interactions.

## A pneumatological approach to corporate theological reflection

The Elim Pentecostal church at the centre of my study was birthed following the success of a three-week revival campaign led by George Jeffreys in 1927. Today the church is still going strong, comprising approximately 150 regular attenders (90 adult members), representing a range of ethnicities, ages, and social backgrounds.[17] Whilst it is not my intention here to share the wider detail of this study, it is perhaps useful to note that before I embarked on my focus groups, I conducted a congregational survey to ascertain whether congregants did indeed hold views on the Bible and the Holy Spirit consistent with the Elim movement's doctrine. From this survey, I was able to establish that 95.5% of adult congregants believed that the Bible is 'as originally given, to be without error, the fully inspired and infallible word of God'[18] and 92.5% believed that the signs and wonders recorded in the book of Acts can be experienced today.[19] In view of this, I felt that if I modelled my corporate theological reflection sessions on Acts 15, seemingly my approach would authentically represent the theology of my participants. In total, therefore, I conducted four small focus groups, consisting of 16 self-selected participants.[20] One group was made up of church leaders (elders and deacons) and the other three, non-leaders. This segregation was intentional to reduce any 'significant power imbalances between recruited participants.'[21]

Given (as we are about to see) that I would be asking participants to engage in ways not too dissimilar to how they ordinarily engaged in group Bible study,[22] it was especially important that I clarified that the session was part of an academic research project. At the start of each of the group sessions, therefore, I began by articulating the aims of my research (also displayed for clarity) before moving on to deal with matters of ethical protocol.

After attending to these important formalities, I commenced each of the group theological reflection sessions by praying for the Holy Spirit to 'mediate' through *our* individual thoughts and collective discussions. I was aware in doing this that it may not be well received by some within the academy. As Butler writes, '[t]here is a suspicion of prayer within practical theology, not whether it is a suitable area for research, but as something which might be part of the research process.'[23] I was, nevertheless, intentional in my pneumatological approach, attempting to 'do' practical theology in a manner authentic to the community.

Whilst I was all for being open to the Spirit's leading,[24] this did not mean, however, that I could negate my responsibilities as a facilitator. Namely, it was important that in advance of the event I had thought through how I could structure the discussion to enable *all* participants to contribute and also to ensure that any experiences shared were interpreted in light of Scripture (as the 'final authority in all matters of faith…'[25]). Prior to the focus groups, therefore, I selected key texts from the book of Acts to form the basis of our shared theological reflections. I did this for several reasons. First, I was aware that it would be impractical to refer to the whole book in a 90-minute session, therefore selection was required for logistical reasons. Having said that, participants were encouraged to make reference to other Scriptures as they saw fit. Second, I was conscious that if I did not pre-select some biblical texts on which to focus the discussion, participants may well not make any reference to Scripture at all. And third, I wanted to ensure that the group engaged with more contentious texts, not just those that are a comfortable read. After prayerful reflection, therefore, I selected 21 passages relating to Spirit baptism and to a variety of different examples of 'signs following'.[26] Having selected these texts, I scrolled through a bank of online images, choosing a corresponding image for each text. These were then printed onto double-sided postcards (see Figure 13.1).[27]

In terms, of facilitating the discussion, I loosely made use of Krueger's five different categories of question. Those questions were the: 'Opening' (to allow participants to get acquainted); 'Introductory' (to begin the discussion); 'Transition' (to move smoothly into key questions); 'Key' (to obtain insight on areas of central concern) and 'Ending' (to bring closure to the discussion).[28]

My 'opening' question was designed to encourage everyone to speak early in the group.[29] Given that participants were known to one another, I did not feel it was necessary to ask them to introduce themselves or to engage in an icebreaker activity. Instead (and in line with my pneumatological approach), I invited them to individually pray and ask the Holy Spirit to lead them in choosing one (or more if they felt led) of the 21 images that I had placed on a side table in the room.

*Figure 13.1* Examples of Image/Bible Text Cards

In order to give all participants an unrestricted choice of images, I asked them to refrain from picking up their chosen card(s) until everyone had made their selection. This allowed more than one person to choose the same card if they felt that that was where the Holy Spirit was leading them. When each person had selected their card(s) from the side table, they brought their chosen images and corresponding numbers back to the group.[30]

As a trained adult facilitator, I had some prior experience of using images as a tool to enable critical engagement. As Plouffe explains, people's response to images is a physiological one that 'happens immediately, regardless of language or cultural norms.'[31] This means that as soon as people start to share their ideas about the images, they begin to connect with one another and it is this connection that leads to effective collaboration.[32] Since some of my participants were not native English speakers, the use of images was one of the ways that I used to break down language barriers and create a more even playing field for everyone to take part. Given that I wanted to facilitate theological reflection *corporately*, purposefully creating this connection within the group was vital. Indeed, using images to reflect theologically is certainly not a new concept. For example, Killen and De Beer in, *The Art of Theological Reflection*, observed how '[b]y entering the space of the image we open ourselves to new insight, to new learning, to being changed, and potentially to revelation.'[33] Also, Thompson et al., in *Theological Reflection*, identify how cards imprinted with frequently found images from the Bible can be used to catalyse reflections and help make links with Scripture and tradition.[34]

When I made the decision to ask my participants to wait on the Holy Spirit's leading to choose their image(s), I knew that such a task would be well received, since it was in keeping with the belief that the Spirit does speak today,[35] and what's more, that He can use various mediums in which to do so, such as 'life circumstances, events in the news, a random saying in a book or magazine, a dream ....'[36] As anticipated, therefore, when invited, each of my participants expectantly waited upon the Holy Spirit, listening to what He might say prophetically through the images.[37]

After each participant had shared their thoughts concerning their image(s), I asked them my 'introductory' question, which was to turn over their card(s) and, *if* they were comfortable in doing so, to read aloud the text that was on the back. I also displayed the image and text so that everyone else could follow. When the text had been read, and I had checked that participants understood the context of the story, I asked my 'transition' question. That is, I invited the participant(s) who had chosen the card to comment on whether they had experienced anything in their own lives that they associated with the reading. After they had been given an opportunity to share their testimony(ies) or thoughts concerning the particular Bible passage, I opened the discussion up to the rest of the participants, so that *together* we could reflect theologically on the experiences shared. In taking this approach I drew on the fact that, for Pentecostals, 'the concept of testimony, the telling of one's personal story of God's activity, is central to the ordinary expression of faith.'[38] As such, it was a mode of theology that my participants were naturally comfortable with. I also took into consideration 'what constitutes for Pentecostals the original hermeneutics of Pentecost.'[39] That is, I embraced the fact that many Pentecostals interpret their experiences in line with the biblical texts by applying a 'this *is* that' approach, as modelled by Peter in Acts 2 when he explained the Pentecostal event (this) as a fulfilment of Joel's prophecy (that).[40] As Vondey explains, Pentecostals are not calling for 'the return to biblical history but to participation in an enduring theological symbol.'[41] Namely, they 'relate their experience to scripture … because they interpret and authenticate their present experiences as participating in the biblical events thrust anew into the present.'[42]

Whilst I had prepared in advance 'key' questions that needed to be addressed (relating to my research project aims[43]), I found that I did not need to pose them directly, since my choice of Scriptures (and images) enabled the answers to naturally emerge through the free flowing discussion. As such, I felt I was able to create space for the Spirit to mediate through our deliberations. When the discussion came to a natural close, I then posed my 'ending' question, which was simply to ask participants if they had anything to add in relation to my research question, before I summed up the key themes of our discussion and asked them whether they felt it was an adequate summary. I finished by closing in prayer.

## Conclusion

On reflection, I was encouraged by how Elim congregants pneumatologically engaged in my corporate theological reflection sessions. That said, I would not wish to give the impression that the above approach can be indiscriminately applied to all research topics and/or congregational contexts. By way of conclusion, therefore, I first make brief comment on my own experience of the process before I offer three caveats for anyone intending to take a similar approach to my own.

Accordingly, in terms of my own experience, I found that Elim congregants were eager to engage pneumatologically in reflecting upon their experiences of Spirit baptism in relation to the book of Acts. Seemingly, there was a real sense within the group that the Spirit could be discerned as He mediated the discussion, guiding participants to specific images and Scriptures and prompting them to testify to signs and wonders.[44] In addition to this, some participants perceived that the Spirit was mediated to them personally through the discussion. For example, after the sessions had taken place, comments were made, such as: 'thank you for allowing me to take part in it, I was truly blessed'; 'it was a wonderful time in the presence of God'; and 'it was powerful'. One participant testified that she had experienced emotional release from a difficult work situation, stating that she now understood why God had wanted her to take part in the group.[45] Another shared how (through reading Acts 16 and reflecting on the loosed chains image, see Figure 13.1) she sensed God was encouraging the wider church to 'keep going'.

In terms of my offer of three caveats, my first relates to how I engaged with the Bible. That is, my research topic was such that it lent itself to congregants applying a 'this *is* that' hermeneutic to standalone texts. For obvious reasons, such a hermeneutic would not have been appropriate if I had chosen, for example, certain Old Testament passages as a basis for our theological reflections.[46]

My second caveat relates to how I engaged participants in 'waiting upon' the Spirit. Namely, when I designed my focus groups, I was already aware that the Elim community (on the whole) would be comfortable taking a Spirit-led approach to prayer and Bible reading. Clearly in churches where participation in the pneumatic is not the norm, this approach may be less effective.[47]

My third and final caveat concerns the messiness of engaging in such an approach. That is, as I facilitated my focus groups, I had to be willing, if necessary, to depart from my carefully made plans and trust that the reflective community would *together* discern and follow the Spirit's lead. No doubt, not everyone will feel comfortable with the unpredictable nature of such a process.

In conclusion, my narrated approach illustrates one possible way of engaging (as a Pentecostal or/and with Pentecostals) in corporate theological reflection. Notably, as my identified caveats show, giving consideration to the theological starting point of participants requires a theologically tailored approach to research design. Whilst, inevitably, this may be time-consuming and not always straightforward, approaching research in this way does, nonetheless, positively empower congregants to work *with* the researcher in authentically representing their faith and praxis.

## Notes

1 Frederick Dale Bruner, *A Theology of the Holy Spirit: The Pentecostal Experience and the New Testament Witness* (Grand Rapids: Eerdmans, 1970), 57.
2 Keith Warrington, "The Holy Spirit," in *The Message: Elim's Core Beliefs*, ed. Keith Warrington (Malvern: Elim, no date), 24–25.
3 Elim, "How to Administer the Baptism in the Spirit," in *The Message: Elim's Core Beliefs*, ed. Keith Warrington (Malvern: Elim, no date), 60.
4 See Wolfgang Vondey, *Pentecostalism: A Guide for the Perplexed* (London: T&T Clark, 2013), 33.
5 That is a movement (Elim) of Pentecostal churches working in the UK, Ireland and over 40 nations around the world. The Elim movement is a member of the Evangelical Alliance. See: Elim, "We are Elim," Elim, no date, accessed August 30, 2020, www.elim.org.uk/Groups/243050/About_Elim.aspx.
6 Mark Cartledge, *The Mediation of the Spirit: Interventions in Practical Theology* (Grand Rapids: Eerdmans, 2015).
7 Heather Walton, *Writing Methods in Theological Reflection* (London: SCM, 2014), xx.
8 Walton, *Writing Methods*, xx.
9 He focuses on: Acts 2; Acts 8:5–25; Acts 9:1–19a; Acts 10:23b–48; Acts 15:1–29; Acts 19:1–7.
10 Cartledge, *Mediation of the Spirit*, 113.
11 Cartledge, *Mediation of the Spirit*, 108.

12 For example, John C. Thomas, "Women, Pentecostals and the Bible: An Experiment in Pentecostal Hermeneutics," *Journal of Pentecostal Theology* 2, no. 5 (1994): 41–56; Kenneth J. Archer, *A Pentecostal Hermeneutic for the Twenty-First Century: Spirit, Scripture and Community* (London: T&T Clark International, 2004) and Amos Yong, *Spirit-Word-Community: Theological Hermeneutics in Trinitarian Perspective* (Eugene: Wipf & Stock, 2006).
13 Cartledge, *Mediation of the Spirit*, 116.
14 Simo Frestadius, *Pentecostal Rationality: Epistemology and Theological Hermeneutics in the Foursquare Tradition* (London: T&T Clark, 2020), 182.
15 Jamys Jeremy Carter, "A Critical Analysis of the Pentecostal Hermeneutics used by Elim Local Church Leadership Teams in Relation to the Topic of Women in Ministry," (PhD diss., University of Leeds, 2019), 179. http://etheses.whiterose.ac.uk/25608/1/Carter_JJ_PRHS_PhD_2019.pdf.
16 This wording is taken from Elim's first Foundational Truth on 'The Bible'. See "What We Believe," Elim, no date, accessed April 17, 2020, www.elim.org.uk/Publisher/Article.aspx?id=417857&redirected=1
17 There are approximately 200 people who would call the church their 'home', although not all are regular attenders.
18 Elim, "What We Believe."
19 These statistics were taken from those adult congregants (73 in total) who filled out the survey during a Sunday service in November 2019.
20 This represented 18% of adult congregants in attendance on the Sunday when I conducted the congregational survey.
21 Helen Cameron and Catherine Duce, *Researching Practice in Ministry and Mission: A Companion* (London: SCM, 2013), 112.
22 Johns and Johns, for example, propose an approach to Pentecostal Bible study that includes: the sharing of testimony; searching the Scriptures; yielding to the Spirit and responding to the call. See Jackie David Johns and Cheryl Bridges Johns, "Yielding to the Spirit: A Pentecostal Approach to Group Bible Study," *Journal of Pentecostal Theology* 1, no. 1 (1992): 124. Found via Mark J Cartledge, *Testimony: Its Importance, Place and Potential* (Cambridge: Grove Books Limited, 2002), 6–7.
23 James Butler, "Prayer as a Research Practice? What Corporate Practices of Prayer Disclose about Theological Action Research," *Ecclesial Practices* 7, no. 2 (2020): 241–257, 241.
24 Parker's explanation of the '*leading of the Spirit*' is helpful here. He defines it as '*inclinations to act in one way or another that are believed to arise from the Holy Spirit.*' He clarifies that '[t]hese inclinations may arise as spontaneous thoughts and feelings within the person but may at times be generated by the suggestions of another Spirit-filled person.' Stephen E. Parker, *Led by the Spirit: Toward a Practical Theology of Pentecostal Discernment and Decision Making*, expanded ed. (Cleveland: CPT Press, 1996), 6.
25 Elim, "What We Believe."
26 These texts were: Acts 1:8; Acts 2:2–6; Acts 2:16–17; Acts 4:24, 27–31; Acts 5:1–5a; Acts 5:12–16; Acts 8:14–17; Acts 8:38b–40; Acts 9:1–6a; Acts 9:17–18; Acts 9:36–38, 40–42; Acts 10:3–6, 44–48; Acts 11:27–28; Acts 12:5–11; Acts 14:1–6; Acts 16:16–19; Acts 16:22–23, 25–26, 29–30; Acts 19:4–6; Acts 19:11–12; Acts 21:10–13 and Acts 28:3–6.
27 Images shown: Jacub Gomez, *Silhouette Photography of Man at Beach during Sunset*, 2018, Pexels, accessed August 27, 2020, www.pexels.com/photo/backlit-beach-clouds-dusk-1142941/; Pixabay, *Low Section of Man Against Sky*, 2016, Pexels, accessed August 27, 2020 www.pexels.com/photo/low-section-of-man-against-sky-247851/.
28 Richard A. Krueger, *Focus Group Kit 3, Developing Questions for Focus Groups* (Thousand Oaks, CA: SAGE Publications, 1998), 22.
29 Krueger, *Focus Group Kit 3*, 23.

30 The use of numbers simply enabled me to keep a record of the images that were chosen.
31 Tammie Plouffe, *The Art of Connection: Using Images in Training Facilitation*, Training Industry, 2018, accessed Mar 10, 2020, https://trainingindustry.com/articles/content-development/the-art-of-connection-using-images-in-training-facilitation/.
32 Plouffe, *The Art of Connection*.
33 Patricia O'Connell Killen and John De Beer, *The Art of Theological Reflection*, (New York, NY: Crossroad, 2002), 41.
34 Judith Thompson with Ross Thompson and Stephen Pattison, *SCM Studyguide: Theological Reflection*, 2nd ed. (London: SCM, 2019), 230.
35 Warrington, "The Holy Spirit," 26.
36 Michael J. McClymond, "The Bible and Pentecostalism," in *The Oxford Handbook of the Bible in America*, ed. Paul C. Gutjahr (Oxford: Oxford University Press, 2017), 598, www-oxfordhandbooks-com.roe.idm.oclc.org/view/10.1093/oxfordhb/9780190258849.001.0001/oxfordhb-9780190258849-e-25.
37 Prophetic art is commonplace in many charismatic/Pentecostal worship settings. I was partly inspired to use images in my research after attending a workshop led by Mayra Pankow at the European Leaders Advance Conference held in Harrogate in July 2019.
38 Mark J. Cartledge, *Testimony in the Spirit: Rescripting Ordinary Pentecostal Theology*, 2nd ed. (London: Routledge, 2017), 17.
39 Wolfgang Vondey, *Pentecostal Theology: Living the Full Gospel* (London: T&T Clark, 2017), 16.
40 Vondey, *Pentecostal Theology*, 16.
41 Vondey, *Pentecostal Theology*, 17.
42 Vondey, *Pentecostal Theology*, 16.
43 As stated at the start of this chapter, my primary research aim is to explore how Elim Pentecostal believers interpret their lived experiences of Spirit baptism in relation to those experiences recorded in the book of Acts.
44 Examples included: physical healings; deliverance; giving and receiving prophetic words; angel visitations and receiving the gift of tongues.
45 I was interested to read that when Carter (an Elim pastor) conducted focus groups based on his Pentecostal methodology (which included starting with prayer), he also received feedback from participants testifying to how God had spoken/ministered to them personally through the group discussion. See Carter, "A Critical Analysis of the Pentecostal Hermeneutics," 56, 58.
46 To make sense of such texts, more contextual information would have been required, not least because most Pentecostals (in line with many other Christians) see the Bible as a progressive revelation. Namely, 'later revelation builds upon the earlier.' See William, L. Oliverio, *Theological Hermeneutics in the Classical Pentecostal Tradition: A Typological Account* (Leiden & Boston: Brill, 2012), 162, commenting on the theology of Arrington in: French Arrington, *Christian Doctrine: A Pentecostal Perspective, vol 1* (Cleveland: Pathway, 1992), 39.
47 I use the term 'pneumatic' in a Pentecostal sense. Vondey's definition is helpful: 'as the experience resulting from the encounter with the Spirit.' See Vondey, *Pentecostal Theology*, 18.

Part V

# Theology that impacts church and world

# 14 Evangelical practical theology
## Reviewing the past, analysing the present and anticipating the future

*Mark J. Cartledge*

### Introduction

I am grateful to the editors for the invitation to write this chapter. My previous overview chapters on the subject of practical theology have been written for volumes either in Pentecostal studies,[1] or from the perspective of Pentecostalism in a volume on practical theology.[2] While there is a significant overlap between evangelicalism and Pentecostalism, they are not coterminous and this is especially seen in the USA, where there can be considerable tension between the two camps for historical and theological reasons. Pentecostalism in America is also more multicultural and ethnically diverse, whereas evangelicalism tends to be predominately Caucasian, although not exclusively so. In the British context, evangelicalism contains Pentecostalism as a subset (for example, many Pentecostal groups are members of the Evangelical Alliance) and this is how I shall treat the relationship here, but I do so with some caution since there are variations globally that need to be taken into account.

At the outset, it is worth noting that there have been at least a couple of attempts at an overview of evangelical practical theology in order to set the scene for this present discussion. The first is by Charles J. Scalise who discusses evangelical identity from a brief historical sketch that includes Pentecostalism, the alliance of North Americans, the new Christian right and politics, the role of Billy Graham, and its relationship with Roman Catholicism, before considering evangelical scholarship.[3] With regard to the latter, he notes the turn of evangelical practical theology towards psychology, social work and family ministry before highlighting Ray S. Anderson's trinitarian model and David Augsburger's model of cross-cultural pastoral counselling. Finally, he observes the British scene and notes the work of Allan H. Anderson and myself at the University of Birmingham among Pentecostals in 2012. On the whole this is a very American-centric account and does not really engage with the substance of academic practical theology (for example, there is no reference to the International Academy of Practical Theology, or any national association); it is more of a general description of evangelicalism in North America, as such it provides only limited insight for our task.

The second is by Andrew Root who has given an overview of evangelical practical theology, again from an American context, giving some historical

DOI: 10.4324/9781003094975-20

background with a discussion of fundamentalism, neo-evangelicalism, the origins of Fuller seminary, and the work of Ray S. Anderson in particular (see below).[4] He notes key figures in the American scene, such as Robert Banks on the subject of education, as well as Mark Lau Branson, Kara Powell and Chap Clark on the subjects of ministry, culture and leadership. He also discusses the sources of authority and the centrality of the Bible for evangelical practical theology (also see below). He then outlines the relationship between theory and practice, before offering a discussion of contexts, the interdisciplinary nature of practical theology and suggests areas for future research, including a Christopraxis of the cross. Some of these themes will be treated later.

It is also worth acknowledging at the outset that there are at least three different levels of practical theology as found in the academy, mostly in the seminary but also found in some university contexts. The first is what might be called skill-based training. There is certainly some theory involved in the teaching of these skills, but the fundamental goal is to form people who have a sufficient level of competence to go into church ministry. This is found in courses that address areas such as preaching, administration, pastoral care, and evangelism. Most undergraduate programmes that are designed to produce ministers for the church tend to work at this level. The second level is what has been called 'reflective practice' and it is focused around helping existing leaders or pastors to reflect on their current practices in order to improve them in some way. So, the standard experiential learning models are often applied, as well as professional reflective practices, in order to identify areas of weakness and improve both competence and integration within a theologically reflective process. This most often works at an individual level, but it can be designed to be led by a minister or facilitator at a congregational level. This approach is typically located at the master's level of theological education, but it can also be found at undergraduate level training. The third level is the research level, and which may be present to some extent at the second level but comes into its own in doctoral studies. This is where a subject of interest is investigated in detail. The investigation can be theoretical or empirical. It can be focused on others beyond the ministry domain of the researcher or it can be part of an action research model. In professional doctoral programmes there can be a combination of levels two and three, thus a reflection on professional practice can be combined with original research of some kind. It is important to note that most evangelical practical theology functions at level one, and occasionally at level two, whereas most academic practical theology functions at level three. For the most part in the recent history of the discipline there has been a significant distance between evangelicals and the rest of the academy, which in part, at least, is explained by these differences.

Therefore, given this disciplinary context, the aim of this chapter is to do three main things: (1) to describe some prominent examples of past and present evangelical practical theology; (2) to revisit a discussion of the sources for theology and how it relates to practical theology; and (3) to suggest ways in which this tradition might develop in the future, given the current state of academic practical theology. This account will draw from the literature, but also my own experience of engaging with the discipline from the mid-1980s as a priest in the Church of England, as an academic, training students for ministry and as a researcher of contemporary evangelical Christianity, especially Pentecostalism.

## Examples of evangelical practical theology

There are four examples of evangelical practical theology that are worth noting for the purpose of this discussion.

Derek Tidball's book entitled *Skilful Shepherds* is a pastoral theology in the Seward Hiltner tradition.[5] It uses the shepherding metaphor as a way of coordinating key ideas around ministry. In Tidball's book he explains the biblical foundations for the shepherding metaphor before offering an historical survey and then applying his ideas to a series of pastoral issues in the church, for example forgiveness and suffering. In this method he uses a standard evangelical approach to practical theology. First, consider what the Bible might contribute on a subject area, which in Tidball's approach means offering a survey of Old Testament, Synoptic Gospels and Acts, Johannine and Pauline literature and finally the general epistles. Then these ideas are applied in a fairly linear fashion to an issue in the contemporary church. On the whole, we might regard this as the 'homiletical' model: first understand the biblical text and then apply it to today's situation. It is a kind of 'then and now' approach that takes seriously the authority of the biblical text to shape the practices of today. In between these two poles, Tidball does include some historical material, but it is something of a whistle-stop tour through the early centuries, the Middle Ages, the Reformation, evangelical revivals and the twentieth century. It includes some useful historical reflection, but ultimately it is biblical themes that are applied to contemporary practice. It would be a good example of 'applied theology' from the mid-1980s.[6]

Ray S. Anderson's book, *The Shape of Practical Theology*, is probably the most cited evangelical book on practical theology.[7] It differs from Tidball's book in using the term practical theology (rather than pastoral theology) and engages with the current academic discipline at the time of writing, especially the work of Don Browning.[8] He reframes Browning's approach, and seeks to place practical theology within a trinitarian framework before seeing it as a form of Christopraxis. He defines Christopraxis in the following manner:

> The praxis of Christ's ministry in the first century was completed (telos) in his resurrection and continued through the gift of the Holy Spirit at Pentecost. Following Pentecost, the early church interpreted the praxis of the Holy Spirit as the continued ministry of the risen Christ, thrusting the community into the world as a mission community and preparing the church to be the church for the last century—the century when Christ returns. With Scripture as its authority, the church engages in the hermeneutical task of interpreting the Word of Christ in the context of the work of Christ.[9]

This particular take on praxis is then expanded with reference to the ministry as the *latreia* of Christ. He then addresses issues in ministry using concepts such as *paraclesis*, ethics and pastoral care, therapeutic culture, the family and postmodern culture, homosexuality, clergy burnout, forgiveness, and suffering. In this respect it lands in the same place as Tidball's work but uses a different approach because of his indebtedness to Browning's model. Although these two books are different in many ways neither of them considers the empirical turn in practical theology (even though Browning does so).

Andrew Root's book, *Christopraxis: A Practical Theology of the Cross*,[10] argues for the place of divine action and places it next to human experience and agency. In many respects he builds on the work of Anderson and extends it. He argues that such divine action is understood in terms of the relationship between the transcendence and immanence of God. He observes that while practical theology has become a significant area of theology, it has still struggled to articulate its normative character. This is related to the focus of its attention, namely human action, while being weak in its articulation of divine action. This is because, in Root's view, divine action is regarded as *impractical*, and while dialogue exists with the social and empirical sciences there has been a lack of interest in the discussion of divine agency. By contrast, Root aims to show that divine action is deeply practical and embedded in concrete lived reality. However, most practical theology has failed to attend to this 'practical' (= experiential) deficiency and has thereby failed to address the theological dimensions of people's experiences. It has missed people's 'evangelical experience', by which he means the call to confess our sins and follow Jesus, as distinct from a commitment to 'evangelicalism' as a theological tradition. For Root, this commitment to 'evangelical experience' is a realist one, understanding that God does truly come to people and they do truly experience him. In his view, practical theology should attend to the lived experiences of Jesus by Christians. He uses the term *Christopraxis* to capture the 'continued ministering presence of Christ.'[11] This means that practical theology is concerned with ministry and this experience of ministry should be regarded as 'theological'. God is the one who ministers to his people through others. Therefore, practical theology directs human action towards divine action as demonstrated in the cross of Christ.[12] He uses a broad definition of ministry that goes beyond the clerical paradigm and includes any encounter of love and care that joins others in their concrete lives and aims to influence them towards new life in Christ.

Pete Ward's book, *Introducing Practical Theology*,[13] is not an explicitly 'evangelical' book, but because he comes from an evangelical background and addresses the issues with some evangelical sympathies, it is worth noting his approach. He sees practical theology as part of the church's existing life and that ordinary believers, whether they know it or not, are already engaged in practical theology because they are reflecting on their faith. He addresses the so-called rejection of the 'clerical paradigm' and sees the ministry of the whole church as providing a concrete reference point. Formal study enhances the ordinary theology that students bring to the study of practical theology and it is developed by the discipline. He also discusses the rejection of the notion of 'applied theology' and makes an appeal for its rehabilitation by observing that the attention to the Scriptures is part and parcel of the everyday life of the church and it flies in face of pedagogical experience to say that students can only start with 'practice'. In any case, we have all been shaped by a communal context and all practices are shaped by some theological content and we cannot bracket out our doctrine from our experience. This 'affective gravitational pull' of the church means that 'starting points' can be blurred.[14] Finally, Ward thinks that the move to experience as a starting point is a political one that privileges modern liberal theology, prioritising experience over theology. Therefore, this move places the discipline distinctly within the 'liberal' tradition. It is asserted as the very basis of the discipline and it is to this manoeuvre that Ward objects. His response is to see practical theology as a broad discipline that takes seriously both practice and theology. He wishes to offer a much more expansive vision of what practical theology can include in its orbit of interest and theological sources.[15] For Ward, practical theology should see itself as 'theology' and therefore attend to the knowledge of God, which is participatory in nature and shares in the life of God. It assumes a relational engagement with God as the basis for an epistemology and, therefore, should be connected to prayer and worship, and an encounter with what is beyond belief.[16] This posture of worship should inculcate both humility and confidence among practical theologians.

As I reflect on my own experience of being taught and researching practical theology over this period, one of the problems that evangelicalism has faced over the latter half of the twentieth century and on into the twenty-first is its sectarian attitude to the wider academy. It started many of its seminaries or theological colleges in the early to mid-twentieth century as part of a reaction against liberalism and so-called 'higher criticism'. These alternative 'spaces' for education and scholarship were created specifically to guard against the influence of liberal thinking so that its perceived negative effects could be ameliorated and countered. There were two main concerns, one was the unbridled affection for and elevation of human reason and the other was the fear of different forms of experientialism, rooted in an anthropocentricism. Both, it was feared, would subvert the objective authority of the Scriptures, which stood above both of them in the evangelical mindset. However, the effects of its theological sectarianism have meant that in many places there is simply no or little conversation between evangelical practical theologians and the wider academy. This has changed to some extent in the British context, where the British and Irish Association of Practical Theology (BIAPT) has become a place where evangelicals participate, and their presence is accepted and to some extent appreciated. It was, however, noticeable that the issue of Association's journal, *Practical Theology*, published to celebrate its twenty-fifth anniversary, omitted major contributions from British evangelical theologians and was dominated by liberal and liberationist perspectives.[17] This is so commonplace that it is hardly noticed by the academy.

## Attending to scripture, history and tradition

One of the major issues in the academic approaches to practical theology has been the rather limited way in which it has engaged with the sources of theology. There have been good examples, of course, but on the whole the turn to contemporary issues in belief and practice, as the focus of research, has nevertheless caused some significant problems for the discipline. For the sake of this discussion, let me consider the three sources of Scripture, tradition, reason (although possibly not really a 'source'), and experience (the standard Wesleyan Quadrilateral). For most level one and two types of practical theology (as noted above), experience has become the focus of enquiry and this is often expanded to include contemporary beliefs and practices, as well as attitudes and values. In other words, there is a turn to contemporary ecclesial or public life and a theological reflection on that life. In order to analyse the contemporary end of the question empirical research is used, and this also means engaging with the empirical social sciences to understand how they would frame and interpret these things. In my view, this is positive and leads to some creative interdisciplinary conversations and debates. But at times it feels like 'theology' has been left behind or reduced to a descriptive element rather than a constructive one. What makes these explorations theological? The answer to this question will largely depend on the kinds of other questions that are being asked and whether the overarching question is in fact a theological one and whether it is being answered within an overarching theological framework or not. For many in the practical theology world there is a problem with how they have used the standard sources.

One of the reactions to this state of play among evangelical practical theologians is to critique the use of Scripture among colleagues in the discipline. This is something I did some years ago.[18] In that study I concluded that the use of Scripture was rather shallow in the academy and that ultimately it demonstrated either a 'proof-text' approach or a thin thematic treatment. The use of more rigorous exegetical and hermeneutically aware appropriations of the text were extremely limited.[19] As a counter to this tendency, I attempted to illustrate what I considered to be a deeper engagement with Scripture, showing how this might enhance the work of scholars. In my *Mediation of the Spirit* book,[20] I analysed the work of Mary McClintock Fulkerson in her celebrated work, *Places of Redemption*.[21] I suggested that she had missed some important dimensions in her reflection on the congregational hermeneutic that could be explored more fruitfully. As I reflect on the state of practical theology around the world at this point in time (2020), I cannot see a change in this tendency towards superficiality in the use of biblical texts. For the most part the Bible is simply ignored, which I have to say is a classic 'liberal' move and something I highlighted back in 2013.

The question has been raised whether evangelical practical theologians should start with Scripture because that is the evangelical theological method.[22] Of course, it is entirely possible to 'start' with Scripture in the sense that for the sake of a piece of work one decides to place all other influences and commitments aside in a kind of suspension in order to read what the text is saying. I regard it as the 'homiletical' model to practical theology, from 'then to now', often mediated without any attention to historical or cultural issues. However, this notion can also be seen as artificial and, while it might cohere with an evangelical intuition to give primacy to Scripture, we cannot bracket out other considerations for long. All Christians work from within a 'reading tradition', as well as other cultural and social factors, that influences how we read the text of Scripture. This does not mean that we cannot 'hear' Scripture on its own terms and certainly it does not mean that Scripture cannot 'read us'. The history of the interpretation of Scripture clearly shows how biblical texts have the capacity to address individuals and groups with remarkable power to transform its readers. For me, the issue is not really a chronological one. The idea that we should start with Scripture suggests that if we do not then we are somehow not giving it the due weight it deserves, and this is the point. It is not really a question of chronology but rather of *weight*. Authority in the sources of theology is more about weighting rather than the sequence in which they can be set, which is also artificial to some extent as well. So, while I am sympathetic to the countering of reason and experience as sources of authority, I do not think a mere resequencing is adequate to address the issue; most of us, even evangelicals, do not actually start with Scripture even when we say that we do. We are part of traditions that shape how we think about and use Scripture, even the idea of 'starting' with Scripture is itself a 'traditioned' understanding.[23]

It is very rare for practical theologians to quarry the riches of the Christian tradition as part of their theological reflection. It does happen occasionally and Ellen T. Charry's work is a good example of this use of traditional sources.[24] The challenge for practical theologians is to understand strands of the evangelical tradition so that they can be more explicit in both stating their 'reading tradition' as well as using the sources from that tradition in their work.[25] It is possible that where this use of tradition is most obvious is in the teaching of skills of preaching and pastoral care. Courses on preaching will often invite students to read some of the classic texts from significant historical and contemporary figures. This does not happen in the same way for theological reflection on practice and it does not appear to inform how evangelical research is shaped.[26] If the research is empirical and requires that the group or congregation being studied be contextualised, then some historical material is provided. But often this is a sketch for the sake of background information, and it tends not to make a return in the constructive chapter towards the end of the study. In this way, it needs to be said that the riches of the evangelical sources are often ignored in evangelical practical theology, as they are (I might add) for the discipline as a whole. Is this the price to pay for the turn to the contemporary end of the question? Quite probably the answer is 'yes', but the next question is what can be done about it?

Allied to this historical problem is also a doctrinal one. For example, if we ask the question, 'how many evangelical studies in practical theology actually engage with standard evangelical doctrines?', the answer is likely to be 'not many'. Where do they inform how the theological reflection or construction proceeds? Again, this is where there is a gap in the manner in which practical theologians engage with the doctrinal tradition. There seems a similar reluctance to engage with the wider doctrinal resources of the church. There are exceptions to this tendency, but, on the whole, it remains largely the case. Of course, there may be readers of this chapter who then say, 'Hang on a minute, does this mean that we have to be biblical, historical and systematic theological experts as well as empirical ones? That is simply not possible!' And I have to agree. We all need to make choices with the sources and methods that we use, how we use them, what tradition of enquiry within which we place ourselves and what kinds of constructions we make. No one person can do everything. What I am suggesting may be practically impossible, certainly for a single individual. Perhaps there is a need to create dialogue and synergy between different types of practical theologians for the sake of more robust and rigorous theological practice. But, given the scarcity of resources, the challenge is a real one that I do not underestimate.

## Areas for future development

Given the discussion above, I would like to suggest that the guild of evangelical practical theology needs to develop particular kinds of expertise in conversation with the wider theological academy. It would seem that the practical theological academy has located itself around liberal, liberationist, or empiricist sets of commitments. A number of evangelicals have found acceptance because of a willingness to engage with these approaches. But it might be possible for a group of evangelical practical theologians to develop the use of different approaches that places evangelicalism as a theological tradition at the centre of the conversation rather than at the periphery.[27] My suggestion for a possible collaborative approach includes attention to the following seven areas, which are not exhaustive but are perhaps significant for evangelical practical theology's development.

First, there needs to be a greater commitment to quarrying the tradition for the sake of contemporary praxis.[28] The evangelical tradition has many examples of how people have engaged with their contexts, proclaimed the gospel, and sought to transform society for the betterment of all. There are different emphases and strands of evangelicalism; and some ways of thinking that could resonate especially today, for example different forms of pietism as opposed to scholasticism. It is rare to find a practical theology project that drills down into the tradition in a significant way in order to provide resources for contemporary theological reflection. If better models could be provided for how this could be done, a younger generation of scholars might be inspired to know their tradition better and engage with it more deeply for the sake of contemporary praxis.

Second, there is a need for individuals to cross theological sub-disciplinary boundaries. Of course, no one person could be expected to cross all of them, but the evangelical approach to practical theology will be enhanced if scholars can engage more intentionally with the other theological sub-disciplines, such as biblical studies and systematic theology.[29] This is an important dimension if we are going to address the fragmentation due to the specialisms in theology. In a sense this is what Don Browning hoped to achieve however imperfectly.[30] Although Ray Anderson followed his model, as noted above, and gave it a distinctively evangelical twist, he did not address the need to integrate the various sub-disciplines of theology as clearly as he might have done, although his attention to a trinitarian framework is worth noting.[31]

Third, one of the developments in practical theology that has been extremely positive at one level but also extremely negative at another level is the engagement with the social and human sciences. There is a real value in the dialogue with social science and the empirical literature largely framed by the social science of religion. The empirical turn in practical theology has been hugely significant and, at the research level, the leading centres of practical theology have trained people at an extremely high level in qualitative and quantitative research methods. But the cost of this empirical turn has also been high. This is because the vision to explore theological beliefs and practices empirically and to situate them within an explanatory theoretical framework that is theological has been difficult to fulfil. Even the *Journal of Empirical Theology* has moved in a Religious Studies direction in my view with theology being used in a descriptive rather than explanatory manner (i.e. descriptive theological beliefs and practices are explained by means of other kinds of theory, typically sociological or social-psychological).[32] Alternative groups, like the 'Ecclesiology and Ethnography Network', have made some important contributions, but there are still some basic issues to be debated in terms of the exact nature of theology and its relationship to practical theology. Some evangelicals are involved in these groups, but as yet there is no clear proposal for how evangelicals can contribute to a model of interdisciplinarity for the sake of the discipline.[33]

Fourth, linked to this interdisciplinarity, and despite my critique above, is the need for evangelical practical theologians to embrace empirical research with a bit more enthusiasm. While many scholars ignore the need for empirical research, there are evangelicals who have embraced it,[34] and some of them have attempted to foreground their theological commitments. For example, when I wrote my PhD thesis many years ago, I wrestled with van der Ven's hermeneutical framework.[35] I could not use Habermas' Communicative Action theory following van der Ven. It felt totally alien to me as an evangelical, so I replaced it with a hermeneutical framework based on the Paraclete sayings in John's Gospel. For me, this was a way of integrating Scripture in a strategic place that changed the lens through which I was interpreting the project. The attempt emerged from my own evangelical (and charismatic location). This also meant that the questions I was raising and the sources I was using in the constructive part of my work were also connected to my spiritual tradition as well as a scholarly tradition. For me, personally, this standpoint has resulted in an expansion into the world of global Pentecostal scholarship and, while there is certainly an overlap with evangelicalism (as noted above), this overlap is played out very differently in different parts of the world. For example, in America there can be a sharp difference because of the fundamentalist-modernist debate of the early twentieth century,[36] while in Vietnam evangelicalism overlaps extensively with Pentecostalism such that they are virtually synonymous.[37]

Fifth, one of the problems that practical theology has as an academic discipline is that it is dominated by western and white (Caucasian) theology (I would say male, but actually this is not the case since there are a high proportion of female practical theologians). If you look at the literature, it is predominantly liberal, white, sometimes feminist, but only occasionally non-white and non-western.[38] Emmanuel Larty is one of those scholars who has championed an intercultural perspective, influenced by his own Ghanaian background and his time at the University of Birmingham with its emphasis in mission studies on the intercultural approach led by Walter J. Hollenweger.[39] Of course, there are other standpoint theologies, such as African American,[40] Asian American,[41] Feminist and Womanist,[42] and Latino/a.[43] While the American field of practical theology does engage a range of standpoints, the British field appears more limited in scope. Similarly, evangelical practical theologians have either ignored the wider academy or simply followed its western cultural dominance. This where a real engagement with the global nature of evangelicalism is important. Its growth is in Africa and Asia and yet these voices have not been as prominent as they should be in the academy. There are signs of change, but this needs to be addressed much more intentionally in the coming years. Allied to this greater interest in intercultural theology is an attention to race and ethnicity. The voices of evangelicals from the global south as well as Black, Asian and minority ethnic voices in the global north need to be heard more clearly and their contributions welcomed.

Sixth, one of the areas facing evangelicals is their relationship to wider society and their contribution to theology and public life. At times they are criticised for being outdated in their thinking. This is most obviously the case around human sexuality, gender identity and same-sex marriage.[44] Often, these themes are ignored by evangelical practical theologians and it is understandable in light of the stress of identity politics. There are social and public issues that evangelicals have addressed in the past, such as slavery, poverty, health, and the economy, but it is rare for an evangelical practical theologian to look beyond the parameters of the church, or its specific mission to evangelise.[45] Missiologists quite rightly address these issues, but, once again, it is unclear just how practical theologians interface with the field of mission studies since they appear to be quite separate spheres. 'Public theology', or a 'theology of public life' should be an item on the agenda for future evangelical practical theology.[46]

Seventh, in the age of 'lockdown' and COVID-19, it has become very clear that the church needs to address its ministry and mission via the Internet. Many churches have been forced to go online and provide worship services via websites, video conferencing tools and social media. This has raised the question as to how the church can function in an online environment and how its interface with off-line (or concrete) church works once the lockdown eases around the world. Of course, there are scholars who have been exploring online religion, including Christianity, and some of this literature is extremely perceptive and useful.[47] Virtual churches, including evangelical churches, have been the focus of online research for a number of years. But, on the whole, and like concrete empirical research, this virtual ethnography (or netnography) has been conducted by sociologists of religion. There has been some theological study, but this tends to come from a more systematic perspective rather than a netnographical one.[48] In my previous job at Regent University School of Divinity, VA, I was asked to construct a pathway through the Master of Divinity Programme that focused on cyber ministry and mission. As part of this pathway, I devised an online course entitled 'Theological Netnography'.[49] It fused together models of theological reflection with Internet research literature in order to give students a basis for conducting their own research and to assist them with their own reflective practice. This pedagogical experiment is only the beginning of an engagement with the Internet as a location of practical theology. There is considerable room for further work and future technological developments will only expand the opportunities available to practical theologians.[50]

## Conclusion

As I conclude this 'state-of-the-art' chapter, reviewing something of the limited past of evangelical practical theology, analysing some of the current patterns and anticipating the possible future of the discipline, it seems to me that there are important features to observe in closing, and some of these have been highlighted to some extent already.

Evangelical practical theology serves the church of Jesus Christ and the society in which it is situated. It is a discipline that is a servant of the church rather than a master of it. It is a discipline that seeks to capture something of the life of the church, offer critical reflection on its life, and then suggest constructive ways forward. It is not critical for the sake of being critical in and of itself. Rather, it is critical in order to illuminate the gospel of the kingdom of God in ways that enhance the flourishing of the community of faith and the common good. Its criticality needs always to be understood as provisional and always open to revision in the light of Scripture and the inspiration of the Holy Spirit.

Evangelical practical theology does not simply reinforce old stereotypes of theology, or indeed celebrate the new fads of theology, but rather it interrogates them in terms of their intrinsic coherence and value for the life of faith and Christian discipleship. It is neither simply about a repetition of what is given, nor is it about being 'relevant' to a changing social and cultural context. Rather, it is about being disciplined in its attentiveness to Scripture and tradition on the one hand, as well as contemporary culture and society on the other hand. This multiple attentiveness will mean that it is pulled in different directions and this too is part of the nature of a discipline that looks in different directions as part of its attempt to make sense of the world and resource the church.

Evangelical practical theology can adopt different scholarly postures. Sometimes it will be about skills-based training and at other times it will be facilitating reflective practice on ministry. In some cases, it will be expressed via academic conventions that are apparently 'objective' and 'academic' and appear to transcend evangelical confessional constraints. Of course, we all know that these constraints are never truly transcended because all theology is hermeneutical from start to finish and we cannot jump outside of our tradition into some 'neutral zone'. But, for the sake of scholarly convention, there are times when evangelical practical theology is done under the guise of 'objective' scholarship, especially when using quantitative methods. This is only a problem when we fail to realise this is merely a convention and ascribe some elevated epistemological virtue to what is otherwise a particular version of scholarly discourse.

Finally, evangelical practical theology is surely developing, and, potentially, it can move in many different directions. New circumstances in which evangelical churches are located will give rise to many different problems and issues that need to be addressed. Each new set of circumstances will be brought into dialogue with evangelical history and tradition, as well as new ways of reading Scripture. But one thing will surely remain and that is the supreme authority of Scripture for the construction of theological accounts. There will always be hermeneutical issues and we cannot step outside of our own time, place and reading context, but Scripture has the capacity to be *transcontextual*, to address the church and its mission across these different times and places;[51] and it is this capacity that shapes *all* evangelical theology, including evangelical practical theology.

## Notes

1 Mark J. Cartledge, "Practical Theology," in *Studying Global Pentecostalism: Theories and Methods*, eds. Allan H. Anderson, Michael Bergner, André Droogers, and Cornelius van der Laan (Berkeley: University of California Press, 2010), 268–285; and Mark J. Cartledge, "Practical Theology: Attending to Pneumatologically-Driven Praxis," in *The Handbook of Pentecostal Theology*, ed. Wolfgang Vondey (London: Routledge, 2020), 163–172.
2 Mark J. Cartledge, "Pentecostalism," in *The Wiley-Blackwell Companion to Practical Theology*, ed. Bonnie J. Miller-McLemore (New York: Wiley-Blackwell, 2012), 587–595.
3 Charles J. Scalise, "Protestant Evangelicalism," in *The Wiley-Blackwell Companion to Practical Theology*, ed. Bonnie J. Miller-McLemore (New York: Wiley-Blackwell, 2012), 576–586.
4 Andrew Root, "Evangelical Practical Theology," in *Opening the Field of Practical Theology: An Introduction*, eds. Kathleen A. Cahalan and Gordon S. Mikoski (Lanham: Rowman & Littlefield, 2014), 79–96.
5 Derek Tidball, *Skilful Shepherds: An Introduction to Pastoral Theology* (Leicester: InterVarsity Press, 1986), 21; Seward Hiltner, *Preface to Pastoral Theology* (Nashville: Abingdon Press, 1958).
6 'Applied theology' is often traced back to Friedrich Schleiermacher, *Brief Outline of the Study of Theology*, Trans. T. N. Tice (Atlanta: John Knox Press, 1996); also see

Nigel Cameron, *Method without Madness? An Evangelical Approach to 'Doing' Theology* (Leicester: UCCF, 1983), 22–25, which uses the classic encyclopaedia approach proceeding from biblical languages and exegesis, biblical theology, systematic theology, ecclesiastical history, historical theology and finally to practical theology.

7 Ray S. Anderson, *The Shape of Practical Theology: Empowering Ministry with Theological Praxis* (Downers Grove: IVP Academic, 2001).
8 Don Browning, *A Fundamental Practical Theology: Descriptive and Strategic Proposals* (Minneapolis: Fortress Press, 1991).
9 Anderson, *The Shape of Practical Theology*, 52.
10 Andrew Root, *Christopraxis: A Practical Theology of the Cross* (Minneapolis: Fortress Press, 2014).
11 Root, *Christopraxis*, xii, 90.
12 Root, *Christopraxis*, 110–113.
13 Pete Ward, *Introducing Practical Theology: Mission, Ministry, and the Life of the Church* (Grand Rapids: Baker Academic, 2017).
14 Ward, *Introducing Practical Theology*, 4.
15 This includes a positive use of Root's *Christopraxis*; also see Ward, *Introducing Practical Theology*, 44–47.
16 See my *Practical Theology: Charismatic and Empirical Perspectives* (Carlisle: Paternoster, 2003), 17–30, 41–68.
17 See *Practical Theology* 13, no. 1–2 (2020), although I note that Andrew Rogers as an evangelical was one of the editors of the issue.
18 See my "The Use of Scripture in Practical Theology: A Study of Academic Practice," *Practical Theology* 6 no. 3 (2013), 271–283; republished in *Mediation of the Spirit: Interventions in Practical Theology* (Grand Rapids: Eerdmans, 2015), 32–59.
19 Even a book by a leading British practical theologian does not ultimately deal with biblical texts in any real depth but tends to treat hermeneutical issues in a broader manner, see Zoë Bennett, *Using the Bible in Practical Theology: Historical and Contemporary Perspectives* (Farnham: Ashgate, 2013).
20 Cartledge, *Mediation of the Spirit*, 125–139.
21 Mary McClintock Fulkerson, *Places of Redemption: Theology for a Worldly Church* (Oxford: Oxford University Press, 2007).
22 See Helen Collins, *Reordering Theological Reflection: Starting with Scripture* (London: SCM, 2020). Collins in my view is largely dealing with a level two type of approach, i.e., reflection on practice. There is a similar use of the metaphor of 'biblical foundations', as found in Tidball. But key differences are found in the use of pneumatology (the Spirit as the architect) and the process of theological reflection. In this way it is a development beyond both Tidball (no significant pneumatology) and Anderson (no theological reflection as a process).
23 Pentecostals and charismatic scholarship tend to place Scripture in a 'trialectic' with the Holy Spirit and the Community. I discussed this in relation to evangelical theology in my "Text-Community-Spirit: The Challenged Posed by Pentecostal Theological Method to Evangelical Theology," in *Spirit and Scripture: Examining a Pneumatic Hermeneutic*, eds. Kevin L. Spawn and Archie T. Wright (London: T&T Clark, 2012), 130–142.
24 Ellen T. Charry, *By the Renewing of Your Minds: The Pastoral Function of Christian Doctrine* (Oxford: Oxford University Press, 1999).
25 Ward, *Introducing Practical Theology*, 86–88, does include a discussion of classic tradition, but does not really unpack the nature of 'evangelical' tradition.
26 One good example is the book by Elaine Graham, Heather Walton, and Frances Ward, *Theological Reflection: Sources* (London: SCM, 2007), although they are not evangelical authors.

216  *Mark J. Cartledge*

27 This would be different to Root's 'evangelical experience' approach. My own approach is more pneumatological; see Mark J. Cartledge, "Locating the Spirit in Meaningful Experience: Empirical Theology and Pentecostal Hermeneutics," in *Constructing Pneumatological Hermeneutics in Pentecostal Christianity*, eds. Kenneth J. Archer and L. William Oliverio, Jr. (New York: Palgrave Macmillan, 2016), 251–266.
28 This may be regarded as a form of 'standpoint epistemology'; see my "Can Theology be "Practical"? Part II: A Reflection on Renewal Methodology and the Practice of Research," *Journal of Contemporary Ministry* 3 (2017): 20–36.
29 This is also noted by Ward, *Introducing Practical Theology*, 119–127.
30 Browning, *A Fundamental Practical Theology*, 7–8.
31 Anderson, *The Shape of Practical Theology*, 35–46.
32 See a statement of the original vision in Johannes A. van der Ven, "Practical Theology: from Applied to Empirical Theology," *Journal of Empirical Theology* 1 no. 1 (1988), 7–27.
33 Early in my research I adopted van der Ven's 'intra-disciplinary' approach and have maintained it when the 'empirical theology' sector moved away from it, see my "Empirical Theology: Inter- or Intra-disciplinary?" *Journal of Beliefs & Values* 20 no. 1 (1999), 98–104, reiterated in *Practical Theology*, 14–16.
34 For example, see Andrew Rogers, *Congregational Hermeneutics: How Do We Read?* (London: Routledge, 2016).
35 See my *Charismatic Glossolalia: An Empirical-Theological Study* (Aldershot: Ashgate, 2002), 17–22; and Johannes A. van der Ven, *Practical Theology: An Empirical Approach* (Kampen: Kok Pharos, 1993), 89–112.
36 See Gerald W. King, *Disfellowshipped: Pentecostal Responses to Fundamentalism in the United States, 1906–1943* (Eugene: Pickwick Publications, 2011).
37 Vince Le, *Vietnamese Evangelicals and Pentecostalism: The Politics of Divine Intervention* (Leiden: Brill, 2018).
38 This is noted by Tom Beaudoin and Katherine Turpin, "White Practical Theology," in *Opening the Field of Practical Theology: An Introduction*, eds. Kathleen A. Cahalan and Gordon S. Mikoski (Lanham: Rowman & Littlefield, 2014), 251–269.
39 Emmanuel Y. Lartey, *In Living Color: An Intercultural Approach to Pastoral Care and Counseling* (New York: Jessica Kingsley Publishers, 2003); Walter J. Hollenweger, *Pentecostalism: Origins and Developments Worldwide* (Grand Rapids, MI: Baker Academic, 2005), 129–131; also see Mark J. Cartledge and David Cheetham, eds., *Intercultural Theology: Approaches and Themes* (London: SCM, 2011). Note the collection of essays in Henry S. Wilson, et al., eds., *Pastoral Theology from a Global Perspective: A Case Study Approach* (Maryknoll: Orbis Books, 1996).
40 Dale P. Andrews, "African American Practical Theology," in *Opening the Field of Practical Theology: An Introduction*, eds. Kathleen A. Cahalan and Gordon S. Mikoski (Lanham: Rowman & Littlefield, 2014), 11–29. Also see Dale P. Andrews, *Practical Theology for Black Churches: Bridging Black Theology and African American Folk Religion* (Louisville: Westminster John Knox Press, 2002); and Dale P. Andrews and Robert London Smith Jr., eds., *Black Practical Theology* (Waco: Baylor University Press, 2015).
41 Courtney T. Goto, "Asian American Practical Theology," in *Opening the Field of Practical Theology: An Introduction*, eds. Kathleen A. Cahalan and Gordon S. Mikoski (Lanham: Rowman & Littlefield, 2014), 31–44.
42 Joyce Ann Mercer, "Feminist and Womanist Practical Theology," in *Opening the Field of Practical Theology: An Introduction*, eds. Kathleen A. Cahalan and Gordon S. Mikoski (Lanham, MD: Rowman & Littlefield, 2014), 97–114.
43 Hosffman Ospino, "U.S. Latino/a Practical Theology," in *Opening the Field of Practical Theology: An Introduction*, eds. Kathleen A. Cahalan and Gordon S. Mikoski (Lanham, MD: Rowman & Littlefield, 2014), 233–249.

44 See Andrew Goddard, "Theology and Practice in Evangelical Churches," in *The Oxford Handbook of Theology, Sexuality, and Gender*, ed. Adrian Thatcher (Oxford: Oxford University Press, 2015), 377–394.
45 My own work has moved in this direction, although not from an explicitly evangelical perspective. My forthcoming book is entitled: *The Holy Spirit and Public Life: Empowering Ecclesial Praxis* (Lanham: Lexington Books/Fortress Academic, 2022) and addresses the themes of poverty, healthcare and healing, race and 'whiteness', sex trafficking, domestic or intimate partner violence, and the common good.
46 See Sebastian Kim and Katie Day, eds., *A Companion to Public Theology* (Leiden: Brill, 2017).
47 See, for example, Rachel Wagner, *Godwired: Religion, Ritual and Virtual Reality* (London: Routledge, 2012); Heidi A. Campbell, ed., *Digital Religion: Understanding Religious Practice in New Media Worlds* (London: Routledge, 2013); Heidi A. Campbell and Stephen Garner, *Networked Theology: Negotiating Faith in a Digital Culture* (Grand Rapids: Baker Academic, 2016); and Tim Hutchings, *Creating Church Online: Ritual, Community and New Media* (London: Routledge, 2017).
48 For example, see Antonio Spadaro, *Cybertheology: Thinking Christianity in the Era of the Internet* (New York: Fordham University Press, 2014); and Katherine G. Schmidt, *Virtual Communion: Theology of the Internet and the Catholic Sacramental Imagination* (Lanham: Lexington Books and Fortress Academic, 2020).
49 For examples of netnography, see Tom Boellstorff, Bonnie Nardi, Celia Pearce, and T. L. Taylor, *Ethnography and Virtual Worlds: A Handbook of Method* (Princeton: Princeton University Press, 2012); Robert V. Kozinets, *Netnography: Doing Ethnographic Research Online* (Los Angeles, CA: Sage, 2013); and Christine Hine, *Ethnography for the Internet: Embedded, Embodies and Everyday* (London: Bloomsbury Academic, 2015). A book on 'Theological Netnography' has yet to be written.
50 Spurgeon's College MA (previously at Durham University) is making these connections but does not appear to fuse theological reflection with netnography as explicitly as I am suggesting, see "MA in Digital Theology," Spurgeon's College, accessed December 16, 2021, https://www.spurgeons.ac.uk/ma-in-digital-theology/.
51 See Cartledge, *Practical Theology*, 23; and Anthony Thiselton, *New Horizon in Hermeneutics: The Theory and Practice of Transforming Biblical Reading* (London: HarperCollins, 1992), 393.

# Conclusion

*Helen Morris and Helen Cameron*

To conclude this book, we have reflected as editors on what we have learned from the different contributors and how this book might shape future engagements by evangelicals with practical theology. Andrew Thomas' contribution[1] sets the scene well for chapters that follow. His affirmation and qualification of Bebbington's quadrilateral exemplifies a persistent theme throughout the book; this is a simultaneous commitment to the evangelical priorities identified by Bebbington alongside a challenge to the exact delineation of these priorities in light of experience of and reflection on practice. Therefore, we thought it fruitful to collate these challenges and propose some avenues of further exploration that flow from them.

## Biblicism

The contributors to this book affirm the centrality and authority of Scripture within the Christian faith. Helen Morris, for example, notes in relation to 1 Kings 21 that, when a clash of narratives occurs, the biblical authors do not present the different perspectives as simply alternative and morally neutral options. Rather, the behaviour and character of the one whose perspective aligns with God's character and revelation is good and right; those behaviours and attitudes that are against God's design are distorted and corrupt. Similarly, in his exploration of the role of theodrama, Samuel Norman contends that an emphasis on 'improvisation' within theodramatic approaches to Scripture flows from, rather than negates, the givenness of the original script of Scripture. The 'characters', and thereby Christian identity, are not self-defined but determined by the script-writer, God. Chloe Lynch maintains that grief and repentance are the most appropriate first response when a discrepancy is observed between the world's current broken state and the hope of God-given newness. Such discrepancies are observed when the prophet (or practical theologian) is rooted in the divine revelation of Scripture and alert to the realities around them. Liz Hoare observes how evangelical practical theologians have provided theological reflectors with methodologies that more robustly and explicitly maintain the authority of Scripture. This contrasts with other expressions and models of theological reflection that, she argues, have been rightly critiqued for being Bible-lite. Other contributors also note the tensions that arise for evangelicals by expressions of practical theology that do not share their prioritising of Scripture.

However, alongside promoting the centrality of Scripture, the authors of this book challenge articulations of biblicism that are overly simplistic or unhelpful. Both Andrew Thomas and Mark Cartledge challenge the misconception that giving final authority to Scripture necessarily means 'starting' with Scripture in a chronological sense. As Cartledge contends, the issue is not one of chronology but weight. No-one can read Scripture without their experience informing their view of the text, just as no-one who is familiar with Scripture can put their biblical knowledge, or the corollary shaping of their worldview, aside when reflecting on experience. Sheryl Arthur's chapter indicates the importance of identifying and examining congregational hermeneutics. Her observation that the participants intuitively adopted a 'this is that' hermeneutical approach[2] enabled her to caution that, whilst this produced fruitful results for the passages selected for her fieldwork, it may not have been appropriate for other texts in Scripture. Andrew Thomas promotes a crucicentric approach to the Bible, wherein the humility and love evidenced so powerfully on the cross characterise evangelical scholars' engagement with the Bible. This is vital, he argues, to avoid the danger that 'being under the text' (which evangelicals regard positively as highlighting the authoritative role of Scripture) becomes a veil for manipulation and domination, whereby others are coerced to be under the interpreters of the text rather than the text itself. Helen Cameron affirms this caution noting that, whilst Scripture is the shared text around which Christian conversation develops, there are questions around the extent to which normativity should be ascribed to particular traditions of interpretation.

In summary, therefore, while the contributors affirm the centrality of the Bible within evangelical practical theologising (Bebbington's 'biblicism'), they also raise important questions about theological method. The use of the Bible in practical theology is thus an area requiring further attention. Mark Cartledge suggests a fruitful way forwards through his assertion that engagement across different theological subdisciplines could develop evangelical practical theology further. He lists the fields of biblical studies and systematic theology as two subdisciplines in particular that could enhance an evangelical approach to practical theology. However, there is more work to be done on how this cross-disciplinary dialogue and engagement can best be facilitated and what methodological approaches could assist in this endeavour.

## Crucicentrism

Alongside affirming the authority of Scripture, the authors of this book demonstrate a commitment to the gospel of Jesus Christ, within which the crucifixion of Jesus has central place. For instance, in reflecting on her location within evangelicalism, Chloe Lynch refers to the 'irrevocable Christocentrism' that participation in evangelical communities has formed her in. Mark Cartledge refers to both Anderson and Root's influence on evangelical practical theology through their emphasis on 'Christopraxis', which the subtitle of Root's book defines as 'a practical theology of the cross.' Both texts are indicative of the impact of evangelicalism's Christocentrism on evangelicals' practical theologising. Helen Morris engages with Ward's assessment of the UK evangelical church's espoused and operant (lived) conception of the gospel, noting the centrality of the cross within evangelical gospel presentations. As noted above, Andrew Thomas promotes the importance of crucicentrism for healthy conceptions of authority in relation to biblical interpretation.

However, whilst affirming an evangelical emphasis on the cross of Christ, the contributors challenge expressions of crucicentrism that are deemed reductionist. Andrew Thomas, for example, highlights the importance of relating the crucifixion to the lordship of Christ and locating the story of Christ in the grand narrative of Scripture. Similarly, whilst affirming the evangelical evangelistic impulse to convey the gospel succinctly, Helen Morris encourages gospel presenters to draw their hearers into the wider narrative of Scripture to avoid implying that what can be communicated about the gospel in a couple of minutes can convey the gospel's fullness. Alistair McKitterick warns against an unwitting conflation of God's *telos* (goal) in redemption with the *teloi* of creation, incarnation, and eschatological consummation. He notes that there would be greater transparency and open dialogue if practical theologians were self-aware and critical as to which of these 'irreducible *teloi*' is governing praxis in any one situation. In addition, he highlights the importance of recognising that 'creation, (incarnation), redemption, and new creation are movements in the one story of God.' Therefore, while affirming an evangelical focus on the cross of Christ, this book's contributors highlight the importance of Jesus' crucifixion being understood and articulated in reference to the whole Christ-event (Jesus' incarnation, ministry, death, resurrection, ascension, and future return) and the Christ-event, in turn, being interpreted in reference to the full biblical narrative.

As regards crucicentrism, it is also important to note the contributors' emphasis on the person and work of the Spirit alongside the person and work of Christ. For instance, in encouraging practical theologians to have their imaginations shaped by the revelation of Christ in Scripture, Chloe Lynch highlights the role of the Spirit in this shaping. It is through 'pneumatic encounters,' she argues, that 'human imagination is transformed to be fundamentally Christological.' Reflecting on his experience teaching practical theology to Pentecostal students, Andrew Rogers stresses the importance of thoughtful attention to the role of the Holy Spirit within practical theology. He refers to Mark Cartledge's writings as an example of the work that has already been done to fill the former 'lacuna' in practical theology regarding the Spirit's role and encourages increased exploration in this area. Sheryl Arthur's chapter contributes further to this topic, exploring 'what a pneumatological approach to corporate theological reflection might "look" like from a classical Pentecostal perspective.' Helen Cameron focuses on the Spirit's role within theological education. She argues that greater attention to students' questions and concerns in shaping the curriculum enables receptivity to the Spirit-given revelation that a conversational approach can evoke. Other contributors too, such as Andy Thomas and Alistair McKitterick, emphasise the importance of pneumatology within practical theology. Therefore, whilst affirming the Christocentrism implicit in evangelicalism's crucicentrism, the contributors of this book do not appear to accord with John Stackhouse's claim that 'the Holy Spirit remains—despite some impressive expositions by evangelicals of late—a relatively minor, shadowy figure in the New Testament compared with the center stage, fully lit person of Jesus.'[3] Rather, in the chapters of this book, the Spirit's work is front and centre alongside that of Christ, albeit with the acknowledgement that there is yet more work to be done in the development of evangelical pneumatological approaches to practical theologising.

## Conversionism

This book's contributors note the centrality of conversionism within evangelical expressions of Christianity. Matt Spencer, for instance, observes the central place of conversion within the Salvation Army tradition of which he is part. Andy Thomas reflects on own experience of evangelism, noting the emphasis that was placed on people 'making a decision for Jesus' within the tent crusades that he participated in. In the context of assessing the evangelical church's presentation of the gospel, Helen Morris reflects on how her findings informed a particular evangelistic opportunity she was given through an invitation to deliver a Good Friday online sermon. This emphasis on conversionism derives from the conviction that the gospel of Jesus Christ truly is good news. The gospel provides future hope but also, as is emphasised by a number of this book's authors, it also provides the surest foundation for flourishing in the here and now, even though, as Morris contends, the biblical notion of human flourishing differs markedly from its secular counterpart. Therefore, the contributors accord with the evangelical emphasis on the reconciliation with God and life transformation that result from the gospel of Jesus Christ.

However, this book's authors challenge notions of conversionism that are overly cerebral and/or individualistic, in addition to evangelistic practices that are too formulaic and/or disconnect evangelism from discipleship. Andy Thomas, for instance, notes that although over 400 people were 'converted' in one evangelistic event he participated in, one year later only 30 were still involved in the life of the church that was planted in response to this conversion. He argues that a reductionist and overly professionalised presentation of the gospel was a key factor in the discrepancy between how many 'made a decision for Jesus' and how many persevered in following him. In contrast, Thomas emphasises the role of the Christian community in proclaiming and demonstrating the richness of the good news of Jesus, referring to what Newbigin terms 'the congregation as Hermeneutic of the Gospel.'[4] With similar focus on the importance of the community in the context of his work with a community choir, Matt Spencer affirms the contemporary missiological emphasis on belonging (to a Christian community) before believing (the core tenets of the Christian faith). Such a focus suggests that rather than a conversion opportunity being the necessary gateway into the Christian community, participation in a Christian community can facilitate a process of transformation that, perhaps over a long period of time, leads to a commitment to Christ. In addition to this, Spencer contends that participating in Christian practices, including bearing witness to others through the lyrics of the songs that are sung, can move people closer to conversion. In this he accords with Michael Moynagh's contention that engagement with Christian practices can play a key role in an unchurched person's faith journey and therefore that the evangelistic model behave-belong-believe should be promoted alongside the more established belong-believe-behave.[5]

The role of the Christian community in conversion and growth is also highlighted by Isaac McNish's reflection on the role of critical thinking within a small group Bible study. McNish notes that the ongoing transformation that results from and is part of salvation is corporate in nature and therefore uses the phrase 'shared journey of faith' to express the purpose of the Bible study group. In addition, in highlighting the significance of behaviour alongside belief, McNish observes that the goal of transformation is 'is not merely mental assent to new ideas but is chiefly manifested in transformed living.' Samuel Norman also affirms the importance of discipleship that encourages both beliefs and behaviour to align with the gospel of Jesus. He proposes that a theodramatic approach to the teaching of doctrine, for instance, could be a means by which a greater synergy between beliefs and behaviour can be encouraged within theological education.

A further challenge to any formulaic conversionism is provided by Fiona Moore and Helen Cameron's emphasis on listening. Moore notes that it was in a moment of silence, not speaking, that a woman she had got to know through her chaplaincy work was challenged afresh by Jesus' sacrifice on the cross. By resisting the temptation to fill the silence with speech, Moore created space for the woman to hear God's voice speaking to her through a distant memory that, in the stillness, had floated to the forefront of her mind. Cameron also highlights the importance of creating space to listen. She gives the example of a conversation in which she too had to resist the temptation to speak, in this instance to explain a biblical story, and chose instead to listen to the concerns and questions that the story had evoked in the hearer. Reflecting on Jesus' encounter with the disciples on the Road to Emmaus (Luke 24:13–35), Cameron suggests that where knowledge of Scripture and the salvation story are lacking, it is necessary to engage with people 'on the road' before opening Scripture and before recognition of the living Christ.

## Activism

The evangelical priority of activism is evident among the contributors to this book. Olwyn Mark, for example, contends that Christians should not withdraw from the public and political world in relation to contentious topics such as Relationships and Sex Education (RSE). She argues that a Christian understanding of human flourishing provides a foundation for effective engagement with schools and communities on the topic of RSE, within which Government guidance accommodates confessional diversity. Her own work with Love for Life in Northern Ireland exemplifies effective Christian engagement in this area wherein, from the foundation of creational flourishing and love of neighbour, Christians contribute to RSE for the common good and in pursuit of the *shalom* (peace) of God's kingdom.

An emphasis on activism is also evident in Helen Cameron, Liz Hoare, and Andrew Roger's reflections on the teaching of practical theology. Rogers notes how teaching theological reflection has developed his students' 'So what?' reflex, increasing their expectation that theologising leads to action. Hoare identifies how rooting her teaching more deeply in her students' own practice, reflecting together on particular students' experiences, has helped them grasp the relevance of theological reflection for their ongoing ministry. Cameron encourages theological educators to give students time to undertake action research into questions that arise from their experience and practice, rather than delivering a curriculum that is established apart from the students' own questions and concerns. In addition, in noting that identifying the Bible as the 'starting point' of theology regards authority and not chronology, Mark Cartledge and Andrew Thomas affirm that activism can be a legitimate starting point for theological reflection. Indeed, the inclusion of students and practitioners in this current text, alongside teachers and researchers, demonstrates how the desire to reflect theologically both after and prior to action is developing as an evangelical practice.

However, alongside affirming the need for and call to action, the contributors of this book also warn that activism can become unhealthy if not balanced by attention to such things as silence, listening, and slowness. Liz Hoare, for instance, warns that evangelicalism's activism can result in a rush to action rather than attentive listening to God's plans and purposes. Andrew Thomas draws on John Swinton's work to warn that Western churches have unwittingly absorbed Western notions of time, leading to a 'driven busyness' that can limit, or even exclude, reception of and response to God's love. Chloe Lynch emphasises the role of grief and lament in the prophetic mode of practical theology that she promotes. She notes that identifying the affective dimension to the practical theologian's task permitted her to sit in her grief as a church leader when she became aware of an unhealthy leadership activism within Western evangelicalism. Although she maintains that '[e]motion is not the acid test of pathos: action ... is,' this should not short cut the process of lament, through which the practical theologian is able to hear God's voice anew.

## Where next?

Editing this collection started from an event at Moorlands College and spilled over into the editors' networks. Reflecting on the final collection, the way in which these networks confine the perspectives included in the book is obvious.

Within the limitations of one book it hasn't even been possible to encompass the full breadth of evangelicalism in the UK. There is limited engagement with the Pentecostal and Holiness traditions and no representation from black majority traditions. The book has a high proportion of women contributors, no doubt again reflecting the networks of the editors and this is perhaps a challenge to other areas of evangelical theology where men's voices still dominate. The editors felt that bringing in contributors outside the UK would lead to ever greater dilemmas about who to include and so readers will identify some elements of evangelicalism prominent in other parts of the world but missing here. Mark Cartledge makes this clear in his chapter. So for teachers using this volume with students of other traditions these features of the book need to be noted. All we can hope is that it will encourage other collections bringing together other voices.

As researchers we have gained encouragement from the vibrancy of research being undertaken by evangelical students, practitioners, and scholars. We would include in this Hoare researching her practice as a teacher and Rogers auto-ethnographic reflections. There is a significant amount of social scientific research into evangelical practice but there is plenty of room for further qualitative theological research. One important area for further research is the ongoing dialogue between evangelicalism and practical theology. It is evident that, for the contributors to this book, not only does their location within evangelicalism impact their practical theologising, but the observations and reflections that they draw from practice influence their evangelicalism. We have highlighted a few examples in relation to Bebbington's quadrilateral of evangelical priorities above. Within this assessment there are several areas that would benefit from further exploration. We will highlight just two. First, how a cross-disciplinary approach with biblical studies and systematic theology, in particular, could develop the use of the Bible within practical theology. Second, how the role of the Spirit in practical theology could be articulated more precisely. Perhaps these two areas, alongside engagement with a more global perspective on evangelicalism and practical theology, could be topics of study for a further Moorlands College conference.

## Notes

1 'Practical Theology and Evangelicalism: Methodological Considerations.'
2 Arthur illustrates a 'this is that' approach in reference to Peter's speech in Acts 2, within which he interprets the Pentecostal event (this) as a fulfilment of Joel's prophecy (that).
3 John G. Stackhouse, *Evangelical Landscapes: Facing Critical Issues of the Day* (Grand Rapids: Baker Academic, 2002), 168–169.
4 Lesslie Newbigin, *The Gospel in a Pluralist Society* (London: SPCK, 1989), 222–233.
5 Michael Moynagh, *Church for Every Context: An Introduction to Theology and Practice* (London: SPCK, 2012), 334–335 as cited by Helen Morris, *Flexible Church: Being the Church in the Contemporary World* (London: SCM, 2019), 20.

# Bibliography

Ackermann, Denise M. "Engaging Freedom: A Contextual Feminist Theology of Praxis." *Journal of Theology for Southern Africa* 94 (1996): 32–49.
Anderson, Ray S. "A Theology for Ministry." In *Theological Foundations for Ministry*, edited by Ray S. Anderson, 6–21. Edinburgh: T&T Clark, 1979.
Anderson, Ray S. *The Shape of Practical Theology: Empowering Ministry with Theological Praxis*. Downers Grove, IL: IVP Academic, 2001.
Anderson, Ray S. *The Soul of Ministry: Forming Leaders for God's People*. Louisville, KY: Westminster John Knox, 1997.
Andrews, Dale P. *Practical Theology for Black Churches: Bridging Black Theology and African American Folk Religion*. Louisville, KY: Westminster John Knox Press, 2002.
Andrews, Dale P., and Robert London Smith Jr., eds. *Black Practical Theology*. Waco, TX: Baylor University Press, 2015.
Ansdell, Gary. *How Music Helps in Music Therapy and Everyday Life*. London: Routledge, 2014.
Antlitz, Kevin. "Metaphor Matters: An Apology for Theodrama." *Transpositions*. Accessed 10th April 2020. http://www.transpositions.co.uk/metaphor-matters-apology-theodrama/.
Aquinas, Thomas. "SUMMA THEOLOGIAE: The Contemplative Life (Secunda Secundae Partis, Q. 180)." New Advent. Accessed May 2, 2020. https://www.newadvent.org/summa/3180.htm.
Archard, David. "How Should We Teach Sex?" *Journal of Philosophy of Education* 32, no. 3 (1998): 437–449.
Archer, Kenneth J. *A Pentecostal Hermeneutic for the Twenty-First Century: Spirit, Scripture and Community*. London: T&T Clark International, 2004.
Archer, Margaret S., Andrew Collier, and Douglas V. Porpora, eds. *Transcendence, Critical Realism and God*. London: Routledge, 2004.
Aristotle. "Nicomachean Ethics." The Internet Classics Archive. Accessed May 2, 2020. http://classics.mit.edu/Aristotle/nicomachaen.6.vi.html.
Aristotle. "Physics." The Internet Classics Archive. Accessed May 1, 2020. http://classics.mit.edu/Aristotle/physics.2.ii.html.
Arnold, Clinton E. *3 Crucial Questions about Spiritual Warfare*. Grand Rapids, MI: Baker, 1997.
Arrington, French. *Christian Doctrine: A Pentecostal Perspective*, vol 1. Cleveland, TN: Pathway, 1992.

Astley, Jeff. *Ordinary Theology: Looking, Listening and Learning in Theology*. Aldershot: Ashgate, 2002.
Atherstone, Andrew, and David Ceri Jones, eds. *The Routledge Research Companion to the History of Evangelicalism*. Milton: Taylor & Francis Group, 2018.
Avis, Paul D. *God and the Creative Imagination: Metaphor, Symbol and Myth in Religion and Theology*. London: Routledge, 1999.
Ballard, Paul. "The Bible in Theological Reflection: Indications from the History of Scripture." *Practical Theology* 4, no. 1 (2011): 35–47.
Ballard, Paul, and Stephen Pattison. "Practical Theological Education - a Profile." *British Journal of Theological Education* 13, no. 2 (2003): 97.
Ballard, Paul, and John Pritchard. *Practical Theology in Action: Christian Thinking in Service of Church and Society*. 2nd ed. London: SPCK, 2006.
Ballard, Paul, and John Pritchard. *Practical Theology in Action: Christian Thinking in Service of Church and Society*. London: SPCK, 1996.
Ballard, Paul, and Stephen Holmes, eds. *The Bible in Pastoral Practice: Readings in the Place and Function of Scripture in the Church*. London: Darton, Longman and Todd, 2005.
Barth, Karl. *Church Dogmatics III:3: The Doctrine of Creation*. Edinburgh: T&T Clark, 1960.
Barth, Karl. *Church Dogmatics IV:3: The Doctrine of Reconciliation*. Edinburgh: T&T Clark, 1962.
BBC World Service. *Fork in the Road - Two journeys out of gang violence*. Heart and Soul 05.04.19. Jahaziel and Guvna B. London, BBC Sounds. Accessed April 6, 2020.
Beasley-Murray, George R. *John*. WBC 36. Dallas, TX: Word, 1987.
Bebbington, David W. *Evangelicalism in Modern Britain: A History from the 1730s to the 1980s*. London: Unwin Hyman, 1989.
Bebbington, David W. "The Evangelical Quadrilateral: A Response." *Fides et historia* 47, no. 1 (2015): 87–96.
Beck, James R., and Bruce A. Demarest. *The Human Person in Theology and Psychology: A Biblical Anthropology for the Twenty-First Century*. Grand Rapids, MI: Kregel, 2005.
Bediako, Kwame. *Theology and Identity: The Impact of Culture Upon Christian Thought in the Second Century and Modern Africa*. Oxford: Regnum, 1992.
Begbie, Jeremy S. *Theology, Music and Time*. Cambridge: CUP, 2000.
Bell, John L. *The Singing Thing: A Case for Congregational Song*. Glasgow: Wild Goose Publications, 2000.
Bennett, Zoë. *Using the Bible in Practical Theology: Historical and Contemporary Perspectives*. Abingdon: Taylor & Francis, 2016.
Bennett, Zoë, Elaine Graham, Stephen Pattison, and Heather Walton, eds. *Invitation to Research in Practical Theology*. London: Routledge, 2018.
Bevans, Stephen B. *Models of Contextual Theology*. Rev. ed. Maryknoll, NY: Orbis, 2014.
Bevans, Stephen B., and Roger P. Schroeder. *Prophetic Dialogue: Reflections on Christian Mission Today*. Maryknoll, NY: Orbis, 2011.
Bird, Michael F. *Evangelical Theology: A Biblical and Systematic Introduction*. 2nd ed. Grand Rapids, MI: Zondervan Academic, 2020.
Blake, Simon in conversation with and Peter Aggleton. "Young People, Sexuality and Diversity. What Does a Needs-led and Rights-based Approach Look Like?" *Sex Education* 17, no. 3 (2017): 363–369.

Boa, Kenneth, and Robert M. Bowman Jr. *Faith Has Its Reasons: Integrative Approaches to Defending the Christian Faith*. Westmont, IL: IVP, 2006.
Boellstorff, Tom, Bonnie Nardi, Celia Pearce, and T.L. Taylor. *Ethnography and Virtual Worlds: A Handbook of Method*. Princeton, NJ: Princeton University Press, 2012.
Boersma, Hans. "Putting on Clothes: Body, Sex and Gender in Gregory of Nyssa." *Crux* 54, no. 2 (2018): 27–34.
Boersma, Hans. "Thomas Aquinas on the Beatific Vision: A Christological Deficit." *TheoLogica* 2, no. 2 (2018): 129–147.
Bolton, Doug. "The Scientific Community Isn't Happy about a Paper Mentioning a "Creator"." *The Independent*, March 3, 2016. http://www.independent.co.uk/news/science/scientific-study-paper-creator-intelligent-design-plos-one-creatorgate-a6910171.html.
Bolton, Paul. *Higher Education Student Numbers*. London: House of Commons Library, 2020.
Bosch, David J. *Transforming Mission: Paradigm Shifts in Theology of Mission – Twentieth Anniversary Edition*. New York, NY: Orbis Books, 2011.
Bosch, David J. *Transforming Mission: Paradigm Shifts in the Theology of Mission*. Maryknoll, NY: Orbis, 1991.
Breck, John. "Biblical Chiasmus: Exploring Structure for Meaning." *Biblical Theology Bulletin: Journal of Bible and Culture* 17, no. 2 (1987): 70–74.
Bretherton, Luke. *Christ and the Common Life: Political Theology and the Case for Democracy*. Grand Rapids, MI: Eerdmans, 2019.
Bretherton, Luke. *Christianity and Contemporary Politics: The Conditions and Possibilities of Faithful Witness*. Oxford: Wiley-Blackwell, 2010.
Briggs, Richard S. "Biblical Hermeneutics and Practical Theology: Method and Truth in Context." *Anglican Theological Review* 97, no. 2 (2015): 201–217.
Briggs, Richard S. "Election and evangelical thinking: Challenges to our way of conceiving the doctrine of God." In *New perspectives for Evangelical Theology: Engaging with God, Scripture and the World*, edited by Tom Greggs, 14–28. London & New York, NY: Routledge, 2010.
Briggs, Richard S., and Zoë Bennett. "Review Article - Using the Bible in Practical Theology: Historical and Contemporary Perspectives." *Theology and Ministry* 3, no. 1–9 (2014). https://www.dur.ac.uk/resources/theologyandministry/TheologyandMinistry3_7.pdf.
Brookes, Andrew, ed. *The Alpha Phenomenon: Theology, Praxis and Challenges for Mission and Church Today*. London: CTBI, 2007.
Brouard, Susanna. "Using Theological Action Research to Embed Catholic Social Teaching in a Catholic Development Agency: Abseiling on the Road to Emmaus." PhD Thesis, Anglia Ruskin University, 2015.
Browning, Don S. *A Fundamental Practical Theology: Descriptive and Strategic Proposals*. Minneapolis, MN: Fortress Press, 1991.
Browning, Don S. *Christian Ethics and the Moral Psychologies. Religion, Marriage, and Family*. Grand Rapids, MI: Eerdmans, 2006.
Brueggemann, Walter. "Prophetic Leadership: Engagement in Counter Imagination." *Journal of Religious Leadership* 10, no. 1 (2011): 1–23.
Brueggemann, Walter. "Response to Symposium on *The Prophetic Imagination*." *Journal of Pentecostal Theology* 23 (2014): 15–19.
Brueggemann, Walter. *The Practice of Prophetic Imagination: Preaching an Emancipating Word*. Minneapolis, MN: Fortress, 2012.
Brueggemann, Walter. *The Prophetic Imagination*. 2nd ed. Minneapolis, MN: Fortress, 2001.

Bruner, Frederick Dale. *A Theology of the Holy Spirit: The Pentecostal Experience and the New Testament Witness*. Grand Rapids, MI: Eerdmans, 1970.

Burgess, Richard. "Education for Conceptual Change: BME Students' Experiences of Learning Theological Reflection." *Developments in Academic Practice (DiAP online)* University of Roehampton (2014): 1–18.

Butler, James. "Prayer as a Research Practice? What Corporate Practices of Prayer Disclose about Theological Action Research." *Ecclesial Practices* 7, no. 2 (2020): 241–257.

Cahalan, Kathleen A. "Three Approaches to Practical Theology, Theological Education, and the Church's Ministry." *International Journal of Practical Theology* 9, no. 1 (2005): 64–94.

Cahalan Kathleen A., and Gordon S. Mikoski, eds. *Opening the Field of Practical Theology: An Introduction*. Lanham, MD: Rowman & Littlefield, 2014.

Cameron, Helen. *Just Mission: Practical Politics for Local Churches*. London: SCM, 2015.

Cameron, Helen. "*Reflections on the Challenges of Using the Pastoral Cycle in a Faith-Based Organisation*." British and Irish Association of Practical Theology conference 11th July (2012).

Cameron, Helen. *Resourcing Mission: Practical Theology for Changing Churches*. London: SCM, 2010.

Cameron, Helen. "The Morality of the Food Parcel: Emergency Food as a Response to Austerity." *Practical Theology* 7, no. 3 (2014): 194–204.

Cameron, Helen, and Catherine Duce. *Researching Practice in Ministry and Mission: A Companion*. London: SCM, 2013.

Cameron, Helen, Philip Richter, Douglas Davies, and Frances Ward, eds. *Studying Local Churches: A Handbook*. London: SCM, 2005.

Cameron, Helen, Deborah Bhatti, Catherine Duce, James Sweeney, and Clare Watkins. *Talking About God in Practice: Theological Action Research and Practical Theology*. London: SCM, 2010.

Cameron, Helen, John Reader, Victoria Slater, and Chris Rowland. *Theological Reflection for Human Flourishing: Pastoral Practice and Public Theology*. London: SCM, 2012.

Cameron, Nigel. *Method without Madness? An Evangelical Approach to 'Doing' Theology*. Leicester: UCCF, 1983.

Campbell, Heidi A., ed. *Digital Religion: Understanding Religious Practice in New Media Worlds*. London: Routledge, 2013.

Campbell, Heidi A., ed. *The Distanced Church: Reflections on Doing Church Online*. Texas: Digital Religion Publications-Network for New Media, 2020.

Campbell, Heidi A., and Stephen Garner. *Networked Theology: Negotiating Faith in a Digital Culture*. Grand Rapids, MI: Baker Academic, 2016.

Carson, D. A. *The Intolerance of Tolerance*. Grand Rapids, MI: Eerdmans, 2012.

Carter, Jamys Jeremy. "A critical analysis of the Pentecostal hermeneutics used by Elim local church leadership teams in relation to the topic of women in ministry." PhD diss., University of Leeds, 2019. http://etheses.whiterose.ac.uk/25608/1/Carter_JJ_PRHS_PhD_2019.pdf.

Cartledge, Mark J. "Affective Theological Praxis: Understanding the Direct Object of Practical Theology." *International Journal of Practical Theology* 8 (2004): 34–52.

Cartledge, Mark J. "Can Theology be "Practical"? Part II: A Reflection on Renewal Methodology and the Practice of Research." *Journal of Contemporary Ministry* 3 (2017): 20–36.

Cartledge, Mark J. *Charismatic Glossoalia: An Empirical-Theological Study*. Aldershot: Ashgate, 2002.

Cartledge, Mark J. "Empirical Theology: Inter- or Intra-disciplinary?" *Journal of Beliefs & Values* 20, no. 1 (1999): 98–104.
Cartledge, Mark J. "Empirical Theology: Towards an Evangelical-charismatic Hermeneutic." *Journal of Pentecostal Theology* 9 (1996): 115–126.
Cartledge, Mark J. "Locating the Spirit in Meaningful Experience: Empirical Theology and Pentecostal Hermeneutics." In *Constructing Pneumatological Hermeneutics in Pentecostal Christianity*, edited by Kenneth J. Archer and L. William Oliverio, Jr., 251–266. New York, NY: Palgrave Macmillan, 2016.
Cartledge, Mark J. *Mediation of the Spirit: Interventions in Practical Theology*. Grand Rapids, MI: Eerdmans, 2015.
Cartledge, Mark J. "Pentecostalism." in *The Wiley-Blackwell Companion to Practical Theology*, edited by Bonnie J. Miller-McLemore, 587–595. New York, NY: Wiley-Blackwell, 2012.
Cartledge, Mark J. "Practical Theology." In *Studying Global Pentecostalism: Theories and Methods*, edited by Allan H. Anderson, Michael Bergner, André Droogers and Cornelius van der Laan, 268–285. Berkeley, CA: University of California Press, 2010.
Cartledge, Mark J. "Practical Theology: Attending to Pneumatologically-Driven Praxis." In *The Handbook of Pentecostal Theology*, edited by Wolfgang Vondey, 163–172. London: Routledge, 2020.
Cartledge, Mark J. *Practical Theology: Charismatic and Empirical Perspectives*. Carlisle: Paternoster, 2003.
Cartledge, Mark J. *Testimony: Its Importance, Place and Potential*. Cambridge: Grove Books Ltd., 2002.
Cartledge, Mark. J. *Testimony in the Spirit: Rescripting Ordinary Pentecostal Theology*. Aldershot: Ashgate, 2010.
Cartledge. Mark. J. *Testimony in the Spirit. Rescripting Ordinary Pentecostal Theology*. 2nd ed. London: Routledge, 2017.
Cartledge, Mark J. "Text-Community-Spirit: The Challenged Posed by Pentecostal Theological Method to Evangelical Theology." in *Spirit and Scripture: Examining a Pneumatic Hermeneutic*, edited by Kevin L. Spawn and Archie T. Wright, 130–142. London: T&T Clark, 2012.
Cartledge, Mark J. "The Use of Scripture in Practical Theology: A Study of Academic Practice." *Practical Theology* 6, no. 3 (2013): 271–283.
Cartledge, Mark J., and David Cheetham, eds. *Intercultural Theology: Approaches and Themes*. London: SCM, 2011.
Castelo, Daniel. "Tarrying on the Lord: Affections, Virtues and Theological Ethics in Pentecostal Perspective." *Journal of Pentecostal Theology* 13, no. 1 (2004): 31–56.
Charry, Ellen. *By the Renewing of Your Mind. The Pastoral Function of Christian Doctrine*. Oxford: Oxford University Press, 1997.
Childs, James M. "Eschatology, Anthropology, and Sexuality: Helmut Thielicke and the Orders of Creation Revisited." *Journal of the Society of Christian Ethics* 30, no. 1 (2010): 3–20.
Church of England. "Relationships Education, Relationships and Sex Education (RSE) and Health Education in Church of England Schools." Accessed April 14, 2020. https://www.churchofengland.org/sites/default/files/2019-11/RSHE%20Principles%20and%20Charter_0.pdf.
Church of England. "Risk of 'Ghettoising' Faith in Schools." Accessed March 12, 2019. https://www.churchofengland.org/more/media-centre/stories-and-features/risk-ghettoising-faith-schools.

Ciampa, Roy E., and Brian S. Rosner, *The First Letter to the Corinthians*. PNTC. Grand Rapids, MI: Eerdmans, 2010.

Clapper, Gregory S. "Orthokardia: John Wesley's Grammar of the Holy Spirit." In *The Spirit, The Affections, and the Christian Tradition*, edited by Dale M. Coulter and Amos Yong, 259–278. Notre Dame: University of Notre Dame Press, 2016.

Clarke, Anthony J. *"Forming Ministers or Training Leaders? An Exploration of Practice and the Pastoral Imagination."* PhD Thesis, University of Chester, 2017.

Clements, Keith. "Theology Now." In *Companion Encyclopedia of Theology*, edited by Peter Byrne and J. L. Houlden, 272–290. London & New York, NY: Routledge, 1995.

Click. "Understanding Casual Relationships." Accessed April 14, 2020. https://click.clickrelationships.org/content/all-issues/casual-relationships/.

Collins, Helen. *Reordering Theological Reflection: Starting with Scripture*. London: SCM, 2020.

Comer, John Mark. *The Ruthless Elimination of Hurry*. London: Hodder & Stoughton, 2019.

Commission on Evangelism. *Towards the Conversion of England*. London: Church of England, 1945.

Cooling, Trevor. *Doing God in Education*. London: Theos, 2010.

Cooling, Trevor, Beth Green, Andrew Morris, and Lynn Revell. *Christian Faith in English Church Schools: Research Conversations with Classroom Teachers*. Oxford: Peter Lang, 2016.

Cray, Graham. *The Post-Evangelical Debate*. London: Triangle, 1997.

Croasmun, Matthew, and Miroslav Volf. *For the Life of the World: Theology That Makes a Difference*. Grand Rapids, MI: Brazos Press, 2019.

Cruse, Jonathan Landry. *"The Christian's True Identity."* Accessed April 11, 2020. https://www.whitehorseinn.org/2019/11/the-mod-the-christians-true-identity/.

Davie, Martin, Tim Grass, Stephen R. Holmes, John McDowell, and T. A. Noble, eds. *New Dictionary of Theology: Historical and Systematic*. 2nd ed. London: IVP, 2012.

Day, Abby. *The Religious Lives of Older Laywomen: The Last Active Anglican Generation*. Oxford: Oxford University Press, 2017.

Dean, Hartley. *Understanding Human Need: Social Issues, Policy and Practice*. Bristol: Policy Press, 2010.

Dean, Kenda Creasy. *Almost Christians: What the Faith of Our Teenagers is Telling the American Church*. Oxford: Oxford University Press, 2010.

Department for Education. *Relationships Education, Relationships and Sex Education (RSE) and Health Education: Statutory Guidance for Governing Bodies, Proprietors, Head Teachers, Principals, Senior Leadership Teams, Teachers*. London: Department for Education, 2019.

Department for Education. *The Equality Act 2010 and Schools: Departmental Advice for School Leaders, School Staff, Governing Bodies and Local Authorities*. London: Department for Education, 2014.

DePoe, John M. "The Heavens Are Declaring the Glory of God: Contemporary Teleological Arguments." *Review & Expositor* 111, no. 3 (2014): 244–258.

Dillon, Michele. *Introduction to Sociological Theory: Theorists, Concepts, and Their Applicability to the Twenty-First Century*. 2nd ed. Chichester: Wiley Blackwell, 2014.

Dochuk, Darren. "Revisiting Bebbington's classic rendering of modern evangelicalism at points of new departure." *Fides et Historia* 47, no. 1 (2015): 63–72.

Dubé, Sophie, Francine Lavoie, Martin Blais, and Martine Hébert. "Consequences of Casual Sex Relationships and Experiences on Adolescents' Psychological Well-Being: A Prospective Study." *The Journal of Sex Research* 54, no. 8 (2017): 1006–1017.

Dudley, J. A. J. "The Love of God in Aristotle's Ethics." *Neue Zeitschrift Für Systematische Theologie Und Religionsphilosophie* 25, no. 1–3 (2009): 126.

Duncan, Bruce. *Pray Your Way*. London: DLT, 1993.

Dunn, James D. G. "The Bible and Scholarship: On Bridging the Gap between the Academy and the Church." *Anvil* 19, no. 2 (2002): 109–118.

Dunn, James D. G. *The Theology of Paul the Apostle*. 2nd ed. London: T&T Clark, 2003.

Durham University. "MA in Digital Theology." Accessed August 25, 2020. https://www.dur.ac.uk/digitaltheology/courses/.

Dykstra, Craig. "Pastoral and Ecclesial Imagination" In *For Life Abundant: Practical Theology, Theological Education, and Christian Ministry*, edited by Dorothy C. Bass and Craig Dykstra, 41–61. Grand Rapids, MI: Eerdmans, 2008.

Egan, Kieran. *Imagination in Teaching and Learning: Ages 8 to 15*. London: Routledge, 1992.

Elim. "How to administer the baptism in the Spirit." In *The Message: Elim's Core Beliefs*, edited by Keith Warrington, 60–61. Malvern: Elim, no date.

Elim. "We are Elim." Elim. No date. Accessed August 30, 2020. https://www.elim.org.uk/Groups/243050/About_Elim.aspx.

Elim. "What we Believe." Elim. No date. Accessed April 17, 2020. https://www.elim.org.uk/Publisher/Article.aspx?id=417857&redirected=1.

Elliott, Dyan. "Tertullian, the Angelic Life, and the Bride of Christ." In *Gender and Christianity in Medieval Europe: New Perspectives*, edited by Lisa M. Bitel and Felice Lifshitz, 16–33. Philadelphia, PA: University of Pennsylvania Press, 2008.

Emerson, Lucy. "New Relationships and Sex Education Guidance is Here – But Does it Do the Job?" Accessed June 10, 2019. https://schoolsweek.co.uk/new-relationships-and-sex-education-guidance-is-here-but-does-it-do-the-job/.

Fletcher, Garth, Jeffry A.Simpson, LorneCampbell, and Nickola C.Overall. *The Science of Intimate Relationships*. Chichester: Wiley-Blackwell, 2013.

Foster, Richard J. *Streams of Living Water*. London: Fount, 1999.

Fowke, Ruth. *Personality and Prayer*. Guildford: Eagle, 1997.

Frestadius, Simo. *Pentecostal Rationality: Epistemology and Theological Hermeneutics in the Foursquare Tradition*. London: T&T Clark, 2020.

Frost, Rob. "Foreword." In *Into God's Presence*, edited by Liz Babbs, 7–10. Grand Rapids, MI: Zondervan, 2005.

Ganiel, Gladys. "Explaining New Forms of Evangelical Activism in Northern Ireland: Comparative Perspectives from the USA and Canada." *Journal of Church and State* 50, no. 3 (2008): 475–493.

Garner, Mark, Richard Burgess, and Daniel Eshun. "Submitting Convictions to Critical Enquiry: A Challenge for Higher Education." *Occasional Papers on Faith in Higher Education* 1 (2015): 62–76. https://cuac.anglicancommunion.org/.

Goddard, Andrew. "Theology and Practice in Evangelical Churches." In *The Oxford Handbook of Theology, Sexuality, and Gender*, edited by Adrian Thatcher, 377–394. Oxford: Oxford University Press, 2015.

Goldingay, John. *Songs from A Strange Land – Psalms 42–51*. BST. Leicester: IVP, 1978.

Goodhart, David. *Head Hand Heart: The Struggle for Dignity and Status in the 21st Century*. London: Allen Lane, 2020.

Goodhart, David. *The Road to Somewhere: The Populist Revolt and the Future of Politics*. London: Hurst & Company, 2017.

Goodhew, David, ed. *Church Growth in Britain: 1980 to the Present*. Farnham: Ashgate, 2012.

Goto, Courtney T. *Taking on Practical Theology: The Idolization of Context and the Hope of Community*. Leiden: Brill, 2018.

Goto, Courtney T. "The Ubiquity of Ignorance: A Practical Theological Challenge of Our Time." *Practical Theology* 13, no. 1–2 (2020): 138–149.

Graham, Elaine. "Between a Rock and a Hard Place." *Practical Theology* 7, no. 4 (2014): 235–251.

Graham, Elaine. *Between a Rock and a Hard Place: Public Theology in a Post-Secular Age*. London: SCM, 2013.

Graham, Elaine. "Why Practical Theology Must Go Public." *Practical Theology* 1, no. 1 (2008): 11–17.

Graham, Elaine, Heather Walton, and Frances Ward. *Theological Reflection: Methods*. London: SCM, 2005.

Graham, Elaine, Heather Walton, and Frances Ward. *Theological Reflection: Methods*. 2nd ed. London: SCM, 2019.

Graham, Elaine, Heather Walton, and Frances Ward. *Theological Reflection: Sources*. London: SCM, 2007.

Granito, Carmer, Claudia Scorolli, and Anna Maria Borghi. "Naming a Lego World. The Role of Language in the Acquisition of Abstract Concepts." *PLoS ONE* 10, no. 1 (2015): 1–21.

Green, Garrett. *Imagining God: Theology and the Religious Imagination*. Grand Rapids, MI: Eerdmans, 1998.

Green, Laurie. *Let's Do Theology*. London: Continuum, 2001.

Green, Laurie. *Let's Do Theology: A Pastoral Cycles Resource Book*. London: Continuum, 1990.

Greenway, Tyler S., Justin L. Barrett, and James L. Furrow. "Theology and Thriving: Teleological Considerations Based on the Doctrines of Christology and Soteriology." *Journal of Psychology and Theology* 44, no. 3 (2016): 179–189.

Greig, Pete. *How to Pray: A Simple Guide for Normal People*. London: Hodder & Stoughton, 2019.

Grenz, Stanley J. *Renewing the Center: Evangelical Theology in a Post-Theological Era*. 2nd ed. Grand Rapids, MI: Baker Academic, 2006.

Grenz, Stanley J. *Revisioning Evangelical Theology: A Fresh Agenda for the 21st Century* Downers Grove, IL: IVP, 1993.

Gross, Richard. *Psychology: The Science of Mind and Behaviour*. 6th ed. London: Hodder Education, 2010.

Guder, Darrell L. *The Continuing Conversion of the Church*. Grand Rapids, MI: Eerdmans, 2000.

Haack, Denis. "When Spiritual Growth Involves Disequilibrium." *Presbyterion: Covenant Seminary Review* 41, no. 1 (2015): 31–49.

Hall, Gerard. "Prophetic Dialogue: A Foundational Category for Practical Theology." *International Journal of Practical Theology* 14 (2010): 34–46.

Halstead, Mark, and Michael Reiss. *Values in Education: From Principles to Practice*. London: RoutledgeFalmer, 2003.

Hamilton, Victor P. *The Book of Genesis Chapters 1–17*. NICNT. Grand Rapids, MI: Eerdmans, 1990.

Hansen, Jochim, and Michaela Wänke. "Truth from Language and Truth from Fit: The Impact of Linguistic Concreteness and Level of Construal on Subjective Truth." *Personality and Social Psychology Bulletin* 36, no. 11 (2010): 1576–1588.

Harman, Allan. *Psalms Vol 1 (Psalms 1–72) – A Mentor Commentary*. Fearn: Christian Focus, 2011.

Harris, Tania. "Where Pentecostalism and Evangelicalism Part Ways: Towards a Theology of Pentecostal Revelatory Experience Part I & 2." *Asian Journal of Pentecostal Studies* 23, no. 1 (2020): 31–56.

Hart, Trevor. "Imagination for the Kingdom of God? Hope, Promise, and the Transformative Power of an Imagined Future." In *God Will Be All in All: The Eschatology of Jürgen Moltmann*, edited by Richard Bauckham, 49–76. Edinburgh: T&T Clark, 1999.

Hatcher, Andrea. *Political and Religious Identities of British Evangelicals*. London: Palgrave Macmillan, 2017.

Heschel, Abraham J. *The Prophets vol.1*. New York, NY: Harper Torchbooks, 1969.

Heschel, Abraham J. *The Prophets vol.2*. New York, NY: Harper Torchbooks, 1975.

Heyes, Joshua M. "Towards a Virtue Ethical Approach to Relationships and Sex Education." *Journal of Moral Education* 48, no. 2 (2019): 165–178.

Hiltner, Seward. *Preface to Pastoral Theology*. Nashville, TN: Abingdon Press, 1958.

Hine, Christine. *Ethnography for the Internet: Embedded, Embodies and Everyday*. London: Bloomsbury Academic, 2015.

Hirst, Julia. "Developing Sexual Competence? Exploring strategies for the provision of effective sexualities and relationships education." *Sex Education* 8, no. 4 (2008): 399–413.

Hollenweger, Walter J. *Pentecostalism: Origins and Developments Worldwide*. Grand Rapids, MI: Baker Academic, 2005.

Hollinger, Dennis. *The Meaning of Sex: Christian Ethics and the Moral Life*. Grand Rapids, MI: Baker Academic, 2009.

Holmes, Stephen R. "Evangelical Doctrines of Scripture in Transatlantic Perspective: The 2008 Laing Lecture." *Evangelical Quarterly* 81 (2009): 38–63.

Hull, John M. *What Prevents Christian Adults From Learning*. London: SCM, 1985.

Humanists UK. "PSHE and Sex and Relationships Education." Accessed April 6, 2020. https://humanism.org.uk/campaigns/schools-and-education/school-curriculum/pshe-and-sex-and-relationships-education/.

Humanists UK. "Secularism." Accessed April 6, 2020. https://humanism.org.uk/campaigns/secularism/.

Hunt, Cherryl. "Promoting Biblical Engagement among Ordinary Christians in English Churches: Reflections on the Pathfinder Project." PhD Diss. University of Exeter, 2016. https://ore.exeter.ac.uk/repository/handle/10871/23365.

Hurcombe, Rachel. *Child Sexual Abuse in the Context of Religious Institutions*. London: IICSA, 2019.

Hurding, Roger. *Five Pathways to Wholeness*. London: SPCK, 2013.

Hutchings, Tim. *Creating Church Online: Ritual, Community and New Media*. London: Routledge, 2017.

Jamieson, Alan. *A Churchless Faith: Faith Journeys Beyond the Churches*. London: SPCK, 2002.

Janis, Irving L. *Victims of Groupthink*. Boston, MA: Houghton Mifflin, 1972.

Janzen, Waldemar. *Old Testament Ethics*. Louisville, KY: Westminster John Knox, 1994.

Jennings, W. J. *After Whiteness: An Education in Belonging*. Grand Rapids, MI: Eerdmans, 2020.

Johns, Jackie David, and Cheryl Bridges Johns. "Yielding to the Spirit: A Pentecostal Approach to Group Bible Study." *Journal of Pentecostal Theology* 1, no. 1 (1992): 109–134.

Johnson, Trygve David. *The Preacher as Liturgical Artist: Metaphor, Identity, and the Vicarious Humanity of Christ*. Eugene, OR: Cascade, 2014.

Jones, Joshua. "Practical Theology and the Holy Spirit." *Theology and Ministry* 6 (2020): 36–61.
Jordan, Elizabeth. "Conversation as a Tool of Research in Practical Theology." *Practical Theology* 12, no. 5 (2019): 526–536.
Kearsley, Roy. *Church, Community and Power*. Farnham: Ashgate, 2008.
Kelsey, David H. "God and Teleology: Must God Have Only One "Eternal Purpose"?" *Neue Zeitschrift Für Systematische Theologie Und Religionsphilosphie* 54, no. 4 (2012), 361–376.
Kidner, Derek. *Psalms 1–72*. TOTC. Leicester: IVP, 1973.
Killen, Patricia O'Connell, and John De Beer. *The Art of Theological Reflection*. New York, NY: Crossroad, 2002.
Kim, Sebastian, and Katie Day, eds. *A Companion to Public Theology*. Leiden: Brill, 2017.
Kinast, Robert L. *Let Ministry Teach. A Guide to Theological Reflection*. Collegeville: The Liturgical Press, 199.
King, Gerald W. *Disfellowshiped: Pentecostal Responses to Fundamentalism in the United States, 1906–1943*. Eugene, OR: Pickwick Publications, 2011.
King, Pamela Ebstyne, and William B. Whitney. "What's the "Positive" in Positive Psychology? Teleological Considerations Based on Creation and Imago Doctrines." *Journal of Psychology and Theology* 43, no. 1 (March 2015): 47–59.
Knorpp, William Max. "What Relativism Isn't." *Philosophy* 73, no. 284 (1998): 277–300.
Kozinets, Robert V. *Netnography: Doing Ethnographic Research Online*. Los Angeles, CA: Sage, 2013.
Krueger, Richard A. *Focus Group Kit 3, Developing Questions for Focus Groups*. Thousand Oaks, CA: SAGE Publications, 1998.
Kuehne, Dale S. *Sex and the iWorld: Rethinking Relationships beyond an Age of Individualism*. Grand Rapids, MI: Baker Academic, 2009.
Lamb, Sharon. "Just the Facts? The Separation of Sex Education from Moral Education." *Educational Theory* 63, no. 5 (2013): 443–460.
Land, Stephen J. *Pentecostal Spirituality: A Passion for the Kingdom*. Sheffield: Sheffield Academic Press, 1993.
Larsen, Timothy, and Daniel J. Treier, eds. *The Cambridge Companion to Evangelical Theology*. Cambridge: Cambridge University Press, 2007.
Lartey, Emmanuel Y. *In Living Color: An Intercultural Approach to Pastoral Care and Counseling*. New York, NY: Jessica Kingsley Publishers, 2003.
Law, Stephen. *The War for Children's Minds*. Abingdon: Routledge, 2006.
Lawrence. *The Practice of The Presence of God*. USA: Mockingbird Classics Publishing, 2015.
Le, Vince. *Vietnamese Evangelicals and Pentecostalism: The Politics of Divine Intervention*. Leiden: Brill, 2018.
Lewis, C. S. *The Abolition of Man: Or, Reflections on Education with Special Reference to the Teaching of English in the Upper Forms of Schools*. London: HarperCollins, 1944. https://www.overdrive.com/search?q=070B1E2B-45C4-4C43-AB6D-A5C3594E07D9.
Lewis, C. S. *The Four Loves*. London: HarperCollins, 2002.
Lipton, Peter. "What Good Is an Explanation?" In *Explanation*, edited by Giora Hon and Sam S. Rakover, 43–60. Synthese Library 302. Dordrecht: Springer, 2001.
Loder, James E. *The Transforming Moment*. 2nd ed. Colorado Springs, CO: Helmers & Howard, 1989.
Lugt, Wesley Vander. *Living Theodrama: Reimagining Theological Ethics*. Farnham: Ashgate, 2014.

Lunn, J. "Paying Attention: The Task of Attending in Spiritual Direction and Practical Theology." *Practical Theology* 2, no. 2 (2009): 219–229.
Lyall, David, and Paul Ballard. "Soil, Roots and Shoots: The Emergence of BIAPT." *Practical Theology* 13, no. 1–2 (2020): 8–18.
Lynch, Chloe. *Ecclesial Leadership as Friendship*. Abingdon: Routledge, 2019.
MacDonald, Raymond, Gunter Kreutz, and Laura Mitchell. *Music, Health, And Wellbeing*. Oxford: Oxford University Press, 2013.
Macintyre, Alasdair. *After Virtue: A Study in Moral Theory*. 2nd ed. Notre Dame: University of Notre Dame Press, 1984.
Maddox, Randy L. "The Recovery of Theology as a Practical Discipline." *Theological Studies* 51 (1990): 650–672.
Male, David, and Paul Weston. *The Word's Out: Principles and Strategies for Effective Evangelism Today*. Rev. ed. Abingdon: The Bible Reading Fellowship, 2019.
Mark, Olwyn E. *Educating for Sexual Virtue: A Moral Vision for Relationships and Sex Education*. Oxford: Peter Lang, 2018.
Martin, Lee Roy. "'Your sons and daughters will prophesy': A Pentecostal Review of Walter Brueggemann's *The Practice of Prophetic Imagination*." *Journal of Pentecostal Theology* 22 (2013): 155–163.
Matera, Frank J. *Romans*. Paideia Commentaries on the New Testament. Grand Rapids, MI: Baker Academic, 2010.
McClintock Fulkerson, Mary. *Places of Redemption: Theology for a Worldly Church*. Oxford: Oxford University Press, 2007.
McClymond, Michael J. "The Bible and Pentecostalism." In *The Oxford Handbook of the Bible in America*, edited by Paul C. Gutjahr, 591–602. Oxford: Oxford University Press, 2017.
McFarlane, Graham. *A Model for Evangelical Theology: Integrating Scripture, Tradition, Reason, Experience, and Community*. Grand Rapids, MI: Baker Academic, 2020.
McGrath, Alister. *Surprised by Meaning: Science, Faith, and How We Make Sense of Things*. London: Westminster John Knox Press, 2010.
McInerney, Dennis M., and David W. Putwain. *Developmental and Educational Psychology for Teachers: An Applied Approach*. London: Routledge, 2016.
McKeown, James. *Genesis*. Two Horizons New Testament Commentary. Grand Rapids, MI: Eerdmans, 2008.
McKitterick, Alistair J. "The Theological Imperative Model for Practice Theology." *Journal of European Baptist Studies* 16, no. 4 (2016): 5–20.
McKnight, Scot. *The King Jesus Gospel: The Original Good News Revisited*. Grand Rapids, MI: Zondervan, 2011.
McRay, Barrett. "How People Develop in Their Thinking." In *Teaching the Next Generations: A Comprehensive Guide for Teaching Christian Formation*, edited by Terence D. Linhart, 58–70. Grand Rapids, MI: Baker Academic, 2016.
Meadowcroft, Tim. "Method and Old Testament Theology: Barr, Brueggemann and Goldingay Considered." *Tyndale Bulletin* 57, no. 1 (2006): 35–56.
Medawar, Peter. *The Limits of Science*. Oxford: Oxford University Press, 1984.
Middleton, J. Richard, and Brian J. Walsh. *Truth is Stranger Than it Used to Be: Biblical Faith in a Postmodern Age*. Gospel and Culture. London: SPCK, 1995.
Miller-McLemore, Bonnie J. "Five Misunderstandings about Practical Theology." *International Journal for Practical Theology* 16, no. 1 (2012): 5–26.

Miller-McLemore, Bonnie J. "Introduction: The Contributions of Practical Theology." In *The Wiley-Blackwell Companion to Practical Theology*, edited by Bonnie J. Miller-McLemore, 1–20. Chichester: Wiley-Blackwell, 2012.

Moon, Jennifer A. *A Handbook of Reflective and Experiential Learning: Theory and Practice*. Abingdon: RoutledgeFalmer, 2004.

Moore, Rickie D. "Walter Brueggemann's *Prophetic Imagination*: Not without Honor." *Journal of Pentecostal Theology* 23 (2014): 1–6.

Moorlands College. "*Our Core Values*." Accessed April 4, 2019. www.moorlands.ac.uk/our-core-values/.

Moreau, A. Scott, ed. *Evangelical Dictionary of World Missions*. Grand Rapids, MI: Baker, 2000.

Moreland, J. P. "Science and Theology." In *Evangelical Dictionary of Theology*, edited by Daniel J. Treier and Walter A. Elwell, 1427–1432. 3rd ed. Grand Rapids, MI: Baker Academic, 2017.

Morris, Helen. *Flexible Church: Being the Church in the Contemporary World*. London: SCM, 2019.

Moxon, John R. L. "Biblical Studies - Troublesome or Catastrophic? Strategies in Ministerial Formation." *Practical Theology* 13, no. 4 (2020): 355–371.

Moynagh, Michael. *Church for Every Context: An Introduction to Theology and Practice*. London: SPCK, 2012.

Muir, R. David. "Theological Education and Training among British Pentecostals and Charismatics." In *Pentecostals and Charismatics in Britain: An Anthology*, edited by Joe Aldred. London: SCM Press, 2019.

Mulholland Jr., M. Robert. "Spiritual Journey." In *Dictionary of Christian Spirituality*, edited by Glen G. Scorgie, 551–552. Grand Rapids, MI: Zondervan, 2011.

Murphy, Nancey. "Constructing a Radical-Reformation Research Program in Psychology." In *Why Psychology Needs Theology: A Radical-Reformation Perspective*, edited by Alvin C. Dueck and Cameron Lee, 53–78. Grand Rapids, MI: Eerdmans, 2005.

Mwangi, James K. "An Integrated Competency-Based Training Model for theological training." *HTS Teologiese/Theological Studies* 62, vol. 2 (2010): 1–10.

Myers, Ched. *Binding the Strong Man: A Political Reading of Mark's Story of Jesus*. Maryknoll, NY: Orbis Books, 1988.

Nash, Sally, Jo Pimlott, and Paul Nash. *Skills for Collaborative Ministry*. 2nd ed. London: SPCK, 2011.

Netherwood, Anne. *The Voice of this Calling: An Evangelical Encounters the Ignatian Exercises*. London: SPCK, 1990.

Newbigin, Lesslie. *The Gospel in a Pluralist Society*. London: SPCK, 1989.

Newbigin, Lesslie. *The Open Secret*. Rev. ed. Grand Rapids, MI: Eerdmans, 1995.

NHS. "Are you Ready for Sex?" Accessed April 14, 2020. https://www.nhs.uk/live-well/sexual-health/are-you-ready-for-sex/.

Notman, Alison. *Faith and Vision: The Moorlands Story*. Sopley: Moorlands College, 1998.

Nouwen, Henri J. M. *Life of The Beloved*. London: Hodder and Stoughton, 1992.

Nouwen, Henri J. M. *Primacy of the Heart*. Madison, WI: St Benedict Center, 1988.

O'Connell Killen, Patricia and John De Beer. *The Art of Theological Reflection*. New York, NY: Crossroad, 2008.

O'Neill, Gary, and Liz Shercliff, eds. *Straw for the Bricks: Theological Reflection in Practice*. London: SCM Press, 2018.

Oliver, Simon. "Teleology Revived? Cooperation and the Ends of Nature." *Studies in Christian Ethics* 26, no. 2 (May 2013): 158–165.
Oliverio, William, L. *Theological Hermeneutics in the Classical Pentecostal Tradition: A Typological Account*. Leiden & Boston, MA: Brill, 2012.
Osborne, Grant R. *Romans*. IVP New Testament Commentary Series. Downers Grove, IL: IVP Academic, 2004.
Osmer, Richard R. *Practical Theology*. Grand Rapids, MI: Eerdmans, 2008.
Osmer, Richard R. "Toward a New Story of Practical Theology." *International Journal of Practical Theology* 16, no. 1 (2012): 66–78.
Palmer, Melissa J., Linda Clarke, George B. Ploubidis, and Kaye Wellings. "Prevalence and Correlates of 'Sexual Competence' at First Heterosexual Intercourse Among Young People in Britain." *BMJ Sex Reprod Health* 45 (2019): 127–137.
Parker, Stephen E. *Led by the Spirit: Toward a Practical Theology of Pentecostal Discernment and Decision Making*. Expanded ed. Cleveland, TN: CPT Press, 2015.
Pattison, Stephen. "Conversations in Practical Theology." *Practical Theology* 13, no. 1–2 (2020): 87–94.
Pattison, Stephen. "Is Pastoral Care Dead in a Mission-Led Church?" *Practical Theology* 1, no. 1 (2008): 7–10.
Pattison, Stephen. "Pastoral Studies." In *The Challenge of Practical Theology*, edited by Stephen Pattison, 247–252. London: Jessica Kingsley Publishers, 2007.
Pattison, Stephen. "Some Straw for the Bricks: A Basic Introduction to Theological Reflection." *Contact* 99, no. 1 (1989): 2–9.
Pattison, Stephen. "Some Straw for the Bricks: A Basic Introduction to Theological Reflection." In *The Blackwell Reader in Pastoral and Practical Theology*, edited by James Woodward and Stephen Pattison, 135–145. Oxford: Blackwell, 2000.
Pattison, Stephen. *The Challenge of Practical Theology: Selected Essays*. London: Jessica Kingsley, 2007.
Paul, Ian. *Revelation: An Introduction and Commentary*. TNTC. Nottingham: IVP, 2018.
Pennington, Donald. C. *The Social Psychology of Behaviour in Small Groups*. London: Routledge, 2014.
Percy, Emma. "Can a Eunuch Be Baptized?: Insights for Gender Inclusion from Acts 8." *Theology* 119, no. 5 (2016): 327–334.
Perry, Samuel L., and Cyrus Schleifer. "Are Bivocational Clergy Becoming the New Normal? An Analysis of the Current Population Survey, 1996–2017." *Journal for the Scientific Study of Religion* 58, no. 2 (2019): 513–525.
Piaget, Jean. "Genetic Epistemology." In Richard L'Evans, *Jean Piaget: The Man and His Ideas*. Translated by Eleanor Duckworth. New York, NY: E. P. Dutton & Company, 1973.
Pieterse, Hendrik J. "Practical Theology in South Africa." *International Journal of Practical Theology* 2 (1998): 155–165.
Pike, Mark A. "British values and virtues: schooling in Christianity and character?" *British Journal of Religious Education* 41, no. 3 (2019): 352–360.
Pike, Mark A. "Christianity and Character Education: Faith in Core Values?" *Journal of Beliefs and Values* 31, no. 3 (2010): 311–321.
Plouffe, Tammie. "The Art of Connection: Using Images in Training Facilitation." Training Industry, 2018. Accessed March 10, 2020. https://trainingindustry.com/articles/content-development/the-art-of-connection-using-images-in-training-facilitation/.

Polanco, Rodrigo. "Understanding Von Balthasar's Trilogy." *Theologica Xaveriana* 67, no. 184 (2017): 411–430.
Pölzler, Thomas, and Jennifer Cole Wright. "Anti-Realist Pluralism: A New Approach to Folk Metaethics." *Review of Philosophy and Psychology* 11 (2020): 53–82.
Pound, Pandora, Sarah Denford, Janet Shucksmith, Clare Tanton, Anne M. Johnson, Jenny Owen, Rebecca Huttenet al. "What is Best Practice in Sex and Relationship Education? A Synthesis of Evidence, including Stakeholders' Views." *BMJ Open* (2017): 1–11.
Punt, Jeremy. "Post Apartheid Racism in South Africa: The Bible, Social Identity and Stereotyping." *Religion & Theology* 16 (2009): 246–272.
Reber, Jeffrey S. "Secular Psychology: What's the Problem?" *Journal of Psychology and Theology* 34, no. 3 (2006): 193–204.
Regnerus, Mark. *Cheap Sex: The Transformation of Men, Marriage, and Monogamy*. Oxford: Oxford University Press, 2017.
Ringer, T. Martin. *Group Action: The Dynamics of Groups in Therapeutic, Educational and Corporate Settings*. London: Jessica Kingsley, 2002.
Roberts, Stephen B. "Keeping Contact: Traditions and Trajectories of British and Irish Practical Theology as Evidenced in the History of BIAPT's Journal." *Practical Theology* 13, no. 1–2 (2020): 19–31.
Rodrigue, Carl, and Mylène Fernet. "A Metasynthesis of Qualitative Studies on Casual Sexual Relationships and Experiences." *The Canadian Journal of Human Sexuality* 25, no. 3 (2016): 225–242.
Roest, Henk. de. *Collaborative Practical Theology: Engaging Practitioners in Research on Christian Practices*. Leiden: Brill, 2019.
Rogers, Andrew P. *Being Built Together: Final Report*. London: University of Roehampton, 2013. http://www.roehampton.ac.uk/BeingBuiltTogether/.
Rogers, Andrew P. *Congregational Hermeneutics: How Do We Read?* London: Routledge, 2016.
Rogers, Andrew P. *Congregational Hermeneutics: How Do We Read? Explorations in Practical, Pastoral and Empirical Theology*. Farnham: Ashgate, 2015.
Rogers, Andrew P. "How Are Black Majority Churches Growing in the UK? A London Borough Case Study." *Religion and Global Society blog* (2016). https://blogs.lse.ac.uk/religionglobalsociety/2016/12/how-are-black-majority-churches-growing-in-the-uk-a-london-borough-case-study/#.
Rogers, Andrew P. "Ordinary Biblical Hermeneutics and the Transformation of Congregational Horizons within English Evangelicalism: A Theological Ethnographic Study." PhD diss., King's College, London, 2009.
Rogers, Andrew P. "Reading Scripture in Congregations: Towards an Ordinary Hermeneutics." In *Remembering Our Future: Explorations in Deep Church*, edited by Luke Bretherton and Andrew Walker. Deep Church, 81–107. Milton Keynes: Paternoster, 2007.
Rogers, Andrew P. "Walking Down the Old Kent Road: New Black Majority Churches in the London Borough of Southwark." In *The Desecularisation of the City: London's Churches, 1980 to the Present*, edited by David Goodhew and Anthony-Paul Cooper, 86–104. London: Routledge, 2018.
Rooms, Nigel, and Zoë Bennett, eds. *Practical Theology in Progress: Showcasing an Emerging Discipline*. London: Routledge, 2019.
Root, Andrew. *Christopraxis: A Practical Theology of the Cross*. Minneapolis, MN: Fortress, 2014.

Root, Andrew. "Evangelical Practical Theology." In *Opening the Field of Practical Theology: An Introduction*, edited by Kathleen A. Cahalan and Gordon S. Mikoski, 79–96. Plymouth: Rowman and Littlefield, 2014.

Root, Andrew. *Faith Formation in a Secular Age: Responding to the Church's Obsession with Youthfulness*. Grand Rapids, MI: Baker Academic, 2017.

Rosado, Nicholas. "My Experience with (Cultural) Relativism in the University." *Medium*, March 21, 2020. https://medium.com/@NickRosado/my-experience-with-cultural-relativism-in-the-university-53a1733b49e6.

Ross, Cathy. "Hospitality: The Church as 'A Mother with an Open Heart'." In *Mission on the Road to Emmaus: Constants, Context and Prophetic Dialogue*, edited by Cathy Ross and Stephen B. Bevans, 67–84. London: SCM Press, 2015.

Ross, Cathy, and Colin Smith, eds. *Missional Conversations: A Dialogue between Theory and Praxis in World Mission*. London: SCM, 2018.

Sacks, Jonathan. *Genesis: The Book of Beginnings*. Covenant and Conversation. Jerusalem: Maggid Books, 2009.

Saliers, Don E. *The Soul in Paraphrase: Prayer and the Religious Affections*. Ashland City, TN: OSL, 2011.

Samushonga, Hartness M. "A Theological Reflection of Bivocational Pastoral Ministry: A Personal Reflective Account of a Decade of Bivocational Ministry Practice Experience." *Practical Theology* 12, no. 1 (2019): 66–80.

Samushonga, Hartness M. "On Bivocational Ministry-Focused Training in British Theological Schools: Dialoguing with British Theological Educationalists." *Practical Theology* 13, no. 4 (2020): 385–399.

Sandberg-Thoma, Sara E., and Claire M. Kamp Dush. "Casual Sexual Relationships and Mental Health in Adolescence and Emerging Adulthood." *Journal of Sex Research* 51, no. 2 (2014): 121–130.

Sanders, Donald. "From Critical Thinking to Spiritual Maturity: Connecting the Apostle Paul and John Dewey." *Christian Education Journal* 15, no. 1 (2018): 90–104.

Satris, Stephen A. "Student Relativism." *Teaching Philosophy* 9, no. 3 (1986): 193–205.

Scalise, Charles J. "Protestant Evangelicalism." In *The Wiley-Blackwell Companion to Practical Theology*, edited by Bonnie J. Miller-McLemore, 576–586. New York, NY: Wiley-Blackwell, 2012.

Scharen, Christian, ed. *Explorations in Ecclesiology and Ethnography*. Grand Rapids, MI: Eerdmans, 2012.

Schleiermacher, Friedrich. *Brief Outline of the Study of Theology*. Translated by T.N. Tice. Atlanta, GA: John Knox Press, 1996.

Schmidt, Katherine G. *Virtual Communion: Theology of the Internet and the Catholic Sacramental Imagination*. Lanham, MD: Lexington Books and Fortress Academic, 2020.

Schussler Fiorenza, Elizabeth. *In Memory of Her: A Feminist Theological Reconstruction of Christian Origins*. London: SCM, 1983.

Sex Education Forum. "The New RSE Guidance – Your Questions Answered." Accessed June 10, 2019. https://www.sexeducationforum.org.uk/news/news/new-rse-guidance-your-questions-answered.

Sheldrake, Philip. "Spiritual Journey." In *The New SCM Dictionary of Christian Spirituality*, edited by Philip Sheldrake, 388–390. London: SCM, 2005.

Shepherd, Nick. "Action Research as Professional Development." *Journal of Adult Theological Education* 9, no. 2 (2012): 121–138.

Silf, Margaret. *Taste and See - Adventuring into Prayer*. London: Darton, Longman & Todd, 1999.

Simmonds, Paul. *From Maintenance to Mission*. Grove Booklets Evangelism, Series 32. London: Grove Books, 1995.

Sloboda, John. "Music and Worship: A Psychologist's Perspective." In *Creative Chords: Studies in Music, Theology and Christian Formation*, edited by Jeff Astley, Timothy Hone and Mark Savage, 110–125. Leominster: Gracewing, 2000.

Smail, Tom. "The Cross and the Spirit: Towards a Theology of Renewal." In *Charismatic Renewal*, edited by Tom Smail, Andrew Walker and Nigel Wright, 49–70. London: SPCK, 1995.

Smith, C. Christopher, and Pattison, John. *Slow Church: Cultivating Community in the patient way of Jesus*. Downers Grove, IL: IVP, 2014.

Smith, Christian, and Melinda Lunquist Denton. *Soul Searching: The Religious and Spiritual Lives of American Teenagers*. Oxford: Oxford University Press, 2005.

Smith, Gordon T. *Transforming Conversion: Rethinking the language and contours of Christian initiation*. Grand Rapids, MI: Baker, 2010.

Smith, Greg, and Linda Woodhead. "Religion and Brexit: Populism and the Church of England." *Religion, State and Society* 46, no. 3 (2018): 206–223.

Smith, James K. A. *Awaiting the King: Reforming Public Theology*. Grand Rapids, MI: Baker Academic, 2017.

Smith, James K. A. *Desiring the Kingdom: Worship, Worldview, and Cultural Formation*. Grand Rapids, MI: Baker Academic, 2009.

Smith, James K. A. "The Reformed (Transformationist) View." In *Five Views on the Church and Politics*, edited by Amy E. Black, 139–162. Grand Rapids, MI: Zondervan, 2015.

Smith, James K. A. *Who's Afraid of Relativism?: Community, Contingency, and Creaturehood*. Grand Rapids, MI: Baker Academic, 2014.

Smith, Mark, ed. *British Evangelical Identities Past and Present: Aspects of the History and Sociology of Evangelicalism in Britain and Ireland*. Milton Keynes: Paternoster, 2008.

Sobrino, Jon. *Spirituality of Liberation: Toward Political Holiness*. Translated by Robert R. Barr. Maryknoll, NY: Orbis, 1988.

Spadaro, Antonio. *Cybertheology: Thinking Christianity in the Era of the Internet*. New York, NY: Fordham University Press, 2014.

Spencer, Matthew. "Salvation's Song: Insights into Salvationist Missiology from Practices of Communal Singing at New Addington Salvation Army Community Church." PhD diss., Anglia Ruskin University, 2019.

St Augustine. "Entering into Joy." *Bmcm.Org*. Accessed April 20, 2020. https://www.bmcm.org/inspiration/passages/entering-joy/.

Stackhouse, John G., ed. *Evangelical Futures: A Conversation on Theological Method*. Grand Rapids, MI: Baker Books, 2000.

Stackhouse, John G. *Evangelical Landscapes: Facing Critical Issues of the Day*. Grand Rapids, MI: Baker Academic, 2002.

Stanley, Brian. *The Global Diffusion of Evangelicalism: The Age of Billy Graham and John Stott*. Downers Grove, IL: InterVarsity Press, 2013.

Stevens, R. Paul. "Living Theologically: Toward a Theology of Christian practice." *Themelios* 20, no. 3 (1995): 4–8.

Stone, Nicole L., Sophie A. Millar, Philip J. J. Herrod, David A. Barrett, Catharine A. Ortori, Valerie A. Mellon, and Saoirse E. O'Sullivan. "An Analysis of Endocannabinoid Concentrations and Mood Following Singing and Exercise in Healthy Volunteers." *Frontiers in Behavioural Neuroscience* 12, no. 269 (2018).

Stott, John. *Evangelical Truth: A Personal plea for unity, Integrity and Faithfulness.* Leicester: IVP, 2003.
Stott, John. *Issues Facing Christians Today.* Rev. ed. London: Marshall Pickering, 1999.
Stott, John. *The Message of Acts.* Leicester: IVP, 1990.
Swinton, John. *Becoming Friends of Time: Disability, Timefullness and Gentle Discipleship.* London: SCM, 2016.
Swinton, John. *Dementia: Living in the Memories of God.* London: SCM, 2012.
Swinton, John, and Harriet Mowat. *Practical Theology and Qualitative Research.* London: SCM Press, 2006.
Swinton, John and Harriet Mowat. *Practical Theology and Qualitative Research.* 2nd ed. London: SCM, 2016.
Taylor, Charles. *A Secular Age.* Cambridge, MA: Harvard University Press, 2007.
Taylor, Charles. *Sources of Self: The Making of Modern Identity.* Cambridge, MA: Harvard University Press, 1989.
The General of The Salvation Army. *The Salvation Army Handbook of Doctrine.* London: Salvation Books, 2010.
The Salvation Army. *Building Deeper Relationships: A Guide to Faith-Based Facilitation.* London: International Headquarters, 2010.
The Salvation Army. "Salvation Army launches group singing programme for people living with dementia." Published 30 January 2018, https://www.salvationarmy.org.uk/salvation-army-launches-group-singing-programme-people-living-dementia.
Thiselton, Anthony. *Discovering Romans: Content, Interpretation, Reception.* Discovering Biblical Texts. London: SPCK, 2016.
Thiselton, Anthony. *New Horizon in Hermeneutics: The Theory and Practice of Transforming Biblical Reading.* London: HarperCollins, 1992.
Thomas, Andrew J. "Pathways to Healing: An empirical theological study of the healing praxis of 'the Group' Assemblies of God in Kwa-Zulu-Natal, South Africa." DTh diss., UNISA, 2010.
Thomas, John C. "Women, Pentecostals and the Bible: An Experiment in Pentecostal Hermeneutics." *Journal of Pentecostal Theology* 2, no. 5 (1994): 41–56.
Thompson, Judith, Stephen Pattison, and Ross Thompson. *SCM Studyguide to Theological Reflection.* London: SCM, 2008.
Thompson, Judith, Stephen Pattison, and Ross Thompson. *SCM Studyguide to Theological Reflection.* 2nd ed. London: SCM, 2019.
Tidball, Derek. *Skilful Shepherds: An Introduction to Pastoral Theology.* Leicester: InterVarsity Press, 1986.
Tobin, Thomas H. *Paul's Rhetoric in Context: The Argument of Romans.* Peabody, MA: Hendrickson, 2004.
Todd, Scott C. *Fast Living: How the Church Will End Extreme Poverty.* Grand Rapids, MI: Somersault, 2011.
Tomlin, Graham. "The Telos of Theological Education." *Theological Education* 51, no. 2 (2018): 113–125.
Tomlinson, Dave. *The Post-Evangelical.* London: Triangle, 1995.
Treier, Daniel J. *Introducing Theological Interpretation of Scripture: Recovering a Christian Practice.* Nottingham: Apollos, 2008.
Trueman, Carl. "Postmoderism, Free Markets and Prophetic Margins." *Themelios* 30, no. 2 (2005). https://themelios.thegospelcoalition.org/article/postmodernism-free-markets-and-prophetic-margins/.

Ukpong, Justin S. "Rereading the Bible with African Eyes: Inculturation and Hermeneutics." *Journal of Theology for Southern Africa* 91 (1995): 3–14.
Urs von Balthasar, Hans. *My Work: In Retrospect*. San Francisco, CA: Ignatius Press, 1993.
Van den Toren, B., and E. Hoare. "Evangelicals and Contextual Theology: Lessons from Missiology for Theological Reflection." *Practical Theology* 8, no. 2 (2015): 77–98.
Van der Ven, Johannes A. *Practical Theology: An Empirical Approach*. Kampen: Kok Pharos, 1993.
Van der Ven, Johannes A. "Practical Theology: from Applied to Empirical Theology." *Journal of Empirical Theology* 1, no. 1 (1988): 7–27.
Vanhoozer, Kevin J. "A Drama-of-Redemption Model: Always Performing?" in *Four Views on Moving Beyond the Bible to Theology*, edited by Stanley N. Gundry and Gary T. Meadors, 151–214. Grand Rapids, MI: Zondervan. 2009.
Vanhoozer, Kevin J. *Faith Speaking Understanding: Performing the Drama of Doctrine*. Louisville, KY: Westminster John Knox Press. 2014.
Vanhoozer, Kevin J. "Putting on Christ: Spiritual Formation and the Drama of Discipleship." *Journal of Spiritual Formation & Soul Care* 8, no. 2 (2015): 147–171.
Vanhoozer, Kevin J. *The Drama of Doctrine: A Canonical Linguistic Approach to Christian Theology*. Louisville, KY: Westminster John Knox Press, 2005.
Vanhoozer, Kevin J. and Daniel J. Treier. *Theology and the Mirror of Scripture: A Mere Evangelical Account*. London: IVP, 2016.
Village, Andrew. *The Bible and Lay People*. Aldershot: Ashgate Publishing, 2007.
Volf, Miroslav. *A Public Faith: How Followers of Christ Should Serve the Common Good*. Grand Rapids, MI: Brazos Press, 2011.
Volf, Miroslav. *Exclusion and Embrace: A Theological Exploration of Identity, Otherness, and Reconciliation*. 2nd ed. Nashville, TN: Abingdon, 2019.
Volf, Miroslav, and Matthew Croasmun. *Life of the World: Theology That Makes a Difference*. Grand Rapids, MI: Brazos, 2019.
Vondey, Wolfgang. *Beyond Pentecostalism: The Crisis of Global Christianity and the Renewal of the Theological Agenda*. Cambridge: Eerdmans, 2010.
Vondey, Wolfgang. *Pentecostal Theology: Living the Full Gospel*. London: T&T Clark, 2017.
Vondey, Wolfgang. *Pentecostalism: A Guide for the Perplexed*. London: T&T Clark, 2013.
Vygotsky, Lev S. *Mind in Society: The Development of Higher Psychological Processes*, edited by Michael Cole, Vera John-Steiner, Sylvia Scribner and Ellen Souberman. London: Harvard University Press, 1978.
Wagner, Rachel. *Godwired: Religion, Ritual and Virtual Reality*. London: Routledge, 2012.
Wainwright, William J. *Reason and the Heart: A Prolegomenon to a Critique of Passional Reason*. Ithaca, NY: Cornell University Press, 1995.
Walker, Andrew. *Telling the Story*. London: SPCK, 1996.
Walker, Andrew. "The Devil You Think You Know: Demonology and the Charismatic Movement." In *Charismatic Renewal*, edited by Tom Smail, Andrew Walker and Nigel Wright, 86–105. London: SPCK, 1995.
Waltner, James H. *Psalms: Believers Church Bible Commentary*. Scottdale, PA: Herald, 2006.
Walton, Heather. *Writing Methods in Theological Reflection*. London: SCM, 2014.
Walton, Roger. *The Reflective Disciple*. London: Epworth, 2009.

Walton, Roger. "Using the Bible and Christian Tradition in Theological Reflection." *British Journal of Theological Education* 13, no. 2 (2003): 133–151.

Wang, Henry. "Rethinking the Validity and Significance of Final Causation: From the Aristotelian to the Peircean Teleology." *Transactions of the Charles S. Peirce Society* 41, no. 3 (2005): 603–625.

Ward, Frances. *Lifelong Learning: Theological Education and Supervision.* London: SCM, 2005.

Ward, Pete. *Celebrity Worship.* Abingdon: Routledge, 2020.

Ward, Pete. *Introducing Practical Theology: Mission, Ministry and the Life of the Church.* Grand Rapids, MI: Baker Academic, 2017.

Ward, Pete. *Liquid Ecclesiology: The Gospel and the Church.* Leiden: Brill, 2017.

Ward, Pete. *Participation and Mediation: A Practical Theology for the Liquid Church.* London: SCM, 2008.

Ward, Pete, ed. *Perspectives on Ecclesiology and Ethnography.* Grand Rapids, MI: Eerdmans, 2012.

Ward, Pete. *Selling Worship: How What We Sing Has Changed the Church.* Milton Keynes: Paternoster, 2005.

Warner, Rob. *Reinventing English Evangelicalism, 1966–2001: A Theological and Sociological Study.* Milton Keynes: Paternoster, 2007.

Warren, Robert. *Building Missionary Congregations.* London: Church House Publishing, 1995.

Warrington, Keith. "The Holy Spirit." In *The Message: Elim's Core Beliefs*, edited by Keith Warrington, 24–26. Malvern: Elim, no date.

Watkins, Clare. *Disclosing Church: An Ecclesiology Learned through Conversations in Practice.* London: Routledge, 2020.

Watkins, Clare, and Bridget Shepherd. "The Challenge of 'Fresh Expressions' to Ecclesiology." *Ecclesial Practices* 1, no. 1 (2014): 92–110.

Watts, Fraser, Rebecca Nye, and Sara Savage. *Psychology for Christian Ministry.* London: Routledge, 2002.

Welch, John W, ed. *Chiasmus in Antiquity: Structures, Analyses, Exegesis.* Maxwell Institute Publications 22: Brigham Young University Scholars Archive, 1998.

Wells, Samuel. *Improvisation: The Drama of Christian Ethics.* London: SPCK, 2004.

Wells, Samuel. *Incarnational Ministry: Being with the Church.* Grand Rapids, MI: Eerdmans, 2017.

What If Learning. "The Prize is Virtue: Subject Teaching and Character Development." Accessed April 14, 2020. http://www.whatiflearning.com/big-picture/virtues/.

Whipp, Margaret. "Lucky Lections: On Using the Bible in Practical Theology." *Practical Theology* 5, no. 3 (2012): 341–344.

Wilcock, Penelope. *Spiritual Care: Of Dying and Bereaved People.* Abingdon: BRF, 2013.

Williams, Garry J. "Was Evangelicalism Created by the Enlightenment?" *Tyndale Bulletin* 53, no. 2 (2002): 283–314.

Williams, Rowan. "To Stand Where Christ Stands." In *An Introduction to Christian Spirituality*, edited by Ralph Waller and Benedicta Ward, 1–13. London: SPCK, 1999. http://catalog.hathitrust.org/api/volumes/oclc/43248292.html.

Wilson, Henry S., Takatso Mofokeng, Judo Poerwowidagdo, Robert A. Evans, and Alice Frazer Evans, eds. *Pastoral Theology from a Global Perspective: A Case Study Approach.* Maryknoll, NY: Orbis Books, 1996.

Wink, Walter. *The Powers That Be: Theology for a New Millenium.* New York, NY: Doubleday, 1998.

Witherington III, Ben. *Matthew*. Macon, GA: Smyth & Helwys, 2006.

Witherington III, Ben. *Romans: A Socio-Cultural Commentary*. In collaboration with Darlene Hyatt. Grand Rapids, MI: Eerdmans, 2004.

Woodward, James, and Stephen Pattison, eds. *The Blackwell Reader in Pastoral and Practical Theology*. Oxford: Blackwell, 2000.

Woodward, Scott. "The Telos of Theological Education: A Theological Reflection." *CrossCurrents* 69, no. 1 (March 2019): 39–44.

Wright, Andrew. *Christianity and Critical Realism: Ambiguity, Truth and Theological Literacy*. London: Routledge, 2014.

Wright, N. T. "How can the Bible be Authoritative?" *Vox Evangelica* 21 (1991): 7–32.

Wright, N. T. *Scripture and the Authority of God*. London: SPCK, 2005.

Wright, N. T. *Scripture and the Authority of God*. New ed. London: SPCK, 2013.

Wright, N. T. *The New Testament and the People of God*. London: SPCK, 1992.

Wright, Tom. *Luke for Everyone*. London: SPCK, 2001.

Yancey, Philip. *Prayer*. London: Hodder & Stoughton, 2006.

Yarhouse, Mark A. *Understanding Gender Dysphoria: Navigating Transgender Issues in a Changing Culture*. Downers Grove, IL: IVP Academic, 2015.

Yoder, John Howard. *The Politics of Jesus: Vicit Agnus Noster*. Grand Rapids, MI: Eerdmans, 1994.

Yong, Amos. *Spirit-Word-Community: Theological Hermeneutics in Trinitarian Perspective*. Farnham: Ashgate, 2002.

Zehr, Paul M. *1 and 2 Timothy, Titus: Believers Church Bible Commentary*. Scottdale, PA: Herald, 2010.

Zenger, Erich. "The Composition and Theology of the Fifth Book of Psalms, Psalms 107–145." *Journal for the Study of the Old Testament* 80 (1998): 77–102.

# Subject Index

action: divine action/human action 40, 42–43, 46–47, 52n19, 126–27, 206; external action 156–58; social action 90–91, 133; telos of 64; theological reflection and 110, 118, 119
action research 94, 204, 223
activism 4, 26, 34–36, 51, 157, 222–23
affect 48–50
Africa/African 25, 29, 101, 103, 106, 212
apologetic 56, 89, 134, 144, 159
Aristotle 58–59, 62
assessment (academic) 91, 94, 95, 121
atonement 181
authority/authoritative 29–31, 46, 57, 92–93, 103, 116–17, 173, 180, 193, 205, 209, 218
autobiographical 100, 110

BIAPT 105–6, 107, 111, 207
Bible 26–28, 72–73, 159, 194; bible commentaries 102; Bible and Practical Theology Special Interest Group 106; Bible Society 104; bible study 109, 119, 169–75; practical theology and 92–3, 205, 208; student engagement with 108, 116–18, 121; *see also* scripture
biblicism 4, 10, 26–29, 218–19
black majority churches 89, 106, 224
Bridge to Life Diagram 73

chaos 189
chapel 185–190
chaplaincy 185
character 71–72, 124, 140–41, 177, 181–82
Church 2–3, 31–32, 62–63, 89–91, 101–02, 164, 205
Common Good 79, 134–39, 213
Common Grace 133–34
Common Life 135–41

community 28–29, 41–42, 47–48, 94, 98n34, 151–53, 192–93; epistemic community 95
community choir 150–64
congregants 192–98
congregation 34, 48, 192–98
constructivism 171, 174
conversionism 4, 10, 26, 31–34, 221–22
creativity 66, 181
critical correlation 56, 61, 66, 104, 173
criticality 107–10, 213
crucicentrism 26, 29–31, 219–21
culture 59, 76, 89, 101, 121, 133–34, 178
curriculum 94–95, 103–04, 109, 117, 125–26

descriptive 7, 11, 56–57, 60–61, 208, 211; descriptive-empirical 46
dialogue 171, 214; with social sciences 56–57, 206, 211
discipleship 123–26, 181, 213
disequilibrium 171–74
diversity 65, 135–38, 152, 159–160; within BIAPT 106–06; within evangelicalism 7
divine action 40–43, 46–47, 206
doctrine 28, 62, 64, 108–09, 180–82, 207

ecclesial 48, 98; ecclesial imagination 44, 48, 50–51; ecclesial practice 37, 40
Elim 192–98
empirical 46–47, 206, 208, 211
enculturation 89, 97n30, 173
equipping 70, 88
ethnicity 106, 212
evangelical 26, 44, 70; engagement with practical theology 5–6, 203–214; evangelical church 43, 70, 81, 125

## Subject Index

evangelicalism 3, 5, 6–7, 32, 43–44, 203, 210–12, 224
evangelism 31–34, 73–74, 88, 123, 221–2
evangelization 34, 94
experience 72, 74–75, 110–11; and imagination 45–46; as a source of theology 5, 26–28, 117–18, 208; lived experience 29, 73, 150

faith 174, 179; authority of the bible and 26, 29, 158, 193; community of 41, 49, 213; inter-faith 89; perspectives 138–139; reflective faith 26, 102, 206; schools 135–38
Final Cause 58–61
formation 94–95, 110–11, 177, 182
Four Spiritual Laws 73
Four Voices of Theology 73, 91–2

goal 2, 56, 66–67, see also telos
gospel 3, 31–34, 73–75, 78–80, 143, 220–22

healthy relationships 139
hermeneutics 104–05, 193, 219
Holy Spirit 8, 153, 172, 192–97, 205; and scripture 61, 213
hope 41–42, 46–47, 162–64
hospice 185–190
human flourishing 15, 76–81, 144–45

identity 76, 94, 177, 182–83
illumination 28–29
imagination 40–51, 189
inter-faith, see faith
Internet 89, 212–13
interpretation 29, 181, 209
inward turn 75–76

journey 29, 80, 120, 127, 172–74

*kairos* moment 172–73

learning 91, 94, 107, 109–11, 171–74

mediation 193
medium and message 74, 75
memory/memories 47–48, 158
metaphor 41, 56, 172, 180, 205
method 2, 6, 26, 47–48, 122, 208–09
methodology 25, 31–32, 117
ministry 36, 153–56, 163, 205–6; preparation for 88–91, 107, 204
missiology 89, 122, 150, 163
mission 32, 89, 101, 150–64, 212–13

moralistic therapeutic deism 77
music 74, 152, 157

narrative 31, 66–67, 70–73, 78–79, 141–42, 177, 180
normative 33, 46, 93, 139, 145, 173, 206; and scripture 13, 43, 105, 174; normative theology 61–62, 170; normative voice 92

ordinands 116–27
orthodoxy 29, 103, 177, 179, 183
orthopraxy 29, 35, 177, 179, 182

pain 41–42, 189
pathos 41, 49–50, 172
peace 77, 223
pedagogy 120, 156
pedagogical 87, 107, 110, 127, 207, 213
Pentecostal 5, 106–10, 192–98, 203
Pentecostalism 111, 198n4, 203, 205
personality/personalities 188
pneumatology 5, 67, 111, 192
political theology 136
power 30–31, 48–50, 60, 71–73, 108, 194
practical theology 5–6, 36–37, 40–43, 48–50, 66–67, 110–11, 203–14, 224; BIAPT and 105–6; definitions of 1–3, 25–26, 56, 72–73
practice 2–3, 92, 110, 180–82 evangelistic 32–34; theological reflection as 118, 128
praxis 64–67, 123, 174, 205–6
prayer 3, 65, 125–27, 174, 187–89, 194
presence 187–90
prophetic imagination 40–51
prophetic-imaginative mode 42, 51
psychology 57–58, 62, 170–71
public 75, 133, 145, 212
public space 135–38
public theology 61, 134, 212
purpose 1, 42, 52n20, 119, 135–45, 160; see also telos

race 125, 212
reductionism 32–34, 78
reformation 6, 33, 205
Regeneration 94
Relationships and Sex Education (RSE) 133–45
relativism 93, 177–79, 182–83
relevance 88–89, 95, 101, 116; cultural 35

salvation 4, 33, 63, 75, 103, 117, 122–23, 150, 158–63

Salvation Army 8, 150, 156–59, 221
scripture 26–29, 78–79, 87–88, 92–93, 95–96, 208–10, 218–19; evangelical theology and 4–5, 111, 117; interpretation of 31, 46, 180–82, 193; practical theology and 2–3, 5–6, 213–14; *see also* bible
secular humanism 136, 137
secularism 75–76, 136
silence 186–90
singing 150–64
social sciences 56–58, 104, 134, 170, 208
space 17, 151, 152–53, 156–58, 163, 185–90, 197; *see also* public space
Spiritual Direction 126–27
Spiritual Growth 119, 128
spirituality 124–27, 162, 187
stillness 186–89
suffering 79, 162, 206

teaching 180–81; of practical theology 61, 89, 100, 106–10, 118–20, 112, 204; in ministerial education 63, 116; school 102, 133–45; *see also* theological education
teleology 56–67
*telos* 56–67, 76, 205
theodrama 177–84

theological education 2, 62–63, 93–95, 102–04, 106–7, 177
theological imperative 61–66, 173–74
Theological Imperative Model 169–74
theological reflection 89, 107–11, 116–28, 209–10; corporate theological reflection 192–98; definition of 2, 71–72; models of 5, 91–92, 107, 210
theology shock 103, 105, 108
timefull 35–37
tradition 57, 89, 91–92, 98n31, 108, 208–10; charismatic tradition 121; Christian 1, 42, 107; evangelical 1, 4–5, 73, 101, 119, 206–7; Holiness tradition 8; quadrilateral, element in 5, 26, 43, 117, 208; Reformed tradition 63; turn to 94–5, 173
transformation 145, 154–55, 162–63, 173–74, 221
trialogue 60, 170
truth 33, 77, 117, 124, 143–44, 158–62, 177–83

wellbeing 79, 151–56, 163
Wesleyan Quadrilateral 20n25, 208; *see also* tradition
women 30, 90, 108, 121, 224
worship 74–75, 154, 187

# Author Index

Ackermann, D. M. 38n30
Adey, Lionel 74
Anderson, R. S. 47, 54n43, 54n45, 203, 204, 205, 206, 211, 215n7, 215n9, 215n22, 216n31, 219
Andrews, D. P. 216n40
Antlitz, K. 184n31
Apostle Paul 12, 78, 124
Aquinas, T. 48, 62, 63, 68n38
Archard, D. 148n60
Archer, K. J. 199n12
Archer, M. S. 113n26
Aristotle 58, 59, 61, 62, 68n18, 68n19, 68n20, 68n22, 68n39
Arnold, C. E. 38n27, 38n28
Arrington, F. 200n46
Astley, J. 37n5
Atherstone, A. 4, 18n6, 19n8, 19n20
Augustine of Hippo 35, 48, 62, 76, 189
Avis, P. D. 53n35

Ballard, P. 96n13, 97n16, 98n42, 111n1, 113n39, 117, 128, 128n4, 128n15, 129n23, 129n25, 173, 176n49
Banks, R. 204
Barrett, D. A. 165n15
Barrett, J. L. 63, 69n50,
Barth, Karl 35, 159, 160
Beasley-Murray, G. R. 38n25
Bebbington, D. W. 4, 6, 10, 26, 100, 101, 218, 219, 224
Beck, J. R. 67n8
Bediako, K. 112n19
Begbie, J. S. 157, 164n13
Bell, J. L. 161, 165n22, 165n23
Bennett, Z. 27, 30, 37n13, 37n14, 38n31, 72, 81n8, 81n9, 93, 98n42, 99n45, 111, 111n1, 114n40, 114n41, 115n74, 215n19
Bevans, S. B. 52n5, 122, 123, 128n14

Bhatti, D. 20n40, 82n15, 82n16, 98n37, 184n32
Bird, M. F. 3, 19n7, 19n10
Blais, M. 148n69
Blake, S. 148n54
Boa, K. 178, 183n4
Boellstorff, T. 217n49
Boersma, H. 68n37, 69n59
Bolton, D. 67n9
Bolton, P. 98n35
Borghi, A. M. 170, 175n11
Bosch, D. J. 33, 38n49, 158, 164n14
Bowman Jr., R. M. 178, 183n4
Branson, M. L. 204
Breck, J. 99n53
Bretherton, L. 97n20, 136, 146n17
Briggs, R. S. 30, 31, 38n33, 114n40
Brookes, A. 96n12
Brouard, S. 99n51
Browning, D. S. 57, 58, 67n12, 68n14, 68n15, 68n32, 205, 206, 211, 215n8, 216n30
Brueggemann, Walter 10, 40, 41, 47, 48, 49, 50, 52n6, 52n7, 52n8, 52n9, 52n10, 52n11, 52n12, 52n13, 52n14, 52n15, 52n16, 52n17, 53n21, 53n25, 54n44, 54n46, 54n47, 54n48, 54n49, 54n50, 54n51, 54n52, 54n53, 54n54, 54n55, 54n59, 54n60, 54n62, 54n63, 54n64, 55n65, 55n68, 55n79
Bruner, F. D. 198n1
Burgess, R. 106, 114n48, 114n53, 114n57, 114n58, 114n59, 115n64
Butler, J. 194, 199n23

Cahalan K. A. 177, 183n1
Cameron, H. 9, 12, 20n40, 79, 82n15, 83n50, 97n14, 97n22, 97n25, 98n37, 99n47, 113n30, 114n40, 184n32, 199n21, 219, 220, 222, 223

# Author Index 249

Cameron, N. 214n6
Campbell, H. A. 97n24, 217n47
Campbell, L. 149n70
Carson, D. A. 178, 183n5
Carter, J. J. 193, 199n15, 200n45
Cartledge, M. J. 5, 6, 10, 18, 19n22, 20n31, 20n32, 20n33, 27, 37n12, 37n16, 38n29, 38n40, 55n67, 104, 115n67, 115n68, 192, 193, 198n6, 198n10, 198n11, 199n13, 199n22, 200n38, 214n1, 214n2, 215n20, 216n27, 216n39, 217n51, 219, 220, 223, 224
Castelo, D. 55n72
Charry, E. 128n2, 209, 215n24
Childs, J. M. 69n59
Ciampa, R. E. 20n41
Clapper, G. S. 55n69
Clark, C. 204
Clarke, A. J. 98n41
Clarke, L. 148n48
Clements, K. 69n66
Cole Wright, J. 178, 183n11
Collier, A. 113n26
Collins, H. 5, 20n29, 20n30, 20n31, 113n36, 115n68, 115n72, 115n73, 128n10, 215n22
Comer, J. M. 189, 191n23, 191n24, 191n25, 191n30
Cooling, T. 136, 146n18
Cray, G. 113n24
Croasmun, M. 77, 79, 83n37, 83n38, 83n48, 83n49, 83n52, 83n53, 135, 146n8
Cruse, J. L. 184n41

Davie, M. 19n9
Davies, D. 97n14
Day, A. 97n29
Day, K. 217n46
De Beer, J. 196, 200n33
Dean, H. 83n51
Dean, K. C. 77, 83n41
Demarest, B. A. 67n8
Denford, S. 146n4
Denton, M. 77, 83n41
DePoe, J. M. 67n1
Descartes, R. 68n24, 76
Dillon, M. 68n16
Dochuk, D. 37n7, 37n8
Dubé, S. 148n69
Duce, C. 20n40, 82n15, 82n16, 98n37, 184n32, 199n21
Dudley, J. A. J. 58, 59, 68n21, 68n23
Duncan, B. 188, 191n14, 191n15

Dunn, J. D. G. 112n12, 173, 176n53, 176n54
Dykstra, C. 45, 48, 53n28, 54n58

Egan, K. 53n33, 53n34
Elliott, D. 69n60
Emerson, L. 148n44
Eshun, D. 114n48, 114n53, 115n64
Evans, A. F. 216n39
Evans, R. A. 216n39

Fernet, M. 148n69
Fiddes, P. 74
Finney, C. 73
Fletcher, G.149n70, 149n71
Foster, R. J. 187, 191n11
Fowke, R. 188, 191n12, 191n13, 191n14, 191n16
Frestadius, S. 193, 199n14
Freud, S. 76
Frost, R. 187, 190n7
Furrow, J. L. 63, 69n50

Ganiel, G. 39n64
Garner, M. 106, 114n48, 114n53, 115n64
Garner, S. 217n47
Goddard, A. 217n44
Goldingay, J. 53n25, 187, 190n2, 190n6, 191n27
Goodhart, D. 97n26, 98n34
Goodhew, D. 97n18, 114n47
Goto, C. T. 52n5, 54n60, 98n31, 216n41
Graham, B. 73, 203
Graham, E. 68n33, 69n45, 93, 97n20, 99n45, 105, 113n34, 113n35, 113n37, 113n38, 115n62, 128n15, 129n23, 134, 146n6, 146n7, 215n26
Granito, C. 170, 175n11
Grass, T. 19n9
Green, B. 147n40
Green, G. 45, 46, 53n36, 53n37, 53n38, 53n39, 54n40
Green, L. 107, 114n50, 128n15
Greenway, T. S. 63, 69n50
Greig, P. 189, 191n22
Grenz, S. J. 3, 19n12, 28, 29, 37n19, 37n20, 37n21, 62, 63, 69n43, 69n49
Gross, R. 171, 175n19
Guder, D. L. 32, 33, 34, 38n44, 38n45, 38n46, 38n47, 38n48, 38n50, 38n51, 38n55, 38n56
GuvnaB 93

Haack, D. 171, 174, 175n26, 176n56
Hall, G. 52n5

Halstead, M. 146n20
Hamilton, V. P. 176n32
Hansen, J. 170, 172, 175n12, 175n13, 176n36
Harman, A. 187, 190n5
Harris, T. 112n4
Hart, T. 53n29, 53n30, 53n31, 53n32, 53n33
Hatcher, A. 112n6
Hébert, M. 148n69
Herrod, P. J. J. 165n15
Heschel, A. J. 52n11, 55n70, 55n71, 55n73, 55n74, 55n76
Heyes, J. M. 140, 147n41, 147n42
Hiltner, S. 205, 214n5
Hine, C. 217n49
Hirst, J. 129n17, 142, 143, 148n51, 148n52, 148n53, 148n55, 148n56, 148n57
Hoare, E. 5, 14, 20n28, 128n13, 218, 223, 224
Hollenweger, W. J. 212, 216n39
Hollinger, D. 145, 149n73
Holmes, S. R. 98n42 112n7
Hull, J. M. 171, 175n21
Hunt, C. 113n31
Hurcombe, R. 98n33
Hurding, R. 128n5
Hutchings, T. 217n47
Hutten, R. 146n4

Jahaziel 93
Jamieson, A. 112n5
Janis, I. L. 170, 175n15
Janzen, W. 70, 71, 72, 81n1, 81n2
Jennings, W. J. 97n27
Johns, C. B. 199n22
Johns, J. D. 199n22
Johnson, A. M. 146n4
Johnson, T. D. 53n33
Jones, D. C. 4, 18n6, 19n8, 19n20, 20n28
Jones, J. 115n68
Jordan, E. 98n39
Jung, C. 76

Kearsley, R. 54n61
Kelsey, D. H. 11, 63, 64, 65, 66, 69n51, 69n52, 69n53, 69n54, 69n55, 69n56, 69n57
Kidner, D. 187, 190n3, 190n4
Kim, S. 217n46
Kinast, R. L. 129n18
King, G. W. 216n36
King, Martin Luther, Jr. 35
King, P. E. 62, 68n40, 68n41, 68n42, 69n43, 69n44, 69n49

Knorpp, W. M. 178, 183n10
Koyama, K. 36
Kozinets, R. V. 217n49
Kreutz, G. 164n12
Krueger, R. A. 199n28, 199n29
Kuehne, D. S. 139, 147n32, 147n33

Lamb, S. 140, 147n37,
Land, S. J. 55n77
Larsen, T. 3, 5, 19n11, 19n17, 19n23, 19n24, 83n45
Lartey, E. Y. 216n39
Lavoie, F. 148n68
Law, S. 143, 148n63
Lawrence 187, 190n8, 190n9, 190n10
Le, V. 216n37
Lewis, C. S. 68n36, 145, 149n72
Lipton, P. 67n7
Loder, J. E. 53n31
Lugt, W. V. 21n42, 180, 181, 184n19, 184n28, 184n34
Lunn, J. 190n10, 191n20
Lyall, D. 96n13, 111n1, 113n39
Lynch, C. 10, 11, 53n25, 98n42, 218, 219, 220, 223

MacDonald, R. 164n12
Maddox, R. L. 184n17
Male, D. 164n8, 164n11
Mark, O. 15, 79, 83n52, 93, 146n19, 222
Martin, L. R. 55n67
Matera, F. J. 173, 176n52
McClintock Fulkerson, M. 208, 215n21
McClymond, M. J. 200n36
McDowell, J. 19n9
McFarlane, G. 5, 6, 20n25, 20n35, 113n38, 115n69, 115n70
McGrath, A. 4, 6, 19n21, 20n34, 97n20
McInerney, D. M. 176n28
McKeown, J. 176n31, 176n35
McKitterick, A. J. 11, 68n34, 69n62, 75, 82n26, 169, 175n2, 175n3, 175n5, 175n9, 175n10, 176n39, 176n41, 176n42, 176n44, 176n45, 176n57, 220, 221
McKnight, S. 33, 34, 38n52, 38n53, 38n54, 78, 83n46
McRay, B. 171, 175n24
Meadowcroft, T. 53n25
Medawar, P. 68n17
Mellon, V. A. 165n15
Middleton, J. R. 113n23
Mikoski, G. S. 112n4, 214n4, 216n38, 216n40, 216n41, 216n42, 216n43

Millar, S. A. 165n15
Miller-McLemore, B. J. 2, 9, 18n1, 20n37, 25, 37n3, 37n4, 40, 52n2, 52n4, 54n41, 67n2, 112n14, 173, 176n43, 214n2, 214n3
Mitchell, L. 164n12
Mofokeng, T. 216n39
Moody, D. L. 73
Moon, J. A. 171, 175n20
Moore, R. D. 55n66
Moreau, A. S. 39n57
Moreland, J. P. 170, 175n7
Morris, A. 147n40
Morris, H. 8, 12, 20n38, 82n35 218, 220, 221, 224n5
Moxon, J. R. L. 114n48, 114n49, 115n61, 115n66
Mowat, H. 1, 14, 18n1, 25, 37n1, 53n22, 56, 60, 61, 66, 67n3, 67n4, 67n5, 68n31, 68n35, 69n65, 71, 72, 81n4, 81n5, 81n6, 81n7, 83n55, 104, 113n27, 114n56, 170, 172, 175n6, 176n40, 179, 183n16, 184n18, 186, 190n1
Moynagh, M. 224n5
Muir, R. D. 114n46
Mulholland Jr., M. R. 172, 176n30
Murphy, N. 57, 68n13
Mwangi, J. K. 183n3
Myers, C. 112n20

Nardi, B. 217n49
Nash, P. 175n17
Nash, S. 175n17
Netherwood, A. 129n22
Newbigin, L. 34, 39n57, 143, 148n62, 160, 164n10, 165n20, 221, 224n4
Noble, T. A. 19n9
Notman, A. 96n7, 96n11, 97n28
Nouwen, H. J. M. 189, 191n26, 191n28
Nye, R. 175n23, 176n29

O'Connell Killen, P. 200n33
O'Neill, G. 114n52
O'Sullivan, S. E. 165n15
Oliver, S. 57, 59, 60, 67n10, 68n25, 68n26, 68n28, 68n29
Oliverio, W. L. 200n46, 216n27
Ortori, C. A. 165n15
Osmer, R. R. 52n5, 113n38
Overall. N. C. 149n70
Owen, J. 146n4

Palmer, M. J. 148n48, 148n49, 148n50, 148n58
Parker, S. E. 199n24

Pattison, J. 35, 39n60
Pattison, S. 45, 53n27, 88, 93, 96n10, 97n16, 96n19, 99n45, 107, 114n50, 114n52, 128n15, 200n34
Paul, I. 77, 83n40
Pearce, C. 217n49
Pennington, D. C. 170, 175n16, 175n18
Percy, E. 69n58
Perry, S. L. 99n52
Piaget, J. 171, 175n25
Pierson, A.T. 34
Pieterse, H. J. 27, 37n10, 37n11
Pike, M. A. 147n39, 148n61
Pimlott, J. 175n17
Plato 76
Ploubidis, G. B. 148n48
Plouffe, T. 196, 200n31, 200n32
Poerwowidagdo, J. 216n39
Polanco, R. 184n20
Pölzler, T. 178, 183n11
Porpora, D. V. 113n26
Pound, P. 146n4
Powell, K. 204
Pritchard, J. 128, 128n15, 129n23, 129n25, 173, 176n49
Punt, J. 38n32
Putwain, D. W. 176n28

Reader, J. 83n50
Reber, J. S. 175n8
Regnerus, M. 141, 148n47
Reiss, M. 146n20
Revell, L. 147n40
Richter, P. 97n14
Ringer, T. M. 170, 175n14
Roberts, S. B. 96n6
Rodrigue, C. 148n69
Roest, H. de. 98n36
Rogers, A. 13, 14, 98n42, 112n2, 112n4, 112n9, 112n5, 113n24, 113n29, 114n40, 114n47, 115n60, 215n17, 216n34, 220, 223, 224
Rooms, N. 111, 111n1, 114n40, 115n74
Root, A. 52n3, 54n42, 54n48, 97n15, 98n32, 110, 112n4, 113n38, 115n70, 115n73, 203, 206, 214n4, 215n10, 215n11, 215n12
Rosado, N. 183n13
Rosner, B. S. 20n41
Ross, C. 98n39, 151, 164n7
Rowland, C. 79, 83n50

Sacks, J. 172, 176n37
Saliers, D. E. 55n77

Samushonga, H. M. 99n52
Sandberg-Thoma, S. E. 148n69
Sanders, D. 169, 173, 175n1, 176n46
Satris, S. A. 179, 183n14
Savage, S. 175n23, 176n29
Scalise, C. J. 203, 214n3
Scharen, C. 113n29
Schleiermacher, F. 214n6
Schleifer, C. 99n52
Schmidt, K. G. 217n48
Schussler, F. E. 99n49
Scorolli, C. 170, 175n11
Shakespeare, William 31, 72
Sheldrake, P. 172, 176n34
Shepherd, N. 97n30, 99n51
Shercliff, L. 114n52
Shucksmith, J. 146n4
Shulevitz, J. 35
Silf, M. 188, 191n17
Simmonds, P. 97n17
Simpson, J. A. 149n70
Slater, V. 79, 83n50
Sloboda, J. 152, 164n9
Smail, T. 30, 31, 38n36, 38n38
Smith, Christian 77, 83n41
Smith, Christopher. C. 39n60
Smith, Colin. 98n39
Smith, G. 97n26
Smith, G. T. 32, 38n42, 38n43
Smith, J. K. A. 135, 137, 138, 143, 146n1, 146n14, 146n15, 147n22, 147n23, 147n24, 148n59, 148n64, 178, 183n7, 183n8, 183n9
Smith, M. 3, 19n8
Smith, W. C. 191n33
Smith Jr., R. L. 216n40
Sobrino, J. 54n62
Spadaro, A. 217n48
Spencer, M. 15, 16, 164n2, 221, 222
Stackhouse, J. G. 3, 4, 19n13, 19n18, 19n21, 221, 224
Stanley, B. 112n3
Stevens, R. P. 179, 183n15
Stone, N. L. 165n15
Stott, J. 27, 30, 31, 37n15, 38n34, 38n39, 73, 116, 128n3
Sweeney, J. 20n40, 82n15, 98n37, 184n32
Swinton, J. 1, 13, 14, 18n1, 25, 35, 36, 37n2, 39n61, 39n62, 39n63, 39n65, 39n66, 39n67, 39n68, 53n22, 56, 60, 61, 66, 67n3, 67n4, 67n5, 68n31, 68n35, 69n65, 71, 72, 81n4, 81n5, 81n6, 81n7, 82n10, 83n55, 99n48, 104, 113n27, 114n56, 170, 172, 175n6, 176n40, 179, 183n16, 184n18, 186, 190n1, 191n21

Tanton, C. 146n4
Taylor, C. 12, 75, 76, 77, 82n27, 82n28, 82n29, 82n30, 82n31, 82n32, 82n33, 82n34, 82n35, 82n36, 83n53, 141, 148n45
Taylor, T. L. 217n49
Thiselton, A. 173, 176n48, 217n51
Thomas, A. J. 10, 38n26, 218, 219, 220, 221, 223
Thomas, J. C. 199n12
Thompson, J. 107, 114n50, 128n15, 196, 200n34
Thompson, R. 114n50, 196, 200n34
Tidball, D. 205, 206, 214n5, 215n22
Tobin, T. H. 176n50
Todd, S. C. 34, 39n59, 98n42, 191n17
Tomlin, G. 62, 63, 69n45, 69n46, 69n47
Tomlinson, D. 113n22, 113n24
Treier, D. J. 19n11, 20n36, 54n57, 83n45, 175n7
Trueman, C. 178, 183n6

Ukpong, J. S. 112n19
Urs von Balthasar, H. 180, 184n20

Van den Toren, B. 5, 14, 20n28, 128n13
Van der Ven, J. A. 37n10, 211, 216n32, 216n35
Vanhoozer, K. J. 20n36, 21n42, 180, 181, 184n24, 184n25, 184n27, 184n29, 184n30, 184n33, 184n35, 184n36, 184n37, 184n38, 184n39, 184n40
Volf, M. 77, 83n37, 83n38, 83n48, 83n49, 83n52, 83n53, 134, 135, 146n1, 146n3, 146n8, 146n9, 172, 176n33, 176n38
Vondey, W. 55n73, 55n75, 197, 198n4, 220n39, 220n40, 220n41, 220n42, 220n47, 214n1
Vygotsky, L. S. 171, 173, 176n27

Wagner, R. 217n47
Wainwright, W. J. 55n73
Walker, A. 30, 38n36, 38n38 78, 83n43, 113n24
Walsh, B. J. 113n23
Waltner, J. H. 28, 37n23
Walton, H. 93, 99n45, 105, 112n8, 113n34, 113n35, 113n37, 115n62, 128n15, 129n23, 192, 198n7, 198n8, 215n26
Walton, R. 111n1, 114n54, 126, 127, 129n19, 129n21, 129n24
Wang, H. 60, 67n11, 68n30
Wänke, M. 170, 172, 175n12, 175n13, 176n36

Ward, F. 97n14, 105, 113n34, 113n35, 113n37, 115n62, 128n15, 129n23, 171, 175n22
Ward, P. 2, 12, 18n3, 18n4, 18n5, 28, 37n17, 37n18, 53n23, 70, 71, 73, 74, 75, 77, 78, 82n11, 82n12, 82n13, 82n14, 82n16, 82n17, 82n18, 82n19, 82n20, 82n21, 82n22, 82n23, 82n24, 82n25, 83n39, 83n41, 83n42, 83n43, 83n44, 83n56, 97n21, 98n40, 112n14, 112n16, 112n18, 113n29, 115n73, 173, 176n55, 177, 183n2, 207, 215n13, 215n14, 215n15, 215n25, 215n26, 216n29
Warner, R. 4, 19n19, 82n11, 112n2
Warren, R. 97n17
Warrington, K. 198n2, 200n35
Watkins, C. 20n40, 82n15, 97n30, 98n37, 98n38, 114n55, 184n32
Watts, F. 175n23, 176n29
Welch, J. W. 96n1, 99n53
Wellings, K. 148n48
Wells, S. 67, 69n64, 69n67
Weston, P. 152, 156, 164n8, 164n11
Whipp, M. 114n40
Whitney, W. B. 62, 68n40, 68n41, 68n42, 69n43, 69n44, 69n49

Wilberforce, W. 35
Wilcock, P. 188, 190, 191n18, 191n19, 191n31, 191n32
Williams, G. J. 4, 19n16, 19n17
Williams, R. 69n63
Wilson, H. S. 216n39
Wink, W. 112n20
Witherington, B. 30, 38n35, 38n37, 173, 176n47, 176n51
Woodhead, L. 97n26
Woodward, J. 128n15
Woodward, S. 63, 69n48
Wright, A. 113n26
Wright, N. T. 31, 38n36, 38n38, 38n40, 38n41, 129n16, 180, 184n21, 184n22, 184n23, 184n26
Wright, T. 96

Yancey, P. 191n28
Yarhouse, M. A. 65, 69n61
Yoder, J. H. 35, 112n20
Yong, A. 54n40, 55n69, 199n12

Zehr, P. M. 37n24
Zenger, E. 28, 37n22

# Biblical Index

Genesis 1:27 65
Genesis 12:1 172

Exodus 3:7–8 47, 49

1 Kings 21:1–29 70, 71, 218
2 Kings 23 29

Job 38:41 57

Psalm 46:10 187
Psalm 119:105 28, 29

Matthew 20:25 30
Matthew 22:30 65
Mark 4:1–20 32
Mark 12:30 187

Luke 2:19 127
Luke 2:41–52 13, 88, 95, 96
Luke 15 65
Luke 20:36 65
Luke 24:13–35 13, 88, 95, 96, 222
Luke 24:32–49 80

John 1:14 164
John 3:16 182
John 14:6 178
John 19:25 96

Acts 1:8 199n26
Acts 2 17, 197, 198n9, 224
Acts 2:2–6 199n26
Acts 2:16–17 199n26
Acts 4:24, 27–31 199n26
Acts 5:1–5a 199n26
Acts 5:12–16 199n26
Acts 8 65

Acts 8:5–25 198n9
Acts 8:14–17 199n26
Acts 8:38b–40 199n26
Acts 9:1–6a 199n26
Acts 9:1–19a 198n9
Acts 9:17–18 199n26
Acts 9:36–38, 40–42 199n26
Acts 10:3–6, 44–48 199n26
Acts 10:23b–48 198n9
Acts 10:28 27
Acts 11:27–28 199n26
Acts 12:5–11 199n26
Acts 14:1–6 199n26
Acts 15:1–29 193
Acts 16:16–19 199n26
Acts 16:22–23 25–26, 29–30, 199n26
Acts 19:1–7 198n9
Acts 19:4–6 199n26
Acts 19:11–12 199n26
Acts 21:10–13 199n26
Acts 28:3–6 199n26

Romans 2:14 156
Romans 6:22 182
Romans 6:23 182
Romans 10:4 56
Romans 12:1–5 173
Romans 12:1b-2a 154
Romans 12:2 173

1 Corinthians 6:19 29
1 Corinthians 10:1–4 80
1 Corinthians 13 20n41
1 Corinthians 15:3b-4 78
2 Corinthians 3:18 62
2 Corinthians 11:2 65

Galatians 3:26 65

Galatians 3:28 65

1 Thessalonians 4:3 182
1 Timothy 6:16 185
2 Timothy 1:12 124
2 Timothy 3:16 29

Hebrews 11:1 179

James 2:17 179

James 3:9 62

1 John 3:10 182
1 John 4:8 159

Revelation 2:8–11 77
Revelation 20:14–15 182
Revelation 21 65
Revelation 21:1–8 182
Revelation 21:4 162

Printed in Great Britain
by Amazon